Introduction to
Computer Programming

Introduction to Computer Programming

A Problem-Solving Approach

John M. Hartling
Larry E. Druffel
F. Jack Hilbing

DIGITAL PRESS

Printed in the U.S.A.
10 9 8 7 6 5 4 3 2 1

Documentation Number: EY-000010-DP
ISBN: 0-932376-21-5
Library of Congress Cataloging in Publication Data

Hartling, John M.
  Introduction to computer programming.

  Includes index.
  1. Electronic digital computers—Programming.
2. Problem solving—Data processing. I. Druffel,
Larry E. II. Hilbing, F. Jack, III. Title.
QA76.6.E382 1983   001.64′2   83-8952
ISBN 0-932376-21-5

Copyeditor: Mary Skousgaard
Illustrations: ANCO/Boston
Designer: Diane Jaroch
Typesetter: The Maple-Vail Book Manufacturing Group
Printer: The Maple-Vail Book Manufacturing Group
Cover Printer: The Lehigh Press, Inc.

To Our Wives

Preface

The fields of Computer Science and Computer Programming are still evolving and there are differences of opinion regarding their definition, relationship, practice, and even their status. While there are diverse views on whether Computer Programming is an art or a science, we think that most authorities would accept the view that Computer Programming is that branch of Computer Science which involves the formulation of algorithms for solution on electronic computers. Unfortunately, most introductory programming courses degenerate into learning a new programming language. Algorithm development, the truly important concept of programming, is usually lost in the details of the specific language. Based upon our experience in both the teaching and the application of Computer Science, we are convinced that algorithm development is the most important concept to be emphasized in learning computer programming. We feel there is a need for a beginning textbook which introduces programming in terms of algorithmic problem solutions, starting in a very simple manner and building up through numerous examples to more sophisticated algorithms that provide insight into other aspects of Computer Science.

This text is presented as a language independent, introductory computer programming text that emphasizes algorithm development. Algorithms are developed as finite sequences of operations which define the process for effectively solving a problem. In the earlier chapters of this book these algorithms are expressed in terms of flowcharts—graphical representation of the flow of operation. In the later chapters, after the student has become familiar and proficient with the flowcharting technique and the development of the more basic algorithms, a shift is made to presenting algorithms through pseudocode. Using pseudocode allows a more concise and less tedious presentation of the more advanced algorithms associated with topics specific to Computer Science. Both methods of presentation are accomplished without reference to a particular programming language. This way the algorithmic aspects of programming are emphasized.

From our experience in teaching introductory computer programming to a wide range of undergraduates, we believe that one of the most effective teaching methods is the use of a large number of examples and problems. Therefore, the book presents algorithm development in a problem-oriented environment. Immediately after discussion of a concept, a solved problem is used to illustrate that concept. These examples are complemented by other solved problems at the end of the chapter, providing reinforcement of the concept as well as alternative applications. The examples in the early chapters are very straightforward. We have deliberately selected some simple and familiar examples in order to illustrate the principles without introducing other complications. The examples and problems in the latter part of the book develop the methodology for handling problems in several important areas of Computer Science.

Organization of the Book

The earlier chapters provide background material and introduce fundamental algorithmic constructs. Chapter 1 is an introduction covering the organization of the computer, representation of information, and the concept of the stored program computer. Although this material is not directly linked to the other chapters, it contains conceptual information which the student should understand. Chapter 2 sets the focus by presenting the concept of decomposing algorithms and their representation as flowcharts. Although we do not use a particular programming language, we recognize that the students will be implementing their algorithms in some high-level language. Therefore, Chapter 3 presents the basic programming constructs needed to convert an algorithm into a program without reference to a specific programming language. Chapters 4 through 6 then cover the algorithmic and programming constructs of conditionals, iteration, and arrays.

Chapter 7 introduces pseudocode, which will be used as an alternative to flowcharts throughout the remainder of the book.

Chapter 8 presents subroutines using pseudocode representation for algorithms. This chapter serves as a transitional chapter from the simpler algorithms of the earlier chapters to the more advanced algorithms of the remaining chapters.

Chapter 9 is devoted to structured programming. Although there are numerous definitions of structured programming, we are basically talking about top-down, structured design. We believe that Chapter 9 is the proper place to introduce structured programming. Attempts have been made to teach only structured programming in some beginning classes. But the implementation of structured programming in such a manner implies the use of a particular programming language, a situation we intentionally avoided. Therefore, we did not introduce structured programming at the start of the book. However, after the presentation of the algorithmic and basic programming concepts in the first eight chapters, describing the concept of structured programming, a concept which can then be discussed independent of programming languages, is appropriate.

In Chapters 10 through 13 we present various Computer Science concepts and develop algorithms applying those concepts in practical applications.

Use of the Book   The organization of introductory computer science courses is as varied as the people teaching them. Each professor has his pet applications and his own emphasis. Our purpose is to present the basic computer programming tools and concepts in sufficient detail that the professor who desires to emphasize a specific application will find sufficient depth. We also provide the necessary diversity for the professor whose purpose is a survey course. Since many introductory courses are service courses, which provide not only an introduction to the Computer Science Department but also serve students in other majors, the professor needs a vehicle for individualizing the course. Sufficient material to permit the liberal arts student to survey the applications, give the business major a solid foundation in data processing applications, and prepare the engineering student for numerical methods is presented. With the increasing emphasis on personalized instruction, the diversity of material should reduce the need to change books.

We assume that the reader has no previous experience with the computer. After completing the early chapters the student should be able to develop algorithms to solve fairly complex problems and to learn higher level languages independently. Upon completion of the remainder of the book, the reader should understand the importance of data structure in the design of an algorithm and be able to design and program larger systems using a top-down approach.

The book can be used in several ways in a basic course:

1. The book is intended primarily as a basic text in a computer programming course at the senior high school and junior college level. There is more than adequate material for a beginning course. In fact, few introductory courses would attempt to cover all of the material in this book. The wide range of material is intended to allow the instructor freedom in selecting appropriate application areas to tailor a course to the specific needs of the students.

2. By segmenting the concepts and immediately reinforcing them by example, the book becomes ideal for self-paced instruction systems, because the student can determine whether the concept is understood or not. Further, the flexibility offered in the later chapters makes the book particularly useful for personalized self-instruction.

3. Since the primary method of explanation in this book is through the liberal use of examples and solved problems, which illustrate basic concepts,

the book will also be useful as a companion text in basic and intermediate Computer Science courses.

In applying the principles of this book and implementing the algorithms on a computer, the student must utilize a programming language. Numerous programming language textbooks are available, which can be used to provide the necessary complementary reference to this book. The organization of this book permits such supplementary language reference texts to be easily cross-referenced for specific programming language concepts.

John M. Hartling
Larry E. Druffel
F. Jack Hilbing

Table of Contents

Introduction to
Computer Programming

1   Introduction to the Computer

1.1 Introduction

In learning any new discipline, it is fundamental to your study that you understand the language and terms of that discipline. In this book, we do not try to teach you everything there is to know about computers and computer science. Rather, our goal is for you to learn how to develop a problem to the point at which it can be solved on a computer. In this chapter, we introduce you to some of the basic terminology of computers and help you to understand what computer science is all about. At the completion of this chapter, you should be able to answer the following questions:

1. What is a computer?
2. How is a computer organized?
3. How does a computer store information?
4. When should I use a computer to solve a problem?
5. What is the advantage to a stored program computer?

1.2 A New Tool

Psychologists and philosophers find great significance in man's ability to develop and use tools. We have learned to use a variety of tools, both mechanical and procedural. Mathematics, for instance, is a procedural tool. In fact, mathematics is a universal tool, providing the means by which people manage to create and develop a great many concepts. In applying mathematics to problem solving, we sometimes rely on such tools as pencil and paper to record intermediate and final solutions. On occasion, we also use other tools such as electronic calculators to assist in the mechanics of calculation.

We only use these tools when they expedite or simplify the performance of some task. In learning to use them, we also learn to appreciate their limitations and applications. Just because we have learned to use a calculator doesn't mean that we would bother to turn it on to multiply 4×8. If we did perform that multiplication with the calculator, we would certainly take care to evaluate the degree of precision of our result. The calculator provides the numeric result to only a limited degree of accuracy and does not necessarily provide the order of magnitude we may find necessary. Aware of the limitations, we are careful to interpret the result correctly.

You are about to learn about another useful tool—the computer. The **computer** is a device capable of accepting data from some external source, processing the data in accordance with a set of prescribed operations, and outputting the results to some external recipient. In accordance with this definition, you might say that a computer is a machine that processes information and can be viewed as in Figure 1–1. The study of information processing through the use of a computer is part of the discipline known as **computer science.**

In essence, the computer is nothing more than an extremely useful tool. Its development is solidly based on accepted principles: it possesses no magical qualities. Because this tool has become very sophisticated, its use has become both a science and an art. Throughout this book, you will learn to use this tool and, through experience, appreciate both its power and its limitations. You will be introduced to the science and exposed to the art.

Although the computer offers many advantages in problem solving, its use is not always appropriate. For instance, would you want to use a computer to solve a simple equation such as

$$X = Y + 2$$

Probably not! You would solve such a trivial problem in your head. However, suppose you were asked to solve the same problem where the values of Y range from -1000 to $+1000$ in increments of .0001. More than likely you would seek the aid of a computer.

The decision to use a computer to solve a given problem usually results from consideration of the two main advantages of a computer. First, the computer can accurately perform specified operations at very high speed. Second, it can store vast amounts of data for rapid retrieval at a later time.

1.3 Computer Organization

Before learning to use the computer as a tool, it is beneficial to make a brief examination of the physical equipment, or hardware, that makes up a computer system. Our concern is not with the details of the hardware operation but rather with the general organization of a computer and its components; we will concentrate on the functions of the components rather than on the intricacies of their operation.

A computer is composed of five basic modules, as illustrated in Figure 1–2. Although these components and their operations will vary among computers, the functions performed by each component must be present in some form in all computers. By analogy, General Motors and Ford produce entirely different cars; however, all cars contain the same essential functional components of engine, drive shaft, steering, and so forth.

Figure 1–1.
Data Processing
System

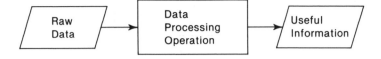

Figure 1–2.
Five Basic
Components
of a Computer

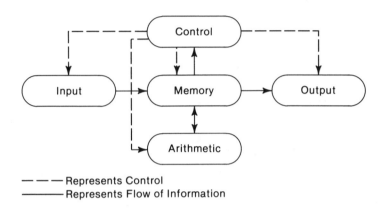

--- Represents Control
——— Represents Flow of Information

A. Memory Unit

The **memory unit** is a physical device capable of holding or storing data until
it is required during processing. Computer memories are capable of storing
millions of pieces of information. Implicit in the usefulness of a memory is
that any piece of information in the memory be accessible.

From a functional standpoint, the memory is analogous to a set of mailboxes, as shown in Figure 1–3. Each pigeonhole, or mailbox, contains a piece
of information, or **contents.** In order to gain access to any particular piece of
information, we refer to its unique location, or **address**. Likewise, a computer memory unit consists of a large number of storage locations, each of
which has a unique address and might contain a specific piece of information. You gain access to the contents of a memory location—the actual information stored in that location—by referencing the address assigned to that
location.

Most devices that lend themselves to the storage of information are binary
in nature; that is, they have only two states. Many electrical devices can be
considered to be two-state devices. A very common example is a light
switch, which is either ON or OFF. The light could very easily be used to
store information consisting of an ON/OFF, 1/0, or TRUE/FALSE nature.
Once the position of the switch is established and as long as no one changes
its position, the information is "remembered." In other words, setting the

Figure 1–3.
Array of Mailboxes

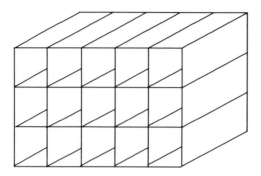

switch is the same as storing one piece of information. A large bank of such switches could easily be connected in such a way as to store information in accordance with some code.

In practice, the number of switches required to build a modern computer memory would be too large to allow practical application. Fortunately, there are many other binary devices that are more adaptable to memory construction. These devices vary greatly in size, cost, and access time. (**Access time** is the time required to retrieve or store information in the memory device.)

Because of these differences, memory is generally subdivided into two categories: **main memory** and **auxiliary memory.** A given memory device fits into one of these categories by consideration of a variety of features, such as size, speed, and amount of storage. The faster a memory device, the more it costs, and because of this tradeoff, most computer systems use a combination of high-speed, small-capacity main memory and slow-speed, large-capacity auxiliary memory.

There are several types of main memory in use:

1. Magnetic cores
2. Semiconductor integrated circuits
3. Magnetic bubbles
4. Thin magnetic films
5. Holographic (laser) disks

These have access times ranging from 1 nanosecond (10^{-9} secs) to 1 millisecond (10^{-3} secs).

In the nineteen-sixties and early seventies, main memory in many computers was magnetic core. Although semiconductor memories have generally replaced core memories, the core provides an excellent example for discussion of how a memory functions.

The magnetic core memory consists of doughnut-shaped ferrite rings less than one-tenth of an inch in diameter threaded together by a network of wires. By passing a current through the wires in a particular ring in the proper direction, we can magnetize the ring with its magnetic lines of force directed either clockwise or counter-clockwise. As shown in Figure 1–4, the clockwise magnetization could be used to represent a 1, the counterclockwise magnetization could represent a 0.

Information is stored in core memory by magnetizing a series of cores in the proper manner. Rather than consider each core separately, a memory address refers to a group of cores that are wired in such a way as to form a **word.**

The number of cores considered as a word varies greatly among the different manufacturers, but it is usually in the range of 8 to 48. Each core in a word is referred to as a **bit,** so you will hear the terminology, an N-bit word. The number of words in memory constitutes the capacity of the memory; each word must be individually addressable. The number of words, then, is equivalent to the number of **addresses,** and the size of a word puts limitations on the contents of an address.

In addition to the high-speed main memory that is used to store small amounts of data during processing, the computer also requires a way of storing large amounts of data for processing, archiving, or filing. This readily accessible but much slower storage is referred to as **mass storage,** or auxiliary memory.

There are several types of auxiliary memory in use:

1. Magnetic tape drives
2. Magnetic disk drives
3. Floppy disk drives

These have access times ranging from milliseconds to minutes. These devices are always electromechanical and require the physical movement of a magnetic surface relative to a sensing device. Because of their lower con-

Figure 1-4.
Ferrite Rings

Representation
of a 0

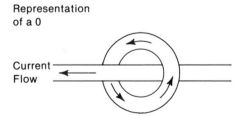

Current
Flow

Magnetic lines of force oriented
in a counterclockwise
direction.

Representation
of a 1

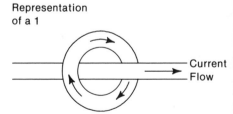

Current
Flow

Magnetic lines of force oriented
in a clockwise
direction.

struction cost and large storage capacity, these devices provide relatively cheaper cost per bit than main memory. However, because of their slow speed, they are used predominantly for storage of large amounts of information that is accessed infrequently. Although these devices serve the purpose of an auxiliary memory, they are generally treated by the computer as input/output devices.

B. Arithmetic Unit

The **arithmetic unit** is perhaps the most obvious component of a computer because nearly everyone is familiar with the computer's ability to perform calculations. The electrical circuitry for performing the basic arithmetic operations of addition, subtraction, multiplication, and division is contained in this unit. The other functions that an arithmetic unit can perform vary among manufacturers; however, some of the more desirable functions are

1. Compare
2. Shift
3. Logical operations—AND, OR, NOT

The arithmetic unit is essentially a very sophisticated calculator capable of doing a well-defined set of arithmetic operations. The arithmetic unit is not allowed to function blindly and at random. It must be told what function is to be performed, when it is to be performed, on what information it is to be performed, and where the results are to be placed. Just as you manually provide all these instructions to your calculator, the control unit provides them to the arithmetic unit. All the required information is stored in memory and is transferred back and forth between memory and the arithmetic unit, through the control unit.

C. Input/Output Units

In order for the computer to serve some useful purpose, it must have **input/output (I/O) devices** as a means of communicating with its external environment. We will only consider those devices used in cases where the external environment is a human being. The necessary communication is performed by electromechanical devices capable of converting information back and forth between a form a human can understand and a form the computer can store and process. Some I/O devices are

Input	Output
Card reader	Card punch
Paper tape reader	Paper tape punch
Teletypewriter	Teletypewriter
Video display key- board	High-speed printers
	Graphic displays

Since these devices are electromechanical and require the movement of mechanical parts, they are inherently slow. I/O devices operate at speeds on the order of milliseconds, while the control unit and memory operate in micro- or nanoseconds. This tremendous difference in time could cause the computer's speed to be limited to the speed of its I/O devices. Thus you may sometimes hear of a computer that is I/O bound or I/O limited. For conceptual purposes, the I/O device can be considered to be communicating directly with memory. However, I/O references are, by necessity, synchronized so that they do not significantly slow down the speeds of the control unit.

D. Control Unit

If each of the devices in a computer were allowed to operate haphazardly, the result would be chaos. Something must provide the coordination to tell the card reader when to read a card, the memory when to transfer information, the arithmetic unit when to add, and the printer when to print. This function is performed by the **control unit,** which coordinates and synchronizes the activities of all the other devices. The control unit receives information from each of the other units to determine what they are doing and what their next action should be. Each of the other units is capable of performing its well-defined functions independently once it receives a directive from the control unit. The control unit contains the master clock and issues timing and synchronization signals to all units of the computer.

1.4 Information Representation

In order to appreciate how a computer stores data and performs operations on that data, you must first understand the relationship between the decimal number system and the binary number system. There is no set standard for representing data within a computer, and methods will vary from one machine to another. In this section, we will discuss how the bits within a word can be arranged to represent data. Let us suppose your name is Joe, age 23, with a pay scale of $9.25 per hour. This would be representative of the three types of information we would like to store in the computer:

1. INTEGER—23
2. REAL (fixed point or floating point)—9.25
3. ALPHANUMERIC characters—Joe

A. INTEGERS

INTEGER data, that is, whole numbers with no fractional part, are the simplest kind of data to represent. Such numbers are simply converted to and stored as binary numbers.

There are some slight differences in the way various computers do this, but in general we can say that in a typical computer with an N-bit word, the leftmost bit is used as a **sign bit** and the remainder of the bits represent the magnitude of the INTEGER shown in Figure 1–5. This means that $N - 1$ bits can be used for representing the magnitude of the INTEGER. The rightmost bit has a weight of 2^0, or 1, the next bit to the left has a weight of 2^1, or 2 and the bit just to the right of the sign bit has a weight of 2^{n-2}. Therefore, the largest INTEGER that can be represented is $2^{n-1} - 1$, which occurs when all the bits except the sign bit are set to 1.

Positive numbers are represented by a sign bit of 0. Negative numbers can be represented in several ways, but the simplest way to represent negative numbers is to use the sign magnitude representation. In this method the sign bit is set to 1 if the number is negative, and the remainder of the word still represents the magnitude of the number, just as if it were positive. So the only difference between a -5 and $+5$ is that the sign bit would be 0 for $+5$ and 1 for -5, as shown in Figure 1–6.

B. REAL Numbers

Because we often work with numbers that are not integers, computers must have a way of representing numbers that have a fractional part. We normally call these numbers **REAL numbers,** and they can be either **fixed point numbers** or **floating point numbers.**

In studying subjects like chemistry or physics, you have probably used scientific notation to write numbers that were extremely large or extremely small. Using this notation, you represent the speed of light as 1.86×10^5 mi/sec instead of 186,000 mi/sec. To convert a number to scientific notation, you normalize it. That is, you move the decimal point to a position in the number where there is just one nonzero digit (and no zero digit) to the left of it. For each position to the left or right that you move the decimal point, you have to multiply the number by 10 or 10^{-1} to compensate. In converting 186,000, you move the decimal point 5 places to the left, so you must multiply by 10^5 to compensate. Thus, the result is 1.86×10^5.

In converting .000000529 to scientific notation, you move the decimal point 7 places to the right, so you must multiply 5.29 by 10^{-7} to compensate. Thus, the result is 5.29×10^{-7}.

The magnitude portion of the number is referred to as the decimal part, or the **mantissa.** Numbers expressed in scientific notation have the form:

Mantissa $\times 10^{\text{Exponent}}$

where the mantissa is normalized so that it has only one digit to the left of the decimal point. Since all such numbers are multiplied by some power of 10, the mantissa and the exponent uniquely identify the number.

Scientific notation is helpful in understanding floating point representation in a computer because it uses similar notation. Floating point numbers have the following general form:

Binary mantissa $\times B^{\text{Binary exponent}}$

Figure 1–5.
N-Bit Integer

	Sign Bit	INTEGER

Weighted   N – 1   N – 2   ·   ·   ·   ·   ·   ·   0
Bit
Positions

Figure 1–6.
Sign Magnitude
Representation
Using Four Bits

Weights	Sign Bit	2	1	0
+5 =	0	1	0	1
–5 =	1	1	0	1

Bit Numbers   0   1   2   3

where the mantissa is normalized and B is some power of 2 (usually 2, 8, or 16). To represent floating point numbers in the computer, a word of memory is divided into two sections. One section contains the exponent; the other contains the mantissa with the binary point assumed to be in a fixed position. Both the mantissa and the exponent have an associated sign bit.

Example 1.1

Suppose that we have a computer with a 12-bit word that represents floating point numbers, as in Figure 1–7. Using the format of Figure 1–7, show how the decimal number 44 would be represented.

Solution

Converting 44 to binary yields 44 = 101100, and after normalizing, we have 1.011×10^{101} (all numbers are binary). Because both the mantissa and exponent are positive, both sign bits are 0, and 44 would be represented as

Sign Bits	Exponent	Mantissa
0 0	0 1 0 1	1 0 1 1 0 0

End Solution

Figure 1-7.
Sample Floating
Point Word

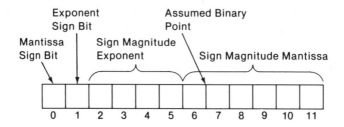

C. ALPHANUMERIC Characters
Even if we used the computer exclusively to perform numerical calculations, we would still want some way of identifying the numbers. For instance, after calculating the distance from San Francisco to New York, we would like our output to appear as follows:

THE DISTANCE FROM SAN FRANCISCO TO NEW YORK = 3056 MILES

or we might want to present the results in tabular form:

ORIGIN	DESTINATION	DISTANCE IN MILES
SAN FRANCISCO	NEW YORK	3056
DENVER	CHICAGO	1047
CLEVELAND	NEW ORLEANS	1103

To provide this capability, we require that the computer be able to store non-numeric information, called **alphanumerics,** which consists of

1. Alphabetics—letters A–Z
2. Numerics—digits 0–9
3. Special characters—+, −, *, %, =, ?, etc.

To provide a unique alphanumeric representation for each of the 26 letters, 10 numbers, and, say, 20 special characters, we would need 56 unique bit configurations, or combinations of bits. What is the minimum number of bits required to represent 56 unique codes? Well, one bit has two distinct states: 0 and 1. Two bits have four distinct states: 00, 01, 10, and 11. With three bits we get eight combinations: 000, 001, 010, 011, 100, 101, 110, and 111. In general, with N bits we get 2^N combinations, so with 5 bits we could represent 2^5 or 32 codes, and with six bits, 2^6 or 64 combinations. Thus it would require six bits to represent 56 alphanumeric characters uniquely. Since six bits can represent 64 unique codes, we could allow for 28 special characters rather than 20.

Some computers use six bits to represent alphanumeric characters by sub-dividing their computer word into groups of six bits. For example, a 48-bit computer word could hold 48/6, or 8 six-bit characters at any address in memory.

Other computer manufacturers divide their computer word into groups of 8 bits, called a **byte.** Each byte can represent 2^8, or 256 different alphanumeric characters. This means that in addition to 26 letters and 10 digits, a byte could represent 220 different special characters. This provides quite a bit of flexibility because it would be easy to code both upper- and lower-case letters, the digits 0–9, all the special symbols, and still allow room for additional symbols.

1.5 The Stored Program Computer

An **instruction** is a command to the computer to perform a specific sequence of steps. The instruction indicates the operation that is to be performed and the data that are to be used in that operation. A **program** is a series of instructions used to solve a problem or accomplish some task. The **coding** of the program is the development of a set of instructions from a logical description of a solution procedure. Two things are important in coding: (1) the preparation of the proper instructions that will perform the operations that are intended, and (2) the organization of these instructions into the proper sequence so that the commands are performed in the order that is intended.

In early computing machinery, the instructions and their sequence were controlled by switches, punched paper tapes, plug boards, or other physical devices. Changes in the sequence of operations could only be made by physically changing these devices. However, the development of the computer was greatly enhanced by the concept of the stored program computer, which was conceived around 1946.

To understand the concept of the stored program computer, it is necessary to be able to differentiate between a storage location, the address of a storage location, and the contents of a storage location. A **storage location** is any storage cell of the computer memory. An **address** uniquely specifies a particular storage location. And the **contents of a storage location** refers to the information that is stored at that address.

A **stored program computer** is a computer in which the instructions are stored in the computer along with the data. Thus, the contents of a storage address can be data or they can be instructions. This is a remarkable concept! It means the program is a sequence of bits that looks exactly like data. The only difference is how the computer treats the computer words. If the computer treats a word as an **instruction,** *it causes an operation* to be performed in the computer. If the computer considers the contents of a storage location to be **data,** then certain *operations are performed upon it.* From this principle evolve the advantages of stored program computers.

Although there are many unique characteristics of the stored program computer, three particularly significant ones should be pointed out. First, there is no need for two types of memory. Since instructions and data are both stored as a sequence of bits, a single type of memory can be used. Thus, the same memory can be used for both a large program that needs a small amount of data and for a small program that needs a large amount of data. Second, there is no need to distinguish between program and data at the input device. Since the program uses the same internal code as for data, both the program and the data can be read into the computer in the same manner. Third, it is relatively easy to make changes to the program.

The stored program computer has its instructions stored in its own memory. Each instruction generally consists of several parts. The two most important parts are the operation code and the address part. The **operation code** is that part of the instruction that triggers the proper action within the computer. For example, the operation might be an add, subtract, or multiply command. The address part will generally contain the addresses of the **operands** involved in the operations (e.g., the addresses of two variables to be added). When an instruction is executed, the bit configuration of the operation code is then decoded into a sequence of control signals that results in the intended action with respect to the decoded operands.

Since an instruction is a sequence of bits, it consists of a long string of 0's and 1's. This makes the instructions difficult to read and introduces many opportunities for error. A shorthand and useful way to write this bit sequence is to use octal numbers to represent the code. In this way, each of the octal numbers from 0 to 7 represents three of these bits.

In the early days of computing, programmers found it necessary to write programs in either the binary or the octal form. The development of programs in this manner was tedious and exacting. In addition, all references to the addresses were in terms of the actual address of a memory location, referred to as an **absolute address.** This required the programmer to keep a storage "map" of the memory in order to be sure that a specific location was used for only one purpose and that the operands and results could be properly addressed.

Another difficulty occurred with inserting a new instruction into the program. It was then necessary to move all subsequent instructions and modify their operands in order to make room in the program for the new instruction.

To overcome some of the difficulties involved in machine language programming, **assembly language programming** was developed. There are two major advantages to assembly languages over the previous methods. First, **mnemonic operation codes** allow the programmer to specify an operation code as a sequence of characters rather than as a series of bits. For example, ADD may mean addition, SUB may mean subtraction, and MUL may be used to show multiplication. These mnemonic operation codes are easier for the programmer to remember and they facilitate the programming task.

Second, symbolic addressing permits the use of names, rather than numbers, to indicate absolute addresses. References to these locations are then made by their names. These symbolic addresses provide a convenient method to reference both data and instructions. The addition or deletion of instructions, and the correction of errors, is considerably easier since the changes need not be in terms of absolute addresses.

The only instructions that the computer can execute are those written in the machine language of that computer. Instructions composed of mnemonic operation codes and symbolic addresses are just conveniences to the programmer; they must be translated to machine language for execution. This translation is performed by another computer program, called an **assembler.** Thus, there is a two-step procedure in running a program: (1) The assembler converts the assembly language program to the machine language, and (2) the sequence of instructions constituting the program is then performed or executed.

The use of assembly languages makes programming considerably easier than coding in machine language, but there are still disadvantages. Two disadvantages are very significant. First, each assembly language instruction is translated to a single machine instruction. This one-for-one correspondence of an assembly language instruction with a machine instruction makes the program somewhat cumbersome and requires the programmer to break down his computation into very detailed steps. Programmers would like to make their instructions look somewhat closer to the algebraic notation or the natural language to which they are accustomed, thus reducing the time devoted to writing the program.

Second, an assembly language program is still very much machine dependent: it is designed for use on only one computer. As computer programming developed, people wanted the ability to run their programs on different machines and to exchange their programs with programmers working on other computers.

Procedural languages, or **higher level languages,** were developed to overcome these disadvantages and make the programming task simpler. Today, there are a large number of these languages, such as FORTRAN, ALGOL, COBOL, PL/I, PASCAL, BASIC, and more recently, ADA. These procedural languages account for the majority of programming effort at the present time. Programs written in these high-level languages are translated by a **compiler** into a sequence of machine language instructions that the computer will execute.

1.6 Summary

As a potential computer user, you will want to learn one of the higher level languages. However, it is not sufficient simply to become a computer linguist. The study of computer science, even at an elementary level, involves more than learning a new language. This book is not the presentation of the mechanics of a particular language. Rather, it is concerned with the process of solving a problem on the computer, regardless of the programming language. The emphasis is on the development of algorithms, a subject introduced in the next chapter.

Solved Problems

1.1

What was the first computer and when was it built?

Solution

The development of the first information processing machine was begun in 1937 by Howard Aiken under the auspices of and with the support of International Business Machines (IBM) and Harvard University. The machine, originally called the IBM Automatic Sequence Controlled Calculator, was presented to Harvard University in 1944 and became known as the Harvard Mark I. The Mark I was the first machine to possess all the fundamental characteristics of our modern-day computers.

The first completely electronic digital computer was developed at the University of Pennsylvania in 1946 by J. P. Eckert and J. W. Mauchly.

1.2

If an arithmetic unit did not have a multiply capability, how could you perform the function $X = 3 \times 4$?

Solution

Multiplication was handled on many of the early computers, which did not have a multiply function, by repeated addition. That is, the function 3×4 implies that the number 4 should be added together 3 times, or

$$3 \times 4 = 4 + 4 + 4 = 12$$

1.3

Assuming a four-bit computer word, show the signed magnitude representation of $+7$ and -7.

Solution

The binary equivalent of the decimal number 7 is 111; therefore the signed magnitude representation would be as follows:

1.	+7	0	1	1	1
2.	−7	1	1	1	1

1.4

Assuming a data word as in Figure 1–7, show the REAL representation of the number 120.

Solution

Converting 120_{10} to binary yields $120_{10} = 1111000_2$, and after normalizing, we have $1111000_2 = 1.111 \times 10^{110}$ (all numbers are binary). Since both the mantissa and exponent are positive, both sign bits are 0, and 120_{10} would be represented as

Sign Bits	Exponent	Mantissa
0 0	0 1 1 0	1 1 1 1 0 0

Supplementary Problems

1.5

Name at least three input and output devices that were not listed in this chapter.

1.6

Can you think of any functions you would like the computer's arithmetic unit to perform besides those given in Section 1.3 B?

1.7

If your computer's arithmetic unit did not have a divide capability, how could you perform the function $Y = 15/3$?

1.8

Label the following as ALPHANUMERIC, REAL, or INTEGER information:

a. The number of students in your class
b. The color of your car
c. The number of wheels on a locomotive
d. A student's grade point agerage
e. A worker's pay scale
f. The number of a worker's dependents
g. The names of the planets

1.9

Show the scientific notation for the following:

a. 2000.15

b. 600000000

c. .00005

1.10

What is the advantage of a stored program computer over a nonprogramma-ble hand calculator?

1.11

Assuming a four-bit computer word, show the signed magnitude representa-tion of +2, −2, and +4, −4.

1.12

Assuming a six-bit computer word and signed magnitude representation, what is the largest positive number you could store in one word?

1.13

Assuming a data word as in Figure 1–7, show the REAL representation of 10_{10} and 76_{10}.

1.14

Given the following floating point number representation, what is its deci-mal equivalent?

Sign Bits	Exponent	Mantissa
0 0	0 1 1 1	1 1 0 0 0 0

2 *Problem-Solving Approach*

2.1 Introduction

The computer is a powerful tool, but it does not inherently "know" anything. The computer is merely an efficient and obedient servant, which will do literally—and only literally—what we tell it to do. Therefore, in order to use the computer to solve a particularly complex problem, we must provide instructions to the computer in a form that describes precisely what operations are to be performed.

In this chapter, we will present a method of preparing a relatively complex problem for solution on the computer. By the end of this chapter, you should be able to answer the following questions:

1. What is meant by decomposition?
2. What are the problem-solving steps?
3. What is an algorithm?
4. What is a flowchart?

We can consider the problem solved when we have developed a formula, sequence of steps, or set of equations that define the solution. This result, called an **algorithm,** will be discussed in more detail in Section 2.5.

2.2 Approach to Problem Solving

The difficulty that faces us when having to solve a rather substantial problem is knowing where to start. The same difficulty is actually present even with small problems. However, the solution to a small problem is usually so readily apparent that you have mentally hurdled the stumbling block of deciding where to start before you even recognize it. For instance, if you were going to wax your car, you would face the problem of deciding what to do first. You would probably begin by gathering the wax, applicator, and chamois cloth. Moreover, you would have reached this decision without consciously recognizing that a decision had to be made.

If you were asked to write the numbers 5, 3, 1, 2, 4 in ascending order, you would unhesitatingly write 1, 2, 3, 4, 5. If you were then asked how you approached the problem, you would have difficulty describing the method you used. Now suppose we presented you with a list of one thousand numbers and asked you to write them in ascending order. You would probably hesitate a few seconds trying to decide how to begin. Asked to describe your method, you might describe a step-by-step process by which you compared the first number with the second, then the second with the third, and so on, exchanging numbers as necessary until the list was in order.

In either situation, whether subconsciously or consciously, the decision as to how to start to solve the problem had to be made. The larger the problem, the tougher the question "Where do I start?" becomes.

Problem solving on a computer poses the same difficulty. If the problem is small enough, we start putting our solution into the language of the computer without hesitating. However, as soon as the problem starts getting so large that it can no longer be kept in mind, the problem of deciding where to start crops up again.

In the next section we propose an answer to the problem of getting started. Once we have overcome the initial problem of how to start, we are then faced with the problem of developing the solution for the computer. In this book we will demonstrate how the solution to any problem can be developed for the computer by the judicious combination and application of three basic control structures: sequential, conditional, and iterative. We will discuss these structures briefly here, and in more detail in the chapters devoted specifically to each one.

In **sequential processing,** instructions are executed in a step-by-step, serial fashion without overlap. Example 2.1 demonstrates sequential processing.

Example 2.1

Given a set of five numbers, compute the average of the numbers in the set.

Solution

1. Add the first two numbers.
2. Add the third number to the number obtained in step 1.
3. Add the fourth number to the result of step 2.
4. Add the fifth number to the result of step 3.
5. Divide the result of step 4 by 5.

End Solution

In **conditional processing,** an instruction or set of instructions is determined by some specified condition or criteria. Example 2.2 demonstrates conditional processing.

Example 2.2

A student should receive a grade of P if the total of his two quiz scores is greater than 64; otherwise he'll receive an F. Given the results of quizzes 1 and 2, find a student's grade.

Solution

1. If quiz score 1 + quiz score 2 is greater than 64, then do step 2; otherwise do step 3.
2. Record the grade of P.
3. Record the grade of F.

It should be clear that if step 2 is performed, then step 3 would be skipped.

End Solution

In **iterative processing,** a specified instruction or set of instructions is executed as long as some condition exists. Example 2.3 demonstrates iterative processing.

Example 2.3

Given a set of N quiz scores, where N is variable, compute the average quiz score.

Solution

1. Set N to 0.
2. Set SUM equal to 0.
3. Repeat steps 4 and 5 as long as there are numbers to be added.
4. Add 1 to N.
5. Add the Nth number to SUM.
6. The average is SUM divided by N.

End Solution

It should be understood that as soon as there are no longer numbers to be added, steps 4 and 5 would be skipped and step 6 would be executed.

In computer problem solving, the algorithms we develop will be restricted to these three control structures. In the course of studying computer problem solving, you will discover that a computer can be instructed to perform numerous operations. However, we will assume that any instruction or combination of instructions fits into one of our three classifications. By limiting ourselves in this way, the problem-solving approach that we will develop will be more straightforward, understandable, and unambiguous.

2.3 Problem Decomposition

Suppose you were faced with the problem of putting a man on the moon. How would you even begin to approach such a problem? Truly, such a terse statement of a problem could boggle the mind; and, at first glance, the solution to the problem would be completely inconceivable by one person. More than likely, you would begin by gathering around you a group of experts who specialize in such areas as astronautics, engineering, physics, and so forth. Together you would start deriving a solution to the problem by breaking it down into smaller modules to investigate separately and independently.

We propose that the idea of breaking the large problem down into smaller, more manageable subproblems, or modules, is the solution to our problem of getting started. This process is called **decomposition.** We have discussed how we could immediately derive a solution when faced with a small enough problem. Therefore, when tackling a large, complex problem, we will start by decomposing it into smaller problems. Then we will decompose the smaller problems into even smaller subproblems. We will continue this decomposition process until each subproblem is small enough to keep in mind and the solution becomes obvious.

At each step in the decomposition, we will ensure that each submodule is functionally independent of its parent module and of all other submodules at the same level. Thereby we ensure that each submodule receives its support only from the solution (i.e., inputs) provided by submodules it has spawned. That is, any particular module should be oblivious of how its output is used and only be concerned that its own output is correct.

Decomposition, as we have described it, is an iterative process. It is applied initially to a large problem and then repetitively to the generated subproblems until all existing subproblems are small enough for solution. We can visualize each module as an independent problem that has an input, a process, and an output. When the solutions, or processes, for all modules are brought together, they form the solution to the original problem.

Example 2.4

We are faced with the problem of designing a new car. Decompose this problem.

Solution

We have not been given any criteria for the capabilities of the car; therefore, we will simply decompose the car through the first stage as follows:

1. Electrical distribution
2. Engine (power plant)
3. Drive train
4. Chassis
5. Interior decor
6. Fuel system
7. Cooling system

At the next stage of decomposition, we would select one of these sub-modules and decompose it. This process would be applied repetitively until we got down to the actual components.

End Solution

Decomposing a problem into numerous subproblems, or modules, has several advantages. First, work can proceed on several modules simultaneously, with the result that the entire problem is solved faster. Second, each module can be tested and its correctness independently verified. Third, problem areas can be isolated to particular modules for correction.

Unfortunately, there are also some disadvantages to decomposition. First, some communications between modules is required, and the **protocol** (i.e., mechanisms and rules) for such communications can be difficult to establish and coordinate. Second, there must be a coordinator able to understand the entire problem and to keep the big picture so that the solutions to all the subproblems can be drawn together to form the solution to the original problem.

2.4 Problem-Solving Steps

At each stage in our process of decomposition we are faced either with having to decompose the problem further or with having to derive the immediate solution. When we have convinced ourselves that a subproblem cannot be decomposed any further, we should apply a set of well-defined problem-solving steps to solve that subproblem. These steps are

1. State the problem in specific terms.
2. Develop an algorithm for solving the problem.
3. Execute the algorithm.
4. Analyze the result.

The first step—a precise statement of the problem—might seem trite. However, it is probably the most important and most overlooked of the four steps. Until the problem solver knows precisely what the problem is, application of the remaining steps would be counterproductive and frustrating. It is implicit in the statement of the first problem-solving step that the inputs to the problem and the outputs derived from its solution be well defined.

The second problem-solving step requires that a procedure be developed that will yield the solution to the specific problem. This procedure has been given the formal name of algorithm. By definition, an **algorithm** is a finite sequence of operations that defines the process for solving a particular problem effectively in a finite period of time.

The third problem-solving step requires that the algorithm developed in step two be executed using some test data.

The fourth problem-solving step requires analysis of the results of executing the algorithm on the test data.

It is difficult to test an algorithm for every conceivable configuration of inputs. However, testing must be thorough. To simplify the analysis step, the data selected for the initial test should yield known results. You are only guessing whether the algorithm executed correctly if you test it with input that doesn't have a known solution to compare with the algorithm's result.

After testing for known results, you should expand and test with experimental inputs for which you do not have an answer. Your analysis might have to be based on whether or not the results are reasonable. The algorithm should be tested to see if it can handle all possible inputs. If the statement of the problem specifies that the input ranges from −5 to +5, then test the algorithm with −5, 0, +5. Why not test for −6, +6? See if the algorithm falls apart or if it can handle extraordinary cases. Many well-stated algorithms have failed dramatically at implementation because the problem solver failed to test and analyze it thoroughly during development.

Throughout this book, as you develop an algorithm you should generate a set of test data to which you can apply the algorithm. This will serve to convince yourself of the correctness of the algorithm and also test your understanding of the algorithm.

2.5 Algorithm Development

We have said that an algorithm is a finite sequence of operations that defines the process for solving a particular problem effectively in a finite period of time. A good algorithm defines a set of instructions that are

1. Well-defined
2. Unambiguous
3. Effective
4. Finite

A well-defined algorithm means that it defines the exact steps to follow and their specific order. An unambiguous algorithm leaves no doubt what action must be taken at each step. An effective algorithm yields the desired solution or results. A finite algorithm terminates, i.e., it does not execute indefinitely.

Examples of poor algorithms are easier to find than good ones. For instance, look at the back of many shampoo bottles and you will see an algorithm stated something like the following:

1. Wet hair.
2. Lather.
3. Rinse with water.
4. Repeat.

This algorithm is not well-defined because it does not specify that shampoo should be applied before lathering. If we assume that shampoo should be applied, then the algorithm should specify how much. Do we apply one capful or two?

The algorithm is not unambiguous. It does not tell us how hard or how long to lather. When it says to repeat, does it mean to apply more shampoo and lather again, or does it mean to rinse again?

The algorithm is not finite because it does not tell us when to stop. Presumably, once we start applying this algorithm, we could continue until we run out of shampoo.

The algorithm is definitely effective, especially if we take it literally, since we do not know when to stop shampooing.

Fortunately, the concept of algorithms is not new to us, although the term itself might be. We have been developing and executing algorithms all our lives. When faced with a poor algorithm, such as the shampoo directions, we unconsciously interpret the directions as they should have been written in the first place and execute the algorithm successfully.

Example 2.5

Describe an algorithm for baking a cake.

Solution

Whether or not you are familiar with the art of cake baking is irrelevant. The simplest solution to this problem is to look on the back of a box of cake mix; you will find a recipe similar to the one shown here.

1. Fill measuring cup with ½ cup of water.
2. Grease an 8- or 9-inch round pan generously and dust with flour.
3. If pan is metal, preheat oven to 350° F; otherwise preheat oven to 325° F.
4. Empty contents of package into small mixing bowl.
5. Add 1 unbeaten egg.
6. Add ¼ cup of water.
7. Beat 2 minutes with standard mixer at medium speed or with portable mixer at high speed. Use 300 strokes if by hand.

8. Add remaining ¼ cup of water and repeat step 7.

9. Bake 25–30 minutes if 8-inch pan, 20–25 minutes if 9-inch pan.

End Solution

Note that Example 2.5 is a well-defined algorithm for baking a cake. Provided that you have at least a rudimentary understanding of the use of kitchen facilities and are familiar with the ingredients, you would be able to execute the algorithm and produce a cake. The recipe is a finite set of specific instructions: precisely the definition of an algorithm. Blindly followed, it will yield the desired result.

There are many examples of algorithms in everyday life. If you have ever built a model airplane, a model boat, or even a kite, you have had to follow the specific directions provided. Given a kit and very detailed instructions, the rest is a matter of implementing the instructions. Very simply, the instructions represent an algorithm.

Development of good algorithms is the key to computer programming. Baking a cake is easy, given the recipe; and building a model is easy, given a good set of instructions. So is the building of a computer program, once the algorithm is fully developed.

In order to develop an algorithm, you must completely understand the operations to be performed. Algorithms can be developed for a variety of everyday situations. But obviously we are not going to be baking cakes, building models, or flying kites on the computer. Instead, we are going to be instructing the computer to perform calculations. We must be able to express the details of a computational procedure in very explicit terms. In other words, successful algorithm development is analogous to giving good directions or writing a good recipe.

Whenever we do a set of calculations by hand, we go through a computational procedure to arrive at a solution. This computational procedure is an algorithm. A simple computational procedure with which we are familiar is that of adding two numbers. Perhaps the procedure has become so natural for us that we combine some of the steps and no longer think about the procedure we are following when we add.

Example 2.6

Develop an algorithm for adding two real decimal numbers.

Solution

1. Place the two numbers one above the other so that the decimal points are in line.

2. Start with the right-hand column.
3. Repeat steps 4 through 8 as long as there are numbers in the column.
4. Sum the digits in the column.
5. If the sum is greater than 9, do step 6.
6. Place the carry digit above the column to the left of the column just added.
7. Record the unit's digit of the sum beneath the column whose digits were summed.
8. Move left one column.
9. The sum is the number you wrote down.

End Solution

In order to execute the algorithm, a person must have a certain amount of ability. We must assume that he can add two digits and that he knows what a carry digit and a unit's digit are. When giving any set of directions, we must assume a certain amount of knowledge on the part of the user of the algorithm. Therefore, in order to develop an algorithm for use on the computer, we must eventually learn what instructions the computer is able to execute. In subsequent chapters we will begin to examine the specific operations that can be performed by the computer, and we will express the algorithms in terms of these computer operations.

The algorithm of Example 2.6 is similar to other algorithms we have seen. Each step is a definite statement of the operation to be performed and is executed in order (i.e., sequential processing). There are provisions for the normal sequence of operations to be varied if certain conditions arise (i.e., conditional processing). The same set of steps is performed repetitively until we run out of digits (i.e., iterative processing). This last is an important concept: if we did not make use of iteration, there would have to be a separate algorithm for numbers of each possible size.

The algorithm specified in Example 2.6 is applicable to a more general type of problem. We will want to take advantage of techniques for making our algorithms applicable to a whole set of problems so that they are not dependent on a specific piece of data.

2.6 Flowcharting   Algorithm development is the key to problem solving. It is also the key to writing computer programs. In most cases the preceding algorithms were quite simple and therefore easy to follow. However, we discovered that algorithms stated in words are sometimes difficult to understand. For instance, Example 2.6 is a fairly simple algorithm, although the logic is not readily apparent at first glance. Even if the logic were straightforward, the wordiness and step-skipping require some concentration in order to understand the exact sequence of operations. When applied to complicated problems of considerable length, the way we have stated the algorithm is cumbersome.

There is nothing inherently wrong with the algorithm development or with the logic of the algorithm in Example 2.6; rather, it is the method of stating the algorithm that causes confusion. Therefore, we want a method of representing an algorithm that is clearer and more descriptive of the logic. One such method is called **flowcharting.**

The algorithm of Example 2.6 is shown in a flowchart in Figure 2–1. Note that although we have not yet formally considered the details of flowcharting, the algorithm is already clearer. A **flowchart** provides a snapshot of the logic of an algorithm. It is a graphic representation of the flow of operations. We use flowcharts to describe algorithms because they are an excellent aid in developing the logic and an accepted means of documenting an algorithm.

All algorithms developed in this text will be expressed in the form of flowcharts using the symbols presented in Figure 2–2 and explained in the following sections.

There are conventions governing the direction of flow when drawing a flowchart. Generally, it is wise to start in the upper left-hand corner and proceed down and to the right. However, this guideline often causes the flowchart to become cluttered. In some organizations the convention is rigidly enforced, while in others it is totally ignored. Quite often the layout is determined by the size of the page or the flow of the logic. We will not rigidly conform to the convention in this text; flowcharts will be drawn using the layout that best illustrates the logic.

A. Terminal Symbol
Every algorithm and consequently every flowchart must have a starting point and an ending point. The oval symbol (see Figure 2–2A) will be used with the word BEGIN to indicate the starting point, and the same symbol with the word END will indicate the ending point of the algorithm.

B. Input Symbol
In the previous examples, when developing the flowchart we assumed that the information to be processed was available as needed. In Figure 2–1, we assumed that the two numbers to be added were available, and consequently we made such statements as "Place the numbers in a column."

When developing algorithms for use on the computer, though, we must have some way to get information, such as the numbers to be added into the algorithm. That is, we must have some means of indicating that the information is to be entered into the computer for processing. So we use the shape of a punched card to indicate input (see Figure 2–2B). The information in the input must be assigned a name so that it can be referenced during processing. This name must appear in the input symbol. The symbol signifies that a value is to be sent from an input device such as a graphics terminal keyboard and is to be converted into an internal binary form and assigned to the variable designated in the box.

Figure 2–1.
Flowchart for Adding
Two REAL Decimal
Numbers

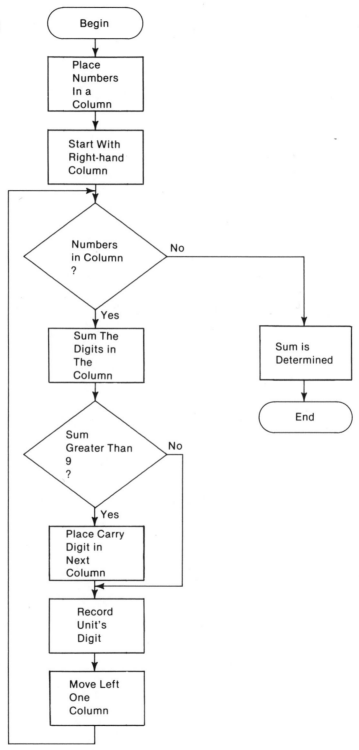

Figure 2-2.
Flowchart Symbols

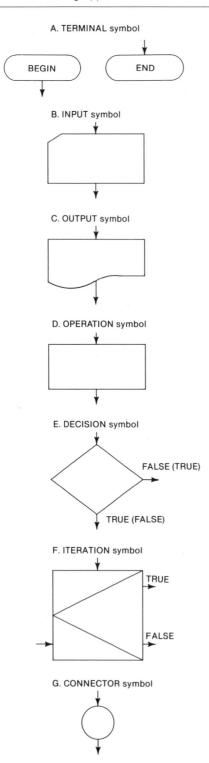

A. TERMINAL symbol

BEGIN   END

B. INPUT symbol

C. OUTPUT symbol

D. OPERATION symbol

E. DECISION symbol

FALSE (TRUE)

TRUE (FALSE)

F. ITERATION symbol

TRUE

FALSE

G. CONNECTOR symbol

C. Output Symbol

Likewise, information contained in the computer will need to be output. So we use the representation of a printed form to indicate the output process (see Figure 2–2C). The name of the information to be sent to the printer or other output device is listed in the symbol.

D. Operation Symbol

A rectangular box (see Figure 2–2D) will be used to represent a particular operation. Although the common practice is to use a separate box for each operation, it will be convenient at times to indicate several operations in one box. Since computer algorithms involve computational procedures, we can expect the normal operation to be a specific calculation. To standardize, we will adopt the convention of allowing only an assignment statement to be represented in the operation symbol. Assignment statements will be discussed in Chapter 3.

E. Decision Symbol

The algorithm of Example 2.6, like most algorithms, requires provision for a variation of the linear sequence of operations. We use a diamond shape to indicate a decision (see Figure 2–2E; also see Figure 2–1).

A question is asked in such a way that the answer is either YES or NO, TRUE or FALSE. (Although a question mark can be used, it is generally understood that the symbol implies a question.) There are two possible paths leading from the symbol, one for the affirmative condition (TRUE) and one for the negative (FALSE). There is only one entry to the symbol.

F. Iteration

Iteration will be indicated on flowcharts by the symbol shown in Figure 2–2F. This iteration construct will be discussed in detail in Chapter 5.

G. Connectors

When necessary to break the flow of logic in a flowchart, a small circle (see Figure 2–2G) can be used to indicate continuity. In the event that a long or complicated flowchart requires the use of a line that would cross other paths or continue onto another page, the line need not be completely drawn. Instead, connectors can be used to indicate the two points to be connected. However, care must be taken so that connectors are not overused to the point that they obscure the logic of the algorithm.

H. Flow Arrow

The symbols of the flowchart are connected with arrows that define the flow of the algorithm. In general, each symbol will have one arrow entering it and one exiting it. There are exceptions. Naturally, the terminal symbol has only one arrow since it is either at the beginning or the end of the flow.

2.7 The Grading Problem

As an example of a problem we can work on, let's consider how grades are assigned to students. Assigning grades to students is an interesting and time-consuming problem that confronts all teachers. Since this problem is sometimes of interest to students, we have chosen to develop it in some detail. One section in each of the next five chapters is devoted to applying what you have learned in that chapter to the grading problem.

Table 2–1 Output of Grading Problem

Course: Math 351				Instructor: Mr. P. J. Smythe		
Section: 3				Room: 304		
Number of Tests: 3						
Number of Students: 10						

Student's Name	Test 1	Test 2	Test 3	CUM PTS	Average	Grade
Adams, M. E.	85	87	90	262	87.33	B
Barnes, L. J.	56	60	72	168	56.00	F
Carlton, P. G.	30	40	59	129	43.00	F
Driscoll, R.	98	99	100	297	99.00	A
Evans, S. T.	90	85	76	251	83.67	C
Orly, A. P.	50	65	78	193	64.33	D
Puget, S.	83	81	84	248	82.67	C
Ryan, M. A.	90	89	72	251	83.67	C
Silve, G. A.	60	65	65	190	63.33	D
Walton, J. J.	88	70	89	247	82.33	C
Test Mean	73.0	74.1	78.5	223.6		
Test Standard Deviation	22.38	17.38	12.42	51.22		

Before proceeding, we will make a more formal statement of the problem. Develop an algorithm that will

1. Input the name and test scores for all students in the class
2. Calculate the mean and standard deviation for each test
3. Calculate the course mean and standard deviation
4. Calculate each student's cumulative points and average
5. Assign each student's letter grade in accordance with the following:
   A.   95–100%
   B.   85–94%
   C.   70–84%
   D.   60–69%
   F.   Below 60%
6. Produce an output listing similar to that shown in Table 2–1.

A. Decomposition

This grading problem is fairly involved. In accordance with what has been discussed in this chapter, we would start by decomposing it into smaller problems. Our first decomposition would yield the following subproblems:

1. Input data
2. Process data
3. Output data

We would normally undertake to decompose the process into a set of sub-problems; however, we note that steps 2 to 5 in the original statement of the problem provide a fairly comprehensive decomposition. We could easily justify decomposing any of these subproblems even further. However, step 4 appears easy enough to solve directly. We will proceed to develop an algorithm by applying the problem-solving steps to step 4 of the problem.

B. Problem-Solving Steps

Applying the problem-solving steps discussed in Section 2.4 to step 4 of the problem, we derive the following:

1. Statement of the problem: Calculate a student's cumulative points and average for three test scores.
2. Develop an algorithm:
   a. Cumulative points = Test 1 + Test 2 + Test 3
   b. Average = Cumulative points ÷ 3
3. Execute the algorithm: Using the data for the first student in the list in Table 2–1, we derive:
   a. Cumulative points = $85 + 87 + 90 = 262$
   b. Average = $262 \div 3 = 87.33$
4. Analyze the results: The answer is entirely consistent with what we would expect, and therefore we assume we have a good algorithm.

C. Flowchart

At this point we would put the algorithm in the form of a flowchart, as shown in Figure 2–3. Since we have discussed the flowchart symbols in detail, you should be able to follow the logic of the diagram. We will leave this problem now and refer back to it in Chapter 3.

2.8 Summary

For the remainder of this book, we will be concerned with the development of algorithms for well-defined problem statements. Before going on, however, it would be good to reflect upon what we have learned about problem solving. The flow diagram in Figure 2–4 is indicative of this entire procedure. Note that the problem-solving process contains several iterative phases and is itself iterative.

Take, for example, the decomposition phase. The problem is continuously decomposed until we are satisfied that we have a subproblem small enough that the problem-solving steps can be applied to it.

Figure 2-3.
Flowchart for Grading Problem

BEGIN
NAME,
TEST1,
TEST2,
TEST3
CUMULATIVE POINTS =
TEST1 + TEST2 + TEST3
AVERAGE =
CUMULATIVE POINTS ÷ 3
NAME, TEST1, TEST2,
TEST3, CUMULATIVE
POINTS, AVERAGE
END

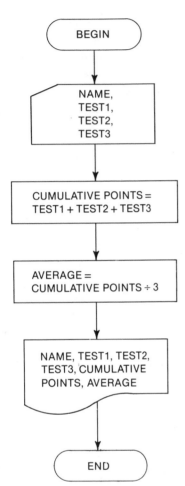

Figure 2-4.
Flowchart for Decomposition Process

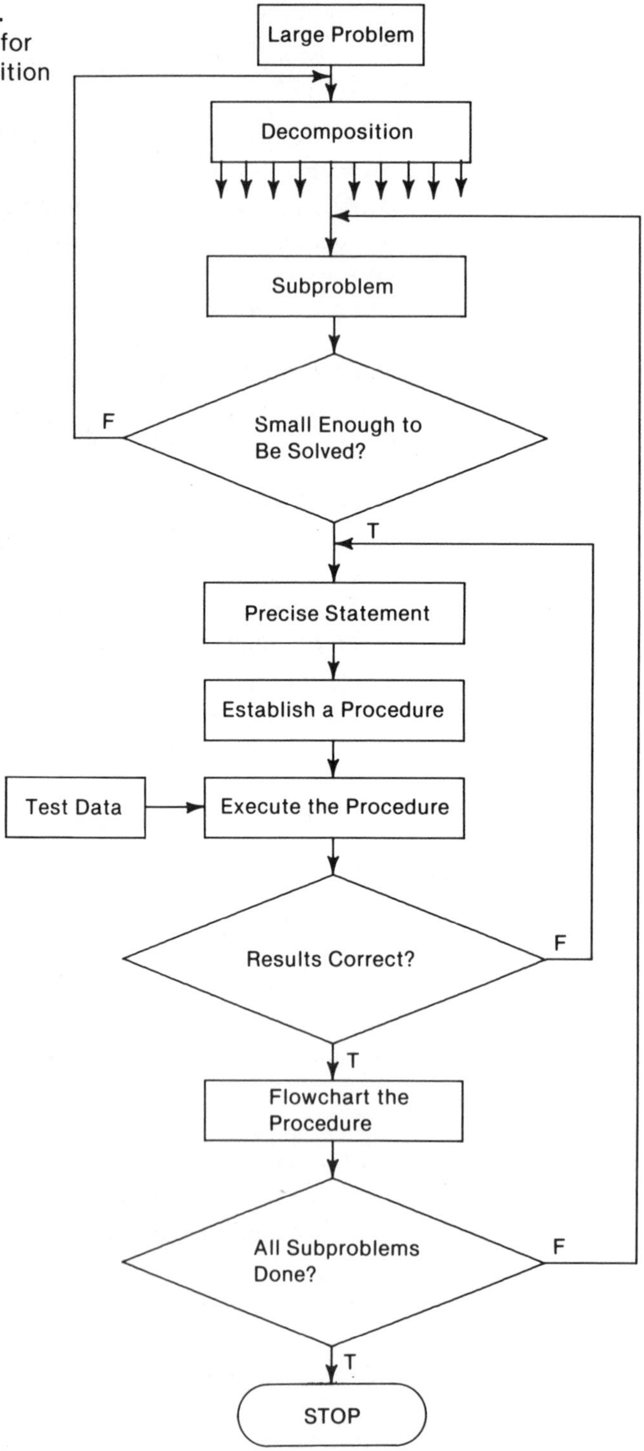

Large Problem
Decomposition
Subproblem
Small Enough to
Be Solved?
F
T
Precise Statement
Establish a Procedure
Test Data
Execute the Procedure
Results Correct?
F
T
Flowchart the
Procedure
All Subproblems
Done?
F
T
STOP

After having developed an algorithm for a particular subproblem, we continually go back until all subproblems have been solved. After all subproblems have been solved and tested, we should be able to test the entire problem and claim an error-free solution. How true this is will depend on how judiciously and thoroughly we applied the execution and analysis steps to each subproblem's solution.

Solved Problems

2.1

Write an algorithm for driving a car out of the garage and into the street.

Solution

The results of decomposing this problem can be enumerated in the following 18 steps. Any one of these could be further decomposed as a separate subprogram if necessary.

1. Walk to garage.
2. Open garage door.
3. If something is in driveway, do step 4.
4. Curse, then remove obstruction from driveway.
5. Open car door.
6. If you do not have key, do steps 7 and 8.
7. Curse and go back to house to get key.
8. Return to car.
9. Turn on ignition.
10. If it is not daytime, do step 11.
11. Turn on lights.
12. If it is raining, do step 13.
13. Turn on windshield wipers.
14. Shift into reverse.
15. Back up to street.
16. Repeat step 17 as long as cars are coming.
17. Mumble.
18. Drive into street.

2.2

Write an algorithm to determine how much paint to buy for a 10-foot-by-12-foot room including the ceiling, which is 9 feet high. One gallon of paint covers 200 square feet.

Solution

1. Find the ceiling area in square feet = $10' \times 12' = 120'$
2. Find the end wall area in square feet = $2 \times 9' \times 10' = 180'$
3. Find the side wall area in square feet = $2 \times 9' \times 12' = 216'$
4. Total the areas = $120' + 180' + 216' = 516'$
5. Paint needed is $516' \div 200' = 2.58$ gallons

2.3

At a recent track meet, the relay team established the following times:

	Distance	Time	Speed
Leg 1	500 meters	60 secs	8.33 m/sec
Leg 2	500 meters	53 secs	9.43 m/sec
Leg 3	500 meters	59 secs	8.47 m/sec
Leg 4	500 meters	51 secs	9.80 m/sec

Develop an algorithm for calculating the average speed for the race.

Solution

1. Distance = $4 \times 500 = 2000$ meters.
2. Time = $60 + 53 + 59 + 51 = 223$ seconds.
3. Average = 8.97 m/sec.

Notice how tempting it is to take the sum of the averages $(8.33 + 9.43 + 8.47 + 9.80)$ and divide by 4. However, this would yield the average speed per leg of the race and not the average speed for the race.

2.4

Generalize and flowchart the algorithm of Solved Problem 2.2 for a room of length L and width W with H-foot ceilings and paint that covers P square feet per gallon.

Solution

The flowchart is shown in Figure 2–5.

2.5

Generalize and flowchart the algorithm of Solved Problem 2.3 for a relay race of 4 legs with D meters per leg and respective times of T1, T2, T3, and T4 seconds.

Solution

The flowchart is shown in Figure 2–6.

Figure 2–5.
Flowchart for
Solved
Problem 2.4

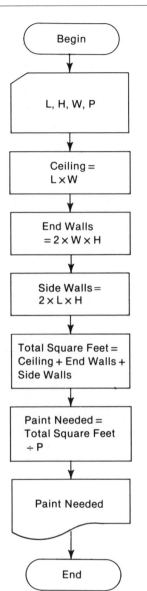

Figure 2–6.
Flowchart for
Solved
Problem 2.5

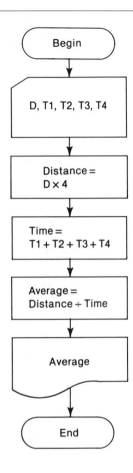

Supplementary Problems

2.6
Write an algorithm for dividing two integers.

2.7
Write an algorithm to describe the process of waking up and getting ready for work in the morning.

2.8
Write an algorithm to describe the steps necessary to buy a car.

2.9
Write an algorithm to describe the process of finding a job.

2.10
Write an algorithm to find the value of 6!, defined as $6! = 6 \times 5 \times 4 \times 3 \times 2 \times 1$.

2.11
Generalize your solution to problem 2.10 to find the value of N!, defined as $N! = N \times (N-1) \times (N-2) \times \cdots \times 1$.

2.12
Assume a person's physical fitness index is defined as weight divided by height. Write an algorithm to find an individual's physical fitness index, given his height and weight.

2.13
Generalize your solution to problem 2.12 to find the physical fitness index of N people.

3 *Programming Concepts*

3.1 Introduction

The process of solving a complex problem on a computer involves several steps. We have discussed the process of successively decomposing a large, involved problem into smaller, more manageable subproblems. We have shown how to apply the four problem-solving steps to the subproblems in order to generate an algorithm. We have discussed the four characteristics of a good algorithm and how it can be pictorially represented as a flowchart.

In this chapter, we will discuss some of the fundamental language constructs needed to understand the development of computer algorithms and the conversion of algorithms to programs. By the completion of this chapter, you should be able to answer the following questions:

1. What is a program?
2. What is a variable?
3. What is an identifier?
4. What is meant by precedence of operators?
5. What is an assignment statement?

3.2 Algorithms and Programs

Let us assume that we have generated a specific set of operations that, when executed, will solve some problem (i.e., an algorithm). Our next step is to convert this algorithm into a form in which it can be executed by a computer. That is, our task is to express our algorithm as a program. A **program** is defined as an explicit set of instructions expressed in a language understandable to the computer. A **language** is a specific set of words and the rules governing their usage from which statements can be constructed for communicating instructions and/or information.

There are two general classes of programming languages: assembly and high-level. Assembly languages are very fundamental and representative of the computer's internal machine codes. **Assembly language** instructions convert to machine instructions, one to one. **High-level languages** (e.g., COBOL, ALGOL, FORTRAN, and so on) are very English-like in structure and have the advantages of converting a single high-level statement to several machine instructions. The process by which the computer converts high-level language instructions to machine instructions is called **compiling.**

The development of an algorithm requires considerable attention to detail and a complete understanding of the process required for resolution of the problem. The process of translating the algorithm into a computer program requires knowledge of the language to be used but does not necessarily require full understanding of the details of the algorithm. While the programming phase is important, it is a less demanding task than algorithm development.

Often these two phases are performed by the same person and the distinction becomes less acute. Unfortunately, in many cases, the beginning programmer becomes so engrossed in learning the details of a language that he neglects the algorithm. In this text, we are concerned with the essence of computer science; we will focus our attention on the development of algorithms. We realize that the student will be translating the algorithms into computer programs of some higher level language. Therefore, the next few chapters will consider those features of higher level languages that are most useful to the programmer.

In general, the statements of higher level languages are designed to assist the programmer in translating his algorithms into computer programs. We must learn to think in terms of these tools when developing our algorithms; however, we do not want to lose sight of the importance of algorithm development by becoming too engrossed in a specific language. Thus we will first examine some of the tools available in higher level languages and then see how those tools are used in more sophisticated applications.

3.3 The Concept of a Variable

A simple analogy was made in Chapter 1 between the memory unit of a computer and a set of mailboxes. Each mailbox has an address (the box number), and letters and packages can be stored in that slot. Likewise, each memory location of a computer has an address, and data or information can be stored in that location. Remember, there is a distinction in both cases between the address of a location and the contents of that location.

It is a great convenience in a programming language to be able to give a name to the address of a storage location. This capability exists in most programming languages. The term **variable** is used to refer to a particular storage location, while the value of that variable denotes the **contents** of the storage location.

Since the contents of a storage location can be changed, the value associated with that variable can be changed. However, the name of the variable does not change. Just as different persons can move in and out of apartments without the address changing, the value of the variable can be altered without a change in the name of the variable, i.e., the address of the storage location. In fact, the concept of different values for a variable is inherent in the name "variable" itself. Remember, the variable is the data name and not the data itself.

Most programming languages refer to a variable as an **identifier,** or a data name. Each language has specific rules governing the construction of data names as identifiers.

Example 3.1

The higher order language PASCAL defines an identifier as a letter, or a letter followed by any combination of letters or digits. Are each of the following items identifiers according to the PASCAL definition?

1. D
2. XI
3. 3AAA
4. CS#A
5. TOTAL$
6. 629 − 10
7. PSHAW
8. TOTAL COST
9. LLANFAIRPWLLGWYNGYLL
10. NET-PROFIT-AFTER-FEDERAL-TAXES
11. SUPERCALIFRAGILISTICEXPIALIDOCIOUS

Solution

1. Yes.
2. Yes.
3. No. PASCAL identifiers must start with a letter.
4. No. PASCAL identifiers consist of only letters and digits (# is neither).
5. No. PASCAL identifiers consist of only letters and digits ($ is neither).
6. No. PASCAL identifiers must start with a letter and consist of only letters and digits (− is neither).
7. Yes.
8. No. PASCAL identifiers consist of only letters and digits (a space is neither). PASCAL would interpret this as two identifiers, TOTAL and COST, separated by a space.
9. Yes.

10. No. PASCAL identifiers consist of only letters and digits (− is neither).

11. Yes. The formal PASCAL definition of an identifier does not place a limit on the number of characters. However, some implementations of the language could limit the number of characters in an identifier.

End Solution

In order to illustrate the concept of an identifier or data name further, we will examine its definition in several well-known programming languages. A symbolic name (i.e., an identifier) in FORTRAN IV must start with a letter followed by any combination of letters and digits. In this respect, the definition is similar to PASCAL's. However, a FORTRAN IV identifier is limited to a total of six characters.

A data name in COBOL consists of combinations of letters, digits, and hyphens. However, it must not end with a hyphen and at least one character must be a letter. The data name is limited to 30 or fewer characters.

In PL/I an identifier must start with a letter, or with a set called the extended alphabet—$, @, or #. The remaining characters can be from the extended alphabet, digits, or the break character (underscore character). Identifiers are limited to 31 or fewer characters.

In the BASIC language, a data name consists of a single letter or a letter followed by a digit. Thus, an identifier in BASIC is never longer than two characters.

Example 3.2

Determine which of the character strings in Example 3.1 are identifiers/data names in FORTRAN, COBOL, PL/I, and BASIC.

Solution

	Language			
Character String	FORTRAN	COBOL	PL/I	BASIC
1. D	YES	YES	YES	YES
2. XI	YES	YES	YES	NO
3. 3AAA	NO	YES	NO	NO
4. CSIA	NO	NO	YES	NO
5. TOTAL $	NO	NO	YES	NO
6. 629-10	NO	NO	NO	NO
7. PSHAW	YES	YES	YES	NO
8. TOTAL COST	NO	NO	NO	NO

9. LLANFAIRPWLLGWYNGYLL	NO	YES	YES	NO
10. NET-PROFIT-AFTER- FEDERAL-TAXES	NO	YES	NO	NO
11. SUPERCALIFRAGILISTIC- EXPIALIDOCIOUS	NO	NO	NO	NO

End Solution

Besides providing a name for memory locations, identifiers can serve as a means of self-documentation in a program. For instance, if you saw the formula

$$V = \frac{\pi \times R^2 \times H}{3}$$

you might or might not recognize that the volume of some object is the product of π divided by 3 times its R (radius?) squared times its h (height?). However, if the formula were written as

$$\text{VOLUMEOFACONE} = \frac{\pi \times \text{RADIUS}^2 \times \text{HEIGHT}}{3}$$

you would have little doubt that the volume of a cone was being derived and that its height and radius were used in the calculation. In the second case, we have assigned the variables meaningful names. The use of such names as identifiers in computer programs not only specifies memory locations but also provides an indication of the meaning of the contents of that location. Throughout this book, we will follow the PASCAL definition for identifiers and use meaningful names wherever possible.

Each programming language has certain reserved words that indicate particular computer operations. Some examples of these reserved words are WHILE, FOR, DO, IF, PRINT, WRITE, READ, and ELSE. In order to avoid confusion and enable the language compiler to function smoothly, most languages require that identifiers be unique from these reserved words. Consequently, this book avoids using, as an identifier, any reserved word in PASCAL, FORTRAN, COBOL, or BASIC.

In Chapter 1, we discussed three different binary representations of data: INTEGER, REAL, and ALPHANUMERIC. Any storage location can contain information in one of these forms. Since a variable indicates a storage location, it is reasonable to expect that the variable name itself can be indicative of the specific type of data stored at that location.

3.4 Constants

A variable is important in a programming language because different values can be associated with that variable. But every entity in an algorithm need not represent a changing value. For example, an algorithm that uses the mathematical constant π (the value obtained from dividing the circumference of any circle by its diameter) would not represent this number as a variable. If a particular value of π is considered to be sufficiently accurate for that algorithm (say $\pi = 3.14159$), then that value remains constant throughout the problem.

Thus, an important feature of any program is the use of constants. A **constant** is merely the use of specific values in the program rather than a reference to a variable. In this text we shall consider three types of constants, corresponding to the three types of data representation: INTEGERS, REAL numbers, and ALPHANUMERIC constants.

A. INTEGER Constants

An **INTEGER constant** is exactly what its name implies: a whole number without a fractional part. An INTEGER can be written with a positive sign (+) or a negative sign (−) and in such cases is usually called a signed INTEGER, or signed number. An INTEGER can also be written without a sign, in which case the number is assumed to be a positive quantity and is referred to as an unsigned INTEGER, or unsigned number.

In representing a constant, there must be some set of conventions. In this book, we will use the following conventions to represent INTEGER values since these rules are followed by a majority of higher level languages:

There are no commas in the INTEGER, e.g., 10,020 will be written as 10020.
A decimal point will not appear in the INTEGER.
An INTEGER cannot contain a space.
If an INTEGER has a sign, it must appear before the digits and there can be no space between the sign and the number.

Example 3.3

Are each of the following items valid INTEGERS according to our set of conventions?

1. 1776
2. 22 314
3. +36.
4. 3,196
5. −213
6. − 662
7. 36768.
8. 69A1

9. 999000000000

10. 0123

Solution

1. Yes.

2. No. A space cannot appear in the INTEGER. This is really two valid IN-TEGERS: 22 followed by 314.

3. No. An INTEGER cannot contain a decimal point.

4. No. An INTEGER cannot contain a comma.

5. Yes.

6. No. There cannot be a space between the sign and the number.

7. No. There cannot be a decimal point even though a fractional part does not follow the decimal point.

8. No. An INTEGER cannot contain a letter.

9. Yes, since we have placed no limit on the number of digits. However, most computer systems will place some restriction on the size of an IN-TEGER and this number would be too large for some computer systems. If required for some calculation, it could be conveniently represented as a REAL constant.

10. Yes. However, the leading 0 is not necessary.

End Solution

B. REAL Constants

Computer algorithms frequently use numerical values with fractional parts. Consequently, programming languages must provide for **REAL constants.** We will use two methods of showing a REAL constant in this book. The first method, called fixed point, uses a decimal point in the number; e.g., 3.14159 is an approximation to π. The second method, called floating point, or scientific notation, is especially useful for representing extremely small or extremely large numbers.

These numbers are stored internally as two parts: the mantissa (or characteristic) and the exponent. For example, 186,000 is the same as 1.86×10^5, where 1.86 is the mantissa and 5 is the exponent. The various languages and computer systems use different methods of expressing this scientific notation. We will use the letter E (for exponent) in the number to divide the mantissa value from the exponent value, and we will require the exponent value to have a sign. Thus, 1.86×10^5 would be written $1.86E+5$. Likewise, .0000234 would be written as $2.34E-5$.

In this book we will use the following conventions in representing REAL constants:

A REAL number is distinguished from an INTEGER by the presence of either a decimal point or the exponent indicator E.

There are no commas in a REAL number.

A REAL number cannot contain a space.

If a REAL number has a sign, it must appear before the number and there can be no space between the sign and the number.

In a REAL number expressed as a mantissa and an exponent, the letter E will serve to separate the two parts, the exponent must be an INTEGER, and the exponent must have a sign.

Example 3.4

Are each of the following items valid REAL numbers according to our set of conventions?

1. 7.45
2. $-$ 2.14
3. 7.102E $-$ 5
4. E2
5. 6291.
6. 7E $+$ 1.5
7. 826
8. 826.0
9. +8E10
10. +8E $+$ 10

Solution

1. Yes.
2. No. There cannot be a space between the sign and the number.
3. Yes.
4. No. There must be a mantissa. Note that most language compilers will interpret this as the variable named E2.
5. Yes.
6. No. The exponent value must be an INTEGER.
7. No. This is an INTEGER.
8. Yes.
9. No. The exponent must have a sign.
10. Yes.

End Solution

C. ALPHANUMERIC Constants

ALPHANUMERIC constants will be represented by the character string enclosed in quotation marks. Thus, "ABC" indicates a three-character string consisting of the letter A, followed by the letter B, followed by the letter C. Note that the character string can consist of ALPHANUMERIC digits. However, the character string "345" will not be equal to the INTEGER 345 since the data representation of the character 3, followed by the character 4, followed by the character 5 is not equal to the binary representation of the INTEGER value 345.

3.5 Arithmetic Expressions

Variables and constants are used to form arithmetic expressions. An **arithmetic expression** is defined as a single variable, a single constant, or a combination of one or more variables and/or constants separated by arithmetic operators that, when evaluated, yield a numerical value. The more interesting arithmetic expressions contain at least one arithmetic operator. Arithmetic expressions are usually formed using the four basic arithmetic operations of addition, subtraction, multiplication, and division. A fifth arithmetic operation, which is sometimes used, is exponentiation, that is, raising a number to some power.

Each high-level language uses special symbols or reserved words to denote arithmetic operations. In describing the arithmetic operations used in algorithms, this text uses the symbols $+$, $-$, $/$, $*$, and $**$ to denote addition, subtraction, division, multiplication, and exponentiation, respectively. The first three symbols correspond to the normal symbols used in mathematics. The symbol $*$ for multiplication avoids the possibility of confusing the multiplication symbol $\times$ with the letter x. Computer languages must have some means of easily depicting exponentiation. The symbol $**$ is generally used for this purpose, e.g., 2^4 is written $2**4$. These symbols are used in several of the programming languages.

The evaluation of an arithmetic expression determines the value of that expression. If the expression contains only constants, the same value will always be obtained whenever the expression is evaluated. But if the expression contains variables, its value at any time will depend upon the values (contents) of the particular variables (memory locations) at the time of the evaluation.

In evaluating an expression, it is necessary to consider the order or sequence of performing arithmetic operations. For instance, if the variables A, B, and C are equal to 4, 5, and 6, respectively, consider the value of the expression $A + B*C$. If the addition is performed first, the result is 54, but a value of 34 is obtained when multiplication is the first operation to be performed. It is therefore necessary to establish the **precedence of arithmetic op-**

erations. Precedence defines the order in which operations must be performed. The arithmetic operations are divided into three precedence levels. From high to low, these are:

Level	Operator	Function
3	**	Exponentiation
2	*, /	Multiplication, Division
1	+, −	Addition, Subtraction

Evaluation of an expression is performed from the highest precedence to the lowest. If more than one operator of the expression is at the same level of precedence, the operations are performed from left to right.

Example 3.5

If A, B, C, and D are algebraic terms, write the following algebraic expressions as algorithmic arithmetic expressions. If A, B, C, and D have the values 4, 5, 6, and 7, respectively, evaluate these arithmetic expressions by the above rules:

1. $A + BC$
2. C^3
3. $AB - CD$
4. $A^2 + B^2$
5. $\frac{1}{2} \pi^2$

Solution

Expression	Value
1. A + B*C	4 + 5*6 = 4 + 30 = 34
2. C**3	6**3 = 216
3. A*B − C*D	4*5 − 6*7 = 20 − 42 = −22
4. A**2 + B**2	4**2 + 5**2 = 16 + 25 = 41
5. 1/2*3.14159**2	1/2*9.86958 = 4.93479

End Solution

Parentheses are used in the algorithmic description of arithmetic expressions just as they are utilized in mathematics. If one really wanted to perform the addition first in Example 3.5(1), the mathematical expression would be (a + b) c; the algorithmic arithmetic expression would be (A + B)*C. In deter-

mining the value of an expression, the expressions enclosed in parentheses are evaluated first, followed by application of the three levels of precedence. Within a set of parentheses, the same precedence rules apply. Thus, inner parentheses are evaluated first.

Example 3.6

Write the arithmetic expressions corresponding to the following algebraic formulas:

1. $\dfrac{C+D}{2}$

2. $A\left(\dfrac{C+D}{2}\right)$

3. $(A+B)^{C-A}$

4. $\dfrac{(A+B)\,(A-B)}{C-D}$

5. $\dfrac{C\,(A+B)+C\,(A-B)}{D}$

6. $\dfrac{2AC}{D}$

Solution

1. $(C+D)/2$
2. $A*((C+D)/2)$. This can also be written as $A*(C+D)/2$, since the performance of the operations according to the above rules will result in the same answer. In such cases as this one, the outer parentheses are optional but the inner parentheses are necessary.
3. $(A+B)**(C-A)$
4. $(A+B)*(A-B)/(C-D)$
5. $(C*(A+B)+C*(A-B))/D$. In this case the inner parentheses are evaluated first. The use of all parentheses in this instance is mandatory.
6. $2*A*C/D$. In this example, no parentheses are needed although one might wish to use them to write the expression as $(2*A*C)/D$. Sometimes this helps the programmer to see more clearly what is intended. Note that this is a simplified form of Example 3.6(5) and is more efficient to evaluate. This expression requires two multiplications and one division, but the evaluation of Example 3.6(5) requires an extra two additions and one subtraction.

End Solution

The programmer must use parentheses whenever it is necessary to override the implied precedence of operators to insure that calculations are executed in the desired sequence. If a specific formula does not require the use of parentheses, the programmer can employ them at his option in order to clarify the meaning and description of the algorithm.

From the examples, it can be seen that an arithmetic operation requires two operands and an arithmetic operator. An arithmetic expression is written such that the two operands are separated by an arithmetic operator. One or both of these operands can be an arithmetic expression enclosed in parentheses. The rules for formulating arithmetic expressions preclude two operators being next to each other. For example, $5 / + Y$ is an invalid arithmetic expression; however, $5 / (+ Y)$ is valid.

In addition to the five binary arithmetic operations $(+, -, *, /, **)$, which require two operands, there are two **unary operators,** namely, plus $(+)$ and minus $(-)$. The unary operators designate the sign of the arithmetic expression that they precede. For instance, $-A$ reverses the sign of the value of A. If we want to indicate the expression C^{-A}, the expression $C ** - A$ is not allowed. We can, however, express this as $C**(-A)$. In this case, the use of parentheses is mandatory with the unary minus.

3.6 Assignment Statement

The most fundamental operation in any high-level programming language is the assignment of a value to a variable. The **assignment statement** assigns a value to a variable. When we think of a value, we generally think of a numerical entity, i.e., an arithmetic value. There can be other types of values (in particular, logical values). However, these will be discussed after we have covered many of the basic concepts of programming. We will restrict the present use of the assignment statement to imply the assignment of an arithmetic value to a variable. Although the assignment operator itself can differ among various programming languages, all languages employ a similar structure for this statement.

There are basically three parts to an assignment statement: the variable that is to be given a value, the value that is to be assigned, and the assignment operator that denotes the assignment process. In this book we will represent the assignment statement in a manner closely related to the usage in the majority of programming languages. An assignment statement will consist of the name of the variable, followed by the assignment operator, followed by the value.

Since the assignment operation has an arithmetic variable on the left, the value on the right can be any arithmetic expression. Some of the symbols that programming languages have used as the assignment operator include $=$, $\leftarrow$, and $:=$. In our flowcharts we will use the reverse arrow, $\leftarrow$, as the assignment operator, to distinguish it from the relational operator (=), which will be introduced in Chapter 4. The symbol := will be introduced in Chapter 7.

Example 3.7

The total area of a sphere is equal to $4\pi R^2$ where R is the radius of the sphere. If the variable AREA is used to represent the area, and the variable RADIUS is used to represent the radius, develop the assignment statement for assigning a value to AREA.

Solution

The value to be assigned is the arithmetic expression $4\pi R^2$. This can be expressed as $4*3.14159*RADIUS**2$. The assignment statement is then

$$A \leftarrow 4*3.14159*RADIUS**2$$

Note that the assignment is an operation and that in developing flowcharts we show operations in a rectangle. Thus, the flowchart representation of the assignment is shown in Figure 3–1.

End Solution

When the assignment statement of Example 3.7 is performed, a value is given to the variable AREA. Note that this value is determined by the value that variable RADIUS contains at the time the assignment is made. For instance, if RADIUS equals 1, the value of AREA will be 12.56636, while AREA will have a value of 113.09724 after the assignment statement, if RADIUS equals 3.

As pointed out previously, the assignment statement consists of a variable and an arithmetic expression, separated by the assignment operator. Since

Figure 3–1.
Flowchart for Area
of a Sphere

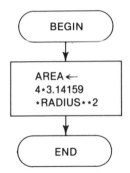

the variable is to the left of the assignment operator, it is sometimes called the left-hand side of the assignment statement. Similarly, the arithmetic expression is called the right-hand side. It is important to note that the left-hand side is a single variable. We point this out because of the similarity in appearance of the assignment statement to the algebraic formula. An algebraic formula shows the relationship of variables. In this sense the equation

$$X + Y = A + B$$

is perfectly legitimate. It merely says the sum of the variables X and Y equals the sum of the variables A and B. But an assignment statement indicates the assignment of a value to a variable. If we attempt to write

$$X + Y \leftarrow A + B$$

we do not have an assignment statement since there is no single variable on the left-hand side to receive the value of the sum of the two variables A and B.

In the case of assigning a REAL number to an INTEGER variable, the programmer must be sensitive to whether the computer language employs truncation or rounding. In truncation, only the numbers to the left of the decimal point are assigned. In rounding, the digit immediately to the right of the decimal point is checked. If 5 or greater, then the number to the left of the decimal point is incremented by 1 before assignment; otherwise it is left alone. The difference between truncation and rounding can significantly affect the results of your algorithm in certain problems.

3.7 Input and Output

The processes of getting data into the computer and getting the results out of the computer are referred to as input and output, respectively.

The actual input/output (I/O) methods used can vary considerably among machines and languages. However, the basic, underlying principles are similar. The same fundamental considerations and requirements must be included in any language, or computer system, in order to provide the I/O operations that are needed in programming.

A. Basic Elements of Input/Output

There are four basic elements of input/output included in all I/O constructs. These are

1. The Input/Output Statement
I/O statements generally include some key word that signifies that the input/output statement is to be executed by the system. Examples of key words that have been used in various languages are WRITE, READ, PRINT, PUNCH, INPUT, and OUTPUT.

2. The Hardware Device

The I/O statement must indicate what specific physical equipment is to be used to perform the operation. There are a large number of I/O devices. These include the card reader, card punch, line printer, magnetic disk, magnetic tape, and video terminal.

3. The Format

When reading data, or writing out the results of a program, it is necessary to consider how the input is to be organized and how the printed output is to look. Is a number to be written as an INTEGER, as a REAL number with a decimal point, or as a REAL number in a scientific or floating point notation? How many decimal places are to be included? Is it desirable to write a message out on the page? Should the number be written on the left side of the page, in the center of the page, or on the right side? This type of information is usually provided to the computer by the format portion of the I/O statement.

4. Variable List

On input, the **variable list** consists of the names of those memory locations where the data is to be stored when it is read from the input device. On output, the variable list consists of the names of those memory locations from which information is to be copied to the output device. The variable list usually consists of one or more variables. In some cases, there may be no variables in the variable list, implying that the I/O statement is being used for device control (e.g., advancing the printer to the top of a page).

B. Flowchart Symbols

The input flowchart symbol (see Figure 2–2B) with the variables NAME and HOURS inside would indicate that two items are to be read from the input device in accordance with a specific format, be converted into their internal binary representation, and be stored at the memory locations NAME and HOURS. The previous value of NAME and of HOURS would be destroyed.

The output flowchart symbol (see Figure 2–2C) with the names PAY and TAX inside would indicate that the values stored in the memory locations PAY and TAX must be translated from their internal binary representation into their associated output code and be sent to the designated output device in accordance with a specified format. The contents of PAY and TAX *remain unaltered.*

Two of the four basic components of the I/O statements are represented by the flowchart symbol. The shape of the symbol indicates whether the command is input or output, and the name of the variable list is written inside the flowchart symbol. The hardware device and format are not identified in the symbol. Unless the hardware device is specifically stated, we will assume that **default devices** are being used, that is, all input is to be entered from a video terminal and all output is to be written to a video terminal or line printer. Formats are generally language dependent and consequently a general exposition of formats is not included in this book. Refer to specific programming language texts for format details.

The next example provides an illustration of simple I/O including the use of an echo check. An **echo check** dictates that the value of all input variables must be immediately displayed (i.e., echoed) before any changes are made in these values. There are many ways for incorrect data to be inadvertently entered into the computer, such as typing errors, incorrect formats, and transposed digits. Therefore, it is important to verify that the input data is accurate. An audit, or an echo check, is one way of ensuring that the program receives the correct data for its execution.

Example 3.8

The total resistance of two resistors connected in parallel is given by the following formula:

$$RTOT = \frac{R1 * R2}{R1 + R2}$$

Develop an algorithm to read the data, provide the echo check, perform the computation, and print the result.

Solution

Let the three variables be denoted by RTOT, R1, and R2. The algorithm in Figure 3–2 consists of four operations: one for each of the four tasks listed in the problem statement. Note that the simple calculation occurs between the echo check and the output.

End Solution

3.8 The Grading Problem and Programming Concepts

Applying some of the programming concepts we discussed in this chapter, we should be able to refine the grading problem developed in Chapter 2. Note that the constant, 3, was used in Figure 2–3. Although it is an INTEGER and occupies a memory location, there is no need to assign it a name. The address, or name, of the 3 may be considered to be the same as its value.

Figure 2–3 makes reference to certain names whose value would change each time this algorithm is executed. These values can be treated as variables and be assigned specific names as follows:

VARIABLE NAME	DATA TYPE	CONTENTS
NAME	ALPHA	Student's name
TEST1	INTEGER	Test score 1
TEST2	INTEGER	Test score 2
TEST3	INTEGER	Test score 3
CUMPTS	INTEGER	Cumulative points
AVERAGE	REAL	Grade point average

Note that the equals symbol, "=," is used as an assignment operator in Figure 2–3. This will be changed to the reverse arrow, "←," for all future flowcharts. Likewise the division sign "÷" will be changed to a slash "/."

Code and execute this algorithm using the sample data and have your output listing match the following output, which was extracted from Table 2–1:

Student's Name	Test 1	Test 2	Test 3	Cumulative Points	Average	Grade
Adams, M. E.	85	87	90	262	87.33	

We have deliberately left GRADE blank for now, since we have not yet shown how it will be assigned. The changes we have discussed for Table 2–1 are shown in Figure 3–3.

Figure 3-2.
Flowchart for
Example 3.8

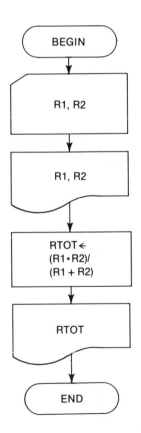

Figure 3-3.
Flowchart for
Grading Problem

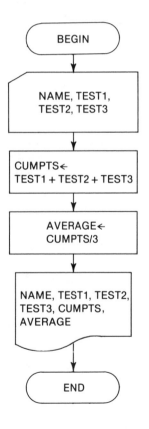

3.9 Summary

This chapter has presented the basic concepts needed to translate simple algorithms to computer programs. A flowchart can be used as a graphic representation of that algorithm. The algorithm can be expressed independently of the computer language in which the problem will be programmed. Throughout this book we strive to express algorithms in general terms, and we try to avoid depicting the problem as being dependent on a specific language.

Solved Problems

3.1

Assume that X, Y, and Z are REAL variables and are initially 0. Show the contents of the variables after the algorithm in Figure 3–4 is executed.

Solution

Action	X	Y	Z
Begin	0.0	0.0	0.0
X←3.4	3.4	0.0	0.0
Y←4.0	3.4	4.0	0.0
Z←X∗Y	3.4	4.0	13.6

The final values of X, Y, and Z are 3.4, 4.0, and 13.6, respectively.

3.2

Assume X, Y, and Z are REAL variables and that the following two data lines are provided as input:

Line 1   5.0
Line 2   2.5

Show the results of executing the algorithm in Figure 3–5.

Solution

Action	X	Y	Z
Begin	0.0	0.0	0.0
Read X	5.0	0.0	0.0
Read Y	5.0	2.5	0.0
Z←X+Y	5.0	2.5	7.5
Write Z	5.0	2.5	7.5

Notice that the READs and the assignment statements destroyed the previous contents of the associated variables, but the WRITE did not affect the contents. Thus there are two ways to alter the contents of memory—by a READ and by an assignment. The WRITE sends a copy of the contents of the

Figure 3-4.
Flowchart for
Solved Problem 3.1

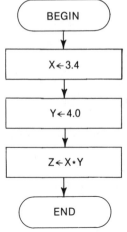

Figure 3-5.
Flowchart for
Solved Problem 3.2

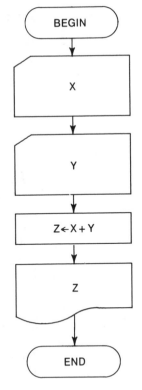

memory location to the output device but does not alter the actual memory contents.

3.3
Show the results of Solved Problem 3.1, assuming X and Y are REAL, Z is an INTEGER, and the computer uses truncation.

Solution

Action	X	Y	Z
Begin	0.0	0.0	0
X←3.4	3.4	0.0	0
Y←4.0	3.4	4.0	0
Z←X*Y	3.4	4.0	13.

The product of X and Y is 13.6; however, before assignment to Z, an INTEGER, the result is truncated to 13.

3.4
Show the results of Example 3.1, assuming X and Y are REAL, Z is an INTEGER, and the computer uses rounding.

Solution

Action	X	Y	Z
Begin	0.0	0.0	0
X←3.4	3.4	0.0	0
Y←4.0	3.4	4.0	0
Z←X*Y	3.4	4.0	14

The product of X*Y is 13.6 but was rounded to 14 before assignment to Z.

3.5

Write an algorithm to find the circumference and area of a circle for some given value of radius.

Solution

The algorithm is shown in Figure 3–6.

3.6

Write an algorithm to calculate a student's new grade point average, given his cumulative score, latest test score, and number of tests.

Solution

The algorithm is shown in Figure 3–7.

Supplementary Problems

3.7

If the REAL variables X, Y, and Z have the values 1.5, 2.3, and 4.6, respectively, evaluate the following assignment statements:

1. $Z \leftarrow Z + X / Z - X$
2. $Z \leftarrow (Z + X) / Z - X$
3. $Z \leftarrow Z + X / (Z - X)$
4. $Z \leftarrow (Z + X) / (Z - X)$
5. $X \leftarrow X * Y + Z$
6. $X \leftarrow X + Y * Z$
7. $Y \leftarrow X + Y * Z - Y$
8. $Y \leftarrow X + Y * (Z - Y)$
9. $Y \leftarrow (X + Y) * Z - Y$
10. $Y \leftarrow (X + Y) * (Z - Y)$

Figure 3-6.
Flowchart for
Solved Problem 3.5

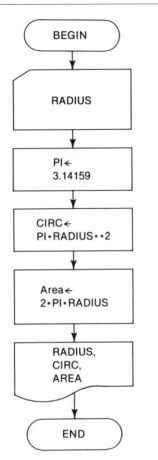

Figure 3-7.
Flowchart for
Solved Problem 3.6

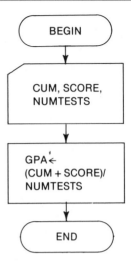

3.8
Write an algorithm to calculate a student's tuition fee based on the following inputs:

1. Number of credit hours
2. Cost per credit hour
3. Parking fee
4. Athletic fee

3.9
Write an algorithm to calculate a worker's take-home pay based on the following inputs:

1. Total hours
2. Rate per hour
3. Rate per overtime hour

Assume any hours over 40 are considered overtime.

4   BOOLEAN Expressions and Conditional Statements

4.1 Introduction

To this point we have developed and discussed algorithms in which the operations occurred sequentially. That is, upon completion of the action required by one statement, the next statement in order was executed. Thus the term **sequential processing.**

The computer is a very powerful and useful tool for problem solving. However, its usefulness is not only derived from its ability to rapidly do sequential processing but also from its ability to choose alternative courses of action based on some decision. This capability is known as **conditional processing.** By the end of this chapter you should be able to answer the following questions:

1. What are BOOLEAN expressions?
2. What are the relational operators?
3. What are conditional statements?

4.2 BOOLEAN Expressions

Fundamental to the development of conditional statements in any program language are BOOLEAN expressions. You might recall that an arithmetic expression is formed by a simple variable, or by two or more variables and constants separated by arithmetic operators, that, when evaluated, will yield a numeric value.

A BOOLEAN expression is very similar in structure to an arithmetic expression. A **BOOLEAN expression** is defined as a simple variable, or two or more variables and constants separated by relational operators, that, when evaluated, will yield a BOOLEAN value. A **BOOLEAN value** is TRUE or FALSE. Therefore, we could say that a BOOLEAN expression is any expression that yields a TRUE or FALSE.

A BOOLEAN expression can be used to establish the relationship between two arithmetic expressions. The relationship in question is established by one of the following six **relational operators:**

Operator	Meaning
<	less than
<=	less than or equal to
>	greater than
>=	greater than or equal to
=	equal to
<>	not equal to

For example, the BOOLEAN expression

$A + B > C$

establishes a relation between the sum of A and B, and the variable C. If the sum of A and B is larger than C at the time of comparison, then this expression would have a value of TRUE; otherwise it would have a value of FALSE.

In order to evaluate a BOOLEAN expression, we must know how the relational operators fit into our hierarchy for the precedence of operators. The relational operators are on an equal precedence level with each other. However, the relational operators have the lowest priority discussed so far and are thus evaluated immediately after the arithmetic operators $(+, -)$. As we scan a statement from left to right, all arithmetic expressions would be evaluated first before a relational operator is applied. Remember, however, that parentheses override all implied precedence levels.

Example 4.1
Evaluate the following expression:

$5 - 3**(3-1) > 12/(3*4) + 6$

Solution
Scan from left to right, continually applying the rules of precedence, as shown in Figure 4–1.

End Solution

Figure 4-1.
BOOLEAN
Evaluation of
Example 4.1

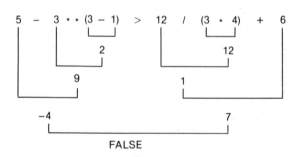

Example 4.2

Is each of the following items a valid BOOLEAN expression according to our set of conventions?

1. X>Y
2. X+3
3. 3=4+4
4. 3+A>=B+4
5. 3−5
6. 6**2<5

Solution

1. Yes.
2. No. (X+3) is an arithmetic expression.
3. Yes.
4. Yes.
5. No. (3−5) is an arithmetic expression.
6. Yes.

End Solution

Example 4.3

Evaluate the following BOOLEAN expressions, given that X=3, Y=5.

1. X+Y>Y**2
2. X>Y
3. X+Y−2=3+Y−5
4. X*Y<=X**2+6
5. X<>Y−2

Solution

1. False. $3+5>5^2$ or $8>25$
2. False. 3>5
3. False. 3+5−2=3+5−5 or 6=3
4. True. 3*5<=3**2+6 or 15<=15
5. False. 3<>5−2 or 3<>3

End Solution

4.3 Logical Operations

In the previous section, we discussed how very simple relationships between arithmetic expressions could be established by the use of relational operators. Although a very useful mechanism, the simple BOOLEAN expression is severely limiting.

Most programming languages allow us to enhance the BOOLEAN expression through judicious applications of logical operators. The **logical operators** are AND, OR, and NOT. They can be used to connect BOOLEAN expressions in order to form new BOOLEAN expressions according to a specific set of rules. The rules for applying logical operators are defined by a set of truth tables (see Table 4–1).

The precedence level of the logical operators is below that of the relational operators. NOT has the highest precedence among the logical operators, followed by AND, and then OR. The overall precedence of the operators we have discussed to this point is shown below:

Arithmetic Operators	* *
	*, /
	+, −
Relational Operators	<, <=, >, >=, =, <>
Logical Operators	NOT
	AND
	OR

The logical operators AND and OR are **binary operators** and establish the relationships between the BOOLEAN expressions immediately preceding and following their appearance. For example,

1. 5<3 AND 2>4 evaluates to FALSE.
2. 3=5−2 AND 4/2=2 evaluates to TRUE.
3. 5<3 OR 4/2=2 evaluates to TRUE.
4. 6−5>3 OR 2>7 evaluates to FALSE.

The logical operator NOT is a **unary operator** and alters the BOOLEAN value of the BOOLEAN expression immediately following it. For example,

1. NOT 5<3 evaluates to TRUE.
2. NOT 3<5 evaluates to FALSE.
3. NOT (5<3 AND 2>4) evaluates to TRUE.
4. NOT (5<3 OR 2<4) evaluates to FALSE.
5. NOT 5<3 OR 2<4 evaluates to TRUE.

Table 4–1 Truth Table for AND, OR, NOT

B1	B2	B1 AND B2	B1 OR B2	NOT B2
T	T	T	T	F
T	F	F	T	T
F	T	F	T	
F	F	F	F	

Example 4.4

Evaluate the following expression:

36**1/2>6 AND 7<3 OR 2**2=4 AND NOT (7>3 OR 5<2)

Solution

Scan from left to right, continually applying the rules of precedence, remembering that parentheses are evaluated first, as shown in Figure 4–2.

End Solution

A word of caution is in order: Sometimes it is tempting to fall into a very common pitfall in using logical operators. Remember, a logical operator references BOOLEAN expressions. Therefore, if we wish to determine if X is greater than 3 and less than 10, we cannot write X>3 AND <10 because <10 is not a BOOLEAN expression. To be syntactically correct, we must write X> 3 AND X<10.

Figure 4–2.
BOOLEAN
Evaluation of
Example 4.4

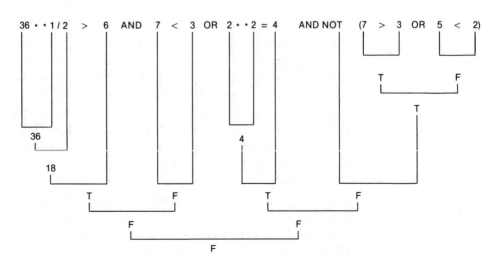

Example 4.5

Is each of the following items a valid BOOLEAN expression according to our set of conventions? If yes, evaluate the expressions.

1. 5<3 AND 6
2. 3<5 AND 6>2
3. 3=2 OR 2=2
4. NOT 3=2 OR 5>6
5. 2**2−3>1 AND 6>7 OR NOT 3
6. 5=10 OR 7=5 OR (6>7 AND NOT 3>2)

SOLUTION

1. No. 6 is not a BOOLEAN expression.
2. Yes. Result is TRUE.
3. Yes. Result is TRUE.
4. Yes. Result is TRUE.
5. No. NOT 3 is not a BOOLEAN expression.
6. Yes. Result is FALSE.

End Solution

4.4 Conditional Statements

The BOOLEAN expression makes it possible to establish a relationship that could be evaluated as either TRUE or FALSE. The conditional statement makes it possible to test the results of a BOOLEAN expression. That is, the conditional statement allows us to decide on alternative courses of action depending on some condition. The conditional statement is implemented in flowcharts through the use of the decision symbol in Figure 2–2E.

This symbol indicates that if the BOOLEAN expression is TRUE, then the TRUE (T) exit is taken; otherwise, the FALSE (F) exit is taken. The meaning of the conditional statement is not affected by which leg is labelled TRUE and which is labelled FALSE; however, we recommend consistency and will follow the convention that the TRUE leg exits to the bottom and the FALSE leg exits to the right.

High-level programming languages derive much of their power from their provision for conditional processing, although it is more straightforward in some languages, such as PASCAL, than it is in others, such as BASIC. During processing, the BOOLEAN expression <BE> is evaluated; if the result is TRUE, the instruction or set of instructions immediately following the TRUE will be executed. If the result is FALSE, then the instruction or set of instructions immediately following the TRUE will be skipped. Graphically, this can be represented as shown in Figure 4–3.

In Figure 4–3 there are no statements to be executed if the BOOLEAN expression is FALSE. In such situations the logic of the BOOLEAN expression can always be reversed to force the required statements to appear in the FALSE leg of the conditional statement.

Example 4.6

Develop an algorithm that will add 1.5 times an individual's hourly pay (HOURLYPAY) to his base pay (BASEPAY) for all hours worked (HOURS-WORKED) over 40.

Solution

The algorithm is shown in Figure 4–4.

End Solution

Figure 4–3.
Flowchart
Symbology for
Conditional
Processing

Figure 4–4.
Flowchart for
Example 4.6

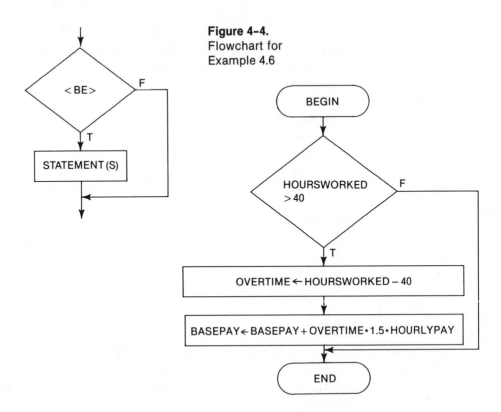

Figure 4–5.
Flowchart
Symbology for
Compound
Conditional
Processing

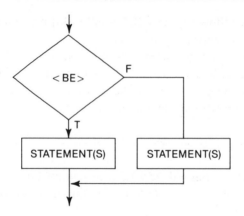

Example 4.6 requires no alternative action to be taken when the BOOLEAN expression (HOURSWORKED > 40) is FALSE. However, we frequently run into problems where the algorithm requires two completely different actions depending on the BOOLEAN expression. For a graphic representation of this requirement, see Figure 4–5.

If <BE> evaluates TRUE, then the statement(s) immediately following the T exit will be executed. If it evaluates FALSE, then the statement(s) immediately following the F exit will be executed.

Example 4.7

Develop an algorithm that will assign a student a "PASS" grade (GRADE) and add 1 to the number of students who passed (NUMBERPASSED) if the score (QUIZ) is 65 or better; otherwise, the grade is "FAIL" and 1 is added to the number of students who failed (NUMBERFAILED).

Solution

The algorithm is shown in Figure 4–6.

End Solution

4.5 Conditional Nesting

In our discussion of the conditional statement, we have put no restrictions on the statement(s) that follow the T or F exits. Consequently, a subsequent conditional statement can be executed as one of the statements controlled by the previous conditional. This logical flow, shown in Figure 4–7, is known as a **nested conditional**.

Figure 4-6.
Flowchart for
Example 4.7

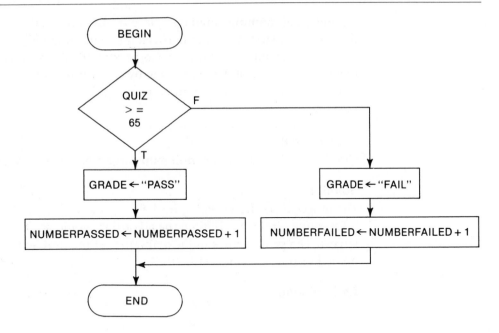

Figure 4-7.
Flowchart
Symbology for
Nested Conditional
Processing

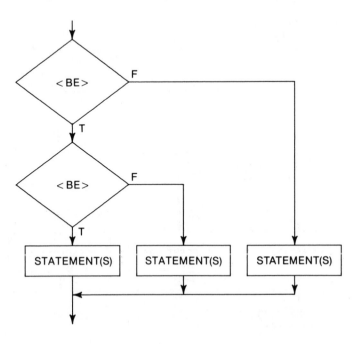

Some programming languages place restrictions on the number of levels that can be nested. You should check the requirements of the language you are using. In many situations, the logic contained in several nested conditionals can be consolidated into one by combining BOOLEAN expressions through the use of logical operators.

Example 4.8

Develop a flowchart to determine the largest of three numbers—X, Y, and Z.

Solution

The flowchart is shown in Figure 4–8.

Of course, if $X = Y = Z$, then the algorithm would still indicate that X is the largest. The problem lies in the ambiguity of the problem statement that did not tell us how to handle equalities.

End Solution

Figure 4–8.
Flowchart for
Example 4.8

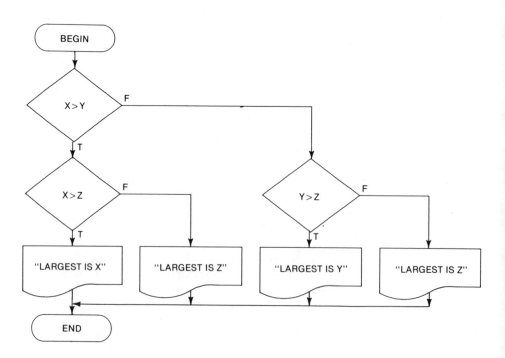

Example 4.9

Simplify Example 4.8 by using logical operators.

Solution

The simplified version is shown in Figure 4–9.

End Solution

Note that in both Example 4.8 and Example 4.9, there was no need to perform a test to see if Z was greater than X or Y. Since X was not greater than Y, and Y was not greater than Z, then by default Z was the largest. Sometimes in using conditionals, we tend to overtest; that is, we test for conditions that have already been eliminated by default. The best way to avoid

Figure 4–9.
Flowchart for
Example 4.9

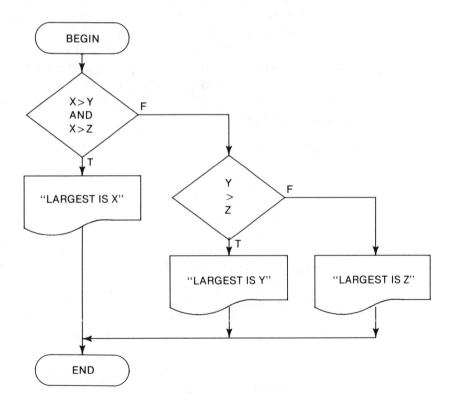

this situation is to do a thorough job during the analysis stage of problem solving and test your algorithm for all possible conditions.

4.6 The Grading Problem and Conditional Statements

Applying some of the concepts discussed in this chapter, we will be able to expand our continuing solution to the grading problem. Specifically, we shall assign each person a letter grade based on the criteria that were established in Chapter 2 as part of the problem definition. We can apply this criteria to the average calculated in Chapter 3. For convenience of reference, we repeat the range of letter grades:

A   95–100%
B   85–94%
C   70–84%
D   60–69%
F   Below 60%

To assign the appropriate letter grade, we simply make use of several nested conditionals to determine the range within which the student's average falls. The logic of this determination is shown as Figure 4–10 and would be placed between the connectors of Figure 4–11. Note that we have used an additional variable, GRADE, which is an ALPHA variable.

We recommend that you actually code the additional steps shown in Figure 4–10. This code should then be inserted in the appropriate place in your program from Chapter 3. Make sure you can duplicate the following output extracted from Table 2–1:

STUDENT'S NAME	TEST 1	TEST 2	TEST 3	CUM PTS	AVERAGE	GRADE
Adams, M. E.	85	87	90	262	87.33	B

4.7 Summary

The conditional statement is an extremely powerful programming construct that is used in all programming languages. The constructs presented in this chapter can be used in all of the high-level languages; however, usage in some is much more straightforward than in others. We strongly recommend that you analyze the language in which you are programming to determine the most direct way to use the material presented in this chapter.

Solved Problems

4.1

Two points can be used to define a straight line. Given any two points, the line segment drawn between the two points can be expressed as $Y = MX + B$,

Figure 4–10.
Flowchart for
Grading Problem

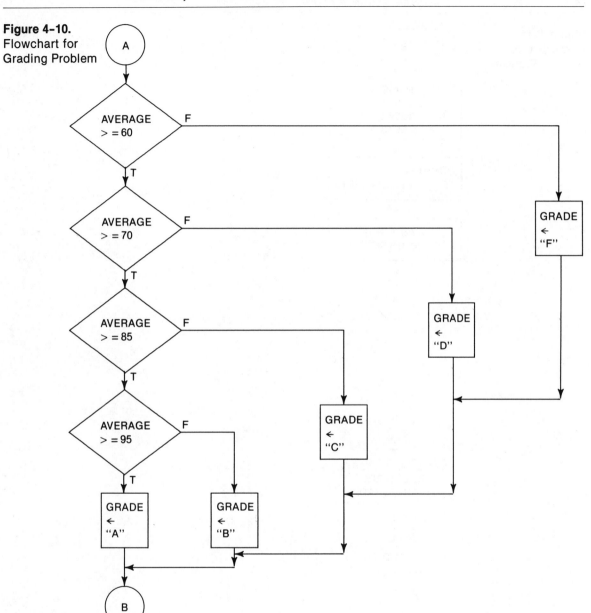

Figure 4–11.
Flowchart for
Grading Problem

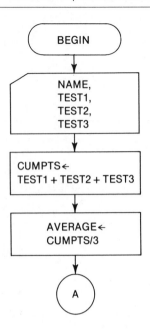

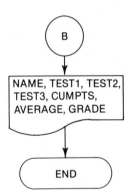

where M is the slope and B is the Y intercept. Develop an algorithm to input two points, (X1, Y1) and (X2, Y2), and determine M and B. The slope M is (Y2 − Y1)/(X2 − X1) and the Y intercept B is Y2 − M (X2).

Solution
Refer to Figure 4–12. The values of M and B can be algebraically determined by relatively simple assignment statements. However, to prevent dividing by 0, test to see if X2 equals X1. If so, merely output a message to that effect.

Figure 4–12.
Flowchart for
Solved Problem 4.1

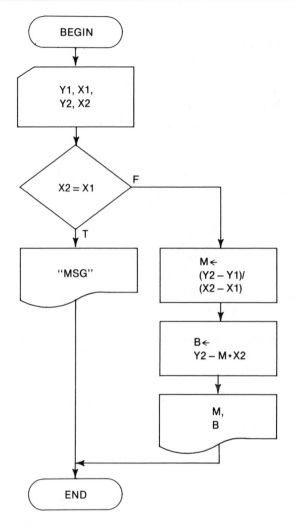

4.2
Given the values of the variables A= 1, B= 2, C= 3, D= 4, E= 5, F= 6, G= 7,
and BOOLEAN variables H= TRUE, I= FALSE, evaluate each of the following BOOLEAN expressions:

1. A= B
2. C<>D
3. D>F
4. 2∗A>= B
5. 4∗C<D∗∗2
6. 4∗E<= G
7. D>F AND C<>D
8. D>F OR C<>D
9. NOT D>F AND C<>D

10. D > F OR NOT C <> D

11. A = B OR 4*E <= G AND D > F

12. NOT (A = B OR 4*E <= G) AND D > F

13. (NOT I OR 4*E <= G) AND C <> D

14. NOT H AND C <> D OR 2*A >= B AND 4*C < D**2

15. NOT (H AND C <> D OR 2*A >= B) AND 4*C < D**2

Solution

The first six example expressions represent each of the six relational operators. Evaluation is a simple matter of arithmetic.

1. A = B	1 = 2	FALSE
2. C <> D	3 <> 4	TRUE
3. D > F	4 > 6	FALSE
4. 2*A >= B	2*1 >= 2	TRUE
5. 4*C < D**2	4*3 < 4**2	TRUE
6. 4*E <= G	4*5 <= 7	FALSE

The remaining expressions are more complicated because of the use of logical operators and require several steps for evaluation.

7. D > F AND C <> D
     F   T
          F

8. D > F OR C <> D
     F   T
          T

9. NOT D > F AND C <> D
        F   T
    T
        T

10. D > F OR NOT C <> D
     F   T
           F
        F

11.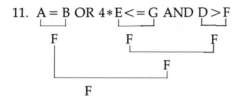

12.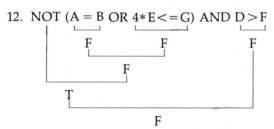

13.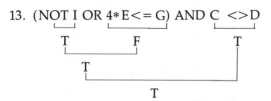

14.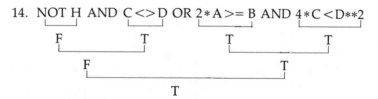

15.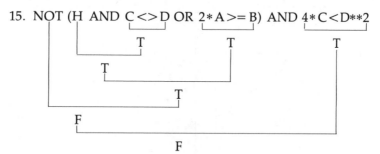

4.3
Develop an algorithm to input five numbers, place the largest number in BIG, and output the resulting value of BIG.

Solution
Refer to Figure 4–13. Read the five numbers into the variables N1, N2, N3, N4, and N5, respectively. Assign N1 to BIG. BIG is then compared to N2, N3, N4, N5 in order. If any of these values is greater than BIG, BIG is assigned that value. As a result, BIG will contain the largest of the five values and is output.

Figure 4-13.
Flowchart for
Solved
Problem 4.3

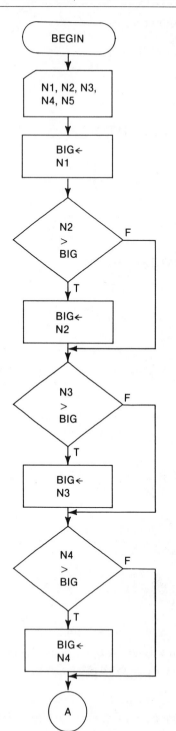
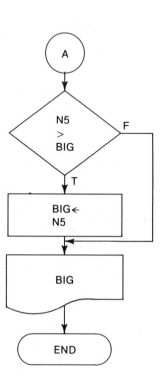

4.4

Income tax is based on a percentage of a person's income minus his deductions. Develop an algorithm to input gross pay (GROSSPAY) and number of dependents (NUMDEP). Compute the taxable income (TAX) according to the following rules:

1) Subtract 10 percent of gross pay from gross pay (GROSSPAY) as a standard deduction.
2) Subtract $1000 for each dependent.

Assign a tax rate (PERCENT) according to the following:

Taxable Income	Percent Tax
>0 AND <10,000	20
>= 10,000 AND <20,000	30
>= 20,000 AND <35,000	40
>= 35,000 AND <55,000	50
>= 55,000	60

Output the resulting tax (TAX) as the product of gross pay and the tax rate.

Solution

Refer to Figure 4–4. The 10 percent standard deduction and the dependent deduction can be expressed in one statement. (Multiplying by .9 is the same as subtracting 10 percent). The appropriate tax rate is determined by a set of conditionals. Note that we must consider the possibility of a negative gross pay, which would result in a negative tax. The Internal Revenue Service would certainly object to a negative tax.

4.5

Develop an algorithm to input X and calculate Y according to the following scale:

X	Y
X < 10	M
10 <= X < 20	M^2
20 <= X < 30	N
30 <= X < 40	$2*N$
40 <= X < 50	N^2
50 <= X < 60	$M*N$
60 <= X < 70	$M*N^2$
70 <= X	M^2*N^2

Figure 4–14.
Flowchart for
Solved Problem 4.4

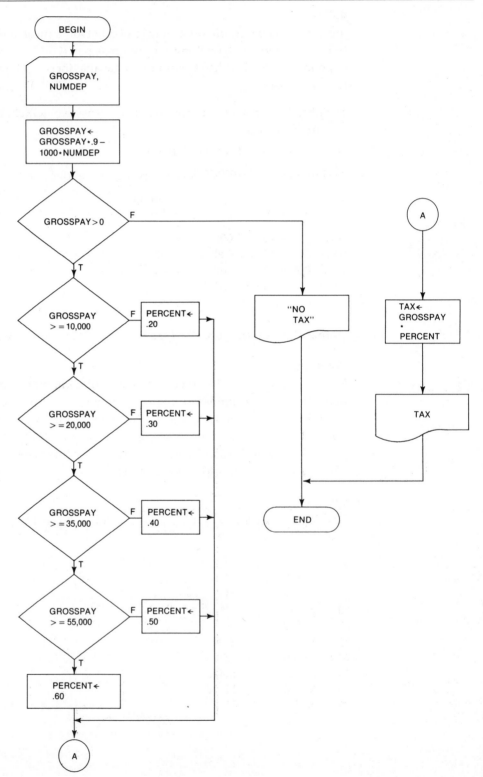

Solution

Although the logic of this problem is very straightforward, there is a very important concept here. It is clear that the algorithm must contain seven conditionals. The sequence in which they are used, however, is important. It is correct to go down the scale asking $X < 10$, $X < 20$, and so forth, as shown in Figure 4–15. However, that is not necessarily the best plan.

Refer to Figure 4–16. It may be more efficient to check the middle of the scale first, essentially breaking the scale into two halves. This procedure is continued until both branches of a conditional lead to an assignment.

From the point of view of the programmer, the first scheme might seem easier and therefore more reasonable. In general, that scheme will require

Figure 4–15.
Flowchart for
Solved Problem 4.5

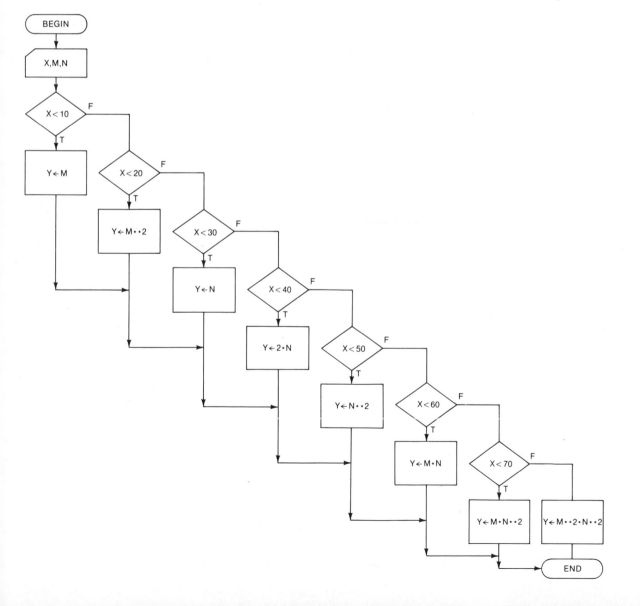

Figure 4–16.
Flowchart for
Solved Problem 4.5
Revised

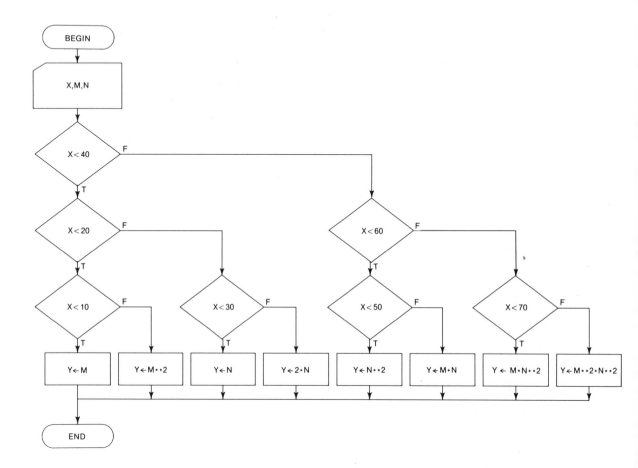

that the executing program step through only one conditional in some cases and in other cases through seven conditionals. On the average, it would require N/2 comparisons, where N = number of alternatives (eight in this case).

The scheme presented in Figure 4–16 requires three comparisons. In general, it will require only log N comparisons, which is significantly less than N/2 for a large N. (For instance, if N = 1000, N/2 = 500, log N ≅ 9.) We will use this later in developing algorithms where efficiency is an important concern.

Note that the relative efficiency of the two schemes was based on the assumption that each range of X was equally likely. If the probability of each range of X were as shown below, then the first scheme would be much more efficient.

X	Probability
X < 10	80%
10 <= X < 20	10%
20 <= X < 30	5%
30 <= X < 40	3%
40 <= X < 50	1%
50 <= X < 60	.5%
60 <= X < 70	.3%
70 <= X	.2%

Often, little is known about the probabilities of occurrence and the assumption of uniform probability is reasonable. The study of information theory is applicable to problems where the probabilities are significantly different.

4.6

Two BOOLEAN operators in addition to those we have presented are equivalence (EQV) and implication (IMP). If two BOOLEAN expressions are denoted B1 and B2, then the truth tables for (B1 EQV B2) and (B1 IMP B2) are as shown in Table 4–2.

The IMP operation has precedence after the OR operation; EQV is applied after the IMP. The full precedence sequence for evaluation of BOOLEAN expressions is then as shown in Table 4–3.

Table 4–2

B1	B2	B1 EQV B2	B1 IMP B2
FALSE	FALSE	TRUE	TRUE
FALSE	TRUE	FALSE	TRUE
TRUE	FALSE	FALSE	FALSE
TRUE	TRUE	TRUE	TRUE

Table 4-3

First:	Arithmetic operations	**
		*, /
		+, −
Second:	Relational Operators	<, <=, >, >=, =, <>
Third:	NOT	
Fourth:	AND	
Fifth:	OR	
Sixth:	IMP	
Seventh:	EQV	

Parentheses can override the implied precedence of operations.
Given $A = 1$, $B = 3$, $C = 5$, $D = 7$, $M = $ TRUE, and $N = $ FALSE, determine the values of the following BOOLEAN expressions:

1. A<3 EQV B<4 AND (NOT N) EQV (NOT M)
2. A+B>C EQV A*D = B*C OR M IMP N
3. NOT (N IMP M) EQV (M IMP N)
4. C+A>B EQV C−A<B OR D−B = C−A AND M IMP NOT N

Solution

1. A<3 EQV B<4 AND (NOT N) EQV (NOT M)

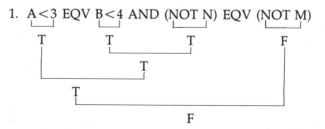

2. A+B>C EQV A∗D=B∗C OR M IMP N

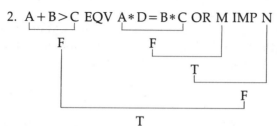

3. NOT   (N IMP M)   EQV (M IMP N)

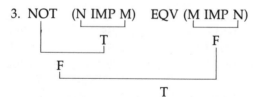

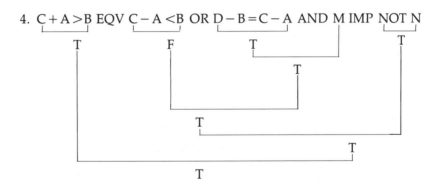

4. $C + A > B$ EQV $C - A < B$ OR $D - B = C - A$ AND M IMP NOT N

4.7

If a programming language does not provide BOOLEAN operators for IMP and EQV, it is easy to derive algorithms for these operations. Develop two algorithms that will do the following:

1. Determine the result of the equivalence operation for two BOOLEAN expressions, BOOL1 and BOOL2, and assign the result to the BOOLEAN variable EQV.
2. Determine the result of the implication operation for two BOOLEAN expressions, BOOL1 and BOOL2, and assign the result to the BOOLEAN variable IMP.

Solution

1. The equivalence algorithm is a very short one, as shown in Figure 4–17. Validate this algorithm by comparing the results with Table 4–2.
2. As shown in Figure 4–18, the implication algorithm is only slightly more complicated than the equivalence algorithm. IMP is assigned a value of TRUE or FALSE consistent with Table 4–2, depending on the values of BOOL1 and BOOL2.

Supplementary Problems

4.8

Given the values of the variables M = 3, J = 2, K = 14, P = 9, Z = 1, and the BOOLEAN variables D = TRUE, S = FALSE, evaluate each of the following expressions:

Figure 4–17.
Flowchart for
Equivalence
Algorithm

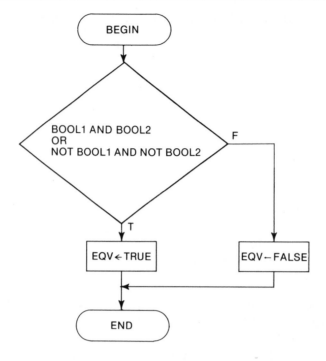

Figure 4–18.
Flowchart for
Implication
Algorithm

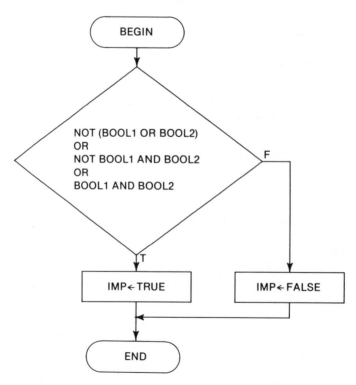

1. NOT D OR J < K
2. S AND M <> J OR P > Z AND Z > J
3. NOT (S AND J = K)
4. NOT (NOT S AND P > M) OR J > M

4.9
Develop an algorithm to input three numbers and find the number that is closest in absolute value to the average of the three.

4.10
Draw a flowchart to determine the value of Y for each of the following problems:

1.
$$Y = \begin{cases} \pi/2 \text{ if } X > 10 \\ 2\pi \text{ if } X <= 10 \end{cases}$$

2.
$$Y = \begin{cases} T^2 \text{ if } X < 0 \\ T^2 - 10 \text{ if } X = 0 \\ T^2 - 25 \text{ if } X > 0 \end{cases}$$

4.11
Given the quadratic equation $AX^2 + BX + C = 0$, its roots are defined as

$$\frac{-B \pm \sqrt{B^2 - 4 * A * C}}{2 * A}$$

Develop an algorithm to input A, B, and C and find the two roots of the equation. Set the roots to 10^{20}, if A is 0.

5   *Iteration*

5.1 Introduction   The algorithms developed up to this point have operated on only a single set of input data. There are very few occasions where it would be economical to implement a computer algorithm to process a single set of inputs. After spending the time and money to develop a program, we hope to use it more than once. We will discuss several problems in which the algorithm developed will apply to numerous sets of data. For example, a payroll algorithm would be developed to process as many people as the company employs.

Likewise, we will find many occasions where we might have to repeat the same set of instructions a number of times. Instead of having to duplicate the set of instructions, all high-level languages provide a programming construct for repetition of the same set of instructions. This process is known as **iteration,** or **looping.** By the completion of this chapter, you should be able to answer the following questions:

1. What are the essential parts to iteration?
2. What is the flowchart symbol for iteration?
3. What is a header value?
4. What is a trailer value?

5.2 Iteration Statement and Counting   Consider the problem of finding your class average for your latest quiz. Assuming for the moment that there are only 4 students in your class, we would solve this problem sequentially, as shown in Figure 5–1, by reading and summing each quiz score (SCORE) and then dividing by 4 to find the average (AVG).

Note that the bracketed instructions in the flowchart are identical. That is, we duplicated the same set of two instructions 4 times. For such a relatively simple problem, this duplication is perfectly reasonable and acceptable.

Now, let us suppose that your class has expanded to 100 students. Would you want to redraw the algorithm repeating the same set of two instructions 100 times? Probably not! Suppose that instead of duplicating the two instructions 100 times, we had some simple mechanism to repeat the same instructions 100 times. In English, we might issue the instructions as follows:

1. Repeat instructions 2 and 3, 100 times.
2. Read a number.
3. Add the number to the sum.
4. Divide the sum by 100 to find the average.
5. Write the average.

Most high-level languages implement some form of this mechanism. But let us expand our problem one step further and assume that instead of 100 students, we have N students. We could apply the same algorithm as before by merely changing 100 to N. However, let's make it more algorithmic in form as follows:

1. Read N.
2. Counter = 1.
3. Repeat instructions 4, 5, and 6 while counter is less than or equal to N.
4. Read Score.
5. Sum = Sum + Score.
6. Counter = Counter + 1.
7. Average = Sum / N.
8. Write Average.

In this algorithm, we have introduced the very important concept of **counting.** In order to control the number of iterations, we counted from 1 to N. We could have accomplished the same thing by counting N down to 1, but then we would not have known by what number to divide to find the average.

We have generalized this algorithm to find the average of any number of numbers without changing any of the instructions. In effect, what we have done is establish an iteration, or loop. You should determine the method used for constructing an iteration statement in whatever language you are using.

By examining our last example a little more closely, we can formalize the process of iteration. First, we required a counter (COUNTER) to control the number of times we iterated. Therefore, COUNTER was used as the **control variable** and was initialized to 1. Second, we terminated the iteration when the control variable exceeded the **terminating value** (N). Third, we determined whether or not to continue iterating by **testing** the control variable against the terminating value. Fourth, we executed several statements inside the loop itself, the last of which was to **increment** the control variable.

As a result of this analysis, we could say that, in general, any iteration consists of four parts:

Figure 5–1.
Flowchart for
Sequential
Processing

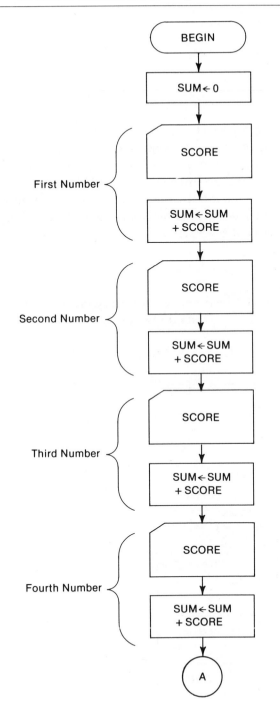
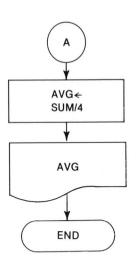

1. Initialize
2. Test
3. Execute
4. Increment

5.3 Flowchart Symbol for Iteration

The iterative control structure is relatively easy to flowchart and recognize. It uses the rectangular box indicating an operation (see Figure 2–2D) and the diamond indicating a decision (see Figure 2–2E). As previously discussed, iteration requires that an instruction or set of instructions be executed repetitively, based on some test. In a flowchart, the instructions to be repeated are very easily delineated and defined as all instructions within the loop. The typical iterative control structure appears as shown in Figure 5–2.

Example 5.1

Using the iterative construct, develop an algorithm to find the average of a set of numbers. Assume the number of numbers is provided by the data element N.

Solution

The solution is shown as Figure 5–3.

End Solution

Figure 5–2.
Flowchart Symbology for Iteration

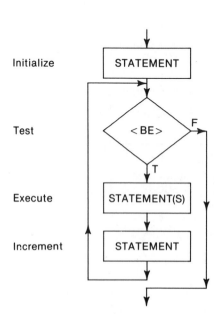

Initialize — STATEMENT

Test — < BE >   F

Execute — STATEMENT(S)

Increment — STATEMENT

Figure 5–3.
Flowchart for
Average of N Scores

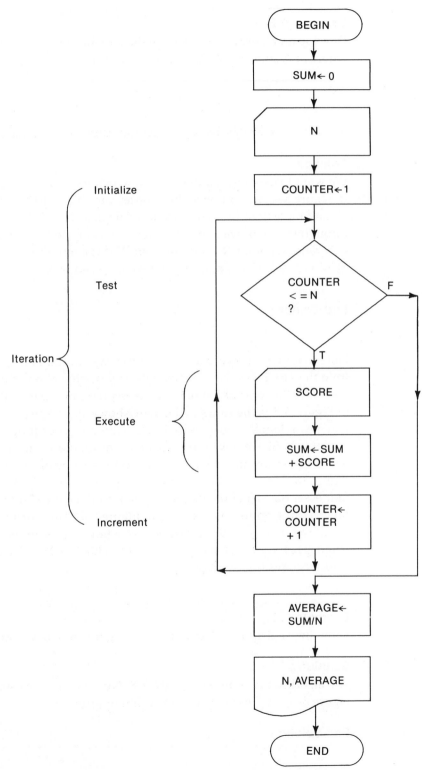

Example 5.2

Develop an algorithm to calculate the sum of the odd integers from 1 to N, where N is some positive number to be input, or

$$\sum_{i=1,+2}^{N} i$$

where the Greek symbol sigma (Σ) indicates the summation process.

Solution

We want to establish an iteration in which we count from 1 to N by 2. Thus, in Figure 5–4, we initialize the counter variable (I) to 1, set up the test against N, and increment by 2 so I assumes values of 1, 3, 5, 7, . . . At each pass through the loop, we add the current value of I to SUM. It does not make any difference whether N is odd or even. If it is even, the last value added to SUM is N − 1; if it is odd, the last value added is N.

End Solution

Note that in the flowchart we use the convention that the loop is formed from the TRUE (T) exit. This could easily be changed to the FALSE (F) exit by reversing the logic of the BOOLEAN expression. That is, the flowchart logic in Figure 5–5 is the same as the logic shown in Figure 5–6. You should use whichever logic is most easily implemented in your programming language.

In this book we have put no restrictions on the value of the increment, and we consider any statement that changes the value of the control variable within the loop to be an increment. In general, iterations contain the same four essential elements; therefore, we introduce the shorthand method of flowcharting an iteration shown in Figure 5–7. This construct includes three out of the four iterative elements in one flowchart symbol. Many high-level languages have a statement (e.g., DO in FORTRAN, FOR in PASCAL) that directly codes this symbol.

Example 5.3

Show the algorithm of Example 5.1 using the new flowchart symbol.

Solution

The algorithm is shown in Figure 5–8. Note that all the essential elements of Figure 5–3 are present, only in a different form.

End Solution

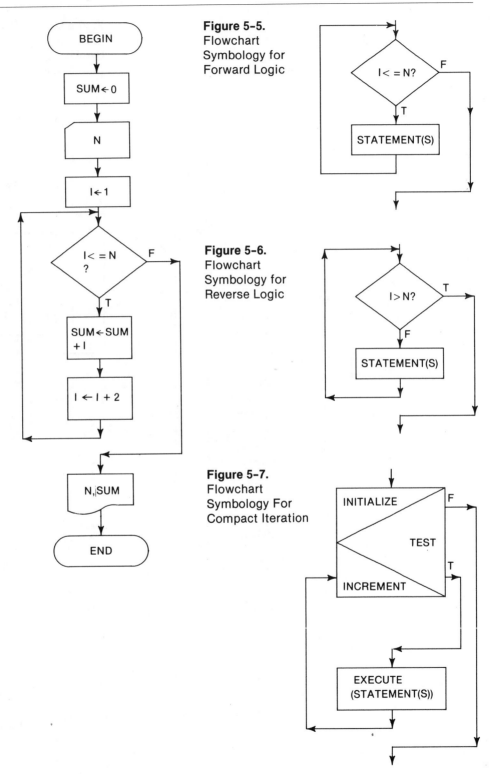

Figure 5-4.
Flowchart for Sum
of Odd Integers

Figure 5-5.
Flowchart
Symbology for
Forward Logic

Figure 5-6.
Flowchart
Symbology for
Reverse Logic

Figure 5-7.
Flowchart
Symbology For
Compact Iteration

Figure 5-8.
Average of N Numbers

Figure 5-9.
Flowchart
Symbology for
Infinite Loop

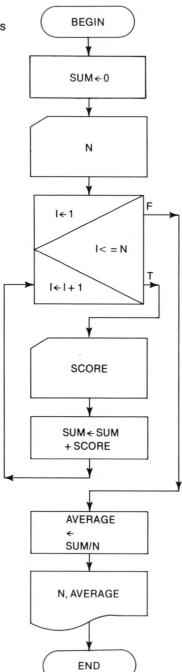

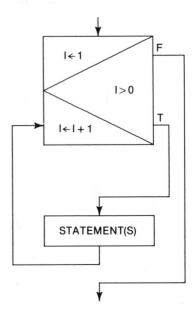

5.4 Terminating Techniques

When implementing the iterative construct, be careful that the loop terminates properly. It is far too easy to enter a loop that never ends by merely forgetting to increment the control variable or by reversing the logic of the test. For example, the loop shown in Figure 5–9 would never terminate normally, because by initializing I to 1 and incrementing by 1, I will always be greater than 0 and the terminating criteria would never be satisfied. This is called an **infinite loop.**

There are many ways to set up the termination of a loop. We will address the three most common methods.

A. Header Value

In the **header value technique,** the first record read establishes how many other records follow and becomes the terminating value. This method has the disadvantage that the number of cases must be established beforehand. Example 5.1 demonstrated the use of the header value technique of data termination.

B. Trailer Value

In the **trailer value technique,** we assume that the number of cases is unknown. The control variable for the loop becomes one of the data items to be read inside the loop. The terminating value is selected to be any value outside the domain of the control variable. When the control variable assumes the terminating value, it implies that the data must have been exhausted and the loop is terminated. In the case of ALPHA data we will use "ZZZZZ" as the terminating value in this text.

This technique requires that the data be read one time before entering the loop. This data is then processed inside the loop. The increment takes the form of the next READ statement. Normally we would not use the compact form of the iteration flowchart symbol for this technique since the initialize and increment statements are both READ statements.

Example 5.4

Develop an algorithm to calculate the take-home pay (THP) for a group (NUM) of employees, given the employee's name (NAME), hourly rate (HR), hours worked (HW), and overtime differential (PERCENT) as input. All hours worked in excess of 40 qualify for the overtime differential.

Solution

The solution is shown in Figure 5–10. A similar solution is shown in Figure 5–11, in which we also count the number of employees and use the compact flowchart symbol. Note that the counter is not the control variable for the loop. It merely forces execution of the loop until the terminating value is read

Figure 5–10.
Flowchart for
Take-home Pay
Calculation

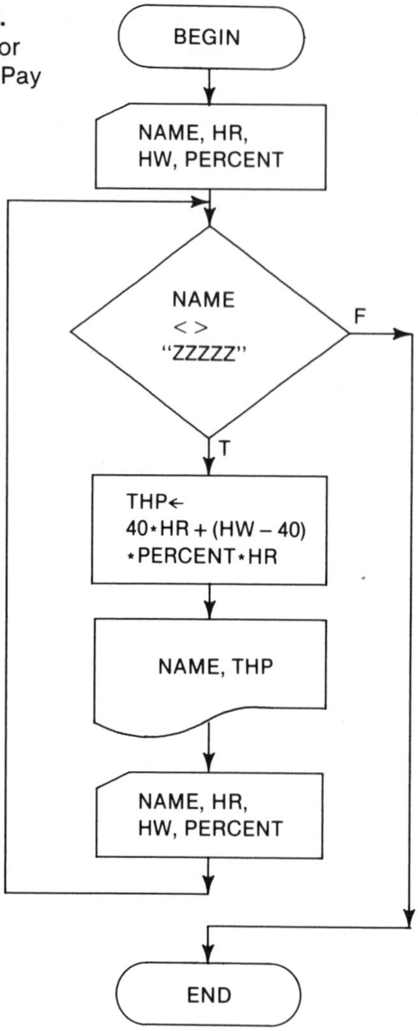

Figure 5–11.
Flowchart for
Takehome Pay
Calculation
(Revised)

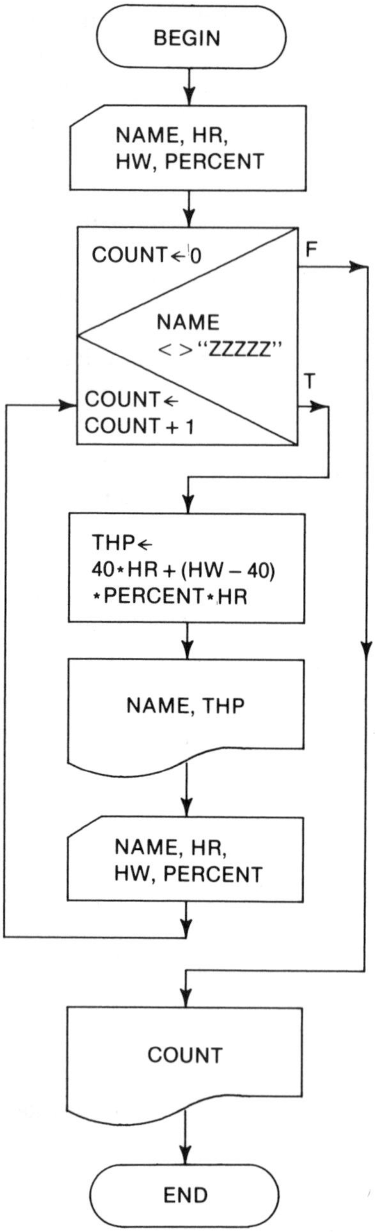

and it records the number of employees processed. The employee's name controls the loop, which terminates when the name "ZZZZZ" is read as the last data value.

End Solution

C. Special Condition

In certain situations neither the header value nor trailer value terminating techniques are applicable. In such cases, the loop is terminated only when **special conditions** are met. Usually these conditions are established by some calculation that takes place within the loop. For instance, we might be looking for the first number between 9 and 100, the product of whose digits is the same as the sum of the square of those digits. We would, therefore, terminate the iteration when the number that satisfied these criteria is found.

This method is very similar to the trailer value technique, except that we might not require any input data and the loop is not controlled by a single control variable. When using the special condition method, you should take care that the terminating condition can be derived; otherwise the loop might not terminate. You should take precautions by terminating the loop after a fixed number of iterations even though the special condition has not been met. This is easy to implement by using a logical operator to establish multiple conditions for termination.

Example 5.5

The value of the sine function can be estimated by the trigonometric series

$$SIN\ (X) = X - \frac{X^3}{3!} + \frac{X^5}{5!} - \frac{X^7}{7!} + \cdots$$

Develop an algorithm to find SIN (X) with an error of less than .001. In the remainder of this text we will define the variable EPS, the abbreviation for the Greek letter epsilon, to have a value equal to the terminating error criteria.

Solution

The trigonometric series lends itself very nicely to implementation through iteration, as shown in Figure 5-12. If we step (i.e., follow the sequence) 3, 5, 7, 9, . . . , I can be used as the exponent in the numerator and as the next term in the factorial. By multiplying the factorial by (−1) at each iteration, we alternate the sign of the next term as required.

If the absolute difference between the new value of sine and the preceding value of sine is less than EPS, (i.e., the error is less than .001), then the solu-

Figure 5–12.
Sine Function Using
Trigonometric
Series

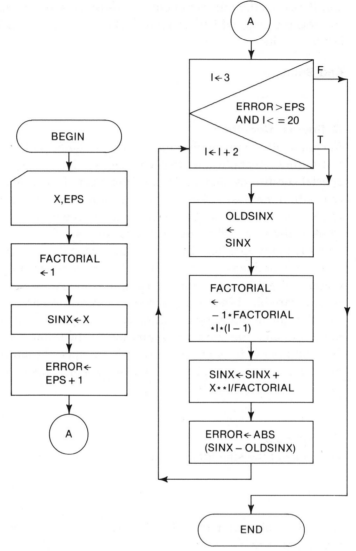

tion is within EPS of the correct answer. This becomes our special condition for termination. The additional criteria (I <= 20) force the iteration to terminate even though the error limit is not achieved after 10 terms are calculated.

End Solution

5.5 Nested Iteration

The purpose of iterative processing is to execute a particular statement or set of statements a number of times. We have not placed any restrictions on the statement(s) to be repeated; thus virtually any statement can appear inside the loop. The case of an iteration inside an iteration is referred to as a **nested iteration.** Some languages restrict the type of statements on which the loop terminates; however, this poses no problem since a special instruction for terminating loops would be provided. You should check to see what, if any, restrictions are in your language.

Example 5.6

Develop an algorithm that will determine whether each student passes or fails the course in accordance with the following criteria:

Points >= Average Points ∗ 60%, then "Passed"

Points < Average Points ∗ 60%, then "Failed"

There is an uncounted number of students. Print each student's name and whether the student passed or failed.

Solution

As shown in Figure 5–13, the solution requires that each student's point total (POINTS) be compared against the average points times 60 percent to determine the assignment of "Passed" or "Failed."

End Solution

In this example we used a condition inside an iteration. From the solution you should be able to determine the termination technique used, the control variable, the terminating value, and the initialize, test, and increment steps.

Example 5.7

In Example 5.5 we developed an algorithm to find the value of SIN (X) with an error less than some desired value epsilon (EPS). Develop an algorithm that incorporates the solution to Example 5.5 and calculates SIN (X) for $0 <= X <= \pi/2$ in increments of .01 π.

Figure 5-13.
Flowchart for
Pass/Fail Grade
Assignment

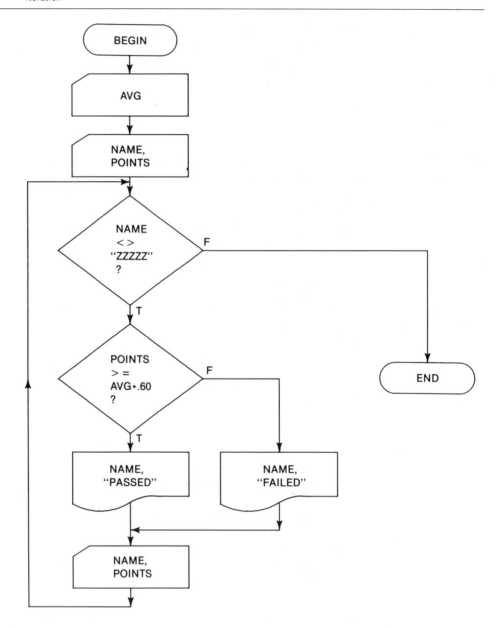

Solution

The flowchart presented in Figure 5–14 differs from Example 5.5 only in the manner in which the variable X obtains its values.

End Solution

The flowchart for Example 5.7 is fairly involved. Before going on, you should make sure that you can follow the flow and that you understand the logic completely. You will find that as we progress and the problems become more sophisticated, we might require conditionals inside of conditionals inside of iterations, and so on.

However, no matter how complex the problem and its solution become, the basic structure remains the same. The structure is easy to determine if you keep in mind the basic components of each of the three types of control structure discussed.

5.6 The Grading Problem and Iteration

Using the concepts of iteration discussed in this chapter, we will apply the grading algorithm developed through Chapter 4 to any number of students. Specifically, in accordance with the original statement of the problem, we desire to assign a letter grade to each student in a class of variable size. To do so, we place Figures 4–10 and 4–11 inside a loop. Since there is a variable number of students, we will use the trailer card technique and terminate the loop when the value of "ZZZZZ" is read as a student's name.

The result is shown in Figure 5–15. Note that we have introduced a new integer variable, (COUNT), which is incremented by 1 for each pass through the loop. Upon termination, COUNT will have a value equal to the number of students in the class. COUNT will eventually be used in calculating the class average and standard deviation.

After you are sure that you understand the logic of Figure 5–15, you should code the algorithm and execute your program with some test data. Be sure that you can duplicate the output shown in Table 5–1, which was extracted from Table 2–1.

5.7 Summary

We have introduced the three control structures required to solve virtually any problem in any programming language. Different high-level languages use different programming constructs to implement the conditional and iterative control structures demonstrated in this book. However, we contend that for algorithmic development, the sequential, conditional, and iterative control structures are all that are necessary, regardless of the method of implementation.

Figure 5-14.
Flowchart for Sine
Calculation

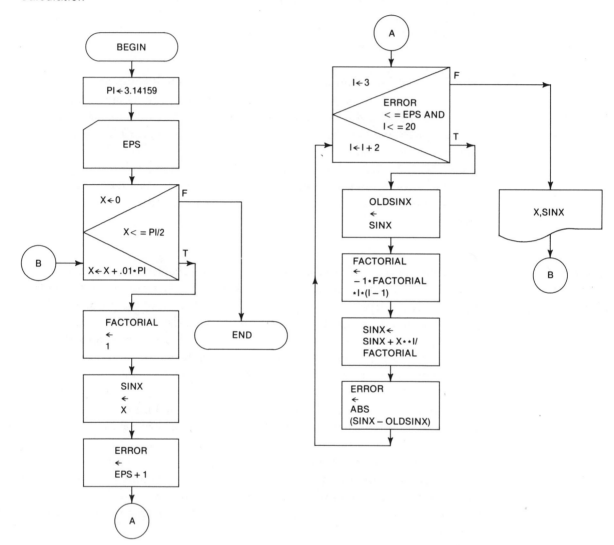

Figure 5–15.
Flowchart for
Grading Problem

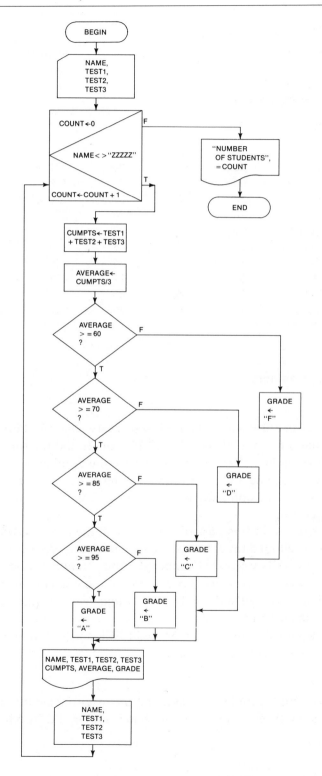

Table 5–1

Course: Math 351					Instructor: Mr. P. J. Smythe	
Section: 3					Room: 304	
Number of Tests: 3						
Number of Students: 10						

Student's Name	Test 1	Test 2	Test 3	CUM PTS	Average	Grade
Adams, M. E.	85	87	90	262	87.33	B
Barnes, L. J.	56	60	72	168	56.00	F
Carlton, P. G.	30	40	59	129	43.00	F
Driscoll, R.	98	99	100	297	99.00	A
Evans, S. T.	90	85	76	251	83.67	C
Orly, A. P.	50	65	78	193	64.33	D
Puget, S.	83	81	84	248	82.67	C
Ryan, M. A.	90	89	72	251	83.67	C
Silve, G. A.	60	65	65	190	63.33	D
Walton, J. J.	88	70	89	247	82.33	C

Solved Problems

5.1

Two cross-country teams, Podunk and Clearwater, are competing in a special nine-mile run. Both teams will start 10 runners and the run will be scored in the following way. Each team will receive the number of points corresponding to the placement of their runners at the finish. The first place runner gets one point, the second place two, and so on. The team with the least number of points wins.

However, since it is possible that some of the runners will not finish within the allotted time, the raw score will be modified according to the formula Score = Raw score * Number starting / Number finishing. The team with the lower score wins. Since we don't know how many runners will actually finish, we will assume that a fictitious team named "ZZZZZ" will be the last name input.

Develop an algorithm to input the PLACE and TEAM of each runner and output the scores of the two teams.

Solution

This is a simple problem of iteration. The resulting algorithm is shown in Figure 5–16. At each iteration, the team is either "PODUNK" or "CLEAR-

Figure 5–16.
Flowchart for
Solved Problem 5.1

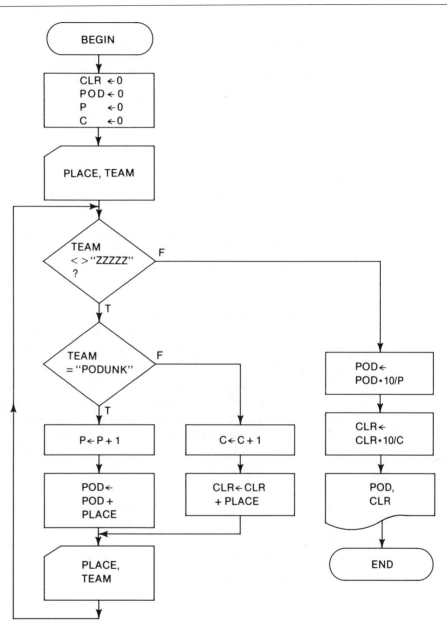

WATER." Depending on the TEAM name, we increment the appropriate count (P or C) and add the PLACE to the appropriate team score (POD or CLR). Note that the counts and team scores are initialized to 0.

After all runners have been input, the respective team scores are calculated. We stop the iteration by recognizing the fictitious team name "ZZZZZ." What would happen in the event that no runner from one team finished in the allotted time? In such a case the value of either P or C would be 0 and we would be trying to divide by 0.

5.2

A survey has been taken to determine the amount of pay that graduates of a certain college are earning. Only the year of graduation, annual income, and degree (B.S., M.S., or Ph.D.) are available. Develop an algorithm to input the available information and find the average pay for B.S. graduates in each of the year groups 1–3, 4–6, and 7–10.

Solution

The solution as shown in Figure 5–17 makes use of an iteration. Since the number of graduates to be processed is unknown, we simply add a trailer value with YEAR= 99, which would not be an expected data value. Since we are only interested in those with DEGREE= "B.S.", we skip all other data.

At this point, we set the variable GROUP equal to the number of years since graduation. Based on the value of GROUP, the appropriate count is increased. Note that there is no counter to increment when GROUP > 10. After all data has been processed, we compute the average for each group. We must check whether or not each group is empty to avoid dividing by 0. The variable names used to refer to year group, pay group, and average are: YRGROUP#, PAYGROUP#, and GROUP#AVG, respectively, where # is a 1, 2, or 3 depending upon the value of GROUP.

5.3

Develop an algorithm to output all the values in the series

1. $1, 2, 4, 8, 16, 32, 64 \ldots < 10^4$
2. $3, 6, 12, 24, 48, 96, 192 \ldots < 10^4$
3. $7, 14, 28, 56, 112, 224, 448 \ldots < 10^4$

Each of the series has a definite progression. Try to take advantage of the progression in developing your algorithm.

Solution

We observe that each of the series is defined by $X_{i+1} = 2X_i$. Refer to Figure 5–18. The algorithm will output any of the three series, depending on the initial value of N:

Figure 5–17.
Flowchart for
Solved Problem 5.2

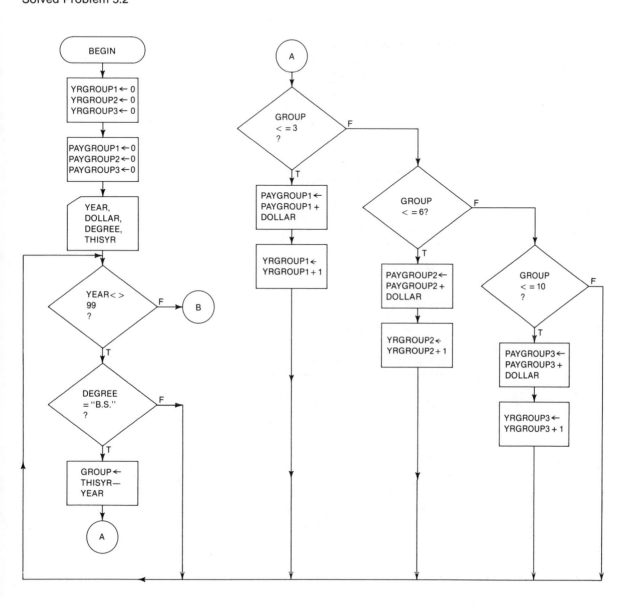

Figure 5–17.
(continued)

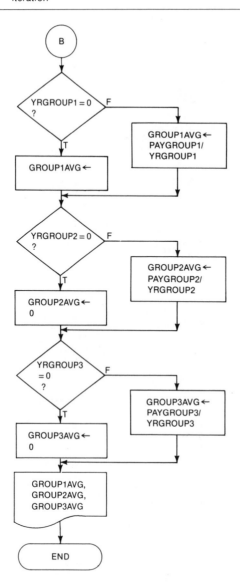

Figure 5–18.
Flowchart for
Solved Problem 5.3

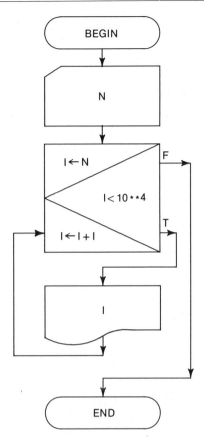

1. 1, 2, 4, 8, 16, 32, 64, . . . , if N = 1;
2. 3, 6, 12, 24, 48, 96, 192, . . . , if N = 3;
3. 7, 14, 28, 56, 112, 224, 448, . . . , if N = 7.

This algorithm presents a useful concept. We are stepping the control variable by a different value each time. In other words, we are using a variable step. This technique is not often used by the beginning programmer, but it is an extremely useful concept at times.

5.4
The angle whose sine is X is called ARCSIN (X) or SIN⁻¹ (X). Develop an algorithm to compute SIN⁻¹ (X) using the power series expansion:

$$SIN^{-1}(X) = X + \frac{1*X^3}{2*3} + \frac{1*3*X^5}{2*4*5} + \frac{1*3*5*X^7}{2*4*6*7} + \cdots$$

Sum the first 20 terms of the series.

Solution

Refer to Figure 5–19. We input a value for X and set the variables SUBTER to 1 and ARCSIN to X. The control variable I serves as both the exponent and divisor of X. It is also used to find the numerator $(I-2)$ and denominator $(I-3)$ of the next coefficient. I starts at 3 and is incremented by 2 until it exceeds 39.

Since a portion of each term was calculated in the previous iteration, we make use of this fact to save some effort. We use SUBTER to calculate a new SUBTER and then use that value to update the value of ARCSIN. This is a useful technique often employed in calculating the value of a series.

5.5

Develop an algorithm to find the arcsine of X using the sum of the first 20 terms of the series:

$$\text{SIN}^{-1}(X) = X + \frac{1}{2} * \frac{X^3}{3} + \frac{1}{2} * \frac{3}{4} * \frac{X^5}{5} + \frac{1}{2} * \frac{3}{4} * \frac{5}{6} * \frac{X^7}{7} \cdots$$

without using the value of the previous term (or any part of it).

Solution

Refer to Figure 5–20. Since the statement of the problem precludes any use of the previous term, we are forced to compute the entire term for each value of I. This requires a second iteration to compute the coefficient of each term. The remainder of the algorithm is unchanged from Figure 5–19.

For each value of I, we recalculate the series by iterating the control variable, J, and using the outer loops control variable I to determine the terminating value for J. Although this is not the most efficient algorithm, it does permit us to appreciate some of the power of nested iterations.

5.6

The Fibonacci series (1, 1, 2, 3, 5, 8, 13, . . .) is an interesting sequence to study because any desired number in the series can only be derived by adding the two numbers preceding it. That is, there is no formula for deriving the tenth Fibonacci number without iteratively proceeding from the first two Fibonacci numbers, which are always 1. Write an algorithm to find the Nth Fibonacci number.

Solution

As shown in Figure 5–21, after we read which Fibonacci number (N) is required, we initialize FIRST and SECOND to 1. If the value of N is 1 or 2, we will not enter the iteration but instead print the value 1 as the answer. For any other positive value of N we repeatedly add the two preceding Fibonacci numbers until we reach the Nth Fibonacci as required.

Figure 5–19.
Flowchart for
Solved Problem 5.4

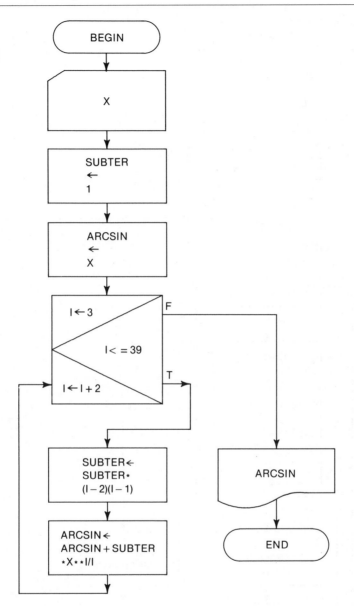

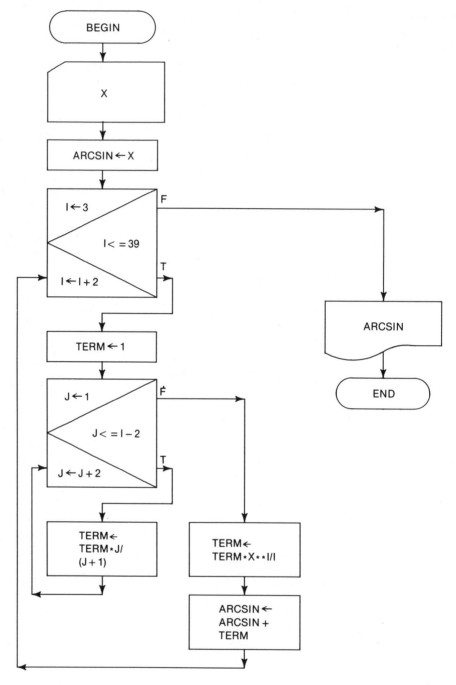

Figure 5-21.
Flowchart for
Solved Problem 5.6

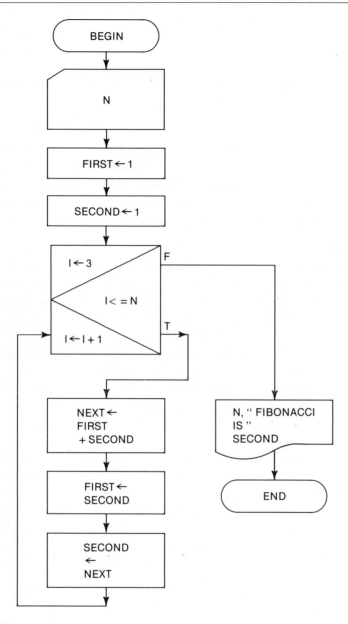

Supplementary Problems

5.7

Write an algorithm to output the first 10 positive terms of the geometric progression 4, −8, 16, −32, 64, . . .

5.8

A certain bank lends money with the following repayment option: the money must be repaid in a specified number of months (M). Each month a payment will consist of AMOUNT BORROWED/M × 1% of the PREVIOUS BALANCE. Write an algorithm to input the loan value (X), the number of months for repayment (M), and output the repayment schedule.

5.9

A charitable institution receives monthly contributions. All cash on hand in excess of $5000 is invested at a guaranteed rate of 2% per month. At month's end after all payments have been made and all contributions have been received, if the balance is less than $4000, money is withdrawn from the investments so that cash on hand is raised to $4000.

   Write an algorithm to input the cash on hand at the beginning of the month, the monthly contributions, and the monthly payments; determine the amount to be invested or withdrawn from investment; and keep track of the amount invested plus interest.

5.10

Each day a computer facility records the amount of computer time used. The information is recorded as three two-digit integers: hours, minutes, seconds. Write an algorithm to input the times recorded for a month and accumulate a total time used. Output the total number of hours, minutes, seconds used.

5.11

Each time Mr. Smith stops for gas during his trip across the country, he records the driving time, miles driven, and gallons of gas consumed. At the end of the trip he wants to know his average speed and his average miles per gallon.

   Write an algorithm to input driving time, miles, and gallons for each leg of his trip. Calculate Mr. Smith's average speed and miles per gallon.

5.12

Write an algorithm to generate the arithmetic progression whose first term is A, last term is L, and common difference is D. Compare the sum of the first N terms with the formula

$$SUM = N/2 * (2 * A - (N - 1) * D)$$

Write an error message if the results are not equal.

5.13
Write an algorithm to derive the number of combinations (M) of N things taken P at a time. The formula for M is given as $M = N!/P! (N - P)!$

6 Arrays

6.1 Introduction

In the preceding chapters, we have described how information can be stored in a computer as simple variables, each with a unique name. We also discussed the three basic control structures available for manipulation, or processing, of this information.

In this chapter we present problems in which the use of simple variables becomes unwieldly. We describe a new data structure called an **array.** We demonstrate how arrays facilitate the solution to these problems and how the three basic control structures are used in manipulating arrays.

By the completion of this chapter, you should be able to answer the following questions:

1. What is an array?
2. What is a subscript?
3. What are the characteristics of a subscript?
4. What are multi-dimensioned arrays?
5. When should an array be used in problem solving?

6.2 The Concept of an Array

There are many applications of computer algorithms in which the set of operations must be performed on several variables. Consider the following example.

Example 6.1
Given a set of five numbers, list those numbers that are greater than the mean.

Solution
As shown in Figure 6–1, the average, or mean, of the numbers must first be found. Then each of the numbers is compared with the average. Those above the average are output.

End Solution

Figure 6-1.
Flowchart for
Numbers Above
Mean

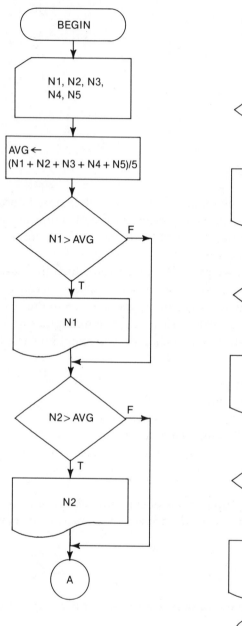
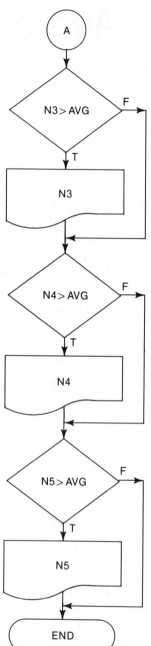

Although the conditional statement itself is simple enough, we note that it had to be performed for each of the numbers since each was stored under a different variable name. This precluded the use of iteration and our algorithm is only effective for five numbers.

Imagine how cumbersome it would be to have to rewrite this algorithm for 1,000 numbers. Suppose we had to write the algorithm to handle N numbers. Since there is no way to generalize the algorithm, we would in fact require N different algorithms.

The algorithm defined by Figure 6–1 is still a good one. The deficiency is in the structuring of the data and not in the algorithm. If, instead of having to place each number into a specific variable, we could address all the numbers by the same variable name, we could then state our algorithm much more concisely, make use of iteration, and generalize one algorithm for N numbers.

Higher level computer languages provide such a feature. A set of values can be assigned to a single variable name and the individual values can then be addressed by subscripting the variable. Such a variable is called a **subscripted variable,** or **array.**

The concept of an array is really quite simple. A group of related items is stored under the name of a single variable. Each individual word of the array is distinguished from the others by its position within the array. This position is called a **subscript,** or an **index.** The subscript, defined as an integer, simply identifies the specific position (first, second, third, and so on) of a referenced variable within an array.

The notion of subscripted variables is not unique to programming languages. On the contrary, their use in computer programming was adapted from well-established mathematical notation, which uses subscripted variables extensively to express complex mathematical formulas concisely. A common example of this notation in mathematics is found in the formula for a polynomial:

$$P_N(x) = a_0 + a_1 x + a_2 x^2 + \cdots + a_i x^i + \cdots a_N x^N$$

where x is a variable, and the a's comprise a set of coefficients, or

$$P_N(x) = \sum_{i=0}^{N} a_i x^i$$

which simply means the sum of terms of the form $a_i x_i$, as i is increased by 1 from 0 through N.

The significant aspect of the above notation is, of course, the set of coefficients. When considered as a group, we can think of the a_i's as an array of values in which each member of the set is identified by its integer subscript i. For example, if we define the set a's to be $A = (15, -3, 0, 7, 12)$, then

$a_0 = 15$, $a_1 = -3$, $a_2 = 0$, $a_3 = 7$, and $a_4 = 12$. This corresponds to the set of coefficients for the equation $P(x) = 15 - 3x + 7x^3 + 12x^4$. Thus the array contains several elements that are uniquely identified by an integer subscript. Note that the subscript merely identifies a specific member of the group; it does not provide that element's content or value.

Since an array name is a variable name, we will use capital letters to denote array identifiers. Because character sets on most peripheral computer equipment do not permit a small lowered subscript, many computer languages indicate subscripts by enclosing them in parentheses. Thus the second element of the array X is denoted X(1).

Although we can use constants for the subscripts, the real advantage to the use of arrays is that they allow integer variables to be used as subscripts. Thus we can refer to the array element X(I), where the specific element is determined by the value of I at the time the element is referenced.

Example 6.2

Restate the algorithm of Example 6.1 using an array.

Solution

See Figure 6–2. First the five numbers are read into the array NUM. Then instead of having five comparisons, we make use of one comparison that we execute five times while varying the subscript (I) from 1 to 5.

End Solution

Compare Figures 6–1 and 6–2. They are logically equivalent except for the input/output of the array, which will be discussed shortly. Execution of either algorithm for a given set of five numbers will yield the same result.

Example 6.3

Generalize the solution to Example 6.2 for a set of N numbers.

Solution

We will assume that the N numbers are in the array NUM. To generalize the solution we need only set up an iteration to find the sum, and then we change the terminating value in the iteration to N. The result is shown as Figure 6–3.

End Solution

Figure 6-2.
Flowchart for
Numbers Above
Mean (Using an
Array of Five
Elements)

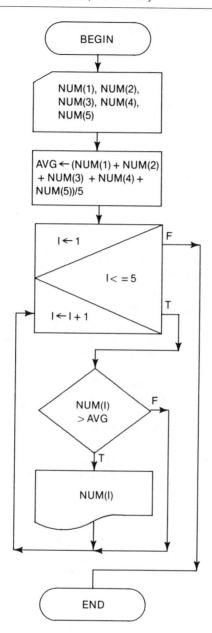

Figure 6-3.
Flowchart for
Numbers Above
Mean (Using an
Array of N
Elements)

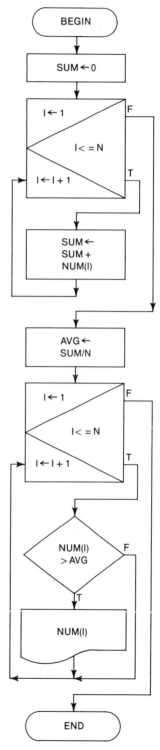

6.3 Rules for Subscripting

Each language has its own specific rules that apply to subscripting of arrays. However, the following simple rules govern the use of subscripts for most languages:

1. The array must be declared. Although all elements of an array are referenced by subscripting the array name, each element must have its own storage location. The management of these storage locations is controlled by the **Operating System** of the computer. The compiler, which converts the higher level language to the machine language, must know in advance how many storage locations to allocate to a given variable name. Therefore, each language will require a declaration of the array name and the range of the array.

2. Indices, or subscripts, to the array must be INTEGERS. Thus reference to the array element X(5.1) is meaningless. Some languages will convert REAL values to INTEGER, either by rounding or truncation.

3. In most languages the subscript can be computed; thus an arithmetic expression that reduces to an INTEGER value can be used as a subscript.

4. The subscript must be within the range of the declaration. In many languages the array is assumed to start with the subscript 1 so that the value X(0) would be undefined in that language. In some languages the lower bound can be declared as well as the upper bound. However, even in these cases, the subscript can not be less than or greater than the declared range.

    Clearly, Figure 6–3 is a more concise statement of the algorithm and can handle any number (N) of numbers. Although the use of an array does not change the logic of the problem, it does frequently allow generalization of the solution and a more concise statement of the algorithm.

5. The number of subscripts used in an array reference must be consistent with the number declared. As we shall see in Section 6.9, multiple subscripts provide added dimension to the use of arrays. In general, the number of subscripts must appear in each reference to the array.

6.4 Input/Output of Arrays

The combination of arrays and iteration provides a powerful means of handling large data sets. Without the versatility afforded by arrays, we would not be able to perform many of the operations efficiently that we need to do on the computer.

In working with arrays, it is necessary to have some means of reading them into memory or writing them on an output device. But although Examples 6.1 through 6.3 provided a glimpse at the usefulness of arrays, we did not discuss the portions of the algorithm that input the array to the computer and that output the array elements.

The input of an array refers to reading the values of the elements of that array into the respective memory cells, or storage locations, of the computer. The output of an array is the opposite of this input operation. During output, the values of the elements of that array are transferred from the internal memory of the computer to some output device.

To avoid the necessity of referring to all I/O devices in the discussion, we will assume throughout the chapter that all input is received from a video terminal keyboard and all output is to the video display. But the concepts, principles, and operations in the chapter are applicable to all the other I/O devices.

There are two basic methods by which the elements of an array can be input into the computer. One method is for the computer to read each element of the array from a separate input line; the other approach is to read several elements from the same input line. The difference is determined by the format of the READ statement and by the manner in which the input statement is executed.

In most programming languages each execution of an input statement involves the reading of the next data line. We will follow this convention throughout this text. This convention is the key to understanding the difference between the method of input of one array element per data line versus the method of input of several array elements per line.

Likewise, the output of the contents of an array can also follow two methods: the printing of each array element on a separate line or the printing of several array elements on one line. The differences between these outputs are closely related to the differences between the two methods of input of arrays. In considering the output of an array, we will always use the convention that each execution of an output statement causes the printing of a new line of output.

A. One Input/Output Data Element Per Line

The most basic type of array input occurs when only one data element is contained on each data line. Since each input statement reads a different data card, there must then be N input statements in order to read N data items. The operations consist of an iteration on the variable I ranging from 1 to N and a reading of the value for each element of the array X.

The flowchart symbol for reading an element of an array is the same as the symbol for reading any other data value. The big difference is that we are reading a value into an element of an array instead of into a simple variable. Notice that in Figure 6–4, the READ occurs within the iteration loop or, equivalently, the iteration symbol is outside of the READ symbol. Thus there will be one READ statement executed N times.

One method of printing the contents of an array is to write the value of each array element on a separate line. The concepts involved in doing this are analogous to those for array input. The WRITE statement occurs inside of the iteration loop as shown in Figure 6–5. Thus the iteration is outside of the output statement, and one WRITE statement will be executed N times.

Figure 6-4.
Flowchart
Symbology for
N Input
Data Lines

Figure 6-5.
Flowchart
Symbology for
N Output
Data Lines

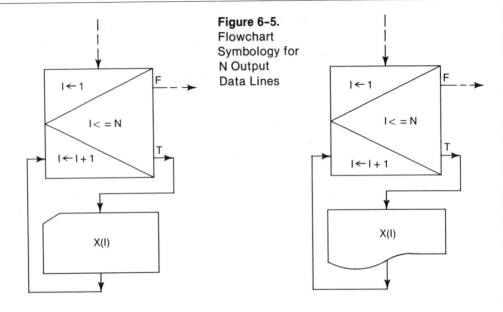

Example 6.4

Modify the algorithm of Example 6.3 to include the input operations when
each input value N(I) is on a separate data line.

Solution

In the revised algorithm shown in Figure 6–6, we read the value N; then each
number NUM(I) is read within the iteration. The I/O operations are basically
depicted as was illustrated in Figures 6–4 and 6–5.

End Solution

B. Multiple Input/Output Elements Per Line

In many cases it is desirable to have several data elements on each input line.
Our flowchart conventions will distinguish between this method of input
and the approach of Section 6.4A. When the input statement is to read several data elements per card, the flowchart symbol of Figure 6–7 will be used.

Note the difference between this symbol and that of Figure 6–1. In Figure
6–1 the iteration is outside of the input statement. In Figure 6–7 we show
X(I), I←1,N inside of the READ symbol. In other words, the *iteration is inside of the input symbol.* This means that the loop occurs inside of the READ
statement instead of having the READ statement occur inside of the loop.
This is sometimes referred to as **implied iteration,** a term we will use
throughout this book.

Figure 6-6.
Flowchart for
Numbers Above
Mean

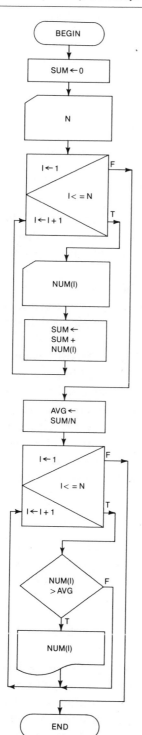

Figure 6–7.
Flowchart
Symbology
for N Input
Date Elements
Per Line

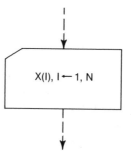

Figure 6–8.
Flowchart
Symbology for N
Output Data
Elements Per Line

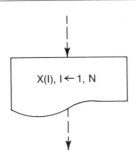

$X(I), I \leftarrow 1, N$

When an input statement contains implied iteration, the computer will read as many items from a data line as indicated by the format. Since formats are language dependent, we will not discuss them specifically in this book. But the general principle is that the next line will be read only when the number of data elements shown in the format is exceeded.

For example, if there are ten data items to be read and the format calls for three values to be on each line, three items each will be read from the first three lines and the tenth item will be read from the fourth line. In this book, we will assume that whenever an implied iteration is performed, as many values are input from a data line as indicated in the corresponding iteration.

The printing of several array elements on one line follows the same general approach as reading several elements from one data line. This output of multiple elements on one line is shown in flowchart form in Figure 6-8. An implied iteration is used within the output symbol of the flowchart, i.e., the *iteration is inside of the output statement*. When this implied iteration is used, the number of items to be printed on each line is determined by the corresponding iteration.

6.5 Using The Array

When we use an array, we are storing all values associated with that array. If there are M elements in the array, M storage locations will be required. In order for the compiler to compute the number of storage locations to allocate for an array, the programmer must declare in advance the maximum size of each array. In Example 6.3 we generalized for an array of size N. The programmer would have to determine the upper limit on the value of N and declare the array NUM accordingly.

We have seen how the use of subscripted variables makes the statement of many algorithms much easier. In the following sections, we are going to find their use even more advantageous. However, we must not become so engrossed in the use of arrays that we permit this data structure to pervade our entire thinking. The following example illustrates a situation in which arrays are not appropriate.

Example 6.5

In a test laboratory a computer is to be used to monitor the performance of a piece of equipment during its operation for a period of 10 days. The monitoring equipment will provide the computer with a value every second. Develop an algorithm to input the value and compute the mean and standard deviation for the 10-day period. The formulas for mean (μ) and standard deviation (σ) are

$$\mu = \frac{\sum_{i=1}^{N} X_i}{N} \qquad \sigma = \sqrt{\frac{\sum_{i=1}^{N}(X_i - \mu)^2}{N}}$$

Solution

Our first inclination is to use an array to store the values received each second, then compute the statistics when the 10-day period is completed. However, a simple calculation will tell us that 864,000 values must be stored if we are going to use an array.

Clearly, no array is needed to compute the mean because we can maintain a running sum of the X_i. It would appear that calculation of the standard deviation requires knowledge of the mean before the formula can be applied so that an array would be needed. But if we substitute for μ we get

$$\sigma = \sqrt{\frac{\sum_{i=1}^{N}\left(X_i - \frac{\sum_{i=1}^{N} X_i}{N}\right)^2}{N}}$$

Expanding the squared term and doing a little algebra yields

$$\sigma = \sqrt{\frac{\sum X_i^2}{N} - \left(\frac{\sum X_i}{N}\right)^2}$$

This formula requires only the sum of the X_i and the sum of the X_i^2, which may be computed without the use of an array. Figure 6–9 shows the resulting algorithm.

By analyzing the problem and looking for alternative methods of expressing the algorithm, we have been able to eliminate the necessity of storing a large array. This type of careful analysis should always be applied.

In Figure 6–9 the following variables are used in applying this formula. SX is the sum of the X's, SXSQ is the sum of the X's squared, and SQRT is a

Figure 6-9.
Flowchart for
Mean and Standard
Deviation
Calculation

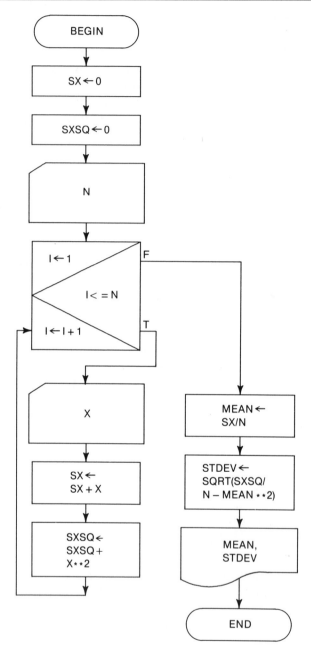

request for a system-level program to provide the square root of the value of the expression in parentheses. STDEV and MEAN should be self-explanatory.

End Solution

6.6 Use of Parallel Arrays

It is sometimes useful to arrange data in several arrays so that the Ith element of each array is related in some way to the Ith element of other arrays. Separate arrays that maintain this one-for-one relationship between corresponding elements are called **parallel arrays.**

Example 6.6

A college course with N students has five graded assignments. Suppose the array STUNBR contains the identification number of each student, and the Ith element of the parallel arrays G1, G2, G3, G4, and G5 contains the five grades for the students identified in the Ith element of STUNBR. Develop an algorithm to print each student's identification number and total point accumulation (TOTAL.)

Solution

Refer to Figure 6–10. We assume that the grades already exist in the arrays. A simple iteration permits us to address each student number. For each value of the control variable I, the five grades can be summed by using the value of I as an index into the five arrays.

End Solution

In Example 6.6, the six parallel arrays can be visualized as the six columns of a table and the index as a row of that table. The technique of parallel arrays is often used in the construction of files for many information retrieval algorithms.

6.7 Double Subscripting

The use of parallel arrays provides a convenient means of correlating information between arrays. With a single index, we were able to address five different values in Example 6.6. Suppose, instead of 5 test scores, there were 25. The algorithm would not change, but we would need an assignment statement:

Figure 6-10.
Flowchart for Student
Data Calculation

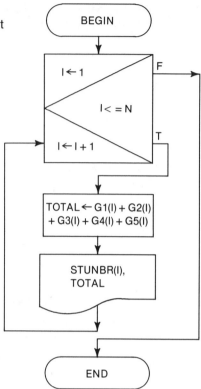

$$TOTAL \leftarrow G1(I) + \cdots + G25(I)$$

Since we can visualize the parallel arrays as columns of a table, it would be advantageous if we could index the columns as well as the rows. This is called **double subscripting** and is permitted in most higher level languages. If we use double subscripting, the problem of summing test scores for 25 tests is as simple as summing the test scores for 5 tests.

Example 6.7
Generalize the algorithm of Example 6.6 to use double subscripting and sum N test scores for each student.

Solution
Refer to Figure 6–11. The array STUNBR is the same as before. Designate the array G to be a doubly subscripted array (also called a two-dimension array). For each value of I up to M students, we sum each test score, $G(I,J)$, where J

Figure 6-11.
Flowchart for
Student Data
Calculation

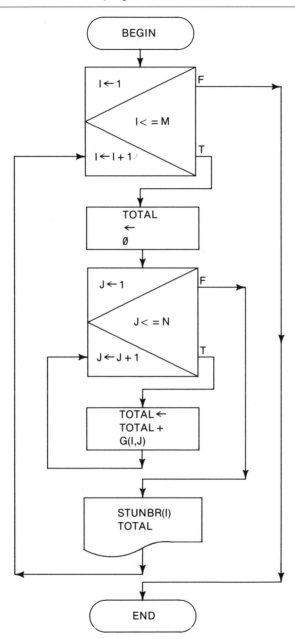

varies from 1 to N. After finding the total for the student represented by row I, we output his identification number and total points.

End Solution

In Example 6.7, we have a more general algorithm. We have employed a number of conventions that make the use of arrays less complicated. For those readers familiar with matrices, the notation should be obvious. A **matrix** is a two-dimension array of numbers. A specific element of a matrix can be identified by specifying its row and column. By convention, the row subscript is specified first. Thus, the matrix **A** can be specified as shown below:

$$A = \begin{bmatrix} 11 & 12 & 13 & 14 \\ 21 & 22 & 23 & 24 \\ 31 & 32 & 33 & 34 \\ 41 & 42 & 43 & 44 \\ 51 & 52 & 53 & 54 \end{bmatrix}$$

Also, by convention, we say that **A** is an $m \times n$ array, where $m = 5$, $n = 4$ in the example of **A** above. In Example 6.7, **G** was an $m \times n$ array. By using nested iteration, we summed the grades in each row by keeping I constant while varying J.

We can also perform operations on the columns of a doubly subscripted array. The technique is similar to that used in Example 6.7.

Example 6.8

A fishing derby is to be held. There will be M children fishing for a total of N days. The number of fish caught by each child will be entered each day into a two-dimension array so that the element FISH (I,J) is the number of fish child I caught on day J. Develop an algorithm to (a) determine the number of fish caught each day, (b) the child catching the largest number of fish on each day, and (c) the largest number of fish caught by a single child on any one day, i.e., the largest element in the matrix.

Solution

There are a number of operations to be performed. We could perform each separately; however, each part requires examination of the entire array so that to do them separately would require three passes over the array. With a little planning, we can do them all in a single pass over the array, as illustrated in Figure 6-12.

The initialization operations appear both outside and inside the iteration on J. Part (c) of the example requires only a single number to represent the

Figure 6-12.
Flowchart for
Fishing Derby

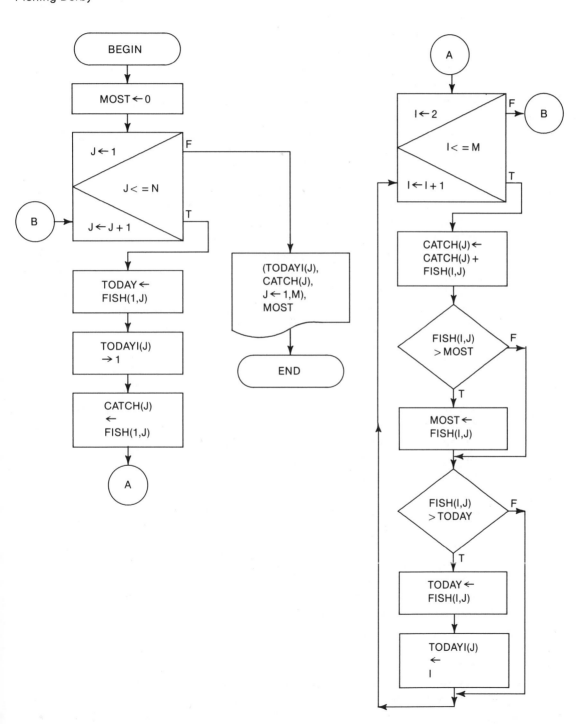

largest element in the array. We therefore initialize the variable MOST to 0, which is the minimum possible value for the largest number of fish. In examining the array, we will be iterating on the columns so that we must vary J.

For each column (i.e., day) we must find the largest number of fish caught that day and the index that identifies the child catching that number. We will create a new array TODAYI for this purpose. We could initialize the simple variable TODAY to 0, but if no fish were caught on day J, then the index contained in TODAYI(J) would be undefined. Therefore, we simply assume that the first child caught the largest number of fish for each day and check that for each iteration.

Part (a) requires a listing of the total catch by day, which we will store in array CATCH. For each J, we initialize CATCH(J) to the number of fish caught by the first child.

For each value of J, we iterate on I (i.e., children), which is equivalent to looking down the column. The summation of CATCH(J) is similar to other summing operations. The value of MOST is checked to see if the current element exceeds it.

Finally, we check to see if the element exceeds the current largest catch for day J. However, if more than one child catches the largest number on a given day, the child with the lowest index who catches that number of fish will be given credit. The same comment applies to the child who caught the most fish.

End Solution

The accomplishment of the three parts of Example 6.8 in one iteration loop rather than in three iterations is more efficient. Remember that iteration control involves several operations that must occur for each element of the array: primarily incrementing and testing of the control variable(s). If there are a large number of elements in the array, the use of one iteration rather than three iterations will provide significant savings.

But the algorithm of Example 6.8 can be further improved for computing the largest number of fish when the number of rows (children) is reasonably greater than the number of columns (days). In general, we would expect this to be true for the example. If we were keeping fishing derby results in the computer, there would probably be a large number of contestants fishing for a small number of days, which would make the value of M (the number of children) much greater than the value of N (the number of days).

Example 6.9
Improve the efficiency of computation of the value of MOST in the algorithm of Example 6.8.

Solution

Part (b) of the example finds the child who caught the largest number of fish each day and stores the index of the row corresponding to that child in TODAYI(J). Note that the child who caught the largest number of fish during the derby—part (c) of the example—must also have caught the largest number of fish on at least one day of the tournament. Thus his row identifier will be in the array TODAYI. Consequently, instead of searching the entire array FISH for the value of the variable MOST, the array TODAYI can be used to determine the value of MOST more efficiently. (As in Example 6.8, cases of ties will result in only the first child being identified.)

Array TODAYI(J) goes from 1 to N and the Ith element of the array contains the index of the Ith row corresponding to the child who caught the largest number of fish that day. Thus the value of TODAYI(J) is a row index I. Consequently, FISH (TODAYI(J), J) contains the value of the largest number of fish caught on the Ith day of the tournament.

Figure 6–13 provides an algorithm based upon this concept. The value of MOST is determined by using the N elements of array TODAYI, rather than searching the $m \times n$ elements of array FISH. Since MOST must be initiated, it is initiated to FISH (TODAYI(1), 1) with the iteration going from $J = 2$ to $J = N$. An alternative method would be to initiate MOST to 0 with the iteration going from $J = 1$ to $J = N$. That would not have been as efficient.

End Solution

In the preceding example, an array subscript consisted of an element of an array, i.e., TODAYI(J). This does not violate any of the subscript rules in Section 6.3. In fact, it is merely another example of the computer subscript mentioned in Rule (3) of that section. We will use this type of array reference when it better describes an algorithm.

6.8 Input/Output of a Doubly Subscripted Array

The input or output of a doubly subscripted, or two-dimension, array involves the use of a nested iteration. This double iteration loop can be performed in several ways. One method of reading the values of the data elements of a two-dimension array is shown in Figure 6–14. The iteration for the row of the array is outside the input symbol, but the iteration for the column of the array is inside the READ symbol. Thus the row subscript will be varied in an iteration statement, but the column subscript will be incremented by the use of an implied iteration.

In keeping with the conventions discussed earlier, each row of the array will be read from a different data line. The method illustrated in Figure 6–14 can be extended to the output of a two-dimension array. If the input symbol

Figure 6-13.
Flowchart for
Fishing Derby
(Revised)

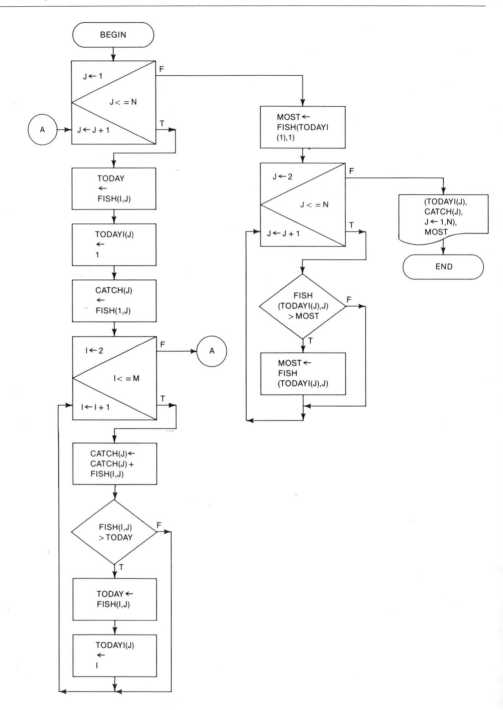

Figure 6-14.
Flowchart
Symbology for
M Lines of N
Data Elements

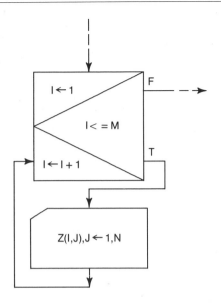

of the figure is replaced by an output symbol, the printing of each row of the array will start on a new line.

In addition to the I/O operation illustrated in the previous example, there are other ways of performing the input/output of a two-dimension array. In some cases, the value of each element of the array will be on a separate data line. In order to read the values of the array in these cases, both iteration loops are outside the READ statement.

This method is shown in Figure 6–15, where each READ statement reads only one data element. There are other I/O cases in which it is desirable or necessary to have the capability to read all data items of the array from the same data line. Figure 6–16 illustrates the manner in which this can be described. Both iterations are inside the READ statement. Thus the input statement contains two implied iterations. In the same manner in which the approach of Figure 6–14 applies to both input and output, the general concepts of Figure 6–15 and Figure 6–16 also apply to output.

There is a great deal of versatility in the input and output of multi-dimension arrays. The iterations required to do the operation can consist entirely of iteration statements outside the I/O statement, entirely of implied iterations inside the I/O statement, or some combination of these.

The following example illustrates this versatility and shows some of the choices available to the programmer when he is performing the output of two-dimension arrays.

Figure 6-15.
Flowchart
Symbology for
M × N Data Lines

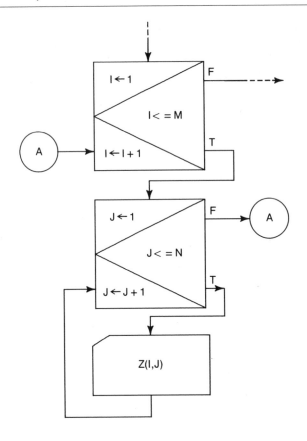

Figure 6–16.
Flowchart
Symbology for
One Line of
M × N Items

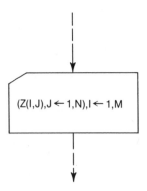

Example 6.10

Develop an algorithm to read a doubly subscripted array (4 × 4) into memory and then output it in a variety of ways. The program should provide an output corresponding to each of the following:

1. Each element of the array on a different line
2. Each row of the array on a separate line
3. All elements of the array on the same line
4. Each column of the array on a separate line
5. Each diagonal element of the array on a different line
6. The diagonal elements of the array on the same line
7. The rearrangement of the elements of the array due to reversing the initial and final values of the iteration variables.

Solution

Each of the individual outputs in Figure 6–17 is preceded by an appropriate output heading. This provides a rapid means of finding a particular part of the program in the flowchart, as well as identifying the results.

1. In Output A, both iteration loops are outside the WRITE statement. Since every WRITE statement causes a new line to be output, each element of the array is printed on a different line.

2. In Output B, each row of the array appears on a separate line. This is due to the outer loop being outside the WRITE statement while the inner loop is an implied loop inside the WRITE statement.

3. In Output C, both loops are inside the WRITE statement. Since the format is assumed to be large enough to hold the entire array on the same line, the whole array is printed on one line.

4. Output D is the transpose of the original array. This output was achieved merely by writing the array in a slightly different order. The outer loop used in Output B (the I loop) and the previous inner loop (the J loop) have been interchanged in this output. Thus, Column 1 values are on the first line, Column 2 values are on the second line, and so forth. Notice that the storage of the array has not been altered in any way.

5. The next output writes out the diagonal of the matrix, i.e., ARR (1,1), ARR (2,2), ARR (3,3), ARR (4,4). Since the row subscript equals the column subscript, the use of only one control variable is sufficient. Output E has the iteration loop on the outside of the WRITE statement and each element of the diagonal appears on a separate line.

Figure 6–17.
Flowchart for
Array I/O Samples

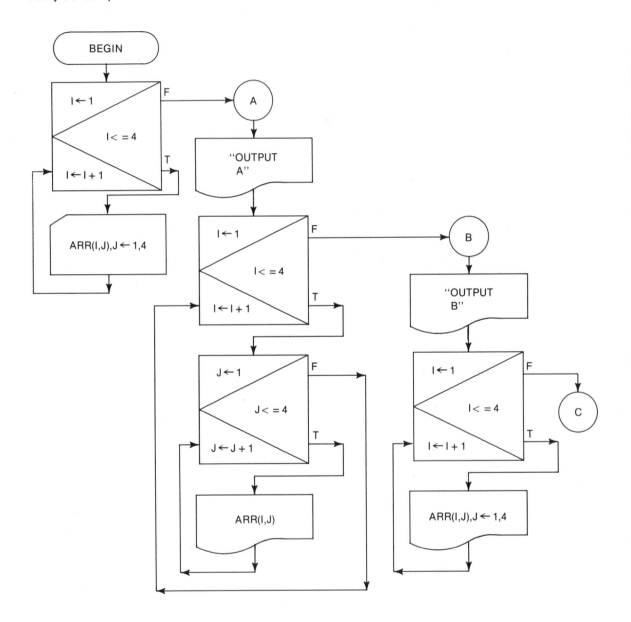

Figure 6–17.
(continued)

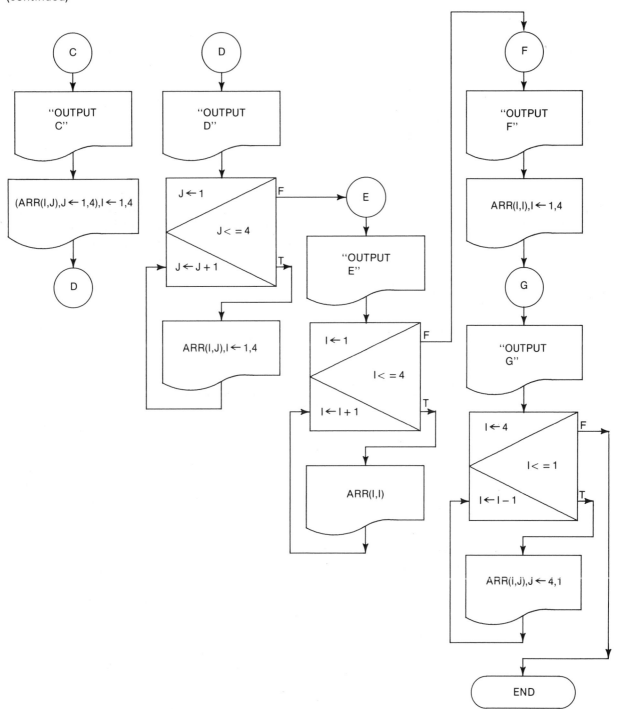

6. Output F provides a contrast to the previous example. Since the iteration is an implied loop within the WRITE statement, all output is on the same line.

7. Output G is the result of using negative stepping in the iteration. Note that the inner and outer loops start at the value of 4 and decrement 1 each time through the loop. As in the case of Output D, the array still holds the original values and the output is merely due to the manner in which the array is printed.

End Solution

6.9 Multiple Subscripting

Most high-level languages do not limit the number of subscripts to two. For some applications, it is convenient to use more than two subscripts **(Multiple Subscripting)** so that the statement of the algorithm remains concise.

Example 6.11
Calculate the mean temperature for the city of Denver for any given day of the year. The average temperature and date are provided as input for the years 1960 to 1982.

Solution
There are three factors to be considered for each temperature given: the year, the month, and the day. Since the data has a natural three-way classification, it would serve our purposes well to declare a three-dimension array TEMP. The first subscript will refer to the year, the second to the month, and the third to the day of the month. The maximum size of the array would have to be 23 (years) by 12 (months) by 31 (days). Note that we have wasted some space since not all months have 31 days. Since there is a variable number of days in each month, we will use a second array called DATE to store the number of days in each month.

We will assume each temperature is on a separate data line along with the month, day, and year. We will use the trailer card technique and terminate when the year is 9999. We use the year as a subscript by subtracting 1959, causing it to range from 1 to 23. To find the mean temperature for any day of the year we need only add the mean temperature from TEMP for that date and divide by 23. We could easily calculate the mean annual temperature and the mean temperature for any given year or month. The algorithm is shown as Figure 6–18. Note that the algorithm ignores the effect of Leap Year. If DATE contained 28 days for February then no average would be generated for February 29. If DATE contained 29 for February then the average pro-

Figure 6–18.
Flowchart for
Mean Temperatures

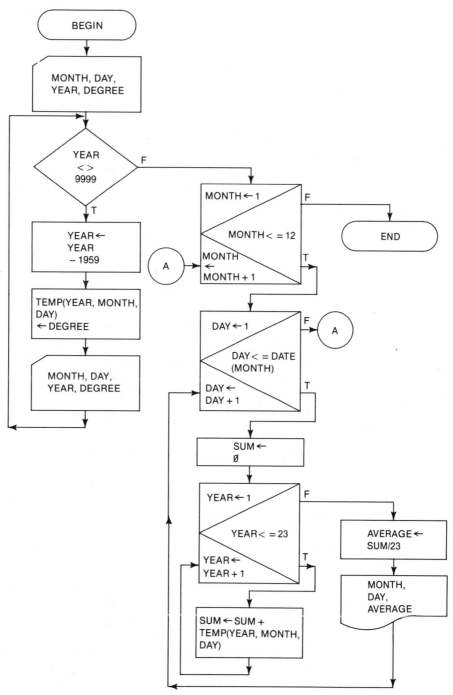

duced for February 29 would be incorrect. The student is asked to enhance the problem to accommodate Leap Years as Supplemental Problem 6.15.

End Solution

6.10 The Grading Problem and Arrays

There are several areas where arrays could be used in the grading problem to make it more compact. First, we could use a one-dimension array, GRADE, to hold the letter grades "A" to "F." Then to determine a student's grade, we merely divide his average by 10, truncate the result, and use the answer as an index into GRADE, thus effectively eliminating the four conditional statements used in Figure 5–15.

Second, we could read each student's information into a two-dimension array, STUDENT. Then to find each student's average, we merely sum the appropriate columns to find CMPTS and divide by 3. To find each test mean and standard deviation, we apply the algorithm of Example 6.5 to the appropriate columns of STUDENT.

However, we do not feel that the use of arrays in either example is warranted. In the first situation the algorithm, though similar, is not nearly as straightforward as the nested conditionals. In the second situation we would be using an excessive amount of memory for information that we really do not need to keep. As the number of students increased, the size of the array would also increase.

The only thing that remains to be done in our problem is to compute the statistics for each test and for the section overall. As shown in Figure 6–19, we will use the two-dimension array POINTS to help generate these statistics.

Applying the algorithm of Example 6.5, we will accumulate the sums in column 1, and the sum of the squares in column 2. The rows will represent TEST1, TEST2, TEST3, and CUMPTS, respectively. We will read each student's test data into a one-dimension array, TEST, to facilitate generating these sums by an iteration.

Our use of arrays in this way makes the algorithm more concise and straightforward. In addition, the amount of storage required remains constant regardless of the number of students in a section.

After you are sure that you understand the logic of Figure 6–19, you should code the algorithm and execute your program with the student data from Table 6–1. Be sure that you can duplicate the output of Table 6–1.

6.11 Summary

Because of our natural orientation toward tabulated information, arrays are easy to visualize, and they offer a straightforward data structure that often

Figure 6-19.
Flowchart for
Grading Problem

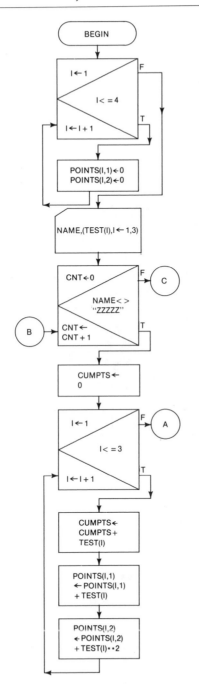

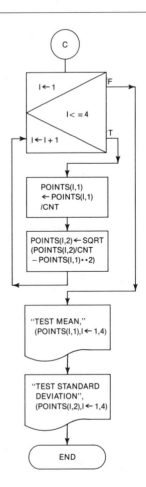

Figure 6–19.
(continued)

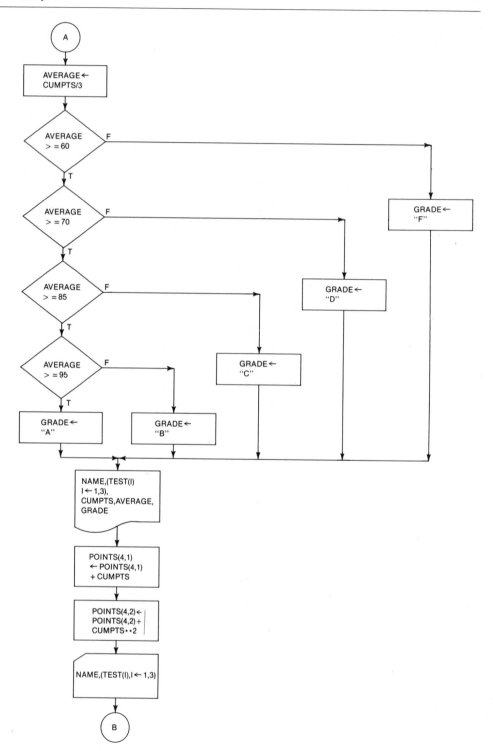

Table 6–1

Course: Math 351				Instructor: Mr. P. J. Smythe		
Section: 3				Room: 304		
Number of Tests: 3						
Number of Students: 10						

Student's Name	Test 1	Test 2	Test 3	CUM PTS	Average	Grade
Adams, M. E.	85	87	90	262	87.33	B
Barnes, L. J.	56	60	72	168	56.00	F
Carlton, P. G.	30	40	59	129	43.00	F
Driscoll, R.	98	99	100	297	99.00	A
Evans, S. T.	90	85	76	251	83.67	C
Orly, A. P.	50	65	78	193	64.33	D
Puget, S.	83	81	84	248	82.67	C
Ryan, M. A.	90	89	72	251	83.67	C
Silve, G. A.	60	65	65	190	63.33	D
Walton, J. J.	88	70	89	247	82.33	C
Test Mean	73.0	74.1	78.5	223.6		
Test Standard Deviation	22.38	17.38	12.42	51.22		

fits the data. However, there are two considerations we must make when contemplating the use of arrays. First, we must be aware of the amount of storage they require. For instance, in Example 6.11, considering only 23 years, we used 8556 storage locations. For each additional year included in the analysis, we would have increased this amount by 372.

Second, the use of arrays slows down execution time considerably, especially arrays with multiple dimensions. This is only logical since each array reference requires that each subscript be calculated separately and added to the base address of the array to determine the actual physical address of the array element.

Therefore, when developing an algorithm, the programmer should take into consideration the trade-off of time and storage requirements against the amount of facility and conciseness provided by array initialization and implementation.

Solved Problems

6.1

Design an algorithm to input an array, remove all data elements with a value of 0, and output the revised array. For example, if the input is the array (2.3,

0, 7, 7.5, 0, 0, 6.2, 2.1, 0, 1.1), then the result will be the array with values (2.3, 7, 7.5, 6.2, 2.1, 1.1). This result is to be achieved by a change in the contents of the input array rather than by the creation of a new array or by the mere printing of the nonzero entries.

Solution

After the number of items in the array NBR is read, each element of the array is input using implied iteration, as reflected in Figure 6–20. The output of the resultant array also uses implied iteration.

The general approach underlying the operation of this algorithm will be useful in a number of different cases. The key to the operation is the use of two different variables as indices to the array ARR. The index MK is used to iterate through each element of the array, comparing the value of that element with the value of 0. The second index, POS, is used to denote the location within the array to which each of the nonzero elements is to be transferred.

Note that the value of POS must be less than or equal to the value of MK at all times. The difference in the values of these two indices will be equal to the number of 0 entries that have been encountered.

In order to provide a further insight into the use of this method, we will consider the values of MK and POS at the time that the flow passes through connector Z of the flowchart. The variables MK and POS can be considered as pointers to locations within the array ARR.

In order to examine a specific case, we will use the small array in Figure 6–21 in analyzing the algorithm. Figure 6–21 depicts the locations of MK and POS after each of the first four iterations and after the completion of the entire loop. For example, after the third iteration, the value of POS is 2 and ARR(2) has been set to the value of 7.

After completion of ten iterations, POS points to the sixth element of the array and the six nonzero values of the original array are in the first six elements of the array. Although the last part of the array contains the original values, this does not cause any difficulty. In the output of the revised array, the upper bound of the implied iteration is POS. Thus in our example only the first six data elements will be printed.

6.2

The **CHI-square goodness-of-fit test** is a statistic that is used to determine how well empirical distributions (obtained from experimental data) fit theoretical distributions (such as Binomial, Poisson, and Normal distributions). In performing the test, the empirical observations are classified into categories, or cells. The observed and expected frequencies are then compared by use of the test. The CHI-square statistic is computed from observed and expected frequencies by the formula:

Figure 6–20.
Flowchart for
Solved Problem 6.1

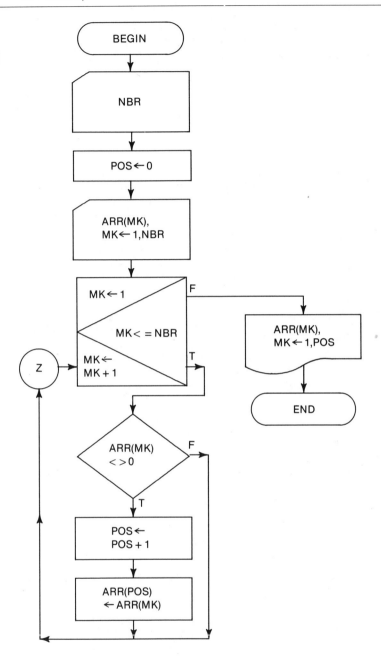

Figure 6-21.
Sample Flow for
Solved Problem 6.1

First Time Through Z:

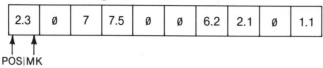

Second Time Through Z:

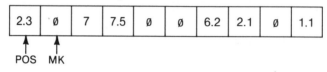

Third Time Through Z:

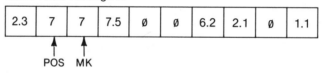

Fourth Time Through Z:

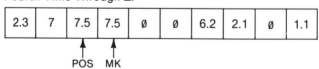

Tenth Time Through Z:

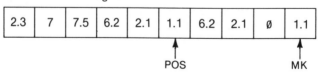

$$\chi^2 = \sum_{j=1}^{N} \frac{(o_j - e_j)^2}{e_j}$$

where o_j is the observed frequency of the jth cell and e_j is the expected frequency of the jth cell. Develop an algorithm that first inputs the values of two arrays corresponding to the observed and expected frequencies and then computes the value of χ^2.

Solution

This algorithm is outlined in Figure 6–22. The algorithm first inputs a value of N, which is the number of intervals, or cells. The number of observations for each cell is then input into the appropriate element of the array OBS, and the corresponding expected frequency is input to the parallel array EXP. This operation consists of an iteration on the variable I ranging from 1 to N and the input of the value for each pair of elements.

Each pair of values must appear on a separate data line, since the iteration is outside of the input operation. Although the two arrays can first be input, then a second iteration used to compute CHI, there is no reason why the two operations cannot be done simultaneously.

It is extremely important to test for an expected value of 0; otherwise the algorithm would fail through an attempt to divide by 0.

6.3

An annuity is a sequence of equal payments made at equal intervals of time. This example considers an annuity in which the payments begin and end on fixed dates, and the payments are made at the end of each payment period (technically this is called an "ordinary annuity certain"). The amount DEP is deposited into a savings account for each of NR months. Interest is compounded monthly at an annual interest of RATE. Develop an algorithm to output an array that will show the amount of combined savings and interest at the end of each month.

Solution

Figure 6–23 shows the values of DEP, RATE, and NR being input to the algorithm. The values of DEP and RATE are then echo-checked and the monthly interest rate is developed from the annual rate. Since the annual rate is not needed after the computation of the monthly rate, the same variable is used to store both the annual and monthly rates. At the end of the first month, the savings consists solely of that month's deposit, i.e., DEP. At the end of each subsequent month, the savings consists of the investment at the end of the previous month, the interest earned during the month, and the monthly deposit. The array SAVNG, which is the table of monthly savings, is then written out.

Figure 6–22.
Flowchart for
Solved Problem 6.2

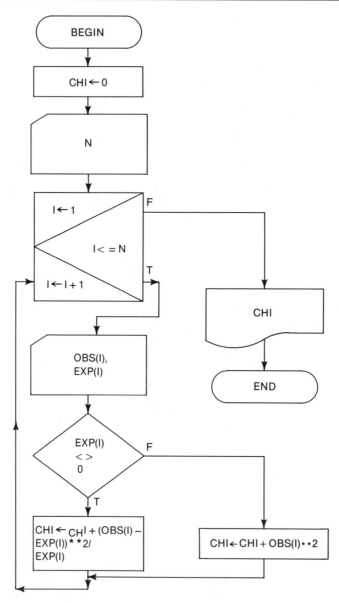

Figure 6–23.
Flowchart for
Solved Problem 6.3

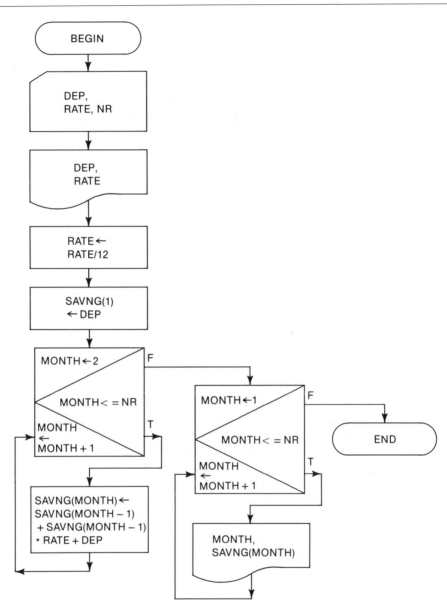

6.4

Develop an algorithm to input two singly subscripted arrays of the same size. The first of these is an array of REAL values; the second contains an array of 0s and 1s. When the value of an element of the second array is 1, the corresponding element of the first array is printed, one data item per line. For example, if the two arrays contain the following values,

(1.1, 2.2, 3.3, 4.4, 5.5, 6.6, 7.7, 8.8, 9.9)

(1, 1, 0, 1, 0, 0, 1, 1, 0)

the results are

1.1
2.2
4.4
7.7
8.8

Solution

The algorithm in Figure 6–24 illustrates two methods of handling the array input. Assume that the array W, which contains REAL values, is input with one data element per line. Thus the READ statement is inside the iteration. On the other hand, the iteration for reading array K is shown as an implied iteration. The output of the elements of array W is inside the iteration. Thus it is the output counterpart of the input method for that array.

6.5

A **square matrix** is a matrix that has the same number of rows as it has columns. A **stochastic matrix** is a square matrix in which all entries in the matrix are nonnegative and the sum of the components in each of the rows is equal to 1. For example, matrix **A** is a stochastic matrix, but matrix **B** is not a stochastic matrix since the sum of the first row is not equal to 1.

$$
A = \begin{bmatrix} \frac{1}{4} & 0 & \frac{3}{4} \\ \frac{1}{2} & \frac{1}{4} & \frac{1}{4} \\ \frac{1}{2} & 0 & \frac{1}{2} \end{bmatrix} \quad B = \begin{bmatrix} \frac{1}{4} & \frac{1}{4} & \frac{1}{4} \\ \frac{1}{2} & 0 & \frac{1}{2} \\ \frac{1}{4} & \frac{1}{2} & \frac{1}{4} \end{bmatrix}
$$

Develop an algorithm that will input a matrix, echo-check the matrix, determine if the matrix is a stochastic matrix, and output an appropriate message.

Solution

The array input and output of this problem use implied iteration. As shown in Figure 6–25, the array XMT is input, row by row. The echo check of the

Figure 6-24.
Flowchart for
Solved Problem 6.4

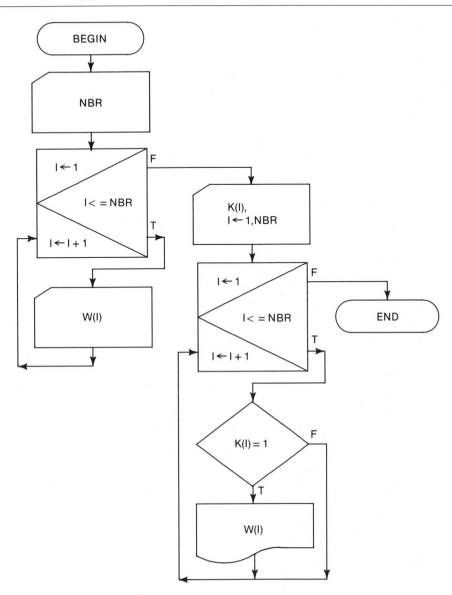

Figure 6-25.
Flowchart for
Solved Problem 6.5

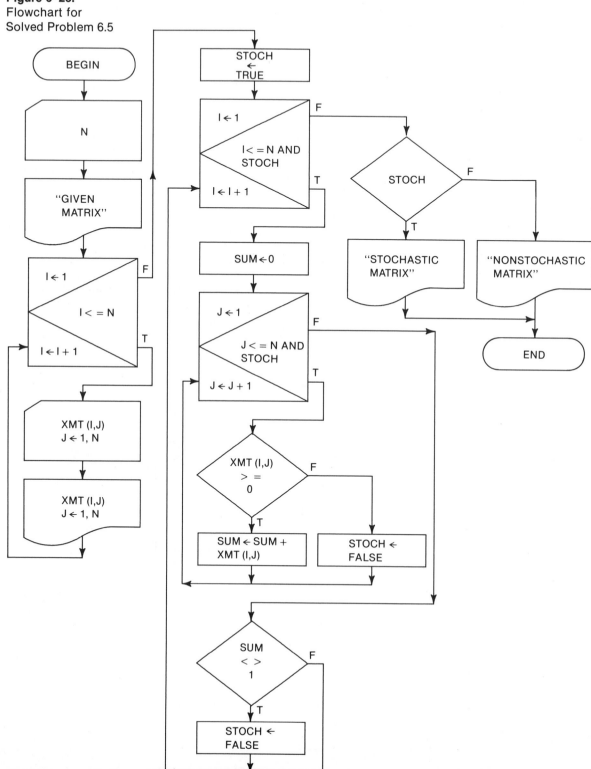

array is printed in the same manner. Each of the N rows of the array is then examined to determine if XMT is a stochastic matrix.

Note that the flowchart makes two tests. Each component of the row is checked to be sure it is nonnegative. In addition, the sum (SUM) of each row is tested to see if it is equal to 1. If either of these tests fails at any time, a message that XMT is nonstochastic is printed immediately and the program stops. There is no need to check the remainder of the array in these instances.

If no test fails, then XMT is a stochastic matrix and the program prints an appropriate message. Note the use of the BOOLEAN variable STOCH to indicate the loop should be terminated when a row with an element less than 0 or a sum not equal to 1 has been found.

End Solution

6.6

Pascal's Triangle is a triangular array of numbers that are binomial coefficients. The first few rows of the triangle are

```
                1
              1   1
            1   2   1
          1   3   3   1
        1   4   6   4   1
      1   5  10  10   5   1
    1   6  15  20  15   6   1
  1   7  21  35  35  21   7   1
```

There are two interesting properties of the triangle:

1. The first and last number of each line is a 1.
2. Each of the remaining numbers is the sum of the two numbers directly above it.

The triangle can be generated very easily by the computer. Develop an algorithm to do this. In order to simplify the output, rearrange the triangle as follows:

```
1
1   1
1   2   1
1   3   3   1
1   4   6   4   1
1   5   10  10  5   1
1   6   15  20  15  6   1
1   7   21  35  35  21  7   1
```

Solution

The program is rather short, as shown in Figure 6–26. The iterations used in the program are not difficult, but they are subtle.

First note that the values for the first two lines are entered by several simple assignment statements. The first iteration loop starts at I = 3 and steps until N. The first and last entry in each row is 1 and again each is entered by a simple assignment statement. The other values in the line are computed on the basis of the values in the preceding row of the array. Be sure to examine closely how the iteration on J is dependent upon the value of I.

Although there is no input into the program, the algorithm is based upon the use of N in the iteration. This allows the algorithm to be general. However, the value of N is initialized through an assignment statement rather than input.

The output iteration uses the value of I in controlling the J iteration loop. The result resembles a triangular matrix. The outer iteration of the output refers to the row. The implied inner iteration is for the columns. The stopping condition of the inner loop is the variable I, which is the control variable of the outer loop. Since the value of I increases by 1 during each iteration, an additional column is printed out for each new row.

6.7

In doing a number of mathematical problems without a computer, it is useful to have a table of squares. Develop an algorithm that will output a table listing the square for the values in the range 0.0 to 24.9 in increments of 0.1. The table should be arranged such that the respective square can be read by entering the row corresponding to the integral part of the number and the column corresponding to the fractional part.

Solution

One possible algorithm, shown in Figure 6–27, is really a very short and simple one. The heading of the table is output to provide columnar headings from 0 to 0.9. The associated squared values are assigned to the array SQ by a nested iteration for 10 entries in each of 25 rows.

Figure 6–26.
Flowchart for
Solved Problem 6.6

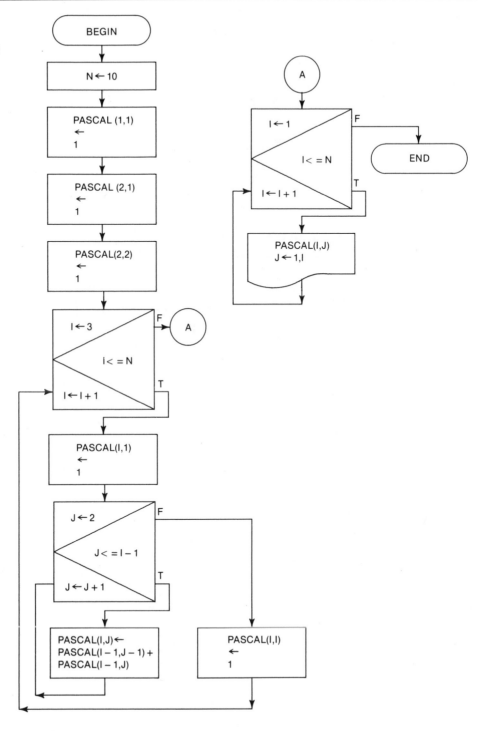

Figure 6–27.
Flowchart for
Solved Problem 6.7

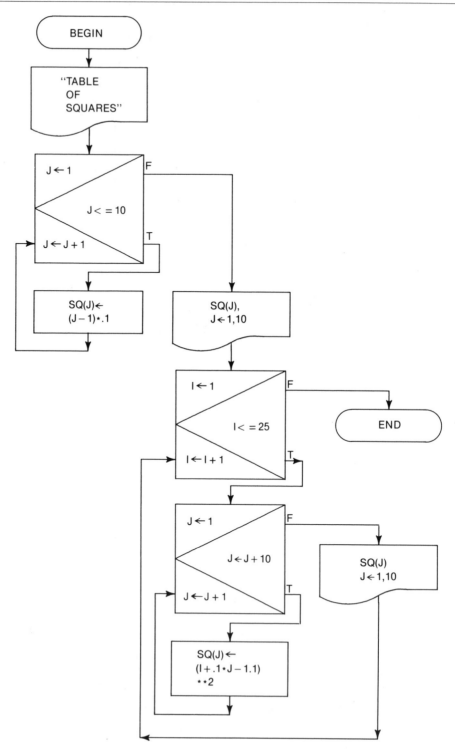

Derivation of the formula for creating the squared values is easier if we consider a specific example. To look up the square of 1.3, it will be necessary to enter the table at the row corresponding to the value of 1 and the column corresponding to the value of 0.3. Assuming that the array starts at (0,0), this is the second row and the fourth column, respectively. Denoting the row subscripts as I and the column subscripts as J, the value for the square of 1.3 is located at $I = 2$ and $J = 4$. Thus we can express the value of 1.3 in terms of the associated coordinates of I and J as $(I - 1) + (J - 1) * (0.1)$.

In fact, any value within the range covered by the table can be expressed as this relationship. Simple algebraic expansion of this term provides the relation $(I + 0.1 * J - 1.1)$. Using this as the basis of the computation in a nested iteration is then the major process of the algorithm.

Note that it is not necessary to use a two-dimension array. Although this could be used, a one-dimension array is adequate. Each row is output immediately after it is generated.

6.8

A triangular matrix is one in which the nonzero elements of the matrix are all on the same side of the diagonal. The name arises from the fact that the nonzero entries form a triangle. A triangular matrix can be completely defined by these nonzero entries, as shown in the following example:

```
11
21   22
31   32   33
41   42   43   44
```

A symmetric matrix is one in which $A(I,J) = A(J,I)$ for all I and J, i.e., it is symmetric about the diagonal. Since $A(J,I)$ is determined if $A(I,J)$ is known, it is possible to store a symmetric matrix as a triangular matrix. This smaller array can then be expanded to a full symmetrical matrix when it is necessary to do so. If the above triangular matrix represented a symmetrical array, the full array would be

```
11   21   31   41
21   22   32   42
31   32   33   43
41   42   43   44
```

Develop an algorithm to input a matrix in triangular form and expand it to a full symmetric matrix.

Solution

As indicated in Figure 6–28, the input starts in a manner similar to a number of the other problems by inputting the number of rows in the array before

Figure 6-28.
Flowchart for
Solved Problem 6.8

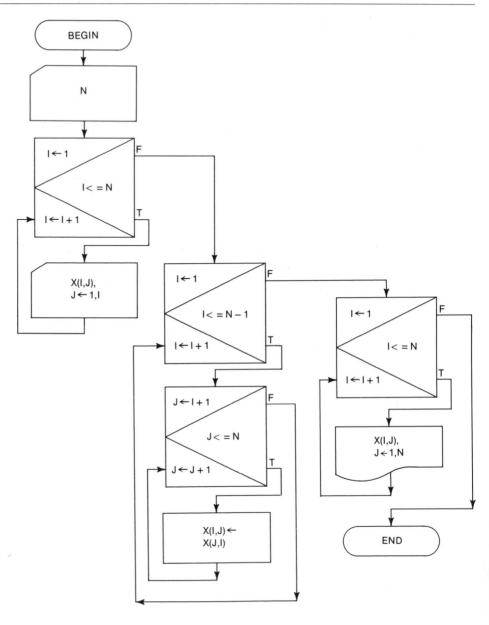

the array is input. The important aspect of the implied iteration on J is that its upper bound is I. Thus one data element will be input for the first row, two elements will be input for the second row, three elements will be input for the third row, and so forth.

The concepts used in establishing the nested iteration to expand the array illustrate the careful attention that must be exercised in setting the limits of iteration loops. The outer iteration on I need only go to $N-1$, since the last row of the array is already full length. The inner iteration on J starts at $I+1$ in order to restrict the data transfer to the elements of the array on the right side of the diagonal of the matrix.

6.9

One business application of the computer is to keep sales records for a company. We will consider a simple example that summarizes the sales record of an organization that has a number of salespeople and sells 15 products.

Develop an algorithm that will input the individual sales record for a specified number of days and compile the sales statistics. Each input consists of a numeric salesperson identifier and the number of each of the 15 products sold by that salesperson for a particular day. The outputs are the dollar value of the sales for each salesperson during the period, the number of each of the 15 products sold, and the value of the sales for each day in the period.

Solution

The information will be stored in a three-dimension array, SALES, where the three subscripts refer to the salesperson, the day, and the product, respectively. The number of salespersons is denoted by NRPERSONS and the variable NRDAY is employed to denote the number of days of data.

The algorithm is shown in Figure 6-29. Initialization includes the input of values for the variables NRPERSON and NRDAY, as well as the values for the singly subscripted array PRICE. The array PRICE contains the unit price of each of the products in elements 1 through 15. This is needed in computing the monetary values of the sales.

Note that the order of the iteration loops in the input statement and the arrangement of the data are closely interrelated. The particular arrangement of this loop necessitates that all data related to a particular salesperson be grouped together; a salesperson's data is then ordered by day. There are other ways of inputting a multi-dimension array, but it is always necessary to be sure that the data and the iteration loops of the READ statement are in agreement.

The actual calculations are accomplished in three loops. The variable used in the outer loop differs for each of the three loops and is determined by the type of analysis: salesperson, product, or day. The loops for computing the salesperson analysis and the computation of the daily sales are almost identi-

Figure 6-29.
Flowchart for
Solved Problem 6.9

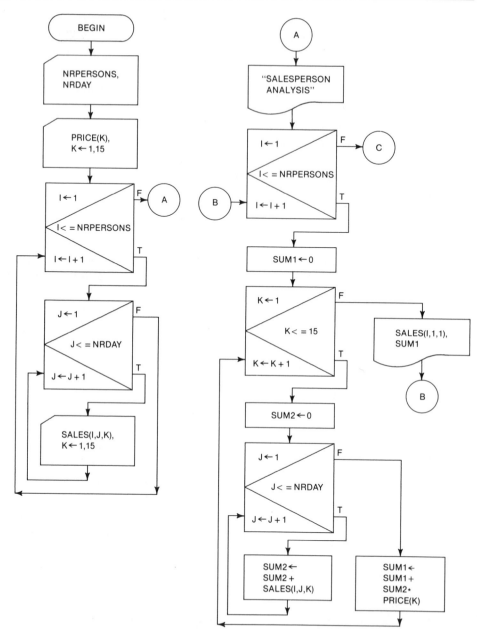

Figure 6–29.
(continued)

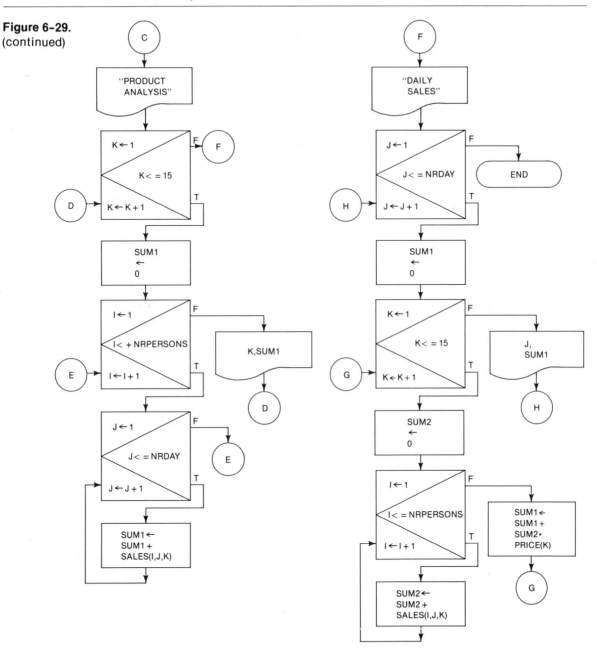

cal. Only the order of the iteration is different. The iteration for the product analysis is quite similar, but it does not require multiplication by the respective element of the array PRICE since only the number of products is included in the output.

Supplemental Problems

6.10

In some applications it is necessary to count the number of data items that exceed a particular value (or conversely, the number of items that are less than a given value). For example, in statistical analysis it might be desirable to know how many data elements are beyond two standard deviations of the mean.

Develop an algorithm that will input an array, count the number of data elements exceeding a particular value, and output this count. Then develop an alternative algorithm to achieve the same result without using an array.

6.11

A row vector $\bar{u}$ is a set of numbers $u_1, u_2, \ldots, u_N$ written in a row. We can then denote the vector $\bar{u}$ as

$$\bar{u} = (u_1, u_2, \ldots, u_N)$$

where the u_i is called the component of the vector. The sum of two row vectors that have the same number of components is defined as

$$\bar{u} + v = (u_1, u_2, \ldots, u_N) + (v_1, v_2, \ldots, v_N)$$
$$= (u_1 + v_1, u_2 + v_2, \ldots, u_N + v_N)$$

Develop an algorithm that reads the component values of two row vectors and then computes and outputs the sum of the two row vectors. Three arrays are to be used in the program, all representing a row vector of the same length.

6.12

The dot product, or scalar product or inner product, is the product of two row vectors. When a vector is expressed in the form shown in Problem 6.11, the dot product of two vectors of equal length is defined as

$$\bar{u} \times \bar{v} = u_1 \times v_1 + u_2 \times v_2 + \cdots + u_N \times v_N = \sum_{i=1}^{N} u_i \times v_i$$

Develop an algorithm that will read two vectors and determine the dot product.

6.13

Develop an algorithm to input a symmetric matrix, store it in triangular form, and output it as a fully expanded symmetric matrix without actually expanding the array in the computer. That is, revise the algorithm of Problem 6.8 to produce the same output without an actual expansion of the input array.

6.14

When a two-dimension array is considered to be in graphic or matrix form, we can define the diagonal of a square array as those elements that form a straight line from one corner of the array to the diagonally opposite corner. For example, in the 4×4 array X, the two diagonals are

X(1,1) X(2,2) X(3,3) X(4,4)

and

X(1,4) X(2,3) X(3,2) X(4,1)

Develop an algorithm that inputs a square array, outputs the echo check of the array, sets all elements of the array to 0 except for the elements of the two diagonals, and prints the revised array.

6.15

Revise Example 6.11 to compute the mean temperature for February 29th in Leap Years. Do not use a separate iteration, rather calculate this figure when February is processed during the existing iteration.

7   *Introduction to Pseudocode*

7.1 Introduction   If you have been conscientiously following the exercises and solved problems, and practicing the supplemental problems, you should be reasonably proficient at expressing an algorithm you have developed in the form of a flowchart. Unfortunately, this pictorial form of representing an algorithm can become somewhat tedious and unwieldy for large, complex problems.

In this chapter, we introduce an alternative method of developing, documenting, and presenting an algorithm. This method is called pseudocode and it will become our standard method of presentation throughout the remainder of this book.

Pseudocode, as the name implies, is not a true code at all, but rather it is a representation of a code. The pseudocode we will develop is not directly applicable to any particular computing system; however, it is closely related to PASCAL. It is our intent that the student become proficient enough at developing pseudocode to represent algorithms that the result can be recoded into the required programming language with minimal effort.

Not all of the constructs we will present are directly transferable to all languages; however, as was the case with some of our flowchart constructs, the recoding effort can be minimized if the logic in conditional and iterative constructs is reversed.

In this chapter we will introduce and discuss the pseudocode counterparts to the flowchart symbology and then demonstrate its syntax. We will recode exercises from previous chapters to use as examples and potential reference.

**7.2 Bracketing/
Declaration/
Comments**

A. Bracketing

In all programming languages it is necessary to be able to determine when a statement begins and ends. Because we desire our pseudocode to be as free-form as possible, we will allow a statement to begin in any column and terminate in any column and to cut across input line boundaries. We will use ";" to indicate the termination of a statement.

In many cases we find it necessary to in some way designate a group of simple statements that are to be treated as a unit or a block. For example, we need to identify all the statements in a program as subordinate to the program header, and all the statements that are controlled by an iteration as subordinate to the iteration statement. The ability to group statements and treat them as a unit is called **bracketing.** We do this in a similar fashion to the flowchart BEGIN and END statements, as follows:

```
BEGIN
      STATEMENT (1);
                  .
                  .
                  .
      STATEMENT (N);
END;
```

Notice that the group of statements started with BEGIN and ended with ";" after END. Although each individual, enclosed statement was in every respect a statement in itself and terminated with ";", we allow the BEGIN/END combination to form a bracket that effectively causes the group of statements enclosed to be treated as a set. We have placed no restriction on the bracketed statements themselves that could in effect also be a set of statements bracketed with another set of BEGIN/END. Thus a portion of a program could actually appear as follows:

```
BEGIN
      STATEMENT (1);
      STATEMENT (2);
      BEGIN
            STATEMENT (3);
            BEGIN
                  STATEMENT (4);
                              .
                              .
                              .
                  STATEMENT (6);
            END;
            STATEMENT (7);
      END;
END;
```

We bracket the entire program as follows:

```
PROGRAM PROGRAMNAME;

DECLARATIONS;

BEGIN
      STATEMENT(S);
END.
```

That is, a program begins with the word PROGRAM followed by the user-assigned reference name, PROGRAMNAME. (Declarations will be discussed in the next subsection.) The actual program code is then bracketed by a BEGIN/END combination, while "." after END signifies the last statement of the program.

B. Declarations

Most languages require that certain data structures, such as arrays, be identified prior to their initial reference in a program statement. This predesignation of variables, arrays, files, and so forth is called a **declaration.** Some languages, such as PASCAL, require that all data structures be explicitly declared in the declaration block. In our pseudocode, we only require that input/output files or devices other than the default devices must be explicitly defined. Recall that we defined the default input device to be the video terminal, and the default output device to be the video terminal or the line printer. Thus if a file were being input from the disk file XYZ, a declaration, FILE XYZ;, should be made prior to the first BEGIN.

C. Comments

Comments may appear anyplace in the pseudocode for documentation purposes and are bracketed by the character combinations "(*" and "*)". Thus a program could appear as follows:

```
PROGRAM DEMO;

BEGIN
        STATEMENT (1);
        (* THIS IS A COMMENT *)
        STATEMENT (2);
        (* SO
                IS
                        THIS *)
        STATEMENT (3);
END.
```

7.3 Sequential Processing

In Chapter 3 we discussed the concept of sequential processing. The flowchart symbol depends upon whether the statement is an assignment, input, or output statement.

A. Assignment Statements

The flowchart symbol for an assignment statement is shown in Figure 7–1 and is interpreted as "A is assigned the value in B." The comparable pseudo-

Figure 7–1.
Flowchart
Symbology for an
Assignment
Statement

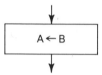

code statement is A:=B;, which is interpreted exactly the same way. Note that the assignment or replacement operator "←" has been changed to the symbol ":=", which has the same meaning. This operator is used to eliminate potential confusion with the BOOLEAN operator "=".

Example 7.1
Recode Solved Problem 3.1 in pseudocode.

Solution

```
BEGIN (* EXAMPLE 7.1 *)
    X := 3.4;
    Y := 4.0;
    Z := X * Y;
END. (* END EXAMPLE 7.1 *)
```

End Solution

B. Input Statements
The flowchart symbol used to signify the input operation as shown in Figure 7–2 indicates that two values are to be read from the default input device and stored in the variables A and B. The pseudocode statement we will use to signify the same process will be READ (list);, where list will be one or more variable names. Thus the corresponding statement to our previous flowchart symbol would be READ (A, B);. If data is to be read from some file other than the default device, then the name of that file must be formally declared and must also appear as the first element in the parentheses. Thus to read A, B from the FILE XYZ, the statement would appear as READ (XYZ, A, B);.

C. Output Statements
The flowchart symbol we have used to signify the output operation as shown in Figure 7–3 indicates that the values contained in variables A, B are to be output to the default output device. The pseudocode statement we will use to signify the same process will be WRITE (list);, where list will be one or more variable names. Thus the corresponding statement to the previous flowchart symbol would be WRITE (A, B);. If data is to be written to some file other than the default output device, then the name of the file must be formally

Figure 7-2.
Flowchart
Symbology for an
Input Statement

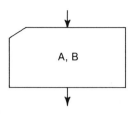

Figure 7-3.
Flowchart
Symbology for an
Output Statement

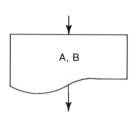

declared and must also appear as the first element in the parentheses. Thus to write A, B to the FILE XYZ, the statement would appear as WRITE (XYZ, A, B);.

Example 7.2
Recode Solved Problem 3.2 in pseudocode.

Solution

```
BEGIN (* EXAMPLE 7.2 *)
    READ (X); (* INPUT VALUE FOR X *)

    READ (Y); (* INPUT VALUE FOR Y *)

    Z := X + Y; (* PERFORM CALCULATION *)

    WRITE (Z); (* OUTPUT RESULTS *)

END. (* END EXAMPLE 7.2 *)
```

End Solution

**7.4 Conditional
Processing**

Recall that in conditional processing the flowchart symbols appeared as shown in Figure 7–4, where the statement(s) in block 1 would be executed if the BOOLEAN expression <BE> were evaluated as TRUE; otherwise the statements in block 2 would be executed. No restrictions were placed on the

Figure 7-4.
Flowchart
Symbology for
Conditional
Processing

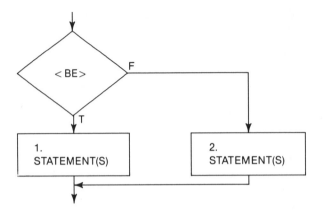

statement(s) within either block; thus we could have a conditional nested within a conditional, and the statement(s) in block 2 could be the null set.

The comparable pseudocode statements would have the following syntax:

```
IF <BE>
      THEN
             1. STATEMENT(S)
      ELSE
             2. STATEMENT(S);
```

Note that the conditional begins with IF and ends with ";". The two blocks could also be multiple statements, in which case they must be bracketed by a BEGIN/END.

Example 7.3

Recode Solved Problem 4.4 in pseudocode.

Solution

```
BEGIN (* EXAMPLE 7.3 *)
   READ (GROSSPAY, NUMDEP); (* INPUT PAY AND NUMBER OF DEPENDENTS *)

   GROSSPAY := GROSSPAY * .9 - 1000 * NUMDEP; (* CALCULATE TAXABLE
   GROSSPAY *)

   (* CALCULATE TAX PERCENTAGE RATE *)
   IF (GROSSPAY > 0)
   THEN
        BEGIN
           IF (GROSSPAY >= 10000)
           THEN
               BEGIN
                   IF (GROSSPAY >= 20000)
                   THEN
```

```
                              BEGIN
                                  IF (GROSSPAY >= 35000)
                                  THEN
                                      BEGIN
                                          IF (GROSSPAY >= 55000)
                                          THEN
                                              PERCENT := .60
                                          ELSE
                                              PERCENT := .50;
                                      END
                                  ELSE
                                          PERCENT := .40;
                              END
                          ELSE
                              PERCENT := .30;
                      END
                  ELSE
                      PERCENT := .20;

                  (* CALCULATE TAXES FROM GROSSPAY AND PERCENT *)
                  TAX := GROSSPAY * PERCENT;

                  WRITE (TAX); (* OUTPUT RESULT *)
          END
      ELSE
          (* IF GROSSPAY <= 0 THEN NO TAX *)
          WRITE ("NO TAX");

  END. (* END EXAMPLE 7.3 *)
```

End Solution

7.5 Iterative Processing

Recall that in conditional processing the flowchart symbols appeared as shown in Figure 7–5, where the statement(s) would be repetitively executed as long as the <BE> was evaluated as TRUE. No restrictions were placed on the statement(s) within the loop; thus we could have an iteration within an iteration.

The comparable pseudocode statements would have the following syntax:

```
STATEMENT; (* INITIALIZE *)
WHILE <BE> DO (* TEST *)
      BEGIN
              STATEMENT(S); (* EXECUTE *)
              STATEMENT; (* INCREMENT *)
      END;
```

Example 7.4
Recode Figure 5–13 in pseudocode.

Figure 7-5.
Flowchart
Symbology for
Iteration

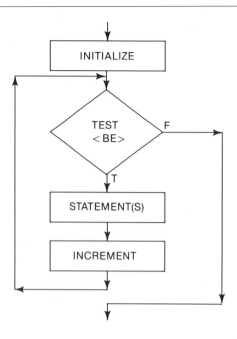

Solution

```
BEGIN (* EXAMPLE 7.4 *)
   READ (AVERAGE); (* INPUT AVERAGE *)

   READ (NAME, POINTS); (* INPUT STUDENT NAME AND POINTS *)

   (* PROCESS ALL STUDENTS UNTIL TRAILER VALUE FOUND *)
   WHILE (NAME <> "ZZZZZ") DO
   BEGIN
       IF (POINTS > AVERAGE * .60)
       THEN
           WRITE (NAME, "PASSED")
       ELSE
           WRITE (NAME, "FAILED");

       READ (NAME, POINTS); (* INPUT NEXT STUDENT *)
   END; (* END OF WHILE *)

END. (* END EXAMPLE 7.4 *)
```

End Solution

We have also used the flowchart symbol shown in Figure 7–6 as an abbreviated method of presenting an iteration. The comparable pseudocode would be as follows:

Figure 7-6.
Flowchart
Symbology for
Compact Iteration

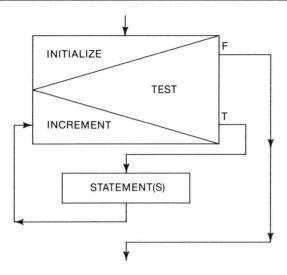

```
FOR VAR := <AE> (* INIT. *) STEP <AE>(* INCR. *) WHILE <BE> (* TEST *) DO
    BEGIN
            STATEMENT(S);
    END;
```

For simplicity's sake, the WHILE (<BE>) can be replaced by UNTIL (<AE>) as the case may allow, where <AE> represents an arithmetic expression.

Example 7.5

Recode Figure 5–20 using pseudocode. Use the FOR construct for the outer loop and the WHILE construct for the inner loop.

Solution

```
BEGIN (* EXAMPLE 7.5 *)

    READ (X); (* INPUT SIN VALUE OF ANGLE *)

    ARCSIN := X; (* INITIALIZE FIRST TERM IN SERIES *)

    FOR I := 3 STEP 2 UNTIL 39 DO (* OUTER LOOP *)
    BEGIN
        TERM := 1;
        J := 1;
        WHILE (J <= I - 2) DO (* START INNER LOOP *)
        BEGIN
            (* CALCULATE NEW COEFFICIENT *)
            TERM := TERM * J / (J + 1);
            J := J + 2;
        END; (* END INNER LOOP *)

        (* CALCULATE NEXT TERM IN SERIES *)
        TERM := TERM * X**I / I;
```

```
          ARCSIN := ARCSIN + TERM; (* ACCUMULATE NEXT TERM *)

      END; (* END OUTER LOOP *)

      WRITE (ARCSIN); (* OUTPUT RESULT *)

  END. (* END EXAMPLE 7.5 *)
```

End Solution

7.6 Arrays

There is no unique flowchart symbol to signify arrays. In our treatment of arrays to this point, we assumed that the array would be dimensioned appropriately. We will continue that assumption, although the student is cautioned that all higher level languages require explicit declaration of the array in order to reserve space and calculate the location of elements of the array. The method of doing so differs among compilers but typically is some variation of

```
DIMENSION ARRAYNAME (SUBSCRIPT RANGE 1, . . . , SUBSCRIPT RANGE N);
```

is used. Some compilers only require the upper bound for the range and assume 1 as the lower bound. Others require an explicit statement of the lower and upper bounds of the range.

Example 7.6

Recode Solved Problem 6.2 using pseudocode.

Solution

```
BEGIN (* EXAMPLE 7.6 *)

  CHI := 0; (* INITIALIZE SUM *)

  READ (N); (* INPUT NUMBER OF INTERVALS *)

  FOR I:=1 STEP 1 UNTIL N DO (* PROCESS N INTERVALS *)
  BEGIN
      READ (OBS(I), EXP(I)); (* INPUT OBSERVATION AND EXPECTED VALUE *)
      IF (EXP(I) <> 0) (* TEST FOR AN EXPECTED VALUE OF ZERO *)
      THEN
          CHI := CHI + (OBS(I) - EXP(I))**2 / EXP(I)
      ELSE
          CHI := CHI + OBS(I)**2;
  END; (* END FOR *)
```

```
        WRITE (CHI); (* OUTPUT RESULTS *)

    END. (* END EXAMPLE 7.6 *)
```

End Solution

7.7 Summary   We have presented the form of pseudocode that we will use to represent algorithms throughout the remainder of this book. Keep in mind that there are numerous ways of presenting a similar form of pseudocode and you should adopt a method most suitable for the language you are using. Do not get bogged down in the syntax of this pseudocode; rather, make sure you understand the flow of the algorithms since the intent is that the code be as English-like as possible, yet translatable directly into code.

Solved Problems
7.1
Recode the Grading Problem from Chapter 6 in pseudocode.

Solution

```
PROGRAM GRADING PROBLEM;

BEGIN
    FOR I := 1 STEP 1 UNTIL 4 DO (* INITIALIZE ARRAYS *)
    BEGIN
        POINTS(I,1) := 0;
        POINTS(I,2) := 0;
    END;

    READ (NAME, (TEST(I),I := 1,3)); (* INPUT FIRST STUDENT IN CLASS *)

    (* PROCESS EACH STUDENT UNTIL TRAILER VALUE READ *)
    FOR CNT := 0 STEP 1 WHILE NAME <> "ZZZZZ" DO
    BEGIN
        CUMPTS := 0;
        FOR I := 1 STEP 1 UNTIL 3 DO (* GATHER STATISTICS *)
        BEGIN
            CUMPTS := CUMPTS + TEST(I); (* SUM STUDENT'S SCORES *)

            POINTS(I,1) := POINTS(I,1) + TEST(I); (* SUM TEST SCORES *)

            (* SUM SQUARES OF TEST SCORES *)
            POINTS(I,2) := POINTS(I,2) + TEST(I)**2;
        END;

        AVERAGE := CUMPTS / 3; (* CALCULATE STUDENT'S AVERAGE *)
```

```
               (* ASSIGN STUDENT'S GRADE *)
               IF (AVERAGE >= 60)
               THEN
                   BEGIN
                       IF (AVERAGE >= 70)
                       THEN
                           BEGIN
                               IF (AVERAGE >= 85)
                               THEN
                                   BEGIN
                                       IF (AVERAGE >= 95)
                                       THEN
                                           GRADE := "A"
                                       ELSE
                                           GRADE := "B";
                                   END
                               ELSE
                                   GRADE := "C";
                           END
                       ELSE
                           GRADE := "D";
                   END
               ELSE
                   GRADE := "F";

               (* OUTPUT INDIVIDUAL STUDENT STATISTICS *)
               WRITE (NAME, (TEST(I),I := 1,3), CUMPTS, AVERAGE, GRADE);

               (* COLLECT COURSE STATISTICS *)
               POINTS(4,1) := POINTS(4,1) + CUMPTS;
               POINTS(4,2) := POINTS(4,2) + CUMPTS**2;

               READ (NAME, (TEST(I),I := 1,3)); (* INPUT NEXT STUDENT IN COURSE *)
           END; (* FOR CNT: = 0 *)

       (* FIND MEAN AND STANDARD DEVIATION PER TEST AND COURSE *)
       FOR I := 1 STEP 1 UNTIL 4 DO
       BEGIN
           POINTS(I,1)**2; := POINTS (I,1) / CNT; (* CALCULATE TEST MEAN *)

           (* CALCULATE TEST STANDARD DEVIATION *)
           POINTS(I,2) := SQRT (POINTS(I,2) / CNT - POINTS(I,2)**2);
           (* CALCULATE TEST MEAN *)
       END;

       (* OUTPUT RESULTS OF CALCULATION FOR TESTS *)
       WRITE ("TEST MEAN:", (POINTS(I,1),I := 1,4));
       WRITE ("TEST STANDARD DEVIATION:", (POINTS(I,2),I := 1,4));

   END. (* END GRADING PROBLEM *)
```

Supplementary Problems

7.2

Recode Solved Problem 6.1 in pseudocode.

7.3

Recode Solved Problem 6.3 in pseudocode.

7.4

Recode Solved Problem 6.8 in pseudocode.

8   *Subprograms*

In Chapter 2 we discussed the desirability of decomposing a large, complex problem into smaller, more manageable subproblems. These problems could then be solved, programmed, and tested independently and when combined, should yield the solution to the large problem. One of the difficulties discussed with regard to decomposition was that of communication and coordination among the modules.

In this chapter, we will present a programming construct that facilitates dividing a large program into smaller, more manageable subprograms, and that minimizes the communication and coordination problems. We will discuss two structures for subprograms, along with the implementation criteria and communication mechanisms associated with each type.

By the completion of this chapter, you should be able to answer the following questions:

1. What are the two types of subprograms?
2. When should each type of subprogram be used?
3. What is the difference between LOCAL and FORMAL parameters?
4. What are GLOBAL variables and COMMON areas?
5. How and when are subprograms executed?

8.2 Subprograms

A **subprogram** is simply a self-contained set of instructions that, when executed, yields a desired result. There are two classes of subprograms: the **open,** or in-line, **subprogram** and the **closed,** or out-of-line, **subprogram.** The distinction is that for an open subprogram, a copy of the subprogram code is inserted into the host program at each place that its execution is required. For a closed subprogram, the subprogram code is generated only once and the same code is executed as required.

As shown in Figure 8–1, a closed subprogram requires a break in the sequence of execution of the main program and a transfer of control to and from the subprogram. Figure 8–2 shows that for an open subprogram, the code is inserted in the host program wherever required. The advantages and

Figure 8-1.
Closed,
or Out-of-Line,
Subprogram

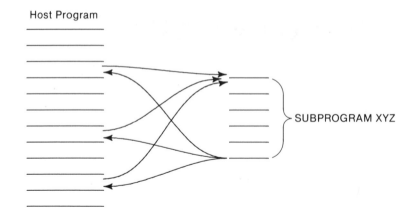

Figure 8-2.
Open,
or In-Line,
Subprogram

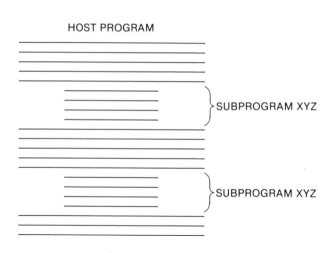

disadvantages of each should be apparent from these figures considering execution time, space requirements, communicating variable information, and compilation time. The transfer of control to a subprogram is referred to as "calling the subprogram" or a "subprogram call."

The closed subprogram is slower because it requires a transfer of control; the open subprogram does not. However, the open subprogram requires additional memory space because the same code is duplicated. There is a trade-off of space versus execution time. Most higher level programming languages implement closed subprograms and do not give the programmer a choice. In this book we will assume all subprograms are of the closed type.

A subprogram provides several advantages in structuring a complex problem:

1. Elimination of redundant code
If the same sequence of steps is performed at a number of places in the program, the steps could be coded as a subprogram. Then each time the sequence is required, the subprogram is called and the same segment of code is executed.

2. Saving of programming time
A programmer may use a pre-existing subprogram that performs a desired function. The subprogram can be written by the programmer or borrowed from someone else.

3. Library generation
Subprograms can be created and made a part of the computer software of a system. The **library** could be made available to all users of the system. A well-documented library of efficient and frequently used algorithms can effectively and significantly reduce programming, development, and debugging time. Consequently, computer usage can be greatly optimized.

4. Modularization
Subprograms provide the mechanism whereby large, complex programs can be broken into many smaller modules. These can then be developed, programmed, and tested independently.

5. Readability
A large program structured into many subprograms is easier to read, analyze, and understand than a continuous string of code. Consequently, it is easier to detect, isolate, and correct errors.

The major disadvantage in using subprograms is the problem of communication between modules. However, this problem can be minimized by a thorough understanding of the structure of subprograms and their various intercommunication channels.

8.3 Subroutines Versus Functions

In addition to the open and closed categories, all subprograms can be classified as either functions or subroutines. A **function** is a subprogram that is used to calculate a single value, which value is assigned to the name of the subprogram itself. A function is executed by using its name in an expression.

A subroutine is a subprogram that is used to calculate several values or provide a particular effect or series of actions. The subroutine does not necessarily return a value. A subroutine is executed whenever its name is called and not as part of an expression, since its name does not assume a value. There is only a minor difference between how a function and a subroutine are coded; therefore, the essential differences between the two are the manner in which they are called and their respective communications links. These differences will be discussed in more detail in the sections devoted to each.

Since subprograms are separate segments of code from the main program, they should always be distinct and identifiable from the main program. The two types of subprograms are referred to by different names among the higher level programming languages. FORTRAN uses the names "FUNC-TION" and "SUBROUTINE." The associated names in PASCAL are "FUNC-TION" and "PROCEDURE." We will use the words "SUBPROGRAM" or "PROCEDURE" as a general category, and "FUNCTION" and "SUBROU-TINE" to differentiate the specific category of subprogram.

8.4 Communicating with a Subprogram

The power of a subprogram is derived from its ability to perform the same computation for different sets of input values. For instance, if a subprogram calculates SIN (X), then the subprogram is written with the variable identifier X used throughout. However, the variable X does not actually take on a value until such time as the subprogram is actually executed.

Variables, such as X, are used for communicating information to and from the subprogram, and when used in the subprogram itself, are known as **formal parameters**. FORMAL parameters can then be viewed as dummy variables, or "place holders." When the subprogram is executed, the actual values of the input parameters are substituted for the FORMAL parameters. These values, which are passed to the subprogram when it is called, are referred to as **actual parameters.** When the subprogram completes its execution, the values of the FORMAL parameters can be returned by assignment to the actual parameters, thus establishing a two-way communication link.

Parameters are the means by which information is communicated between the calling program and the subprogram. Since the FORMAL parameters of a subprogram are replaced by the values of actual parameters, a subprogram may be executed, or called, repeatedly for different values of actual parameters.

Frequently, a subprogram requires the use of temporary variables to perform its calculations. Since such variables are used only within the subprogram and are not communicated outside the subprogram, they are known as **local variables.**

In addition to the communications channel formed by actual and formal parameters, the function subprogram communicates back to its calling expression by assigning a value to its name. This capability will be discussed in more detail in the subsection on functions.

There is generally no restriction on the types of variables that can be used as actual parameters, and they can be simple variables or arrays. Most languages only require that the number and type of the actual parameters must correspond exactly with the number and type of the FORMAL parameters. Moreover, since the actual parameters substitute for the FORMAL parameters, they must also correspond by position. That is, a one-for-one substitution is made between formal and actual parameters by virtue of their relative positions in the subprogram heading and call statements, respectively.

8.5 Pseudocode for Subprograms

Since we defined two separate types of subprograms, i.e., subroutine and function, we have to accommodate each in our pseudocode. Recall that the subprogram is a separate entity that is explicitly called from the main program. In the case of the subroutine, this call is explicit and is written in pseudocode as CALL SUBROUTINENAME (Parameters);.

Functions are treated as expressions and therefore may appear anywhere an expression may be used, for example on the right-hand side of an assignment statement. An example function call in pseudocode is as follows: VARIABLE := FUNCTIONNAME (Parameters);.

The statement of the subprogram code will be identical for both subroutines and functions except that for functions, the type must be explicitly provided. The pseudocode for a subroutine is:

```
SUBROUTINE SUBROUTINENAME (Parameters);
DECLARATIONS;
BEGIN
     STATEMENT(S);
END;
```

The pseudocode for a function is

```
TYPE FUNCTION FUNCTIONNAME (Parameters);
DECLARATIONS;
BEGIN
     STATEMENT(S); (* Calculate Value *)
     FUNCTIONNAME := (Value);
END;
```

In all cases, "Parameters" represents a list of variables similar to the list used in I/O statements that are, in effect, simply calls to system-provided subroutines. Since subprograms are considered separate sections of code from the main program and are not executed until called, they are placed in the declarative block of the program. A complete program could be structured as follows:

```
PROGRAM PROGRAMNAME;
SUBROUTINE;
FUNCTIONS;
BEGIN
     STATEMENT(S);
END.
```

8.6 Functions

A FUNCTION subprogram is a segment of code that, when executed, performs a calculation and provides a single answer. It is called by referencing its name as an expression. Since the name of the FUNCTION itself assumes a value, the FUNCTION must be explicitly declared as a specific type in languages such as PASCAL, or implicitly declared by the first letter of its name in languages such as FORTRAN. The type of expression in which the FUNCTION should be used is generally determined by the type of the FUNCTION itself.

The communications channel of FORMAL and actual parameters is used for passing information to the FUNCTION. In contrast to the SUBROUTINE, the same mechanism is not employed for obtaining the results from the FUNCTION. The last statement of the FUNCTION generally assigns the calculated result to the name of the FUNCTION. The FUNCTION name acts as the output channel of communication and returns a single value to the calling program.

In order to understand the concept of the FUNCTION, it is necessary to study the structure of the FUNCTION subprogram and the call of a FUNCTION. The following example provides an illustration of the structure of the FUNCTION.

Example 8.1

The **factorial** of an INTEGER M is equal to the product of the positive integers from 1 to M and is represented as M! (read M factorial). Thus $M! = 1 \times 2 \times 3 \times \cdots \times (M-2) \times (M-1) \times M$.

By definition, $0! = 1$. The value of the factorial is undefined when M is negative.

Develop an algorithm in the form of an INTEGER FUNCTION to calculate the value of a factorial, given the value of M.

Solution

```
INTEGER FUNCTION FACT (M);
```

```
BEGIN
    PROD := 1; (* INITIALIZE PROD FOR TEMPORARY RESULTS *)

    IF (M > 1) (* TEST FOR POSITIVE INTEGER *)
    THEN
        FOR I := 2 STEP 1 UNTIL M DO (* CALCULATE PRODUCTS THROUGH M *)
            PROD := PROD * I;

    FACT := PROD; (* RETURN VALUE VIA FUNCTION NAME *)

END; (* END FACT *)
```

An important point of the example is that the sole purpose of the algorithm is to calculate the value of the factorial. There is nothing else to be included in the code. Since it is directed to finding a single value, it is a good candidate for use of a FUNCTION.

A FUNCTION is always given a name and this FUNCTION will be called FACT. The formal parameter is M and it is an INTEGER variable. We always indicate the parameters of a subprogram in parentheses after the name of the subprogram, such as FUNCTION FACT (M). In FUNCTION FACT (M) the value of the factorial is calculated by successive multiplications. A temporary product, PROD, is initialized to the value of 1. If the value of M is greater than 1, then the variable PROD is multiplied by each integer from 2 to M. If the value of M is 0 or 1, the value of PROD remains 1.

Notice that the value of the result is dependent upon only one variable, M. However, different values of M will provide different numerical answers. Consequently, it is important to be sure the correct actual parameter corresponds to M whenever FACT is called.

The variable PROD is used as a temporary variable to accumulate the product of the terms. It is not referenced outside the function and it is not used to transfer information between the subprogram and the main program. Thus, it can be declared as a local variable. Note that the last statement of the example assigns PROD to FACT, thus returning the value of the factorial to the main program.

End Solution

This example illustrates several of the major characteristics of a FUNCTION:

1. A FUNCTION subprogram is directed to the calculation of a single value or result.
2. The parameters provide the means to input different values to the FUNCTION, i.e., they furnish the link between the main program and the subprogram.

3. LOCAL variables are used within a FUNCTION and are only applicable within that FUNCTION.
4. In a FUNCTION subprogram, the value of the result must be assigned to the name of the procedure.

A function is executed only when it is called from within the main program. Basically, this means that some statement in the main program causes the corresponding function code to be performed. When the function is completed, program control returns to the main program and execution is resumed from the point at which the subprogram was called.

Since the name of the function itself returns a value, the call of the function must occur within an expression, and each function must be a type similar to that of a simple variable. Since the type of the FUNCTION FACT is assumed to be INTEGER, the call of that function must occur within an expression in which an INTEGER variable can occur. A valid pseudocode call of FACT could be

```
Y := FACT(4);
```

The statement Y := FACT(4) causes the FUNCTION FACT to be executed. Prior to execution, the actual parameter, 4, would be substituted for the FORMAL parameter, M. When the function terminates execution, FACT would have a value of 4! = 4*3*2*1, or 24, which value is then assigned to Y in the calling program.

Example 8.2 illustrates the use of function calls. The program makes three calls on the FUNCTION FACT (M) of Example 8.1. The corresponding pseudocode depicts both the main program and the function in order to demonstrate the relationship between the two segments.

Example 8.2
Develop an algorithm that reads two values, (N, K), and uses the FUNCTION FACT to calculate B, where

$$B = \frac{N!}{K! \, (N-K)!}$$

Solution
The general algorithm is shown on the left side of Figure 8–3. It reads the value of N and K; calls FACT to calculate B1, B2, and B3; computes B; prints the value of B; and then returns to the beginning of the statements to process the next data set. The program terminates when the value of N is equal to 0.

In order to depict the sequence of actions that occurs, FACT is shown on the right of the flowchart. The dashed lines show the transfer of program

Figure 8–3.
Flowchart for Use of
Function Fact(M)

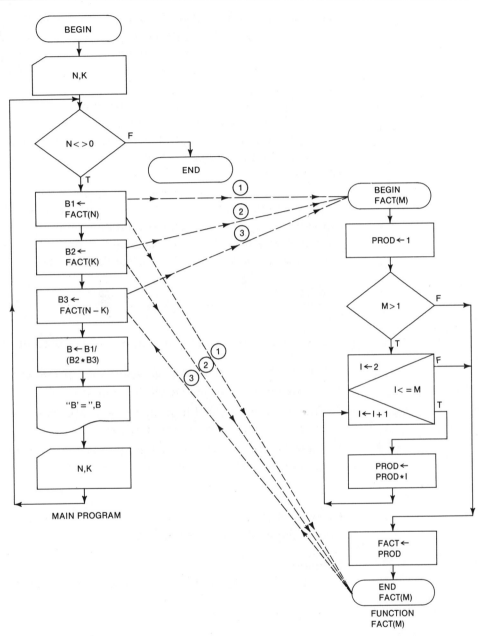

control when FACT is called. For instance, when FACT is called in the assignment statement giving B1 a value, the statements associated with FACT are executed. Control returns to the main program at the point at which FACT had been called. Similar situations occur when the values of B2 and B3 are determined.

It is important to understand the correspondence of actual and formal parameters. In the statement assigning B1 a value, the actual parameter is N. This means that the current value of N is taken as the value of the formal parameter, M. Since N is in a loop, it can have a different value each time FACT is called.

The correspondence of the actual parameter K and the formal parameter M is similar. In the third call to FACT the actual parameter is an arithmetic expression. This is an acceptable alternative in most languages. The value of the actual parameter $N - K$, is calculated, and then the function is executed with the value of $N - K$ substituted for the formal parameter, M.

End Solution

Several characteristics of the function call have been illustrated:

1. The function call must appear within an expression.
2. The function is executed each time that it is called.
3. The function call must indicate the actual parameters that correspond to the formal parameters of the function.
4. After the function is executed, program control returns to the main program immediately following the function call.

Example 8.3
Convert Figure 8–3 into pseudocode.

Solution
Note that FUNCTION FACT appears prior to the code for the main program.

```
PROGRAM EXAMPLE 8.3;

(**** DECLARATION SECTION ****)
INTEGER FUNCTION FACT (M);
BEGIN
    PROD := 1;
    IF (M > 1)
    THEN
        FOR I := 2 STEP 1 UNTIL M DO
            PROD := PROD * I;
    FACT := PROD;
END; (* END FUNCTION FACT *)
```

```
(**** BEGIN MAIN PROGRAM ****)
BEGIN
    READ (N, K); (* INPUT FIRST SET OF VALUES *)

    WHILE (N <> 0) DO (* CALCULATE B FOR THESE VALUES *)
    BEGIN
        B1 := FACT(N);
        B2 := FACT(K);
        B3 := FACT(N-K);
        B  := B1 / (B2 * B3);

        WRITE ("B =", B); (* OUTPUT RESULTS *)

        READ (N, K); (* INPUT NEXT SET OF VALUES *)
    END; (* END WHILE *)

END. (* END EXAMPLE 8.3 *)
```

End Solution

In the pseudocode in Example 8.3 there are four distinct assignment operations involved in determining the value of B. Most languages provide the capability to formulate these into one statement. An example of this is B := FACT(N)/(FACT(K) * FACT(N–K));.

This one assignment statement contains three calls to FACT. This presents no problem, since the only requirement is that the function calls on FACT occur in an expression where an INTEGER variable can occur.

Remember that the right-hand side of any assignment statement is an expression of some type, and the call of a function must appear in an expression. Therefore, most languages are designed such that the appearance of the name of a function in an expression implies an attempt to call that function. Consider the following statement: FACT := FACT * I;.

The second FACT in the statement indicates a call on FACT. Therefore, in practically all languages, the name of a function should not appear on the right-hand side of an assignment statement unless a function call is intended. This makes the use of the LOCAL variable PROD in the FUNCTION FACT mandatory. To maintain a summation or product within a function that will be associated with the function name, a local variable or a parameter should be employed.

Example 8.4

A combination, C, of N objects taken K at a time is a selection of K out of N objects, with no attention being paid to the order of the K objects. The number of such combinations can be represented in a variety of ways including $C(N/K)$, $C_{N,K}$, $C(N,K)$, and $_NC_K$. The value can be determined by the formula

$$C(N,K) = \frac{N!}{K!\,(N-K)!}$$

The algorithm described in Example 8.2 presented one method of calculating the value of C(N,K) by using several calls to FACT to implement this formula.

The evaluation of FACT for any value, M, always requires $M-1$ multiplications. In executing the program in Example 8.3, it is easy to determine the total number of multiplications. For any value of N and K, the calculation of the equation will involve three calls on FACT and $(N-1)+(K-1)+(N-K-1)$, or $2N-3$ multiplications.

There is another method of evaluating this same equation that will take at most N/2 multiplications and N/2 divisions. Assuming the time necessary for the computer to perform multiplication and division is approximately the same, this second method is somewhat more efficient. In fact, the combined number of multiplications and divisions can be considerably less than N, since this is a maximum number.

The alternative method of computation is based upon the fact that C(N,K) can be represented as

$$C(N,K) = \frac{N*(N-1)*(N-2)\cdots(N-K+1)*(N-K)!}{K!\,(N-K)!}$$

Elimination of the COMMON factor $(N-K)!$ from the numerator and denominator provides the following:

$$C(N,K) = \frac{N*(N-1)*(N-2)\cdots(N-K+1)}{1*2*3\cdots(K-1)*K}$$

Develop an algorithm in the form of a REAL FUNCTION, BINOM (N, K), that will implement this formula.

Solution

```
REAL FUNCTION BINOM (N, K);

BEGIN
    TEMP := 1; (* INITIALIZE FIRST TERM *)

    FOR I := 1 STEP 1 UNTIL K DO (* PROCESS PRODUCTS THROUGH K *)
        TEMP := TEMP * (N - I + 1) / I;

    BINOM := TEMP; (* RETURN CALCULATED VALUE *)

END; (* END BINOM *)
```

Both N and K are FORMAL parameters while I and TEMP are LOCAL variables. It is necessary to use the temporary variable, TEMP, in BINOM for the same reason PROD was used in FACT, that is, the name of the function cannot occur on the right-hand side of the assignment statement unless it is a call on the function. An example of the call on the function BINOM can be represented as X := BINOM (20, 4);.

This will provide the number of combinations of 20 objects taken 4 at a time. The combined number of multiplications and divisions to compute the value of BINOM would be 8. By comparison, three calls of FACT would require 37 multiplications.

End Solution

Although Example 8.4 provides an increase in efficiency over Example 8.3, the major point illustrated is the use of more than one parameter in the function. There are two parameters needed in BINOM. Remember that the formal and actual parameters must agree in number, type, and order. That is, there must be as many actual parameters as there are formal parameters; therefore, the call on binom must have two actual parameters.

The second requirement is that the type of the actual parameters must agree with the type of the formal parameters. Thus both actual parameters used in any call to BINOM of Example 8.4 must be INTEGERS.

The third requirement means the first actual parameter corresponds to the first formal parameter, the second actual parameter corresponds to the second formal parameter, and so forth.

Example 8.5

Develop a REAL FUNCTION XMAX (X, N) to find the largest value of the first N elements of the REAL array X.

Solution

```
REAL FUNCTION XMAX (X, N);

BEGIN
   BIG := X(1); (* FIRST VALUE IS LARGEST AT START *)

   FOR I := 2 STEP 1 UNTIL N DO (* COMPARE REMAINING VALUES TO BIG *)
   BEGIN
       IF (X(I) > BIG)
       THEN
           BIG := X(I);
   END;

   XMAX := BIG; (* RETURN RESULT *)

END. (* END XMAX *)
```

The FUNCTION XMAX (X, N) searches X for the largest value. The value of the first element of the array is assigned to a temporary variable, BIG. Then each subsequent element of the array is compared with BIG. If any element is greater than BIG, its value is assigned to BIG. This process continues until the entire array is examined. Then, finally, XMAX is assigned the value of the temporary variable, BIG.

End Solution

Since X is a formal parameter of XMAX(X,N), the search will be performed on whichever array is passed as an actual parameter. For instance, consider the following statement: LARGE := XMAX (EXAM, 50);.

The call of the function results in the first 50 elements of the array EXAM being searched for the largest value. The largest value is returned as the result of the function, which is then assigned to the variable LARGE.

Again, we wish to emphasize the necessity of the formal and actual parameters agreeing in number, type, and order. In the above example, the first formal parameter X is a one-dimension array and the variable N is an INTEGER. Therefore, the first actual parameter must be an array, while the second one must be an INTEGER.

8.7 Intrinsic, or Standard, Functions

A number of COMMON functions are used quite frequently. For instance, there are many occasions when the square root of a number must be determined. If a programmer had a previously developed square root function, he could use it in each program in which he needed to find a square root. However, many other programmers can be calculating square roots and would also need to develop a square root function.

In order to avoid this duplicate effort, many languages include a square root function. The incorporation of this function into a language has the additional advantage of providing an efficiently coded version of the procedure. Those functions that are included in the implementation of the computer language are generally referred to as **intrinsic functions, standard functions,** or **built-in functions.**

The use of an intrinsic function is similar to that of any user-defined function; however, the program calling one of these functions does not include its declaration. The function can be used wherever it is needed in the program. The calls for intrinsic functions are the same as any other function call.

Since sine and cosine can be used to calculate the remaining four trigonometric functions, some languages include only sine and cosine as intrinsic functions. Example 8.6 illustrates the use of intrinsic functions by applying these two trigonometric values.

Example 8.6

Develop an algorithm to read an angle A and print the values of the six trigonometric functions of A. Assume that the intrinsic FUNCTIONS SIN(X) and COS(X) are available for computing the sine and cosine.

The six trigonometric functions of an angle A are the sine, cosine, tangent, cotangent, secant, and cosecant. Given the sine and the cosine, the other four functions can be determined by the following relationships:

tangent A = sine A/cosine A

cotangent A = 1/tangent A

secant A = 1/cosine A

cosecant A = 1/sine A

Solution

```
PROGRAM EXAMPLE 8.6;

BEGIN
   READ (A); (* INPUT ANGLE *)

   WHILE (A <> 0) DO (* CALCULATE TRIG FUNCTIONS *)
   BEGIN
      (* OUTPUT A HEADER FOR EACH ANGLE *)
      WRITE ("TRIG VALUES FOLLOW FOR ANGLE", A);

      SINE := SIN(A);
      COSIN := COS(A);
      TAN := SINE / COSIN;
      COT := 1 / TAN;
      SEC := 1 / COSIN;
      COSEC := 1 / SINE;

      (* OUTPUT RESULTS *)
      WRITE ("ANGLE =", A,
             "SINE =", SINE,
             "COSIN =", COSIN,
             "TANGENT =", TAN,
             "COTANGENT =", COT,
             "SECANT =", SEC,
             "COSECANT =", COSEC);

      READ (A); (* INPUT NEXT ANGLE *)
   END;

END. (* END EXAMPLE 8.6 *)
```

This algorithm reads an angle A and then calculates the value of the six functions by calls on the two FUNCTIONS SIN(X) and COS(X) and the above trigonometric relationships. The results are printed and the program iterated after reading a new angle A. The program terminates on the trailer value 0 for angle A.

End Solution

8.8 Call of a Function From Within a Function

Preceding examples illustrated several calls of function subprograms. All of these calls were assumed to occur in the main program. However, there is no requirement that the call of a function occur within the main program, and, in fact, calls of functions can occur from other subprograms. Example 8.7 is an illustration of a function call from another function.

Example 8.7

The **Poisson distribution** is a **discrete probability distribution** that has considerable usefulness. The distribution is described by the following equation:

$$P(K) = \frac{\lambda^K e^{-\lambda}}{K!} \ (K = 0 , 1 , 2 , \ldots)$$

where P(K) describes the probability of exactly K events occurring. The value of e is 2.71828 . . . and is a given constant.

The Poisson distribution has many uses, among which is the approximation of the binomial distribution when the probability, P, of a single event occurring is close to 0. The approximation holds in practice when the total number of trials, N, is greater than or equal to 50 and the value of the product, NP, is less than 5. In such cases, the Poisson distribution will approximate the binomial distribution when the value of Lambda (λ) is set equal to the product NP.

Develop REAL FUNCTION POISSON (N, P, K) that has as its parameters the total number of trials, N, the probability of a single event occurring, P, and the number of events, K. Using the product of N and P as the value of lambda, the function must calculate the corresponding Poisson probability using the given relationship.

Solution

```
REAL FUNCTION POISSON (N, P, K);

    (* N = NUMBER OF TRIALS,
       P = PROBABILITY OF A SINGLE EVENT OCCURRING,
       K = NUMBER OF EVENTS *)
```

```
BEGIN
   LAMBDA := N * P; (* CALCULATE LAMBDA *)

   (* CALCULATE POISSON PROBABILITY *)
   POISSON := LAMBDA**K * EXP(-LAMBDA) / FACT(K);

END; (* END POISSON *)
```

Although this example reflects a very simple solution, note that there are actually two function calls. FACT determines the factorial of K, as was developed in Example 8.3. EXP(X) computes the value of e^x, that is, the exponential function of X. EXP could be a function developed by the individual programmer; however, it is generally provided as an intrinsic function in most programming languages.

End Solution

8.9 Subroutines

The **subroutine** is similar to the **function** in that it is a separate subprogram, coded separately from the main program. The important aspect of the subroutine is that it is intended to accomplish a specific task or calculate several values, and not necessarily to provide a single value.

Consequently, unlike the function, the name of the subroutine does not receive a value when it is executed. All returned values must be transmitted to the main program by the parameters of the subroutine. Thus formal parameters are used for both input to, and output from, the subroutine.

Example 8.8

Develop SUBROUTINE REVERSE (A, N) that reverses the sequence of the first N data elements in the one-dimension array A. For instance, A(1) is assigned the value of A(N), A(2) is assigned the value of A(N − 1) and A(N) is assigned the value of A(1). The resultant sequence is then in the opposite order of the original sequence.

Solution

```
SUBROUTINE REVERSE (A, N);

   (* A = ARRAY TO BE REVERSED,
      N = NUMBER OF ELEMENTS IN ARRAY *)

BEGIN
   FOR I := 1 STEP 1 UNTIL (N / 2) DO
   BEGIN
      (* CALCULATE ASSOCIATED ARRAY INDEX TO I *)
      J := N - I + 1;
```

```
        (* EXCHANGE A(I) AND A(J) *)
        TEMP := A(I);
        A(I) := A(J);
        A(J) := TEMP;

    END;

END; (* END REVERSE *)
```

Note that the name of the subroutine, REVERSE is *not* assigned a value. Any results from the execution of a subroutine must be conveyed back to the main program via the use of the parameters.

In this example, the parameter A contains values that will affect the operation of the subprogram. Thus it is a means of input to the procedure. On the other hand, the order of the data in array A is changed when the subroutine is completed. Since the result of the procedure is the new order of the array, array A is also an output parameter.

The variable J is used as the index to that element of array A that is to be exchanged with array element A(I). In order to verify that the equation for J is correct, it is helpful to check a few specific values. For I = 1, the value of J is N and the correct exchange will take place. If there are 19 elements in the array and I = 9, then A(9) and A(11) will be exchanged; this is the desired result. Consequently, the formula for J appears correct.

Elements A(I) and A(J) are exchanged using a third variable, TEMP. The use of this third location is necessary. The exchange would not work if the code were:

A(I) := A(J);

A(J) := A(I);

To understand this concept, execute these statements with A(I) = 2 and A(J) = 3. After the first statement is executed, A(I) is set equal to 3. The second statement then causes the value of A(J) to be set to the value of A(I). Since the present value of A(I) is now 3, the new value of A(J) is also equal to 3. Both A(I) and A(J) have the same value and an exchange did not occur.

This is an extremely important concept for you to grasp, so analyze it thoroughly. An effective exchange of two variables requires three instructions. This exchange technique will reoccur in numerous algorithms.

The upper bound of the iteration is N/2. Note that a bound of N will result in each array element being exchanged twice. We would then end up with the original order. Half of the array then appears to be the upper bound of the array.

However, it is still necessary to be sure that exactly the right thing will happen for both even and odd values of N. For N = 20, the upper bound is 10 and A(10) and A(11) are exchanged correctly. In the case of N = 19, the upper bound of the iteration is N/2, or 9.5. If the programming language allows the upper bound to be a fraction, then A(9) is exchanged with A(11). Since A = 10 is the center element, it need not be exchanged. The correct result is then achieved.

If the upper bound must be an INTEGER, as in FORTRAN, then the 9.5 must be truncated to 9 or rounded to 10. If the value is truncated to 9, the result is the same as before. If the variable is rounded to 10, A(10) is exchanged with A(10), giving the same result and everything is still correct.

In deriving many algorithms, it is necessary to consider what will happen at the limits of the iteration bounds or what result will be obtained for special cases. Many algorithms that seem to work will be found to be deficient for some specific instances. Thus, an analysis similar to that presented here is helpful.

End Solution

Some of the major characteristics that were illustrated by Example 8.8 are:

1. A subroutine is directed to the accomplishment of a given task or computation. It is not designed specifically to provide a single value.
2. The parameters communicate in both directions, to input values and output results.
3. LOCAL variables are only applicable within the subroutine.
4. The value of the result must *not* be assigned to the name of the subroutine. Any output must occur through the use of parameters.

Example 8.9

Develop an algorithm that will

1. Generate an array NUMB that contains the integers 1 to 12 in ascending order in the first 12 data elements of the array. Call SUBROUTINE REVERSE to reverse the sequence of this array.
2. Generate an array N2 that contains the powers of 2 from 2^1 to 2^8 in ascending order. Call REVERSE to reverse the order of these 8 numbers.
3. Call REVERSE to reverse the first 7 data elements in NUMB.

Solution

```
PROGRAM EXAMPLE 8.9;

(**** DECLARE SUBROUTINES ****)
SUBROUTINE REVERSE (A, N);
```

```
BEGIN
   FOR I := 1 STEP 1 UNTIL (N / 2) DO
   BEGIN
      J := N - I + 1;
      TEMP := A(I);
      A(I) := A(J);
      A(J) := TEMP;
   END;
END; (* END REVERSE *)


(**** MAIN PROGRAM ****)
BEGIN
   (* ITEM (1) *)
      (* FILL FIRST TWELVE INTEGERS IN NUMB *)
      FOR J := 1 STEP 1 UNTIL 12 DO
         NUMB(J) := J;

      CALL REVERSE (NUMB, 12); (* REVERSE 12 INTEGERS IN NUMB *)

      (* OUTPUT REVERSED ARRAY *)
      WRITE ("REVERSE ORDER =", (NUMB(J),J := 1,12));
   (* END ITEM (1) *)

   (* ITEM (2) *)
      FOR I := 1 STEP 1 UNTIL 8 DO (* FILL FIRST 8 ELEMENTS OF N2 *)
         N2(I) := 2**I;

      CALL REVERSE (N2, 8); (* REVERSE VALUES IN N2 *)

      (* OUTPUT REVERSED ARRAY *)
      WRITE ("POWERS OF 2 REVERSED =", (N2(I),I := 1,8));
   (* END ITEM (2) *)

   (* ITEM (3) *)
      CALL REVERSE (NUMB, 7); (* REVERSE FIRST 7 ELEMENTS OF NUMB *)

      (* OUTPUT REVERSED ARRAY *)
      WRITE ("FIRST SEVEN REVERSED =", (NUMB(I),I := 1,12));
   (* END ITEM (3) *)

END. (* END EXAMPLE 8.9 *)
```

The first two instructions store the integers 1 to 12 in NUMB. REVERSE is then called with formal parameters NUMB and 12. Array NUMB corresponds to the formal parameter A in REVERSE. The actual parameter 12 corresponds to the formal parameter N. After REVERSE is completed, the program returns to the first WRITE statement, which prints the contents of NUMB, i.e., 12, 11, 10, 9, 8, 7, 6, 5, 4, 3, 2, 1.

Array N2 is created by storing the corresponding power of 2 in successive locations. REVERSE is then called and the resulting values that are printed are 256, 128, 64, 32, 16, 8, 4, and 2.

The third call of REVERSE uses array NUMB again. In this case, the actual parameter corresponding to N in REVERSE is 7; therefore, only the first seven elements of NUMB are reversed. In REVERSE, the parameter N is taken as the number of elements to be reversed, starting with the first element. It does not necessarily imply that there are only N elements in the array. There must be at least N; but the use of fewer elements, as shown here, is acceptable. The present sequence of numbers in NUMB is in the reverse order of the starting sequence. Since only the first seven numbers are reversed in this call, the last WRITE statement provides the sequence 6, 7, 8, 9, 10, 11, 12, 5, 4, 3, 2, 1.

End Solution

In summarizing the use of subroutine calls, remember the following:

1. The subroutine call is a separate, executable statement.
2. The subroutine is executed for those actual parameters in the call. Those parameters can be used for input of data to the subroutine, for output of values from the subprogram, or for both purposes.
3. After the execution of the subroutine, program control is returned to the statement immediately following the call.
4. The subroutine can be called many times in a program, with many different actual parameters.

Example 8.10

The least square line approximating a set of points (X_1, Y_1), (X_2, Y_2), . . . , (X_N, Y_N) is the line in which the sum of the squares of the vertical deviation of the points from the line is a minimum. The equation of the line is given by the formula $Y = A_0 + A_1 * X$. The constants A_0 and A_1 can be determined by simultaneously solving the normal equation for the least square line:

$$\Sigma Y = A_0 * N + A_1 * \Sigma X$$

$$\Sigma XY = A_0 * \Sigma X + A_1 * \Sigma X^2$$

The equations for the constants can be stated as follows:

$$A_0 = \frac{(\Sigma Y)(\Sigma X^2) - (\Sigma X)(\Sigma XY)}{N \Sigma X^2 - (\Sigma X)^2}$$

$$A_1 = \frac{N \Sigma XY - (\Sigma X)(\Sigma Y)}{N \Sigma X^2 - (\Sigma X)^2}$$

Develop a subroutine, LSQ, to find the values of A_0 and A_1 using these formulas. The coordinates of the set of points (X_1,Y_1), (X_2,Y_2), . . . , (X_N,Y_N) are contained in the respective elements of the parallel input arrays X and Y.

Solution

```
SUBROUTINE LSQ (X, Y, N, A0, A1);

BEGIN
    (* INITIALIZE LOCAL VARIABLES *)
    SX := 0;
    SY := 0;
    SXSQ := 0;
    SXY := 0;

    FOR I := 1 STEP 1 UNTIL N DO (* ACCUMULATE SUMS *)
    BEGIN
        SX := SX + X(I);
        SY := SY + Y(I);
        SXSQ := SXSQ + X(I)**2;
        SXY := SXY + X(I) * Y(I);
    END;

    (* CALCULATE DENOMINATOR FOR A0 AND A1 *)
    DENOM := N * SXSQ - SX**2;

    (* CALCULATE RESULTS *)
    A0 := (SY * SXSQ - SX * SXY) / DENOM;
    A1 := (N * SXY - SX * SY) / DENOM;

END; (* END LSQ *)
```

The SUBROUTINE is denoted as LSQ(X, Y, N, A0, A1). The first two FORMAL parameters are one-dimension REAL arrays that contain the sets of X and Y coordinates. The parameter N is an INTEGER denoting the number of coordinates; A0 and A1 are REAL variables that are used to provide the results to the main program.

The iteration on I is used to accumulate the necessary sums. This provides the sum of the X(I) coordinates, the sum of the Y(I) coordinates, the sum of the squares of the X(I) coordinates, and the sum of the products of X(I) and Y(I).

There are several local variables in addition to I. These are denoted SX, SY, SXSQ, SXY, and DENOM, corresponding to the given formulas as follows: $SX = \Sigma X$, $SY = \Sigma Y$, $SXSQ = \Sigma X^2$, $SXY = \Sigma XY$, and $DENOM = N\Sigma X^2 - (\Sigma X)^2$. These allow for a single calculation of DENOM, which can be used in deriving A0 and A1. Note that there is no error checking. What if, due to a data error, DENOM = 0?

If we have two arrays of coordinates X1 and X2 with 100 data elements each and we want the answers to be returned in the REAL variables SLOPE and INTERCEPT, the call on the procedure would be similar to CALL LSQ (X1, X2, 100, SLOPE, INTERCEPT).

End Solution

In Examples 8.8 and 8.10 a one-dimension array was used as a parameter of the subroutine. There is, however, no restriction on the dimensions of an array used as a parameter. In the following example, a doubly subscripted array is used as one of the parameters.

Example 8.11

It is sometimes desirable to set all elements of an array to the same value. This is particularly true when initializing the variables in a program.

Develop a subroutine that sets all elements in an $M \times N$ array to the value DAT.

Solution

```
SUBROUTINE SET (A, M, N, DAT);

BEGIN
    (* SET ALL ELEMENTS OF ARRAY A TO DAT *)
    FOR I := 1 STEP 1 UNTIL M DO
        FOR J := 1 STEP 1 UNTIL N DO
            A(I,J) := DAT;

END; (* END SET *)
```

The subroutine has four FORMAL parameters and it can be denoted as SET (A, M, N, DAT). Array A is a doubly subscripted array with the INTEGER parameters M and N denoting the number of rows and columns, respectively. The parameter DAT indicates the value to be stored in each element of the array.

The algorithm for this example is a very simple double iteration loop. The variables I and J are local variables.

End Solution

8.10 Calls of Other Subprograms From Within a Subroutine

We illustrated earlier how one function can call another function. Likewise, a subroutine can call a function or even another subroutine. In this section we consider two subroutines that include calls on other subprograms.

A. Call of a Function From Within a Subroutine

Example 8.12 illustrates a case where functions are called from within a subroutine. As with any other function call, the call must appear in an arithmetic expression if the type of the function is REAL or INTEGER. Likewise, it must be used in a BOOLEAN expression if the type of function is BOOLEAN.

Example 8.12

Frequency distributions are often used to organize and summarize large amounts of raw data. The possible range of values of the data is subdivided into classes, or categories. Each individual data point is then assigned to one of these classes and a count of the data points within each class is then obtained. The resulting tabular arrangement of the classes together with their corresponding counts, or frequencies, is called a **frequency distribution,** or **frequency table.**

This frequency distribution can be used to produce a histogram. A **histogram** is a set of rectangles that have bases on an axis denoting the classes, widths equal to the size of the class interval, and areas proportional to the class frequencies.

Develop a subroutine that performs the following operations:

1. Derives a frequency distribution from an array of raw data
2. Scales the resultant frequencies so that the maximum count within a class does not exceed a specified value

Solution

```
SUBROUTINE FREQ (OCCUR, N, COUNTS, BOUND, INTERVALS, HIGH, NUMBR);

(**** DECLARE FUNCTIONS ****)
REAL FUNCTION XMAX (X, N);
BEGIN
   BIG := X(1); (* FIND LARGEST VALUE IN ARRAY X *)
   FOR I := 2 STEP 1 UNTIL N DO
   BEGIN
       IF (X(I) > BIG)
       THEN
           BIG := X(I);
   END;
   XMAX := BIG;
END; (* END XMAX *)


REAL FUNCTION XMIN (X,N);
BEGIN
   SMALL := X(1); (* FIND SMALLEST VALUE IN ARRAY X *)
   FOR I := 2 STEP 1 UNTIL N DO
```

```
    BEGIN
        IF (X(I) < SMALL)
        THEN
            SMALL := X(I);
    END;
    XMIN := SMALL;
END; (* END XMIN *)


INTEGER FUNCTION ICNT (X, NBR, LOW, HIGH);

(* FIND NUMBER OF ELEMENTS IN X BETWEEN LOW AND HIGH *)
BEGIN
    COUNT := 0;
    FOR I := 1 STEP 1 UNTIL NBR DO
    BEGIN
        IF ((X(I) >= LOW) AND (X(I) < HIGH))
        THEN
            COUNT := COUNT + 1;
    END;

    ICNT := COUNT;

END; (* END ICNT *)


INTEGER FUNCTION IMAX (X, N);
BEGIN
    BIG := X(1); (* FIND LARGEST INTEGER IN ARRAY X *)
    FOR I := 2 STEP 1 UNTIL N DO
    BEGIN
        IF (X(I) > BIG)
        THEN
            BIG := X(I);
    END;
    IMAX := X(I);
END; (* END IMAX *)


(**** BEGIN CODE FOR FREQ ****)
BEGIN
    (* FIND THE SIZE OF EACH INTERVAL *)
    LOWERBOUND := XMIN (OCCUR, N);
    SIZE := (XMAX(OCCUR,N) - LOWERBOUND) / INTERVALS;

    (* BUILD DATA FOR EACH INTERVAL IN TURN *)
    FOR I := 1 STEP 1 UNTIL INTERVALS DO
    BEGIN
        BOUND(I) := LOWERBOUND; (* SAVE LOWER BOUND *)

        (* SAVE NUMBER OF ELEMENTS IN THE INTERVAL *)
        COUNTS(I) := ICNT (OCCUR,N,LOWERBOUND,LOWERBOUND+SIZE);

        (* SET NEXT INTERVAL'S LOWER BOUND *)
        LOWERBOUND := LOWERBOUND + SIZE;
    END;
```

```
          IF (NUMBR = 1) (* TEST TO SEE IF SCALING IS CALLED FOR *)
          THEN
               BEGIN
                    (* TEST TO SEE IF SCALING IS NECESSARY *)
                    IF (IMAX(COUNTS,INTERVALS) > HIGH)
                    THEN
                         BEGIN
                              (* CALCULATE SCALE FACTOR *)
                              NUMBR := TRUNC(IMAX(COUNTS,INTERVALS) / HIGH + 1);

                              (* SCALE ALL COUNTS *)
                              FOR I := 1 STEP 1 UNTIL INTERVALS DO
                                   COUNTS(I) := COUNTS(I) / NUMBR;
                         END; (* IF IMAX > HIGH *)
               END; (* END IF NUMBR = 1 *)

END; (* END FREQ *)
```

Assume that all necessary parameters are assigned values prior to the call to
FREQ. The raw data needed to develop the histogram is in array OCCUR of
length N. The frequency counts are developed in the INTEGER array
COUNTS. The lower bound of each class is stored in the array BOUND,
while the number of intervals is INTERVALS. The parameters HIGH and
NUMBR are used in scaling the data.

This pseudocode utilizes two REAL functions and two INTEGER functions. The XMIN function determines the smallest value in the array OC-
CUR, while the XMAX function of Example 8.5 is used to find the largest
value. Both of these functions are of type REAL.

The INTEGER FUNCTION ICNT counts the number of data points in each
of the classes of the frequency distribution. ICNT is called in an arithmetic
expression within the iteration on I and is therefore called INTERVALS
times. The fourth function used is IMAX, which is similar to XMAX; however, it searches an INTEGER array rather than a REAL array and it provides
an INTEGER result.

To determine if the second part of the subroutine is to be performed, the
parameter NUMBR is tested. If NUMBR is equal to 1, the scaling is to be accomplished if it is necessary; otherwise, the program is terminated.

The maximum height of the frequency distribution is denoted by HIGH. If
the value of the largest element in COUNTS is less than HIGH, the scaling is
not necessary. If the scaling is desired and necessary (NUMBR equals 1 and
the largest element of COUNTS greater than HIGH), a new value of NUMBR
is computed and all elements of COUNTS are divided by NUMBR.

To compute the value of NUMBR, the largest element of COUNTS is divided by HIGH, 1 is added to the quotient, and the result is truncated. Note

that we made use of the function TRUNC for this purpose, which we assume is an intrinsic function available in most languages in one form or another.

End Solution

Remember that the inclusion of a subroutine in a program does not automatically cause that subroutine to be executed. The subroutine must be called by the main program by means of a CALL statement. Example 8.13 demonstrates the use of SUBROUTINE FREQ through a CALL statement.

Example 8.13

Develop a complete program that will read in an array of raw data, call the subroutine FREQ to compute the frequency distribution, and print out the result.

Solution

```
PROGRAM EXAMPLE 8.13;

(**** SUBROUTINE FREQ IS INSERTED HERE ****)

BEGIN
    READ (NRPTS, NINT); (* INPUT NUMBER OF DATA POINTS AND INTERVALS *)

    READ (POINTS(I),I := 1, NRPTS); (* INPUT DATA POINTS *)

    KEY := 2; (* SET SCALING PARAMETERS *)
    HILIMIT := 1;

    (* GET HISTOGRAM STATISTICS *)
    CALL FREQ (POINTS,NRPTS,ICOUNT,LBOUND,NINT,HILIMIT,KEY);

    WRITE ("FREQUENCY DISTRIBUTION");

    (* PRINT LOWER BOUND OF EACH INTERVAL AND THE COUNT *)
    FOR I := 1 STEP 1 UNTIL NINTS DO
        WRITE (I,LBOUND(I),ICOUNT(I));

END. (* END EXERCISE 8.13 *)
```

This program first reads the number of data points, NRPTS, and the number of intervals, NINT. The data array POINTS is input and the SUBROUTINE FREQ is called with seven parameters. FREQ is not recoded in the program; however, notation is made where it would appear. The order and type of the actual parameters in the call to FREQ must match the order and type of the FORMAL parameters in FREQ. Consequently, the first parameter in the call must be a REAL array, the second parameter in the call must be an INTE-GER, and so forth.

The arrays LBOUND and ICOUNT are output parameters. After the completions of FREQ, LBOUND contains the lower bound of each of the NINT intervals with the corresponding element of ICOUNT denoting the count in that interval. The program terminates after these arrays are output.

In this call to FREQ, the data will not be scaled. Scaling is determined by the last parameter, KEY, in the CALL statement, which is set to 2 in the example. The value of HILIMIT is unused in this case. To make the program more general, the values of KEY and HILIMIT should be variables that are entered by the user during processing.

End Solution

B. Call of a Subroutine From Within a Subroutine

A subroutine can be called from another subroutine just as functions can be called from subroutines or other functions. The subroutine of Example 8.14 uses the SUBROUTINE LSQ of Example 8.10.

Example 8.14

SUBROUTINE LSQ in Example 8.10 provides the values of A and B of the equation for a least square line: $Y = A + BX$. If the X and Y coordinates of a number of points are known, the values of A and B can be used to draw the least square line.

Develop a subroutine to determine a set of coordinates of the least square line.

Solution

```
SUBROUTINE GRAPH (X, Y, N, XX, YY, N);

(**** DECLARE SUBROUTINES ****)
SUBROUTINE LSQ (X, Y, N, AO, Al);
BEGIN
    (* INITIALIZE LOCAL VARIABLES *)
    SX := 0;
    SY := 0;
    SXSQ := 0;
    SXY := 0;

    FOR I := 1 STEP 1 UNTIL N DO (* ACCUMULATE SUMS *)
    BEGIN
        SX := SX + X(I);
        SY := SY + Y(I);
```

```
            SXSQ := SXSQ + X(I)**2;
            SXY := SXY + X(I) * Y(I);
        END;

        (* CALCULATE DENOMINATOR FOR AO AND Al *)
        DENOM := N * SXSQ - SX**2;

        (* CALCULATE RESULTS *)
        AO := (SY * SXSQ - SX * SXY) / DENOM;
        Al := (N * SXY - SX * SY) / DENOM;

    END; (* END LSQ *)


    (**** BEGIN CODE FOR GRAPH ****)
    BEGIN
        CALL LSQ (X, Y, N, A, B); (* GET VALUES FOR A AND B *)

        (* CALCULATE SIZE OF INTERVALS *)
        SMALL := XMIN(X,N);
        BIG := XMAX(X,N);
        DELTA := (BIG - SMALL) / (N - 1);

        X1 := SMALL; (* SET STARTING INTERVAL *)
        FOR I := 1 STEP 1 UNTIL N DO
        BEGIN
            (* SET X,Y COORDINATE *)
            XX(I) := X1;
            YY(I) := A + B * X1;

            X1 := X1 + DELTA; (* SET NEXT INTERVAL POINT *)
        END;

    END; (* END GRAPH *)
```

In SUBROUTINE GRAPH (X, Y, N, XX, YY, N), arrays X and Y contain the set of coordinates for the N points. These are used in the call of the SUBROUTINE LSQ to determine the values of the constants A and B of the equation for the least square line.

A and B are subsequently used to determine the coordinates of the least square line. This set of coordinates is arranged such that they start at the X value corresponding to the smallest X(I) and stop at the value corresponding to the highest X(I). This will provide the coordinates necessary to plot the line from XMIN = MIN (X(1), X(2), . . . , X(N)) to XMAX = MAX (X(1), X(2), . . . , X(N)).

The distance from XMIN to XMAX is divided into NR − 1 equal-size intervals, the bounds of each interval comprising the values of the array XX. The Y(I) value for each point is calculated and stored in the corresponding element of YY.

End Solution

8.11 Other Methods of Achieving Correspondence of Variables Between the Main Program and Subprograms

In all of our examples thus far, the variables used in the subprograms were either parameters of the subprogram or variables that were local to the subroutine. When a subprogram is called, the procedure described in terms of the FORMAL parameters is accomplished for the actual parameters provided by the call. Other variables used in the subprogram are valid only for that subprogram and do not exist outside the subprogram.

In some cases it is desirable to have variables that are used in both the main program and the subprograms but that are not passed as parameters. For example, some large programs have a number of subprograms with many of the same variables being used in them. It could be confusing to pass such a large number of variables as parameters. In addition, there is a greater opportunity for error in the type and number of parameters when making the correspondence of the actual and formal parameters in the CALL statements.

Some higher level languages allow the use of the variables in different subprograms without using large numbers of parameters. Although the techniques of doing this are highly dependent upon the languages, it is worthwhile to briefly consider two general methods.

One method is the use of a **COMMON area of storage** that is available to the main program and to the subprograms. For example, a section of storage can be designated as COMMON. An identical COMMON declarative statement can be used to reserve the same space within the main program and within each of the subprograms that utilize the COMMON data. The correspondence of the variables referred to between these programs is established by their relative positions within the COMMON list. This also allows the variables in the COMMON list to be referenced by different names in each subprogram. Several distinct, COMMON areas can be established if desirable.

A second method is to have variables declared outside the subprogram but accessible within the subprogram. These types of variables are generally referred to as **GLOBAL variables.** A variable, X, is declared outside a subprogram. If X is not declared in the subprogram and it is not listed as a formal parameter, then the use of X in the subprogram implies a reference to the GLOBAL variable X declared outside the subprogram. Simple variables, arrays, formats, and a number of other constructs can be handled in this way.

The COMMON variables method of storage is used in FORTRAN, while the use of GLOBAL variables is achieved in PASCAL through the block structure of that language. PL/I uses both concepts. The external variable of PL/I is actually a modification of the COMMON concept of FORTRAN. Likewise, the nesting of procedures in PL/I provides the concepts of GLOBAL variables as in PASCAL. The details and use of these techniques for the various languages are provided in the language texts provided by the vendor.

Example 8.15

Develop a subroutine that will read the values of a number of elements and place them into a COMMON array. The subroutine first reads a number, NBR. If NBR is equal to 0, a BOOLEAN parameter, QUIT, is set equal to TRUE and the subroutine terminates. If NBR is any other value, then NBR data sets are read. The data set consists of an array row number, an array column number, and the data value for that row and column of the array, which is understood to be in the COMMON area.

Solution

```
SUBROUTINE INIT (QUIT);

(* ARR1 IS ASSUMED A COMMON ARRAY VARIABLE *)

BEGIN
   READ (NBR); (* INPUT SIZE OF ARR1 *)

   IF (NBR <> 0) (* TEST TO SEE IF CHANGES ARE CALLED FOR *)
   THEN
       BEGIN
           FOR K := 1 STEP 1 UNTIL NBR DO
               READ (ROW, COL, ARR1(ROW,COL));

           QUIT := FALSE; (* QUIT INDICATES CHANGES WERE MADE *)
       END
   ELSE
       QUIT := TRUE; (* QUIT INDICATES THAT NO CHANGES WERE MADE *)

END; (* END INIT *)
```

SUBROUTINE INIT (QUIT) uses only the BOOLEAN parameter QUIT. The array ARR1 is not a parameter of the subroutine, but the contents of some elements in ARR1 are changed.

If ARR1 was a local parameter, SUBROUTINE INIT would be nonsensical since the information stored in ARR1 would be lost when the INIT subroutine ended. Thus, the information could not be used outside of the subroutine.

But if ARR1 was a GLOBAL array or if it was stored in a COMMON area, the information saved in ARR1 would still exist after INIT completed. Therefore, we will consider ARR1 a GLOBAL array or a part of a COMMON storage area.

Although the above analysis indicates that ARR1 should be GLOBAL, this is not directly apparent from the pseudocode. Since our pseudocode does not prescribe a method to indicate GLOBAL variables, comments in the pseudocode must indicate the variables that are in COMMON storage or GLOBAL variables.

End Solution

8.12 The Grading Problem and Subprograms

Let's closely review the algorithm presented in Figure 6–19, which is the solution to the grading problem as we have developed it so far. If we decided to implement subprograms for the pure sake of efficiency of code, there would be few candidates in this algorithm as it exists.

However, if we agree that the use of subprograms could improve the readability of the program and also possibly facilitate debugging, there immediately appear to be several candidates. In fact, since we have already derived an algorithm for calculating the standard deviation in previous chapters, we could certainly incorporate this algorithm through the use of a function and take advantage of our previous work. We could also consolidate code by accumulating the sum and the sum of the squares through use of a subroutine. To improve the readability and shorten the grading algorithm, a subroutine could be employed to determine the range and assign the letter grade.

```
PROGRAM GRADING PROBLEM;

(**** DECLARE SUBROUTINES ****)
SUBROUTINE ACCUM (SUM, SUMSQ, VALUE);
BEGIN
   SUM := SUM + VALUE;
   SUMSQ := SUMSQ + VALUE**2;
END; (* END ACCUM *)


(**** DECLARE FUNCTIONS ****)
REAL FUNCTION STDEV (MEAN, SUMSQ, NR);
BEGIN
   STDEV := SQRT(SUMSQ / NR - MEAN**2);
END; (* END STDEV *)


ALPHA FUNCTION ASSIGN (SCORE);
BEGIN
   IF (SCORE >= 60)
   THEN
       BEGIN
           IF (SCORE >= 70)
           THEN
               BEGIN
                   IF (SCORE >= 85)
                   THEN
                       BEGIN
                           IF (SCORE >= 95)
                           THEN
```

```
                                    ASSIGN := "A"
                           ELSE
                                    ASSIGN := "B";
                           END (* SCORE >= 85 *)
                      ELSE
                           ASSIGN := "C";
                 END (* SCORE >= 70 *)
           ELSE
                 ASSIGN := "D";
      END (* SCORE >= 60 *)
   ELSE
      ASSIGN := "F";

END; (* END ASSIGN *)


(* ARRAY POINTS ROW 1 = TEST 1 STATS,
                   2 = TEST 2 STATS,
                   3 = TEST 3 STATS,
                   4 = CLASS STATS,
               COL 1 = SUM,
                   2 = SUM**2 *)

(**** MAIN PROGRAM ****)
BEGIN
   (* INPUT HEADER *)
   READ (COURSE, SECTION, INSTRUCTOR, ROOM, NRTESTS, NRSTUDS);

   (* OUTPUT HEADER *)
   WRITE (COURSE, SECTION, INSTRUCTOR, ROOM, NRTESTS, NRSTUDS);
   (* FORMAT AND TITLE COLUMNS *)
   WRITE ("STUDENT'S", "TEST", "TEST", "TEST", "CUM", "AVERAGE", "GRADE");
   WRITE ("NAME", "1", "2", "3", "PTS");

   FOR I := 1 STEP 1 UNTIL 4 DO (* INITIALIZE POINTS *)
   BEGIN
       POINTS(I,1) := 0;
       POINTS(I,2) := 0;
   END;

   FOR CNT := 1 STEP 1 UNTIL NRSTUDS DO
   BEGIN
       READ (NAME, (TEST(I),I := 1,3));

       CUMPTS := 0; (* COLLECT TEST STATISTICS *)
       FOR I := 1 STEP 1 UNTIL 3 DO
       BEGIN
           CALL ACCUM (POINTS(I,1), POINTS(I,2), TEST(I));
           CUMPTS := CUMPTS + TEST(I);
       END;

       AVERAGE := CUMPTS / 3; (* CALCULATE STUDENT AVERAGE *)

       GRADE := ASSIGN (AVERAGE); (* ASSIGN LETTER GRADE *)
```

```
(* OUTPUT STUDENT DATA *)
WRITE (NAME, (TEST(I),I := 1,3), CUMPTS, AVERAGE, GRADE);

(* COLLECT CLASS STATISTICS *)
CALL ACCUM (POINTS(4,1), POINTS(4,2), CUMPTS);

END; (* ALL STUDENTS PROCESSED *)

(* CALCULATE CLASS STATISTICS FOR 3 TESTS AND CUM PTS *)
FOR I := 1 STEP 1 UNTIL 4 DO
BEGIN
    POINTS(I,1) := POINTS(I,1) / NRSTUDS; (* FIND AVERAGE *)

    (* FIND STANDARD DEVIATION *)
    POINTS(I,2) := STDEV(POINTS(I,1),POINTS(I,2),NRSTUDS);
END;

(* OUTPUT CLASS STATISTICS *)
WRITE ("TEST MEAN:", (POINTS(I,1),I := 1,4));
WRITE ("TEST STANDARD DEVIATION:", (POINTS(I,2),I := 1,4));

END. (* END GRADING PROBLEM *)
```

After you feel confident you understand the logic, you should code the algorithm and execute your program with the sample test data. Be sure you can duplicate the output shown in Table 8–1.

Table 8-1

Course: Math 351					Instructor: Mr. P. J. Smythe	
Section: 3					Room: 304	
Number of Tests: 3						
Number of Students: 10						

Student's Name	Test 1	Test 2	Test 3	CUM PTS	Average	Grade
Adams, M. E.	85	87	90	262	87.33	B
Barnes, L. J.	56	60	72	168	56.00	F
Carlton, P. G.	30	40	59	129	43.00	F
Driscoll, R.	98	99	100	297	99.00	A
Evans, S. T.	90	85	76	251	83.67	C
Orly, A. P.	50	65	78	193	64.33	D
Puget, S.	83	81	84	248	82.67	C
Ryan, M. A.	90	89	72	251	83.67	C
Silve, G. A.	60	65	65	190	63.33	D
Walton, J. J.	88	70	89	247	82.33	C
Test Mean	73.0	74.1	78.5	223.6		
Test Standard Deviation	22.38	17.38	12.42	51.22		

Before moving on, let's look at what we have done with this problem. We started at the lowest level and built our way up to a complete solution to the problem. At the very least, we broke it up into modules for debugging, efficiency, and readability. That is, we took a **bottom-up approach**—the results are obvious.

Do you remember now or can you determine the use of POINTS(4,1) or POINTS(4,2)? What would you have to do to accommodate 5 test grades, or 10, or possibly N? In the next chapter, we'll see how an entirely different approach lends itself to modularization, readability, and efficiency of code.

8.13 Summary

In this chapter, we have presented a convenient programming structure for decomposing and modularizing a large problem. This structure, known as a subprogram, is provided in all of the higher level languages, although the name itself can vary from language to language. We have discussed the advantages and disadvantages to subprograms and the reasons for using them.

We have placed no restrictions on the placement of a subprogram call, implying that subprograms can be called from anyplace in a program including another subprogram. We have established the communications channels available to both functions and subroutines. The concepts of GLOBAL variables and COMMON areas were introduced.

One last word of caution before leaving this chapter. The unrestricted use of GLOBAL variables as a communications channel seriously detracts from the readability and modularity of a program and destroys some of the **top-down** structure (see Chapter 9) of the overall algorithm. Because of the convenience and ease of using GLOBAL variables, many programmers fall into the habit of using them for all communications between subprograms. We strongly advocate that GLOBAL variables be used judiciously, that is, only when they greatly simplify the problem and have minimum effect on readability.

Solved Problems
8.1
The summation of the integers from 1 to N can be expressed as

$$\sum_{I=1}^{N} I = 1+2+3+ \cdots +(N-1)+(N) = \frac{N*(N+1)}{2}$$

Develop an INTEGER FUNCTION that provides the value of the summation, given the value of N as a parameter.

Solution

```
REAL FUNCTION SUMI (N);

BEGIN
  (* CALCULATE SUM OF FIRST N INTEGERS *)
```

```
    SUMI := N  *  (N + 1)  / 2;

END; (* END SUMI *)
```

There is only one parameter needed in FUNCTION SUMI (N). This is the value of N. It consists of one assignment statement that assigns the value of the summation to the name of the function, SUMI.

8.2

The sum of the powers of the integers from 1 to N can be expressed as

$$\sum_{K=1}^{N} K^M = 1^M + 2^M + 3^M + \cdots + (N-1)^M + N^M$$

As shown in Solved Problem 8.1, the expression can be simplified for M = 1 and is equal to N (N + 1)/2. In a similar manner, the equations for M = 2 and M = 3 can be stated in a simple method as

$$\sum_{K=1}^{N} K^2 = 1^2 + 2^2 + 3^2 + \cdots + (N-1)^2 + N^2 = \frac{N(N+1)(2N+1)}{6}$$

and

$$\sum_{K=1}^{N} K^3 = 1^3 + 2^3 + 3^3 + \cdots + (N-1)^3 + N^3 = \frac{N^2(N+1)^2}{4}$$

Develop REAL FUNCTION POWR (M,N) that will provide the value of the summation, given the values of M and N.

Solution

```
REAL FUNCTION POWR (M, N);

    (* M = POWER,
       N = NUMBER OF INTEGERS TO PROCESS *)

BEGIN
    IF (M = 1) (* TEST FOR CASE M = 1 *)
    THEN
        POWR := N * (N + 1) / 2
    ELSE
        BEGIN
            IF (M = 2) (* TEST FOR CASE M = 2 *)
            THEN
                POWR := N * (N + 1) * (2 * N + 1) / 6
            ELSE
                BEGIN
                    IF (M = 3) (* TEST FOR CASE M = 3 *)
                    THEN
                        POWR := N**2 * (N + 1)**2 / 4
```

```
                    ELSE
                        BEGIN (* PROCESS ALL OTHER CASES *)
                            SUM := 1;
                            FOR I := 2 STEP 1 UNTIL N DO
                                SUM := SUM + I**M;
                            POWR := SUM;
                        END;
                END;
        END;

END; (* SUBROUTINE POWR *)
```

The function has two parameters. The efficiency of the computation is greatly increased by using the short formulas for M = 1, M = 2, and M = 3. Therefore the value of M is compared to these three constants in order to determine if one of the three simple computations can be used. If M is equal to 4 or higher, the value is computed by initializing SUM to 1 and doing a summation of the appropriate power of each integer from 2 to N. In all cases, the final value is assigned to the name of FUNCTION POWR.

8.3

In managing inventories, the **economic lot size formula** is often used. This is a very simple inventory model, which is based upon several simplifying assumptions. It determines the quantity to be ordered by minimizing the sum of the setup costs of placing an order (C1) and the inventory holding costs (C2). If D is the demand rate per time period, the economic order quantity, EOQ, is

$$EOQ = \sqrt{\frac{2 * C1 * D}{C2}}$$

Develop REAL FUNCTION EOQ (C1,C2,D) that will determine the economic order quantity.

Solution

```
REAL FUNCTION EOQ (C1, C2, D);

    (* C1 = SETUP COSTS,
       C2 = COST OF PLACING ORDER,
       D  = DEMAND RATE PER TIME PERIOD *)

BEGIN
    (* CALCULATE ECONOMIC ORDER QUANTITY *)
    EOQ := SQRT (2 * C1 * D / C2);

END; (* END EOQ *)
```

The function is straightforward. There are no local variables needed and it is assumed that there is an INTRINSIC FUNCTION SQRT that computes the square root.

8.4

If P is a present sum of money invested at interest rate I, which is compounded at the end of each of N interest periods, the future sum of money, S, is given by $S = P (1 + I)^N$. Develop REAL FUNCTION FS (P,I,N) that will compute the future sum, given the present sum, interest rate per period, and the number of periods.

Solution

```
REAL FUNCTION FS (P, I, N);

   (* P = PRESENT SUM,
      I = INTEREST RATE PER PERIOD,
      N = NUMBER OF PERIODS *)

BEGIN
   FS := P * (1 + I)**N; (* CALCULATE FUTURE SUM *)
END;
```

FS consists of a simple assignment statement implementing the formula specified for S, the future sum.

8.5

The following formulas come from elementary solid geometry:

Volume of a cone: $V = \frac{\pi}{3} R^2 H = 1.0472\ R^2 H$
Volume of a cylinder: $V = \pi R^2 H = 3.1416\ R^2 H$
Volume of a sphere: $V = \frac{4}{3}\pi R^3\ = 4.1888\ R^3$

Develop REAL FUNCTION VOL (SHAPE,R,H) that will compute the volume of either a cone, a cylinder, or a sphere, depending upon the value of SHAPE. The parameters R and H represent the value of the radius and the height, respectively.

Solution

```
REAL FUNCTION VOL (SHAPE, R, H);

   (* SHAPE = TYPE OF GEOMETRY,
      R     = RADIUS,
      H     = HEIGHT *)

BEGIN
   IF (SHAPE = 1) (* TEST FOR CONE *)
   THEN
       VOL := 1.0472 * R**2 * H
   ELSE
       BEGIN
```

```
              IF (SHAPE = 2) (* TEST FOR CYLINDER *)
              THEN
                  VOL := 3.1416 * R**2 * H
              ELSE
                  BEGIN
                      IF (SHAPE = 3) (* TEST FOR SPHERE *)
                      THEN
                          VOL := 4.1888 * R**3
                      ELSE
                          (* UNKNOWN SHAPE--SET VOLUME TO ZERO *)
                          VOL := 0;
                  END; (* IF SHAPE = 2 *)
          END; (* IF SHAPE = 1 *)

END; (* END VOL *)
```

This quite simple function contains no local variables. If SHAPE is equal to 1, the volume of a cone is to be computed. When SHAPE is equal to 2, the volume of a cylinder is calculated. The volume of a sphere is computed when SHAPE is equal to 3. If SHAPE is any other value, the result is set equal to 0. The parameters R and H are of type REAL.

8.6

Many people like to keep track of the number of miles that they receive from one gallon of gasoline in their automobile. Assume that the fuel tank is always filled when gasoline is purchased and that the number of gallons and the odometer mileage are recorded at that time. Develop a real function that will use this information to compute the number of miles per gallon for the automobile.

Solution

```
REAL FUNCTION MPG (MILES, GALS, N);

   (* MILES = MILEAGE AT EACH GAS PURCHASE,
      GALS  = GALLONS BOUGHT AT EACH PURCHASE,
      N     = NUMBER OF PURCHASES *)

BEGIN
   SUM := 0;
   FOR I := 2 STEP 1 UNTIL N DO (* CALCULATE TOTAL GALLONS BOUGHT *)
      SUM := SUM + GALS(I);

   MPG := (MILES(N) - MILES(1)) / SUM; (* CALCULATE MILEAGE *)

END; (* END MPG *)
```

In REAL FUNCTION MPG (MILES, GALS, N), MILES is an INTEGER ARRAY containing the mileage, in ascending order, for each gasoline purchase. Each element of the REAL ARRAY GALS contains the number of gallons purchased at the mileage of the corresponding element of MILES. The parameter N denotes the number of elements in MILES and GALS.

The computation of the number of gallons is a simple process. In order to compute the number of miles per gallons correctly, it is necessary to start with a full tank of gasoline. Thus the procedure must ignore the size of the first purchase. The only two mileage figures that are needed for this computation are the starting mileage, MILES(1), and the final mileage, MILES(N).

8.7

Nonparametric statistics is a branch of statistics that compares the distribution of data without specifying the form of the distribution. The name derives from the fact that the parameters of the statistical distribution (e.g., mean and variance) are not needed for the analysis. The **sign test** is one technique of nonparametric statistics. It is appropriate under the following conditions:

1. Two materials, treatments, processes, and so forth, are being compared and there are a number of pairs of observations of these two processes.
2. One observation of a pair refers to the first process and the other observation refers to the second process.
3. Both parts of each pair of observations were made under similar conditions.
4. The different pairs were observed under different conditions.

The sign test is used to test the statistical difference between the two processes. This is done by computing the difference in value between the observations of each pair and counting the number of plus and minus signs of these differences. If there is no significant difference in the two processes, the number of plus and minus signs should be approximately the same and the only variations should be due to random causes.

The sign test computes the number of times the less frequent sign occurs. This number can then be used to determine the level of statistical significance using established reference tables. Assuming that X and Y are arrays containing the paired observations in their respective elements, develop INTEGER FUNCTION NBR that determines the signs of the N differences X(I) − Y(I). The lesser number of plus or minus signs is then returned as the value of the procedure. For the purpose of this function, ignore all ties when X(I) = Y(I).

Solution

```
INTEGER FUNCTION NBR (X, Y, N);

    (* X = FIRST SET OF SAMPLES,
       Y = SECOND SET OF CORRESPONDING SAMPLES,
       N = NUMBER OF SAMPLES *)
```

```
BEGIN
    NBRP := 0; (* INITIALIZE PLUS COUNTER *)
    NBRM := 0; (* INITIALIZE MINUS COUNTER *)

    (* PROCESS ALL N ELEMENTS OF ARRAYS X AND Y *)
    FOR I := 1 STEP 1 UNTIL N DO
    BEGIN
        IF (X(I) <> Y(I)) (* CHECK FOR EQUALITY *)
        THEN
            BEGIN
                IF (X(I) > Y(I))
                THEN
                    NBRP := NBRP + 1
                ELSE
                    NBRM := NBRM + 1;
            END;
    END;

    IF (NBRP < NBRM) (* RETURN SMALLEST VALUE *)
    THEN
        NBR := NBRP
    ELSE
        NBR := NBRM;

END; (* END NBR *)
```

The FUNCTION NBR (X, Y, N) has two REAL ARRAYS, X, Y, and an IN-TEGER, N, as parameters. The local variables, NBRP and NBRM, are used to accumulate the number of plus and minus differences, respectively. Although the sign of the differences is counted, the difference is not calculated since the magnitude of the difference is not used in the algorithm.

If X(I) is larger than Y(I), then the difference must necessarily be positive, and the difference is negative if X(I) is smaller than Y(I). If there is an equal number of plus and minus differences, either NBRP or NBRM can be used as the value of NBR. If there is a difference, the lesser value is returned. Note that the problem does not call for identifying the sign for which the value, NBR, is returned.

8.8

When an individual or business enterprise purchases an asset such as machinery, there is a high initial investment. There are also operating and maintenance costs that tend to increase each year for many types of equipment.

A common example of this occurrence is demonstrated in the purchase of an automobile where there is a high initial purchase cost and where maintenance charges become larger as the vehicle becomes older. The **economic service life** of such an asset is defined as the number of time periods that will minimize the average cost per period of service.

The average cost for N years of service is equal to the sum of the initial investment and the total operating costs for the N years divided by the number of years of operation. If the initial investment is V and the operation cost for any year is C_i, the average cost for N years, AC(N), is equal to

$$AC(N) = \frac{V + \sum_{i=1}^{N} C_i}{N}$$

The economic service life is then the value of N that minimizes the value of AC(N).

Assume that C_i remains the same or gets larger for each successive period, i.e., the operating costs tend to increase as the asset gets older. Since the initial cost, V, is spread over a number of years, its contribution to average cost decreases as N increases, i.e., V/N decreases as N gets larger. Thus one component of the average cost decreases while the other tends to increase. The average cost curve will initially decrease, eventually reach a minimum, and then increase.

Develop INTEGER FUNCTION ESL that will determine the economic service life, given the initial investment and the operating cost for each year of service.

Solution

```
INTEGER FUNCTION ESL (V, C);

    (* V = INITIAL INVESTMENT,
       C = OPERATING COSTS PER YEAR OF SERVICE *)

BEGIN
    ACP := V + C(1); (* INITIALIZE AVERAGE COST OF PREVIOUS PERIOD *)
    AC := ACP;

    SUM := C(1); (* INITIALIZE TOTAL COSTS TO DATE *)

    (* TRACK COSTS UNTIL THEY START TO RISE--UP TO 50 YEARS *)
    FOR N := 2 STEP 1 WHILE (N <= 50 AND AC <= ACP) DO
    BEGIN
        ACP := AC;
        SUM := SUM + C(N);
        AC := (V + SUM) / N;
    END;

    ESL := N - 1; (* RETURN MINIMUM COST YEAR *)

END; (* END ESL *)
```

FUNCTION ESL (V, C) accepts two formal parameters V (the initial investment) and array C (the operating costs for each year of service). There are four LOCAL variables: N (the period under consideration), AC (the average cost for the Nth period), ACP (the average cost for the previous period, i.e., period $N-1$), and SUM (the sum of the operating costs through the Nth period).

ESL starts by initializing ACP and SUM to the average cost of the first period and the operating cost of the first period, respectively. Then an iteration on N considers the periods 2 through 50. For each value of N the operating costs are included in the partial sum of such costs and the average cost is calculated.

The average cost for period N is then compared with the previous average cost for period $N-1$. If AC is greater than ACP, the costs are starting to increase and ACP must be the minimum cost per period. The solution is $N-1$, which is returned through ESL. If AC is less than ACP, costs are still decreasing and the next period must be considered. Therefore, the present value of AC is saved in ACP for later comparison and the value of N is incremented.

The algorithm is based upon the consideration of a maximum of 50 periods. These periods could be years, quarters, months, or any other time period. The number of periods can easily be changed, as long as the C array is at least that size. If a minimum cost is not found by the end of the iteration, the value of 50 is assigned as the value of ESL.

8.9

A **polygon** is a closed plane figure bounded by straight line segments as sides. A **quadrilateral** is any polygon having four sides. There are a number of special cases of quadrilaterals fulfilling certain restrictions, e.g., squares and rectangles.

Develop INTEGER FUNCTION ISHPE (X, Y) that will determine if a given quadrilateral fulfills the definition of one of the restricted polygons. The quadrilateral is represented by four sets of X and Y coordinates. Given these four sets of coordinates, ISHPE determines if the polygon is one of the following:

a. A **trapezoid,** which has two and only two parallel sides.

b. A **parallelogram,** in which the opposite sides are parallel.

c. A **rhombus,** which is a parallelogram with all sides being of equal length (equilateral).

d. A **rectangle,** which is a parallelogram with all angles being equal to 90 degrees (equiangular).

e. A **square,** which is an equilateral and equiangular parallelogram (i.e., all sides are of equal length and all angles are equal).

Examples of these shapes are shown in Figure 8–4.

The value returned by ISHPE will be an INTEGER between 0 and 5. The values 1 to 5 correspond to the above five special cases of the quadrilateral,

Figure 8–4.
Sample
Geometric Figures

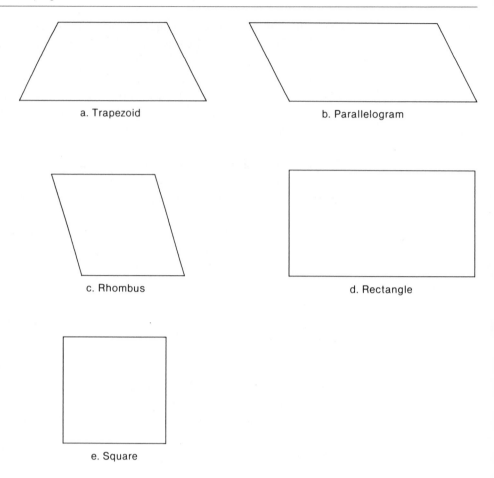

a. Trapezoid

b. Parallelogram

c. Rhombus

d. Rectangle

e. Square

while the value 0 indicates that the quadrilateral does not fulfill any of the above criteria.

Solution

The decisions of the subprogram are based upon the slopes of the four lines and the length of the lines. The slope of a line passing through two points, P_1 and P_2, represented by two sets of coordinates (X_1, Y_1) and (X_2, Y_2), is defined as

$$SLPE1 = \frac{Y_2 - Y_1}{X_2 - X_1}$$

The distance between the two points, P_1 and P_2, is defined as

$$DISTANCE = \sqrt{(X_2 - X_1)^2 + (Y_2 - Y_1)^2}$$

Thus the calculation of the distance involves finding the hypoteneuse of a right triangle. Figure 8–5 is a graphic representation of these concepts. For simplicity, we will assume that the four sets of X and Y coordinates are positive values.

The only parameters of ISHPE are two singly subscripted arrays X and Y, which have four elements each, representing the values of the four X and Y coordinates.

Figure 8–5.
Sample
Calculations for
Slopes and Lengths

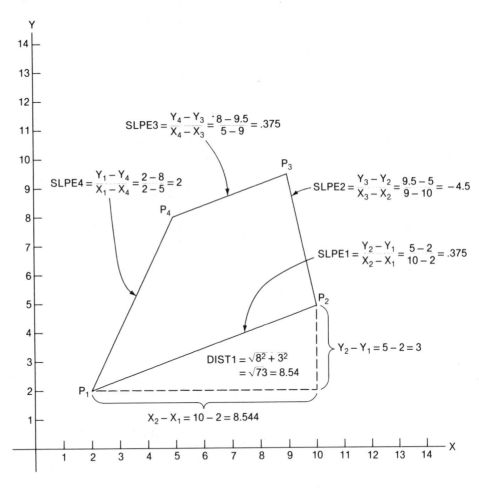

$$SLPE3 = \frac{Y_4 - Y_3}{X_4 - X_3} = \frac{8 - 9.5}{5 - 9} = .375$$

$$SLPE4 = \frac{Y_1 - Y_4}{X_1 - X_4} = \frac{2 - 8}{2 - 5} = 2$$

$$SLPE2 = \frac{Y_3 - Y_2}{X_3 - X_2} = \frac{9.5 - 5}{9 - 10} = -4.5$$

$$SLPE1 = \frac{Y_2 - Y_1}{X_2 - X_1} = \frac{5 - 2}{10 - 2} = .375$$

$$Y_2 - Y_1 = 5 - 2 = 3$$

$$DIST1 = \sqrt{8^2 + 3^2}$$
$$= \sqrt{73} = 8.54$$

$$X_2 - X_1 = 10 - 2 = 8.544$$

```
INTEGER FUNCTION ISHPE (X, Y);

BEGIN
    (* FIND SLOPE OF ALL FOUR SIDES *)
    SLPE1 := (Y(2) - Y(1)) / (X(2) - X(1));
    SLPE2 := (Y(3) - Y(2)) / (X(3) - X(2));
    SLPE3 := (Y(4) - Y(3)) / (X(4) - X(3));
    SLPE4 := (Y(1) - Y(4)) / (X(1) - X(4));

    (* FIND LENGTH OF ADJACENT SIDES *)
    DIST1 := SQRT((X(2) - X(1))**2 + (Y(2) - Y(1))**2);
    DIST2 := SQRT((X(3) - X(2))**2 + (Y(3) - Y(2))**2);

    IF (SLPE1 <> SLPE3) (* TEST FOR OPPOSITE SIDES PARALLEL *)
    THEN
        BEGIN (* TRAPEZOID OR NONE *)
            IF (SLPE2 = SLPE4) (* TEST FOR TRAPEZOID *)
            THEN
                ISHPE := 1 (* TRAPEZOID *)
            ELSE
                ISHPE := 0; (* NOT A SPECIAL SHAPE *)
        END
    ELSE
        BEGIN (* SIDE 1 AND SIDE 3 ARE PARALLEL *)
            IF (SLPE2 <> SLPE4) (* TEST FOR OPPOSITE SIDES PARALLEL *)
            THEN
                ISHPE := 1 (* TRAPEZOID *)
            ELSE
                BEGIN
                    (* SIDE 2 AND SIDE 4 ARE PARALLEL *)
                    (* IT'S A PARALLELOGRAM--WHAT KIND? *)
                    IF (SLPE1 = (-1/SLPE2) (* TEST FOR RIGHT ANGLES *)
                    THEN
                        BEGIN (* SQUARE OR RECTANGLE *)
                            IF (DIST1 = DIST2) (* TEST EQUAL LENGTH LEGS *)
                            THEN
                                ISHPE := 5 (* SQUARE *)
                            ELSE
                                ISHPE := 4; (* RECTANGLE *)
                        END
                    ELSE
                        BEGIN (* PARALLELOGRAM OR RHOMBUS *)
                            IF (DIST1 = DIST2) (* TEST EQUAL LENGTH LEGS *)
```

```
                                THEN
                                        ISHPE := 3 (* RHOMBUS *)
                                ELSE
                                        ISHPE := 2; (* PARALLELOGRAM *)
                            END;
                    END; (* END SLPE2 <> SLPE4 *)

            END; (* END SLPE1 <> SLPE4 *)

    END; (* END ISHPE *)
```

In ISHPE (X, Y), the initial actions involve the calculation of the slopes of the four lines and the distance or length of two adjacent lines. The first conditional determines if SLPE1 and SLPE3 are equal. Since these slopes pertain to opposite sides of the quadrilateral, it is a check to see if one set of opposite sides is parallel. If the sides are not parallel, the figure must be either a trapezoid or not one of the special cases. Therefore, the TRUE path from the first conditional leads to a second conditional that checks the slopes of the other two lines. The test, SLPE2 = SLPE4, determines whether the quadrilateral is a trapezoid. In any case, the process terminates.

Following the FALSE path of the first conditional, the second set of slopes is again tested. If the second set of slopes is not equal, the figure must be a trapezoid. If the set is equal, the next conditional checks to see if the angles are equal, i.e., if they are 90-degree angles. If the angles are 90 degrees, they are perpendicular and the slopes of one set of parallel lines must be the negative reciprocals of the other set. Thus if these are 90-degree angles, SLPE1 = −1/SLPE2. If this conditional is FALSE, the quadrilateral must be either a parallelogram or a rhombus. If the slopes are negative reciprocals, the quadrilateral must be a rectangle or a square. In all of the cases the decision is recorded by assigning the proper value to ISHPE.

8.10

A **recursive procedure** is a procedure that calls itself. This pseudocode depicts a recursive procedure called RECUR(M).

```
INTEGER FUNCTION RECUR (M);

BEGIN
    (* CONTINUE CALLING RECUR UNTIL M = 0 *)
    IF (M <> 0)
    THEN
        RECUR := M + RECUR(M-1)
    ELSE
        RECUR := 0;

END; (* END RECUR *)
```

Determine the result of each of the following calls upon this recursive procedure:

a. RECUR(0)

b. RECUR(2)

c. RECUR(6)

RECUR implements the algorithm for

$$\sum_{i=0}^{M} i.$$

Solution

a. RECUR(0). The value of the actual parameter corresponding to the formal parameter, M, is 0. Since the value of the actual parameter is 0, the FALSE path of the conditional is followed. RECUR is assigned the value of 0 and the process is terminated. This is the **stopping condition,** or **terminating rule,** of this recursive procedure. Each recursive procedure must contain some type of stopping condition.

b. RECUR(2). Since the value of the actual parameter is 2, the result of this call is an addition of the INTEGER 2 plus the call on RECUR(1). Thus RECUR is again called for the value of M = 1. Since M is not equal to 0, the value of this second call is 1 plus the value of the function call RECUR(0). The value of the third call is 0 and the sequence of calls of RECUR is terminated. The final result is 2 + 1 + 0, or 3. A more graphic representation of this series of calls is shown in Table 8–2.

c. RECUR(6). The evaluation for RECUR(6) follows the logic of that for RECUR(2). It is best depicted as in Table 8–2.

Table 8-2 Logic of A Recursive Procedure

```
RECUR (2) = 2 + RECUR (1)
          = 2 + 1 + RECUR (0)
          = 2 + 1 + 0
          = 3

RECUR (6) = 6 + RECUR (5)
          = 6 + 5 + RECUR (4)
          = 6 + 5 + 4 + RECUR (3)
          = 6 + 5 + 4 + 3 + RECUR (2)
          = 6 + 5 + 4 + 3 + 2 + RECUR (1)
          = 6 + 5 + 4 + 3 + 2 + 1 + RECUR (0)
          = 6 + 5 + 4 + 3 + 2 + 1 + 0
          = 21
```

8.11

The traditional problem that most textbooks and instructors use to introduce the recursive procedure is the computation of the factorial. Revise Example 8.1 to develop a recursive procedure for computing the factorial of M.

Solution

```
INTEGER FUNCTION FACT (M);

BEGIN
    (* CONTINUE PROCESSING PRODUCTS UNTIL M = 0 *)
    IF (M <> 0)
    THEN
        FACT := M * FACT(M - 1)
    ELSE
        FACT := 1;

END; (* END FACT *)
```

This pseudocode virtually duplicates the pseudocode of the preceding solved problem. The only difference is that a product of the integers is obtained rather than a sum of the integers. The evaluation of the factorial follows the logic presented in the previous problem.

In studying a large number of examples of subprograms, it is often desirable to have a number of the subprograms related to each other in order to make the examples somewhat more interesting and unified. The next series of examples is related to scheduling theory.

Scheduling theory is the study of the sequencing of a number of tasks on a set of facilities in order to optimize some measure of effectiveness. One problem in this field that has been studied extensively is sometimes called the **N-job—single machine problem.**

Assume that there are N jobs to be scheduled on one machine and the machine can only work on one job at a time. The objective is then to sequence the N jobs in such a manner as to minimize or maximize some effectiveness measure.

8.12

In the N-job–single machine problem, each of the jobs has a due date, D(I) which is the time at which job I is to be completed. For any given sequence, the actual completion times of the jobs can be compared to these due dates in order to determine the effectiveness of the sequence, or schedule.

If C(I) represents the time at which job I is completed for a given sequence of jobs, the lateness, L(I), of job I is the difference between the completion date and the due date, i.e., $L(I) = C(I) - D(I)$. Note that the lateness measure can be a positive or a negative value. If job I is completed after the due date,

L(I) is positive; if job I is completed before the due date, L(I) is negative. The mean lateness is then

$$\frac{\sum\limits_{I=1}^{N} L(I)}{N}$$

Develop REAL FUNCTION ALATE(D, C, N) that will compute the mean lateness of the N jobs of this sequence when array C contains the corresponding time of each job of the sequence. Assume that the elements of an array D are ordered according to a particular job sequence and that the Ith element of the array represents the due date of job I.

Solution

```
REAL FUNCTION ALATE (D, C, N);

    (* D = DUE DATE OF JOB,
       C = COMPLETION DATE OF JOB,
       N = NUMBER OF JOBS *)

BEGIN
    SUM := 0;
    FOR I := 1 STEP 1 UNTIL N DO (* FIND TOTAL LATENESS *)
        SUM := SUM + C(I) - D(I);

    ALATE := SUM / N; (* FIND AVERAGE LATENESS OF ALL JOBS *)

END; (* END ALATE *)
```

SUM is initialized to 0 and used to accumulate the sum of the N values of lateness determined as the difference between completion date C(I) and due date D(I). SUM will contain the total lateness value of the N jobs. The last statement of the function computes the average lateness and assigns the result to ALATE.

8.13

In addition to the average or mean lateness of a schedule, the maximum lateness of any job in the sequence is another measure of effectiveness.

Develop REAL FUNCTION XLATE(D, C, N) that will provide the largest or maximum value of lateness for any job in the sequence. The three parameters of the function are the same as those for FUNCTION ALATE of the preceding problem.

Solution

```
REAL FUNCTION XLATE (D, C, N);

   (* FIND THE MAXIMUM LATENESS IN THE SEQUENCE *)

BEGIN
   BIG := C(1) - D(1); (* CALCULATE LATENESS OF JOB 1 *)

   (* COMPUTE LATENESS OF SUCCEEDING JOBS *)
   FOR I := 2 STEP 1 UNTIL N DO
   BEGIN
       IF ((C(I) - D(I)) > BIG)
       THEN
           BIG := C(I) - D(I);
   END;

   XLATE := BIG;

END; (* END XLATE *)
```

Although the algorithm is patterned after that of the preceding problem, there are three major differences:

1. The starting value of the LOCAL variable, BIG, is set equal to the difference between the completion time of the first job, $C(1)$, and its due date, $D(1)$. Thus the initial value of BIG is the lateness of the first job.
2. Each successive difference of $D(I) - C(I)$ is compared with BIG via a conditional statement. The value of BIG is then changed only if the lateness of the Ith job is larger than the existing value of BIG.
3. The iteration statement starts at I equal to 2. Since BIG is initialized to the lateness of job 1, there is no need to compare $C(1) - D(1)$ with BIG.

8.14

Another interesting measure of effectiveness in the N-job–single machine problem is the number of jobs that are late.

Develop INTEGER FUNCTION NLATE(D, C, N) that will return the number of late jobs in the sequence of N jobs.

Solution

```
INTEGER FUNCTION NLATE (D, C, N);

   (* FIND THE NUMBER OF LATE JOBS *)

BEGIN
   NR := 0;
   FOR I := 1 STEP 1 UNTIL N DO
       IF (C(I) > D(I)) (* JOB IS LATE *)
```

```
         THEN
              NR := NR + 1;

    NLATE := NR;

END; (* END NLATE *)
```

In contrast to functions ALATE and XLATE, this procedure is an INTEGER function. It is similar to ALATE in that NR is a LOCAL variable that is used to accumulate the number of late jobs. The testing criteria is $C(I) - D(I)$. If the difference is greater than 0, the job is late and the counter NR is incremented.

8.15

Given a sequence of N jobs with due dates and completion dates in arrays DD and CC, respectively, develop an algorithm that will determine the average late time, maximum late time, and the number of late jobs for the N jobs.

Solution

```
PROGRAM PROBLEM 8.15;

(* CALCULATE AVERAGE LATE TIME, MAX LATE TIME, NUMBER OF LATE JOBS *)

BEGIN
    READ (N); (* INPUT NUMBER OF JOBS *)

    WRITE ("ECHO CHECK");

    (* INPUT AND ECHO DUE DATES AND COMPLETION DATES *)
    FOR I := 1 STEP 1 UNTIL N DO
    BEGIN
        READ (CC(I), DD(I));
        WRITE (CC(I), DD(I));
    END;

    AVERAGE := ALATE (DD,CC,N); (* FIND AVERAGE LATENESS *)

    LATEST := XLATE (DD,CC,N); (* FIND MAXIMUM LATENESS *)

    NUMBER LATE := NLATE (DD,CC,N); (* FIND NUMBER LATE *)

    (* OUTPUT RESULTS *)
    WRITE ("AVERAGE =", AVERAGE,
           "LATEST JOB =", LATEST,
           "NUMBERLATE =", NUMLATE );

END. (* END PROBLEM 8.15 *)
```

The solution fills the arrays DD and CC with the due dates and completion dates, respectively. After echo-checking the input data, the previously derived FUNCTIONS ALATE, XLATE, and NLATE are called to calculate the desired information, which is then printed out as the variables AVERAGE, LATEST, and NUMLATE.

8.16

Develop SUBROUTINE COPY(A, B, N, M) that will copy the contents of the two-dimension array A into the two-dimension array B. The parameters M and N refer to the number of rows and the number of columns, respectively.

Solution

```
SUBROUTINE COPY (A, B, M, N);

   (* COPY ARRAY A INTO ARRAY B *)

BEGIN
   FOR I := 1 STEP 1 UNTIL M DO
      FOR J := 1 STEP 1 UNTIL N DO
         B(I,J) := A(I,J);

END; (* END COPY *)
```

SUBROUTINE COPY consists of a nested FOR iteration on the control variables I and J for the rows and columns, respectively.

The next three problems are related to the functions based upon scheduling theory as presented in Solved Problems 8.12 through 8.15. They are interesting illustrations of subprograms and provide a unifying theme for a number of problems.

8.17

Solved Problems 8.12 through 8.15 used an array of job completion times as a parameter of the functions. This problem provides a method of computing these completion times, given the processing times of the job. The processing time of a job is the time necessary to perform the tasks associated with that job. In processing a sequence of jobs on a single machine, it can be shown that there is no advantage in delaying the start of a job if the machine is not busy. In other words, the next job should start as soon as the present one is finished.

An array P contains the processing times with the order of the elements in P corresponding to the job sequence. The respective completion time is to be stored in array C. Assuming that the start of processing occurs at time 0, the completion time of the first job is equal to the processing time of that job, i.e., $C(1) = P(1)$. The completion time of any other job is then $C(I) = C(I-1) + P(I)$.

Develop SUBROUTINE CMPLT (P, C, N) that will create the C array, given the P array and the number of elements, N.

Solution

```
SUBROUTINE CMPLT (P, C, N);

    (* P = PROCESSING TIMES OF JOBS,
       C = CALCULATED COMPLETION TIME,
       N = NUMBER OF JOBS *)

BEGIN
    C(1) := P(1);
    FOR I := 2 STEP 1 UNTIL N DO
        C(I) := C(I-1) + P(I);

END; (* END CMPLT *)
```

Supplementary Problems

8.18
The surface of a sphere of radius, R, and diameter, D, is equal to $S = 4\pi R^2 = \pi D^2 = 12.57 R^2$. Develop a REAL FUNCTION to compute S.

8.19
When N is large, the computation of N! by the methods of Example 8.1 involves a number of multiplications. An approximate value of N can be calculated for large N by **Stirling's Formula,** which is

$$N! \approx \sqrt{2 * \pi * N} * (N/e)^N$$

in which $e = 2.71828$, the base of natural logarithms. Develop REAL FUNCTION STRLG that uses Stirling's Formula to approximate N!.

8.20
Solved Problem 8.8 presents an algorithm for economic service life. Using the information of the problem, it can easily be shown that the minimum average cost must be less than the operating cost of the next period. The economic service life can be considered to occur at that value of M that is less than N and for which, AC (M) < C. Develop INTEGER FUNCTION ESL (V, C) based on this relationship. While the algorithm is similar to that of Solved Problem 8.8, there is no need for the local variable ACP, one less statement is used in the initialization, and one less iteration of the loop needs to be performed when the economic service life is less than 50.

8.21

In scheduling theory, the sequence of jobs is determined by various algorithms. For the N-job–single machine problem, some rather simple scheduling algorithms will provide optimal schedules with respect to certain measures of effectiveness. For example, a sequence can be arranged by processing times in non-decreasing order, such that the processing time of job I is equal to or greater than the time for job I-1. This sequence will minimize the maximum lateness of all possible schedules for that set of jobs.

Develop SUBROUTINE SEQ (P, D, N) that will resequence the array P of processing times such that the processing times are non-decreasing. Each element of array D contains the due date of the job represented by the corresponding element of P. Therefore, the sequence of D must be rearranged to correspond to the new sequence of P.

8.22

Supplemental Problem 8.21 presented one sequencing rule for the N-job–single machine problem. Another interesting rule is to sequence the jobs by ascending due dates. This will minimize the maximum tardiness of any job in the sequence. In an algorithm similar to that of Problem 8.21, develop SUBROUTINE SEQD(P, D, N) that will sequence the jobs by ascending due dates.

9 *Structured Programming*

Before starting this chapter it would be a good idea for you to review Chapter 2, in which we presented an approach to problem solving and algorithm development through decomposition and flowcharting. In the subsequent chapters, we developed solutions to a large number of problems through the use of these concepts. Admittedly, the problems we presented have been small enough that you have not been forced to test or refine your problem-solving skills vis-à-vis a large problem.

In this chapter we will return to the task of problem solving per se and enhance your ability to attack a large problem by developing a structured approach to problem solving. We will revisit the grading problem and see how the solution would have evolved differently if we had used a structured approach.

By the end of this chapter you should be able to answer the following questions:

1. What is structured programming?
2. What is the top-down approach?
3. What is meant by stepwise refinement?
4. What are the structured programming standards?
5. How does structured programming aid readability and maintainability?

9.2 Structured Programming Philosophy

It might strike you as strange that we use the term philosophy in the title to this section. However, that is how we view structured programming. It is an attitude, not a recipe. There is no generally accepted, well-defined, unambiguous, finite set of steps to follow in approaching any large problem. We will, however, provide you with a set of guidelines and standards against which you can judge your success in using a structured programming approach.

Structured programming is a method for developing good quality software using a system engineering approach. The emphasis in structured programming is on design and not on code. Certainly the code is the end result of the entire process; however, we consider the code to be a mere implementation of our design or solution. Thus we would like our solution to be language independent, and even when a language has been specified, coding will be postponed to the very last.

Using a structured approach to problem solving requires that we approach the problem from a hierarchical point of view—repeatedly decomposing and refining the problem into successively lower levels in the hierarchy until the lowest satisfactory level is reached. What is a satisfactory level? It would be easy to state that this is the level at which the problem cannot be decomposed any further, but that could lead to an absurd level of refinement.

Rather, the satisfactory level has been reached when the subproblem is so well understood that no further refinement is required, that is, when it can be completely understood in its entirety by an individual. Therefore, we would expect that the required level of refinement will vary with the individual.

Some proponents of structured programming state there are some very specific guidelines for how big a subprogram should be. We will not attempt to quantify the size of a module or subprogram; we believe that it should be as large as the individual feels comfortable with. Decompose to the level of comprehension of the individual—not of the machine.

The suggested approach to structured programming is as follows:

1. Think of the problem in layers of more and more finely detailed functions.
2. Decompose the problem into "modules," "levels," or "levels of abstraction" having:
    A. An inner part, or "resources," which that module alone controls.
    B. An interface to lower level modules from which it receives its input. These inputs determine the state of the module. That is, any module at a given level should be completely oblivious to how a higher level module uses its output. It receives its functional support only from lower level modules.
3. Reduce the amount of interface between modules wherever possible and maximize use of internal, or protected, resources.
4. Implement multi-use modules wherever possible. However, these should be considered an extension of the language and not as part of the hierarchy that evolved from solving the problem.

As stated previously, a program developed using a structured approach has very distinctive qualities that are the inherent benefits of using the approach:

Reliability—A structured program contains very few bugs since its correctness can be determined by obtaining correct answers to functional questions about its structured constructs.

Maintainability—A structured program is easier to update or correct because of its hierarchical structure and well-defined communications protocols and interfaces.

Modifiability—A structured program is easier to change because of its modularity. It is also easy to extract pieces of a structured program for use in other programs because of its modularity. In addition, it is simple to incorporate modules from other programs where applicable.

Understandability—The flow of logic in a structured program is easier to follow because of its modularity and hierarchical design. Modules are logically complete entities that perform a single function, and they are always small enough to be understood.

Readability—Structured programs are easier to read because of a disciplined manner of assigning variable names, indentation, and the use of standard constructs.

Transferability—Structured programs can be transported between systems because only programming language constructs that are supported by compilers that meet the programming standards of the American National Standards Institute are used.

Efficiency—Structured programs are designed and written with a concern for the efficiency of the programmer and not solely for the machine on which they will be executed.

9.3 Top-Down Approach

Top-down design implies starting with a very broad description of an algorithm that completely defines the solution but does so in a very general way. Then the various portions of the algorithms are defined separately in greater detail. Some of these can still be rather general and they are then further defined. The process of development continues in this manner. Thus the system is developed as a hierarchical tree structure with the top segment containing the most general description and the lower levels providing successivly more detailed portions of the algorithm.

Top-down design is different from the traditional approach to computer programming. Traditionally, development of computer programs has started at the lowest level in the hierarchy. Several of these modules, or segments, are then combined into a higher level segment. That segment can then be combined with other modules to form an even higher segment. This corresponds to a **bottom-up design,** which is essentially a "many to one" approach contrasting with the "one to many" approach of top-down design. The bottom-up approach was used in developing the grading problem in previous chapters.

The algorithms developed under our concept of top-down design can be directly translated into a programming language following the rules of structured programming. The concept of top-down design is applicable to the development of larger and more complicated algorithms.

The process of constantly subdividing the problem, as proposed in the top-down approach, is called **stepwise refinement.** That is, the problem is repetitively refined into lower levels of hierarchy until the lowest level has been reached.

In applying the top-down approach to a large, complicated problem, it is helpful to graphically represent progress made in establishing and traversing the hierarchy that is derived. To this end we suggest use of the bubble diagram, as shown in Figure 9–1. In this diagram each level of hierarchy is delineated.

From a programming point of view, each bubble shown on the chart could be considered a separate subprogram for which a separate algorithm, flowchart, or pseudocode must be developed. Each bubble has a single entry path and a single exit. Each bubble receives its input, which determines its states, only from the level below it. Each bubble is indifferent to how the next higher level bubble utilizes its output, and it is completely independent of other bubbles on the same level.

For a truly large problem the bubble diagram can get quite enormous, filling hundreds of sheets of paper. As problems grow in complexity, it becomes imperative that some sort of coding system be used to uniquely identify each bubble and its position on the chart. Additional advantages are derived by making programming assignments against these codes and utilizing the same coding scheme in the users' manual and program documentation manuals.

A suggested coding scheme is presented in Figure 9-2. Note that the number of tasks, or bubbles, at each level is virtually unlimited by this scheme. The same is true of the number of levels. This is important since we don't want our coding scheme to limit our ability to decompose the problem as necessary.

Example 9.1

In a given coded bubble diagram, what information can be derived about the bubble whose code is "2.1.1.2.1".

Solution

We could easily analyze this number to the point of absurdity, but the significant and obvious fact is that this bubble is at the fifth level in the hierarchy, as evidenced by the four decimal points preceding the last digit. It is also subordinate to the second module (2.1) at the first level of decomposition. If necessary, its specific derivation could be traced without looking at a bubble diagram (e.g., Figure 9–2) as follows:

2.0	Level 1
2.1	Level 2
2.1.1	Level 3
2.1.1.2	Level 4
2.1.1.2.1	Level 5

Figure 9-1.
Bubble Diagram
Template

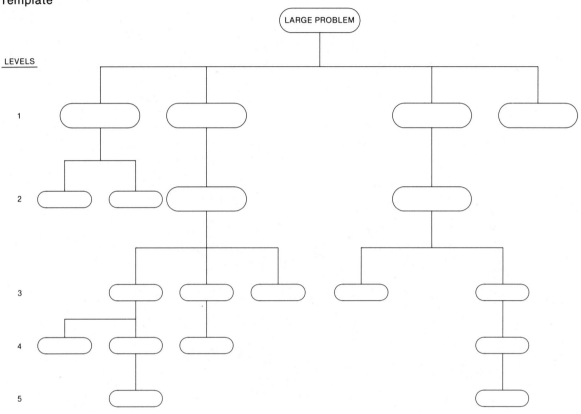

Figure 9-2.
Coded Bubble
Diagram

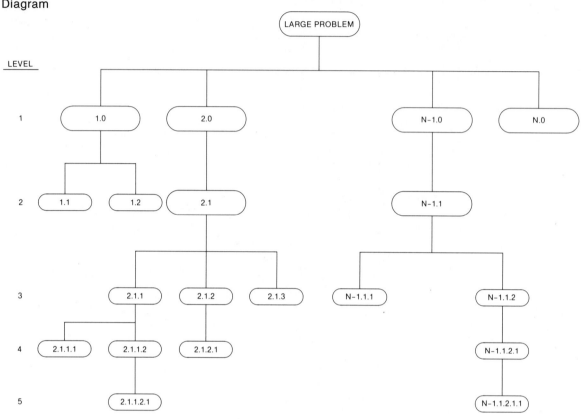

What the number does not tell us is how many subtasks were defined at any given level.

End Solution

The following exercises demonstrate the applicability of the top-down approach to nonprogramming types of problems.

Example 9.2

Graphically demonstrate through a bubble diagram of the results of the top-down approach used in designing this book.

Solution

The solution is provided simply enough by examining the table of contents for the book. The only chore is involved in creating the bubble diagram; however, since the table of contents was derived from a bubble diagram in the first place, the numbering system allows for direct transcription. The result is shown in Figure 9–3. For simplicity's sake, only the numbers of the chapters and sections are provided, and only the first three chapters are displayed.

End Solution

9.4 Structured Programming Constructs

In implementing structured programming techniques, we will restrict ourselves to the three basic constructs we have used so far. That is, the sequential, conditional, and iterative constructs, and combinations thereof, are the only acceptable mechanisms for programming under our structured rules.

The significant and unifying factor among these constructs is that they can be considered submodules within a module. Thus ultimately the solution to all problems is a structured combination of very low-level modules. Significantly, these constructs, like their parent modules, have a single entry point and a single exit point. This fact is the major contributor to what we continually refer to as a structured program.

These three constructs can be implemented in most high-level languages through the use of some form of the following statements for each construct:

1. Sequential—Assignment, I/O
2. Conditional—IF, Logical IF, IF-THEN-ELSE
3. Iterative—WHILE, REPEAT-UNTIL, DO, FOR

Figure 9–3.
Bubble Diagram
For Book
Decomposition

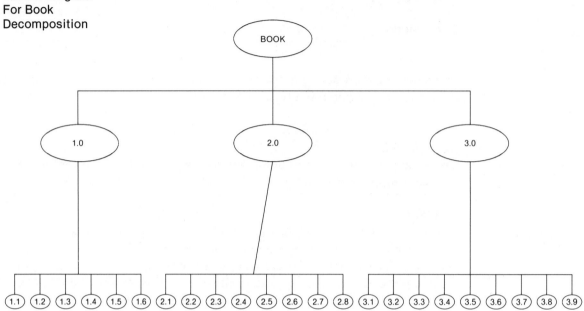

Because of the variations in high-level language statements, the actual implementation of the structured constructs can vary considerably among languages. The code generated from a given flowchart or pseudocode can be much more straightforward in one language than in another.

There is generally very little variation among languages in the implementation of assignment statements, although the assignment operator itself can vary. There can be a tremendous difference in I/O statements, but this would not be reflected as a change in the flowchart symbology. In the following discussion the referenced figure will present the solution flowchart and respective pseudocode side by side.

Consider the conditional construct in Figure 9–4a, which is representative of the swap function used within a sort algorithm for exchanging the contents of A(I) and A(J) when A(I) is greater than A(J). This would be directly implemented in code in both ALGOL and PASCAL.

However, in FORTRAN, the algorithm would be much easier to code if the flowchart were as shown in Figure 9–4b. Note the use of NOT in the pseudocode to reverse the logic. This is not to say that the forward logic pseudocode in Figure 9–4a is not directly implementable in FORTRAN; however, it would require the use of an additional GO TO in that language. Under our structured programming guidelines, the use of GO TOs should be minimized and used only where dictated by the language in the implementation of structured constructs, or where their use actually enhances the readability of the code.

The two versions shown in Figure 9–4 actually represent the same construct; only the logic is reversed. We will adhere to the forward logic shown in Figure 9–4a and leave it to the programmer to reverse logic where necessary in implementing the code.

Consider the iterative construct shown in Figure 9–5, which counts the number of inputs until NAME equals "ZZZZZ." It can be directly coded in ALGOL and PASCAL through the use of a WHILE statement. There is no comparable statement in FORTRAN (FORTRAN-77 does have a WHILE construct); however, the flowchart can be implemented through the use of an IF and two GO TOs in FORTRAN. In this case, the GO TOs are unavoidable.

The important point here is that for some languages, such as FORTRAN, there is no such thing as "GO TO-less" code. The algorithms presented in this book are directly implementable in all languages, although the logic might need to be reversed for some languages.

The following are some specific rules that should be adhered to when implementing code under the guise of structured programming:

1. Code segments should have a single entry point and a single exit point. This is consistent with our specifications for the three structured constructs.
2. There should be a limited amount of code per module. This aids readability and understandability and enforces our philosophy of modules being no larger than a person can understand.

Figure 9–4.
Conditional
Construct

Pseudocode

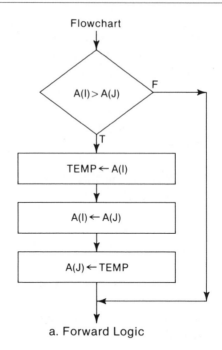

IF (A(I) > A(J))

THEN

    BEGIN

        TEMP : = A(I);

        A(I) : = A(J);

        A(J) : = TEMP;

    END;

a. Forward Logic

PSEUDOCODE

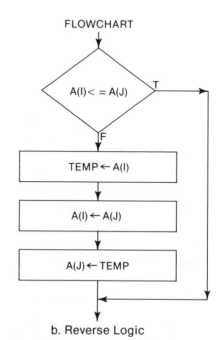

IF (NOT A(I) < = A(J))

THEN

    BEGIN

        TEMP : = A(I);

        A(I) : = A(J);

        A(J) : = TEMP;

    END;

b. Reverse Logic

Figure 9-5.
Iterative
Construct

PSEUDOCODE   FLOWCHART

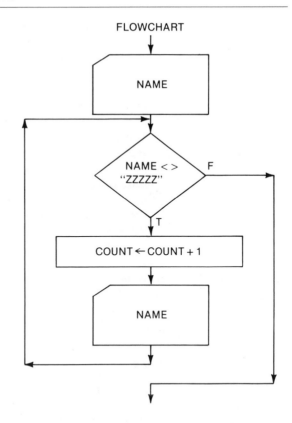

READ (NAME);

WHILE (NAME < > "ZZZZZ") DO

BEGIN

    COUNT : = COUNT + 1;

    READ (NAME);

END;

3. There should be no more than one statement per line, thus aiding readability and maintenance.

4. Indentation should be used freely to graphically indicate "span of control." Avoid the "code starts in Column 6" syndrome.

5. Control proceeds downward. That is, structure the program to be consistent with the hierarchy derived in solving the problem and avoid code that does not flow smoothly from top to bottom.

6. There should be no lateral transfers. Do not allow branches between code segments at the same level of hierarchy.

7. Make free use of comments to explain the situation, conditions, and purpose of code. Make the comments document the process and program flow. Such comments as "The following line increments I" are trite when the code (I←I + 1) is obvious. However, "Increment the sheepcount (I)" could be extremely meaningful.

9.5 Grading Problem

By now you probably have the output from this problem fairly well memorized (Figure 2-1), but let's take a fresh approach from the hierarchical point of view and apply our top-down design process. For convenience of reference, the required output is repeated as Table 9–1.

Table 9-1

Course: Math 351					Instructor: Mr. P. J. Smythe	
Section: 3					Room: 304	
Number of Tests: 3						
Number of Students: 10						

Student's Name	Test 1	Test 2	Test 3	CUM PTS	Average	Grade
Adams, M. E.	85	87	90	262	87.33	B
Barnes, L. J.	56	60	72	168	56.00	F
Carlton, P. G.	30	40	59	129	43.00	F
Driscoll, R.	98	99	100	297	99.00	A
Evans, S. T.	90	85	76	251	83.67	C
Orly, A. P.	50	65	78	193	64.33	D
Puget, S.	83	81	84	248	82.67	C
Ryan, M. A.	90	89	72	251	83.67	C
Silve, G. A.	60	65	65	190	63.33	D
Walton, J. J.	88	70	89	247	82.33	C
Test Mean	73.0	74.1	78.5	223.6		
Test Standard Deviation	22.38	17.38	12.42	51.22		

In looking at the report it should be obvious that we need to output a header or title information; that is, the course, instructor, section, and room data will have to be input, formatted, and output. We'll also need to know the number of tests and students for further processing of averages and standard deviation. For each student, we'll have to input data and perform calculations to derive statistics and grades. For each test, we'll have to retain data in order to calculate and output statistics.

To make the problem as general as possible and be able to handle N students and M tests, it is advisable that some sort of array structure be utilized. So it will be necessary to initialize these arrays and other parameters.

A bubble diagram of the grading problem is given in Figure 9–6. Look at the first level of the diagram. Analyzing the Initialize (1.0) module, we determine that we should only initialize those items at this stage that will be unique to the given course. That is, we should zero out the variables that will contain the cumulative sums for TESTS and CUMPTS. Let's postpone any discussion of the required data structures for now. If this is the major reason for the Initialize (1.0) module, it should be obvious that no futher decomposition is needed over and above what will take place within the module.

Analyzing our requirements for the Header (2.0) module, we also determine that there is no need for a subordinate module. We will simply input the header information, format it nicely, and output it. This module should make the number of tests and number of students for a given section known to all other modules.

Looking closely at the Calculate (3.0) module, we determine that several actions should take place. In general, we see that for every student we must input test scores, calculate cumulative points and average, assign a letter grade, and output the results. When we are done with all students, we must calculate statistics for each test and cumulative points.

The second level of Figure 9–6 illustrates the dual nature of the actions that will take place under the Calculate (3.0) module; they're divided into Studentcalc (3.1) and Coursecalc (3.2).

Now we come to the third level of the grading problem bubble diagram. First, the decomposition for Studentcalc (3.1): In Instudent (3.1.1) we collect the name and test scores for each student. In Studdata (3.1.2) we sum the points for each student and each test, and calculate the student's average. In Studgrade (3.1.3) we assign the actual letter grade. In Outstudent (3.1.4) we print the results for each student. These should be fairly simple modules requiring no further decomposition.

The decomposition for Coursecalc (3.2) has only two modules. In Coursedata (3.2.1) calculate the mean and standard deviation for each test and for the cumulative points. Outcourse (3.2.2) prints the results for the given course.

Figure 9-6.
Bubble Diagram
for Grading
Problem

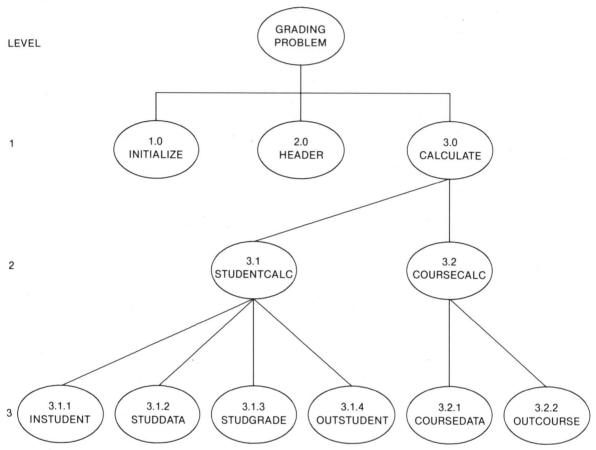

It is time now to give serious consideration to the data structures that must be used in implementing the solution based on the proposed decomposition. The problem statement required that we provide for up to M tests; therefore, an array, TEST (M) should be established. Simple INTEGER variables can be used for the number of tests, NUMTESTS, and the number of students, NUMSTUDS.

The cumulative points, average, and letter grade can be simple variables of the appropriate type kept local to the module STUDENTCALC. Although we have multiple students, it is not necessary to retain their data in an array if we provide for the calculation of each test mean and standard deviation by accumulating the test sum, SUMTEST, and test square, SUMTESTSQ. The same is true of the cumulative points, for which we use CUMPTS and CUMPTSSQ, respectively.

Again, since we have multiple tests, M, for which we provide statistics, it is natural to make SUMTEST and SUMTESTSQ arrays of size M.

Example 9.3

Develop the pseudocode for the grading problem, implementing the precepts of structured programming discussed in this chapter.

Solution

```
PROGRAM GRADING PROBLEM;

(**** DECLARE SUBROUTINES ****)
(* DECOMPOSITION MODULE 1.0 *)
SUBROUTINE  INITIALIZE  (SUMTESTS,   SUMTESTSQ,   SUMCUMPTS,   SUMCUMPTSSQ,
                         NUMTESTS);
BEGIN
   FOR I := 1 STEP 1 UNTIL NUMTESTS DO (* ZERO ALL ARRAYS *)
   BEGIN
       SUMTESTS (I) := 0;
       SUMTESTSQ (I) := 0;
   END;

   (* ZERO CUM VARIABLES *)
   SUMCUMPTS := 0;
   SUMCUMPTSSQ := 0;

END; (* END INITIALIZE *)


(* DECOMPOSITION MODULE 2.0 *)
SUBROUTINE HEADER (NUMTESTS, NUMSTUDS, DONE);
BEGIN
   READ (COURSE); (* INPUT COURSE NAME *)
```

```
            IF (COURSE <> "ZZZZZ") (* TEST FOR TRAILER VALUE *)
            THEN
                BEGIN
                    READ (INSTRNAME, SECTION, ROOM); (* INPUT HEADER DATA *)

                    READ (NUMTESTS, NUMSTUDS); (* INPUT CLASS DATA *)

                    (* OUTPUT HEADER DATA *)
                    WRITE ("COURSE:", COURSE, "INSTRUCTOR NAME:", INSTRNAME);
                    WRITE ("SECTION:", SECTION, "ROOM:", ROOM);
                    WRITE ("NUMBER OF TESTS:", NUMTESTS);
                    WRITE ("NUMBER OF STUDENTS:", NUMSTUDS);
                    WRITE ("STUDENTS", ("TEST",I := 1,NUMTESTS),
                        "CUM", "AVERAGE", "GRADE");
                    WRITE ("NAME", (I, I:= 1,NUMTESTS));

                    DONE := FALSE; (* RESET TERMINATION FLAG *)

                END (* END IF COURSE <> "ZZZZZ" *)
            ELSE
                DONE := TRUE; (* SET TERMINATION FLAG *)

END; (* END HEADER *)

(* DECOMPOSITION MODULE 3.0 *)
SUBROUTINE CALCULATE (SUMTESTS, SUMTESTSQ, SUMCUMPTS, SUMCUMPTSSQ,
                NUMTESTS, NUMSTUDS);
BEGIN
    (* PROCESS ALL STUDENT AND COURSE DATA *)
    (* TEST TO ENSURE CLASS HAS STUDENTS AND TESTS *)
    (* THIS PRECLUDES POSSIBLE DIVISION BY ZERO *)
    IF (NUMSTUDS <> 0 AND NUMTESTS <> 0)
    THEN
        BEGIN
            (* PROCESS EACH STUDENT IN THIS COURSE *)


            FOR I := 1 STEP 1 UNTIL NUMSTUDS DO
                CALL STUDENTCALC (SUMCUMPTS, SUMCUMPTSSQ, SUMTESTS,
                    SUMTESTSQ, NUMSTUDS, NUMTESTS);

            (* PROCESS COURSE STATISTICS *)
            CALL COURSECALC (SUMCUMPTS, SUMCUMPTSSQ, SUMTESTS,
                SUMTESTSQ, NUMSTUDS, NUMTESTS);

END; (* END CALCULATE *)


(* DECOMPOSITION MODULE 3.1 *)
SUBROUTINE STUDENTCALC (SUMCUMPTS, SUMCUMPTSSQ, SUMTESTS, SUMTESTSQ,
                    NUMSTUDS, NUMTESTS);
BEGIN
    CALL INSTUDENT (NAME, TEST, NUMTESTS); (* INPUT STUDENT DATA *)

    (* PROCESS STUDENT DATA *)
```

```
            CALL STUDDATA (TEST, NUMTESTS, SUMTESTS, SUMTESTSQ, CUMPTS, AVERAGE,
                           SUMCUMPTS, SUMCUMPTSSQ);

            GRADE := STUDGRADE (AVERAGE); (* FIND STUDENT'S LETTER GRADE *)

            (* OUTPUT INDIVIDUAL STUDENT'S DATA *)
            CALL OUTSTUDENT (NAME, TEST, NUMTESTS, CUMPTS, AVERAGE, GRADE);

        END; (* END STUDENTCALC *)


        (* DECOMPOSITION MODULE 3.1.1 *)
        SUBROUTINE INSTUDENT (NAME, TESTS, NUMTESTS);
        BEGIN
            (* INPUT STUDENT NAME AND TEST SCORES *)
            READ (NAME, (TESTS(I),I := 1,NUMTESTS));

        END; (* END INSTUDENT *)

        (* DECOMPOSITION MODULE 3.1.2 *)
        SUBROUTINE STUDDATA (TEST, NUMTESTS, SUMTESTS, SUMTESTSQ, CUMPTS,
                             AVERAGE, SUMCUMPTS, SUMCUMPTSSQ);
        BEGIN
            (* COLLECT DATA FOR STUDENT AND TEST STATISTICS *)
            CUMPTS := 0;
            FOR I := 1 STEP 1 UNTIL NUMTESTS DO
            BEGIN
                CUMPTS := CUMPTS + TEST(I);
                SUMTESTS(I) := SUMTESTS(I) + TEST(I);
                SUMTESTSQ(I) := SUMTESTSQ(I) + TEST(I)**2;
            END;

            (* COLLECT DATA FOR COURSE STATISTICS *)
            SUMCUMPTS := SUMCUMPTS + CUMPTS;
            SUMCUMPTSSQ := SUMCUMPTSSQ + CUMPTS**2;

            AVERAGE := CUMPTS / NUMTESTS; (* FIND STUDENT AVERAGE *)

        END; (* END STUDDATA *)


        (* DECOMPOSITION MODULE 3.2 *)
        SUBROUTINE COURSECALC (SUMCUMPTS, SUMCUMPTSSQ, SUMTESTS, SUMTESTSQ,
                          NUMSTUDS, NUMTESTS);
        BEGIN
            (* CALCULATE COURSE STATISTICS *)
            CALL COURSEDATA (SUMTESTS, SUMTESTSQ, TESTMEAN, TESTSD, SUMCUMPTS,
                          SUMCUMPTSSQ, CUMMEAN, CUMSD, NUMSTUDS, NUMTESTS);

            (* OUTPUT COURSE STATISTICS *)
            CALL OUTCOURSE (TESTMEAN, TESTSD, CUMMEAN, CUMSD, NUMTESTS);

        END; (* END COURSECALC *)
```

```
(* DECOMPOSITION MODULE 3.1.4 *)
SUBROUTINE OUTSTUDENT (NAME, TEST, NUMTESTS, CUMPTS, AVERAGE, GRADE);
BEGIN
   (* OUTPUT STUDENT STATISTICS *)
   WRITE (NAME, (TEST(I),I := 1,NUMTESTS), CUMPTS, AVERAGE, GRADE);

END; (* END OUTSTUDENT *)


(* DECOMPOSITION MODULE 3.2.1 *)
SUBROUTINE COURSEDATA (SUMTESTS, SUMTESTSQ, TESTMEAN, TESTSD,
       SUMCUMPTS, SUMCUMPTSSQ, CUMMEAN, CUMSD, NUMSTUDS, NUMTESTS);
BEGIN
   (* COLLECT TEST STATISTICS FOR COURSE *)
   FOR I := 1 STEP 1 UNTIL NUMTESTS DO
   BEGIN
       TESTMEAN(I) := SUMTESTS(I) / NUMSTUDS;
       TESTSD(I) := SQRT(SUMTESTSQ(I) / NUMSTUDS - TESTMEAN(I)**2);
   END;

   (* CALCULATE COURSE MEAN AND STANDARD DEVIATION *)
   CUMMEAN := SUMCUMPTS / NUMSTUDS;
   CUMSD := SQRT(SUMCUMPTSSQ / NUMSTUDS - CUMMEAN**2);

END; (* END COURSEDATA *)

(* DECOMPOSITION MODULE 3.2.2 *)
SUBROUTINE OUTCOURSE (TESTMEAN, TESTSD, CUMMEAN, CUMSD, NUMTESTS);
BEGIN
   (* OUTPUT TEST AND COURSE MEAN *)
   WRITE ((TESTMEAN(I),I := 1,NUMTESTS), CUMMEAN);

   (* OUTPUT TEST AND COURSE STANDARD DEVIATION *)
   WRITE ((TESTSD(I),I := 1,NUMTESTS), CUMSD);

END; (* END OUTCOURSE *)

(**** DECLARE FUNCTIONS ****)
(* DECOMPOSITION MODULE 3.1.3 *)
ALPHA FUNCTION STUDGRADE (AVERAGE);
BEGIN
   IF (AVERAGE >= 60)
   THEN
       BEGIN
           IF (AVERAGE >= 70)
           THEN
               BEGIN
                   IF (AVERAGE >= 85)
                   THEN
                       BEGIN
                           IF (AVERAGE >= 95)
                           THEN
                               STUDGRADE := "A"
```

```
                                ELSE
                                    STUDGRADE := "B";
                             END
                        ELSE
                            STUDGRADE := "C";
                    END
                ELSE
                    STUDGRADE := "D";
            END
        ELSE
            STUDGRADE := "F";

END; (* END STUDGRADE *)

(***** MAIN PROGRAM *****)
BEGIN
    CALL HEADER (NUMTESTS, NUMSTUDS, DONE);

    CALL INITIALIZE (SUMTESTS, SUMTESTSQ, SUMCUMPTS, SUMCUMPTSSQ,
                    NUMTESTS);

    (* REPEAT FOR ALL COURSES UNTIL TRAILER VALUE READ *)
    WHILE (NOT DONE) DO
    BEGIN
        CALL CALCULATE (SUMTESTS, SUMTESTSQ, SUMCUMPTS, SUMCUMPTSSQ,
                        NUMTESTS, NUMSTUDS);

        CALL INITIALIZE (SUMTESTS, SUMTESTSQ, SUMCUMPTS, SUMCUMPTSSQ,
                        NUMTESTS);

        CALL HEADER (NUMTESTS, NUMSTUDS, DONE);

    END; (* END WHILE NOT DONE *)

END. (* END GRADING PROBLEM *)
```

At our first glance at the final decomposition, we see that the main module calls on three other modules. In order to make our solution as general as possible, we would like the program to execute for any number of courses. Since we don't know how many this will be, we elect to use the trailer card technique of terminating the iteration. We assume we will terminate when the course name is read as "ZZZZZ." Since the course name is read by HEADER, we will pass a BOOLEAN variable, DONE, as a formal parameter to indicate that the program is to be terminated.

Note that the given solution iterates the three calls on INITIALIZE, HEADER, and CALCULATE in sequence until terminated by DONE = TRUE. At this point you should be able to follow the algorithm to completion to reproduce the results in Table 9-1. Set up the recommended data structures as required by each subroutine and step through the logic with the given test data. The reader should compare the results of this top-down approach with that of the bottom-up approach provided in Chapter 8.

9.6 Summary   In this chapter, we presented the concepts of structured problem solving through the use of a top-down, disciplined approach. Before proceeding, make sure you understand these concepts and make a personal commitment to exercise these ideas in your approach to all problems. This includes not only problems that find their solution through use of a computer, but also problems you confront in your daily life that don't have a computer application. These could include everything from overhauling a car engine to building a chair.

Remember that structured problem solving is not an algorithm or a set of rules; it is a philosophy by which a problem is approached.

10   Sorting

Quite frequently in our lives we find it necessary to arrange information in some order. For instance, the telephone company organizes its customers alphabetically when it generates a telephone book. The dean of a college requires a list of students organized by grade point average in order to determine who is on the Dean's List. In our own personal affairs we might arrange our class papers by date, or cancelled checks by check number.

This process of rearranging a list of items into some prescribed order or sequence is known as **sorting.** In fact, sorting has become so mechanical and natural to us that we would have difficulty describing the method we use. In this chapter, we will discuss several different algorithms for sorting data on a computer.

Before we introduce sorting algorithms, it is necessary that you understand several of the terms applied to information stored in a computer. These terms will be discussed in detail in Chapter 12; however, the following definitions and explanations will suffice for now:

A **data item** is the smallest element of identifiable information. For instance, a person's age, when stored in a computer, would be considered a data item.

A **record** consists of a collection of related data items. Therefore, a person's name, age, and social security number, when stored together in a computer, would compose a record.

A **file** is a collection of records that are related because they contain the same class of information. If the name, age, and social security number of a group of people were stored together, they would compose a file.

The specific location within a record where a particular data item is located is called a **field.** Therefore, a record consisting of name, age, and social security number contains three fields, with the person's social security number in the third field.

The particular data item that uniquely identifies a record within a file is the **key.** In the preceding example, the key would have to be the person's social security number since it is always unique, but the name and age might not be.

In a formal sense, then, we can say that sorting is the process of rearranging the records within a file by applying a set of rules to one of the fields of the record. The specific field on which the sort takes place is called the **sort key.**

In some situations, the file merely consists of a list of items—for example, the names of students in a class. In most computer applications, such lists would be stored in arrays. Thus, we might have occasion to sort records in a file, items in a list, or elements in an array. The concepts of sorting, however, are the same and we will use all of these phrases in our discussions.

The algorithms we develop are applicable to ALPHA, INTEGER, or REAL data without modification.

Sorting occurs in applications of all types, but one of the most common requirements for sorting is in the area of data processing. In fact, it has been estimated that in some commercial data processing systems, as much as 40 percent of the computer's time is devoted to sorting data. However, there are also applications in which the use of sorting might not at first be apparent.

There are a large number of sorts that can be performed on the computer. The advantages of one sort over another will depend upon a number of factors related to the specific problem. In order to provide you with several methods of sorting, we have included a number of sort algorithms. Most of the more common ones that the beginning programmer might expect to encounter are discussed in this chapter.

10.2 The General Concept of Sorting

Since most readers might not have considered in depth the operations involved in sorting, it is worthwhile to analyze the general sorting process before the specific algorithms are presented in the following sections. First, we will consider a very simple example that we will sort by hand. It should help your understanding of sorting if you perform this simple sort before you study the solution. Be aware of the method that you use and attempt to keep track of the individual steps that you mentally perform in rearranging the list.

Example 10.1
Sort the following sequence of numbers in ascending order (i.e., lowest to highest value):

31   22   16   25   42   38   43

Try to determine the exact sequence of operations needed to perform the sort.

Solution

Obviously, not all of us would use precisely the same method. This solution describes only one.

The first operation of the sort is to scan the list to find the smallest number. For a small list we would mentally examine each of the items in the list and remember the smallest value that we see. If the list consisted of many numbers, we would probably write the smallest of the first few numbers down on a piece of paper. Then we would compare each successive number to the smallest number found to date. When a smaller number was found, we would write it down and compare the rest of the items in the list to that number.

When we finished scanning the list, we would have the smallest number. We could then start a new list with this number as the first one in the list. The smallest number in the original list could then be deleted to assure that it would not be a candidate for the second number in the new list. Then we would search the list for the next lowest number. When found, it would be added to the new list and scratched from the original one. This process would continue until there were no remaining items in the original list.

Figure 10–1 follows this example through each of the steps and shows the status of both lists after each number is transferred from the first list to the sorted list. During the first pass, the number 16 is found to be the smallest. It is placed in the sorted list and crossed out in the original list. The result is depicted in Figure 10–1a. After the second smallest number (22) is placed on the sorted list, the sorted list appears as in Figure 10–1b. The results for each of the steps are shown in a-f of Figure 10–1. The final sorted list is shown in Figure 10–1g.

End Solution

Figure 10-1.
Sample of Manual
Sort

a. Original List	31	22	~~16~~	25	42	38	43
Sorted List	16						
b. Revised List	31	~~22~~	~~16~~	25	42	38	43
Sorted List	16	22					
c. Revised List	31	~~22~~	~~16~~	~~25~~	42	38	43
Sorted List	16	22	25				
d. Revised List	~~31~~	~~22~~	~~16~~	~~25~~	42	38	43
Sorted List	16	22	25	31			
e. Revised List	~~31~~	~~22~~	~~16~~	~~25~~	42	~~38~~	43
Sorted List	16	22	25	31	38		
f. Revised List	~~31~~	~~22~~	~~16~~	~~25~~	~~42~~	~~38~~	43
Sorted List	16	22	25	31	38	42	
g. Revised List	~~31~~	~~22~~	~~16~~	~~25~~	~~42~~	~~38~~	~~43~~
Sorted List	16	22	25	31	38	42	43

The solution to Example 10.1 might seem too formalized for such a small data set. Although this detailed process might not be necessary for this example, it would be necessary in order to hand sort a list of one hundred elements or more. We're looking at this small data set because it is an absolute necessity to understand such detailed steps if we are going to develop a sorting algorithm that can be translated into a computer program.

10.3 The Selection Sort

The procedure described in Example 10.1 is actually very similar to one of the many possible sorts that can be performed on the computer. This method is often called the **selection sort.** Although it is a rather inefficient sort, it is a useful one to start our study of sorting. It follows the manner in which a number of people would handle the sort by manual methods and it is an easy one to program.

The selection sort algorithm selects elements from the first list according to a specified rule and creates a second, ordered list. To sequence a list in ascending order, the algorithm searches the original array for the smallest value and moves this value into the first position of a second array. The element in the original array is then deleted by "crossing out" the value of that element. Then the algorithm searches for the next smallest element (which is now the smallest element in the revised original array). This process is continued until all items in the original list have been transferred into the new list. The resulting new list then contains the values in ascending order.

To implement the selection sort, it is necessary to have some means to cross out the value in the original array. One way to implement this on a computer is to store some artificial or previously defined dummy value in that element. In choosing this dummy value, it is only necessary to be sure that it is outside the range of the data. For example, if all of the data elements are expected to be less than 10^{20}, the algorithm might use 10^{20} as the dummy value. After a number is copied into the second array, that number in the original array would be assigned the value of 10^{20} (i.e., be crossed out).

Example 10.2

Apply the selection sort to the following data, in which each element is a two-character symbol (show each of the intermediate steps):

JM   LD   JH   DW   NM   BF   DS   PW

Solution

The selection sort implies that there are two lists: the original list and the resultant sorted list. We will refer to these lists as A1 and A2, respectively. After selecting the smallest data element in A1 and copying it to A2, the cor-

Figure 10-2.
Sample of Manual
Sort

		A1/A2								
a.	Original List	A1	JM	LD	JH	DW	NM	★ ★	DS	PW
	Sorted List	A2	BF							
b.	Original List	A1	JM	LD	JH	DW	NM	★ ★	★ ★	PW
	Sorted List	A2	BF	DS						
c.	Original List	A1	JM	LD	JH	★ ★	NM	★ ★	★ ★	PW
	Sorted List	A2	BF	DS	DW					
d.	Original List	A1	JM	LD	★ ★	★ ★	NM	★ ★	★ ★	PW
	Sorted List	A2	BF	DS	DW	JH				
e.	Original List	A1	★ ★	LD	★ ★	★ ★	NM	★ ★	★ ★	PW
	Sorted List	A2	BF	DS	DW	JH	JM			
f.	Original List	A1	★ ★	★ ★	★ ★	★ ★	NM	★ ★	★ ★	PW
	Sorted List	A2	BF	DS	DW	JH	JM	LD		
g.	Original List	A1	★ ★	★ ★	★ ★	★ ★	★ ★	★ ★	★ ★	PW
	Sorted List	A2	BF	DS	DW	JH	JM	LD	NM	
h.	Original List	A1	★ ★	★ ★	★ ★	★ ★	★ ★	★ ★	★ ★	★ ★
	Sorted List	A2	BF	DS	DW	JH	JM	LD	NM	PW

responding element in A1 is deleted by assigning it a dummy value of "★★," which is assumed to be larger than any of the strings in A1. Each time a data item is added to A2, the respective data element in A1 is set to ★★.

After the first element is moved into A2, A1 and A2 appear as in Figure 10–2a. Observe that BF has been moved to the second list, while ★★ has been substituted in the corresponding position of A1. The result of each subsequent step is shown in b h of Figure 10–2. At the conclusion of the procedure, the sorted list is A2 and the original list, A1, is completely filled with ★★.

End Solution

As we discuss each of the sorts, we will present the algorithm to perform the operation. Due to the wide use of sort methods, it is convenient to have them in a form in which they can be used for a number of applications. In order to do this, we will present all sort algorithms as subroutines (procedures).

Example 10.3
Write a subroutine to implement the selection sort. The three parameters of the subroutine should be the original input array, the sorted output array, and the number of items in the arrays.

Solution

```
SUBROUTINE SELSORT (A1, A2, N);

    (* A1 = ORIGINAL INPUT ARRAY,
       A2 = OUTPUT SORTED ARRAY,
        N = NUMBER OF ITEMS IN ARRAYS *)

BEGIN
    DUMMY: = 10**20; (* ALL ITEMS ARE ASSUMED LESS THAN DUMMY *)

    INDEX := 1;
    K := 0;
    FOR I := 1 STEP 1 UNTIL N DO
    BEGIN
        SMALL := DUMMY;
        FOR J := 1 STEP 1 UNTIL N DO
            IF (A1(J) < SMALL)
            THEN
                BEGIN
                    SMALL := A1(J);
                    INDEX := J;
                END;

        K := K + 1; (* K IS INDEX INTO ARRAY A2 *)

        A2(K) := SMALL;
        A1(INDEX) := DUMMY;
    END;

END; (* END SELSORT *)
```

The subroutine is named SELSORT. The three parameters are the input array, A1, the output array, A2, and the number of elements N. Thus the reference to the subroutine will be SELSORT (A1, A2, N). It is assumed that all values in A1 are less than 10^{20}, so the artificial or dummy, value used to delete elements from consideration in A1 is 10^{20}. This value is calculated once and assigned to the variable DUMMY to eliminate the need to recalculate at each pass.

The variable K is the index to A2, while J is the index to A1. The control variable I is used to keep track of the number of times that A1 is searched. Each time the list is searched, the variable SMALL is used to hold the value of the smallest element of the array that is found. Prior to each iteration through A1, SMALL is set equal to DUMMY. Since it was predetermined that all actual data items are less than DUMMY, any value in the array not transferred to A2 will be smaller than DUMMY.

Each element of A1 is then compared against SMALL. If A1(J) is less than SMALL, SMALL is assigned the value of A1(J) and the index of the element containing that value J is assigned to INDEX.

At the conclusion of the iteration on J, the smallest remaining value is in SMALL, and the location of the index of the element of A1 containing that value is in INDEX. SMALL is then assigned to the next element of the array A2 after incrementing the index of that array, K, by 1. The corresponding element of A1, i.e., A1(INDEX), is set equal to DUMMY. The iteration on I then continues until all N elements of A1 have been transferred to A2.

End Solution

SUBROUTINE SELSORT presented in Example 10.3 will sort any array into ascending order. The algorithm for sorting a list into descending order (highest to lowest value) differs from SELSORT only in the logic used in the comparison statement in the sort. Solved Problem 10.1 applies the selection sort to arrange a list in descending order.

In some applications, it is necessary to retain the order of the original list, as well as to generate the sorted list. Unfortunately, the selection sort (as well as most sort methods) will destroy the order of the original array. One method of keeping the original list is to copy the contents of the list into another array before performing the sort. If sufficient storage space exists in the computer, this approach will work for all of the sorts. Solved Problem 10.2 presents an alternative technique that can sometimes be applied to the selection sort.

In evaluating the various sort methods, several characteristics will be interesting to us. Two particular terms that are commonly used are "pass" and "comparison."

A **pass** is one iteration through the list, file, or array while performing the sort operation. This can be considered an execution of the group of instructions constituting one loop through the program.

A **comparison** is the act of comparing two variables or two values. In discussing the number of comparisons involved in performing a sort, we refer to either the number of comparisons per pass or to the total number of comparisons. It is important to know the number of passes and comparisons since it provides some measure of the processing workload involved in performing a sort.

In order to determine the number of passes and comparisons required for the selection sort, we will re-examine SUBROUTINE SELSORT of Example 10.3. Each iteration on J results in a complete examination of the array A1. Therefore, each such iteration constitutes a pass.

There would be as many passes as there are iterations in the loop of the I variable. Since the I iteration goes from I = 1 to I = N, and there is no way to exit the iteration sooner, the number of passes is equal to N. Each of the passes results in a comparison for the value of J. Thus N, the upper bound of the J iteration, indicates the number of comparisons per pass. With N passes, the total number of comparisons is equal to $N*N$, or N^2.

Example 10.4
Determine the number of passes and the total number of comparisons when the selection sort is applied to the data of Example 10.2.

Solution
There are 8 elements to be sorted in the example. The number of passes is then equal to 8. The number of comparisons is 8 per pass and the total number of comparisons is 8^2, or 64.

These values can be verified by examining Figure 10–2. Note that there are 8 different configurations listed in the figure. Each of these corresponds to a pass through the data. During each pass, all elements of A1 are compared, resulting in 8 comparisons per pass.

End Solution

The advantage of the selection sort is its simplicity. The straightforward approach of the algorithm makes it easy to program. In addition, the algorithm follows at least one intuitive view of sorting. For small data sets, it is adequate. However, the selection sort has several disadvantages, including

a. It requires considerable storage space. The ordered list is stored in a second array. Therefore, a second array of size N is needed in order to implement the procedure. For a small data set, this will not create a problem, but for larger files or data sets, this could place heavy, and perhaps unreasonable, demand upon the available storage space.

b. The total number of passes and comparisons required to perform a selection sort is very high and is proportional to the square of the number of records. Since this is an indication of the workload involved, the processing time will be high as compared to other sorts. The effect of this inefficiency is greater for the larger data sets.

10.4 The Exchange Sort

There are a number of sorts that reduce the disadvantages of the selection sort. We will discuss two of these at this time: the exchange sort and the bubble sort.

The **exchange sort** algorithm rearranges a list by exchanging the items of the list according to a specified pattern. This sort does not require a second list, but rather the items of the original list are rearranged. This implies that the original list is destroyed during execution.

The procedure is started by comparing the first item in the list with the second—the first pass. If the second item is smaller than the first, the two data items are exchanged; otherwise, the two items retain their original position in the list. The third item is then compared with the first item. If the third item is smaller, the exchange of the first and third items is made; otherwise, the order remains the same. At this point, the first position contains the smallest of the first three items.

The first and fourth items are then compared and the procedure continues in this manner. At the conclusion of the first pass, the smallest item in the list is in the first position.

For the second pass, the procedure is then applied to all of the items in the list except the first one, i.e., the second item is compared to all items in the list except the first. At the end of the second pass, the second smallest value is in the second position.

In the third pass, the third item is the starting point. The procedure terminates when only one item remains and the rearranged list is in ascending order.

Example 10.5

Apply the exchange sort to arrange the following sequence of numbers into ascending order:

3.1   2.2   1.6   2.5   4.2   3.8   4.3

Solution

Figure 10–3 illustrates two conventions that we will follow in presenting the various sorts. First, comparisons are indicated by a line drawn under the list of items and connecting the two items that are being compared. A small vertical line is used to point to a specific item. Note that lines a through c in Figure 10–3 contain six of these vertical lines, indicating the six comparisons used in the first pass. Second, note that a new list is presented each time an exchange occurs in the list; when there is no exchange, the list will not be repeated. Since the first pass involves two exchanges, there are two lists in addition to the original order.

In the first comparison of the first pass, the first item in the list, 3.1, is compared with the second item, 2.2. Since the second item is smaller, the two values are exchanged in the list. The revised list is shown in line b. The third item is then compared with the first one. Since 1.6 is smaller than 2.2, the positions of the two values are exchanged to provide the list shown in line c. The fourth item is then compared with the first, 1.6, and no exchange takes place. The comparisons continue until all items have been compared with the first one. Since they are all larger than 1.6, no more exchanges are made in the first pass.

The first comparison of the second pass is shown in line d. The remaining items in the list are compared with the second item. When the third item, 2.2, is compared with the second item, 3.1, an exchange is made to obtain the list in line e. The fourth and following items are then compared with the second item. Since they are all larger than 2.2, no exchanges occur and the final order of the second pass is as shown in line e.

The third pass is shown in lines f and g of Figure 10-3. Please note that in the fourth pass, line h, no exchanges are made, but it is still necessary to go to the next pass, since the entire list is not yet in order. Even if the original list were in the correct order, all the other passes would still have to be made; the program doesn't "know" the list is in the correct order until all passes are made.

In the fifth pass, lines i and j, an exchange is made after the first comparison, but no exchanges are made in the sixth pass, line k. So the list is finally in the correct, ascending order. The summary of actions is shown in Figure 10-4.

The algorithm necessary for the exchange sort is only slightly more complex than that for the selection sort.

Example 10.6

Develop a subroutine that uses the exchange sort to sequence a list in ascending order. The two parameters are the one-dimension array to be sorted and the variable indicating the number of elements in the array.

Solution

```
SUBROUTINE EXCSORT (A, N);

    (* A = INPUT ARRAY TO BE SORTED AND RESULTING OUTPUT ARRAY,
       N = NUMBER OF ELEMENTS IN ARRAY A *)

BEGIN
    FOR I := 1 STEP 1 UNTIL (N - 1) DO
        FOR J := I + 1 STEP 1 UNTIL N DO
            IF (A(J) < A(I))
            THEN
                BEGIN
                    TEMP := A(I);
                    A(I) := A(J);
                    A(J) := TEMP;
                END;

END; (* END EXCSORT *)
```

Figure 10–3.
Sample of Manual Exchange Sort

									Exchange Following Comparison?
First Pass									
a. First Comparison	3.1	2.2	1.6	2.5	4.2	3.8	4.3		Yes
b. Second Comparison	2.2	3.1	1.6	2.5	4.2	3.8	4.3		Yes
c. Third through Sixth Comparisons	1.6	3.1	2.2	2.5	4.2	3.8	4.3		No
Second Pass									
d. First Comparison	1.6	3.1	2.2	2.5	4.2	3.8	4.3		Yes
e. Second through Fifth Comparisons	1.6	2.2	3.1	2.5	4.2	3.8	4.3		No
Third Pass									
f. First Comparison	1.6	2.2	3.1	2.5	4.2	3.8	4.3		Yes
g. Second through Fourth Comparisons	1.6	2.2	2.5	3.1	4.2	3.8	4.3		No
Fourth Pass									
h. Three Comparisons	1.6	2.2	2.5	3.1	4.2	3.8	4.3		No
Fifth Pass									
i. First Comparison	1.6	2.2	2.5	3.1	4.2	3.8	4.3		Yes
j. Second Comparison	1.6	2.2	2.5	3.1	3.8	4.2	4.3		No
Sixth Pass									
k. Only One Comparison	1.6	2.2	2.5	3.1	3.8	4.2	4.3		No

Figure 10–4.
Results of Each Pass of Manual Exchange Sort Sample

a. Start of pass	3.1	2.2	1.6	2.5	4.2	3.8	4.3
b. After first pass	1.6	3.1	2.2	2.5	4.2	3.8	4.3
c. After second pass	1.6	2.2	3.1	2.5	4.2	3.8	4.3
d. After third pass	1.6	2.2	2.5	3.1	4.2	3.8	4.3
e. After fourth pass	1.6	2.2	2.5	3.1	4.2	3.8	4.3
f. After fifth pass	1.6	2.2	2.5	3.1	3.8	4.2	4.3
g. After sixth pass	1.6	2.2	2.5	3.1	3.8	4.2	4.3

The subroutine will be denoted EXCSORT (A, N), where A is the array to be sorted and N is the variable indicating the number of items in the array. The entire algorithm consists of a double iteration loop. The bounds for the two iteration variables are important and these should be verified from an example. The iteration for the outer loop goes from $I = 1$ to $I = N - 1$, while the inner iteration on J starts at $I + 1$ and goes to N.

The main operation of the loop is the comparison of A(J) with A(I). For $I = 1$, the values A(2) through A(7) are compared with A(1). These are the same comparisons that were made in our previous example, as reflected in lines A–C of Figure 10-3. Likewise, when the second pass is made, the value of A(2) is compared with A(3) through A(7). This is in agreement with the results of the second pass of our previous illustration, as shown in lines D and E of Figure 10-3.

Note that the iteration on I terminates at $N - 1$ since there would be no items remaining to make the comparison when $I = N$. The termination of the outer loop at $N - 1$ rather than at N is important, but it can easily be overlooked. The principle of stopping the iteration at $N - 1$ appears in several of the sorts to be discussed.

The three remaining statements perform the exchange between A(J) and A(I).

End Solution

The number of passes and comparisons is easily determined from the pseudocode in Example 10-6. The variable I is the number of iterations in the sort, that is, it is the number of passes. Since I goes from 1 to $N - 1$, the number of passes for the exchange sort is $N - 1$. Likewise, the iteration on the variable J determines the number of comparisons per pass. Since the bound of J goes from $I + 1$ to N, the number of comparisons on the Ith pass is equal to $N - I$. The total number of comparisons for the $N - 1$ passes is equal to $(N - 1) + (N - 2) + \cdots + 3 + 2 + 1$, or the sum of all the integers from 1 to $N - 1$, or

$$\sum_{i=1}^{N-1} i.$$

Another method of expressing this quantity is:

$$\frac{N(N - 1)}{2} \text{ or } \frac{N^2 - N}{2}$$

This is less than one half the N^2 comparisons needed with the selection sort. The reduced processing time as reflected by the number of comparisons is another of the advantages of the exchange sort over the selection sort.

Example 10.7
Determine the number of passes and the total number of comparisons that are needed when the exchange sort is applied to the data of Example 10.5.

Solution
There are seven data items to be sorted, i.e., $N = 7$. Therefore, from the above formula, we know that $N - 1$, or six, passes are required to sort the list. The total number of comparisons is equal to the sum of the integers from 1 to 6, i.e., $6 + 5 + 4 + 3 + 2 + 1$, or 21. In order to verify these figures, check Figure 10-3. For example, the first pass in Figure 10-3 took six comparisons. The second pass used five comparisons. Likewise, each succeeding pass uses one less comparison until the last pass merely compares the last two values.

End Solution

10.5 The Bubble Sort

The **bubble sort** algorithm rearranges a list by successive comparisons of two adjacent items of the list. The name derives from the fact that the algorithm "bubbles" the lowest value to the top of the list.

In performing the bubble sort, the first item in the list is compared with the second one. If the second item is smaller than the first, the algorithm exchanges the two; otherwise the exchange is not made. Then the algorithm compares the second and third items. An exchange is made only if the third item is smaller than the second. Next, the algorithm compares the third and fourth items of the list and performs an exchange if the fourth item is smaller. The procedure continues in this manner until a comparison is made between the $N - 1$ and the N item.

Then a second pass is made using the same concept of comparing successive items. Because by the end of the first pass, the largest value is at the end of the list, there is no need to examine the last item during the second pass. Likewise, at the end of the second pass, the second largest item is in the $N - 1$ position of the list. Thus this position of the list need not be examined during the third pass. In a similar manner, each successive pass has one less comparison than the previous pass, a situation that is similar to the exchange sort.

The advantage of the bubble sort over the exchange sort is that the number of passes may be less than $N - 1$. Consider the case in which no exchanges are made during a complete pass. This means that the first and second items are in sequence, the second and third items are in order, the third and fourth items are in order, and so on. Thus there is not a single item out of place and there is no need for another pass.

This is the stopping condition for the algorithm: when a pass is completed without any exchanges, the procedure is terminated. This stopping condition is different from that of the exchange sort, in which a pass without an exchange does not necessarily mean the list is in order.

Example 10.8

Apply the bubble sort to arrange the following sequence of names in ascending order:

JIM   DAVID   BRUCE   JOE   LARRY   JACK   JOHN

Solution

This bubble sort is illustrated in Figure 10-5. The column labeled "Comparison on Which an Exchange Is Made" shows which comparison results in an exchange. When an exchange occurs, the new order of items is shown in the next line. And that new order is the order upon which the next comparison is made. Therefore, to indicate the new order after an exchange, reference will be made to the line after an exchange was found to be needed.

The column in Figure 10-5 labeled "Number of Comparisons Made in Pass" shows that the total number of comparisons made decreases by 1 for each pass because the items toward the end of the list (N in the second pass; N and N − 1 in the third pass; N, N − 1, and N − 2 in the fourth pass; and so forth as the bubble sort continues) have already been placed in the correct order and do not have to be compared again.

In the first pass, the first item in the original list is compared with the second item (see line a). Since David should come before Jim, the two are exchanged, resulting in a new order before the second comparison is made (see the order of line b). The third item is then compared with the second item. Since Bruce should come before Jim, an exchange is again made (see line c for the new order).

No exchange is needed after the third or fourth comparison since Jim comes before Joe, and Joe comes before Larry. But the fifth comparison, between Larry and Jack (again, see line c) does result in an exchange. The revised order is shown in line d. And the sixth comparison also results in an exchange, between Larry and John. The final order for the first pass is shown in line e; it is the order that the second pass will begin with. In the first pass, six comparisons have been made on seven items, resulting in four exchanges.

Since exchanges are made during the first pass, another pass must be made. The second pass is shown in lines e through g of Figure 10-5. As can be seen from studying our conventions (discussed in Example 10.5), there are five comparisons and two exchanges. Note that the second pass does not in-

Figure 10-5.
Sample of Manual
Bubble Sort

								Comparison on Which an Exchange Is Made	Number of Comparisons Made in Pass
First Pass									
a. First comparison	Jim	David	Bruce	Joe	Larry	Jack	John	1st	
b. Second comparison	David	Jim	Bruce	Joe	Larry	Jack	John	2nd	
c. Third through fifth	David	Bruce	Jim	Joe	Larry	Jack	John	5th	
d. Sixth (last)	David	Bruce	Jim	Joe	Jack	Larry	John	6th	6
Second Pass									
e. First comparison	David	Bruce	Jim	Joe	Jack	John	Larry	1st	
f. Second through fourth	Bruce	David	Jim	Joe	Jack	John	Larry	4th	
g. Fifth (last)	Bruce	David	Jim	Jack	Joe	John	Larry	None	5
Third Pass									
h. First through third	Bruce	David	Jim	Jack	Joe	John	Larry	3rd	
i. Fourth (last)	Bruce	David	Jack	Jim	Joe	John	Larry	None	4
Fourth Pass									
j. First through third (last)	Bruce	David	Jack	Jim	Joe	John	Larry	None	3

clude a comparison between the sixth and seventh items. The bubble sort ensures that the largest item is in the last position after the first pass. Therefore, the last item (N) need not be considered during the second pass.

After the second pass, the second largest item will be in the second to last position (N − 1). Therefore, the third pass requires one less comparison than the second pass. There are four comparisons in the third pass as shown in lines h and i of Figure 10–5. Since there are no exchanges in the three comparisons of the fourth pass, as seen in line j of Figure 10–5, the sort can terminate at this point.

End Solution

The program to accomplish the bubble sort is about the same size and level of difficulty as the code necessary for the exchange sort. The only addition is a means of determining if an exchange has been made. However, this can be accomplished with the use of one variable, as shown in the following example.

Example 10.9

Implement the bubble sort in the form of a subroutine to arrange a list in ascending order. The input parameters are the one-dimension array to be sorted and an integer variable indicating the number of items in the array.

Solution

```
SUBROUTINE BUBSORT (A, N);

    (* A = INPUT ARRAY TO BE SORTED AND OUTPUT ARRAY,
       N = NUMBER OF ELEMENTS IN ARRAY A *)

BEGIN
    FLAG := TRUE; (* FLAG DETERMINES WHEN SORT IS COMPLETED *)

    FOR I := 1 STEP 1 WHILE (I <= (N - 1) AND FLAG) DO
    BEGIN
        FLAG := FALSE;
        FOR J := 1 STEP 1 UNTIL (N - I) DO
            IF (A(J) > A(J+1))
            THEN
                BEGIN
                    TEMP := A(J);
                    A(J) := A(J+1);
                    A(J+1) := TEMP;
                    FLAG := TRUE;
                END;
```

```
    END;

END; (* END BUBSORT *)
```

The subroutine is called BUBSORT (A, N). A BOOLEAN variable, FLAG, is used in the subroutine as the indicator to determine if an exchange is made during a pass. The variable is set equal to FALSE at the beginning of each pass. Whenever two adjacent items of the array are exchanged, the value of FLAG is set equal to TRUE. The outer loop terminates after $N-1$ passes have been made, or when FLAG has a value of FALSE, indicating that no exchanges were made during the preceding pass. In either case, the array would be in order upon exit from the outer loop.

Each pass of the bubble sort considers one less item than the previous one. This is incorporated in the algorithm by the terminating value, $N-I$, for the inner loop. Since the upper bound of the array is decremented by 1 at the beginning of the inner loop, the last comparison for the first pass will be $A(N-1)$ and $A(N)$, thus providing the right stopping condition for that pass.

End Solution

The number of comparisons made during each pass of the bubble sort is the same as for the exchange sort. There are $N-1$ comparisons for the first pass, $N-2$ comparisons for the second pass, and so on. This is easily seen from an examination of SUBROUTINE BUBSORT (A, N) above and of Example 10.8. Because of the capability to terminate as soon as the array is ordered, the number of passes will not be the same for all cases. The specific starting order of the items will determine the number of passes needed to accomplish the sort.

Example 10.10
Determine the total number of passes and comparisons that are needed when the bubble sort is applied to the data of Example 10.8.

Solution
The easiest solution is to use the results of the sort as shown in Figure 10–5. As shown in this figure, there are 6 comparisons in the first pass, 5 comparisons in the second pass, 4 comparisons in the third pass, and 3 comparisons in the fourth pass. The number of passes is then 4 and the total number of comparisons is 18. This corresponds with the general guidelines for determining the number of passes and comparisons, as outlined above.

End Solution

In considering the selection and exchange sorts, it is possible to calculate the number of passes required before the sort is applied to the data. However, the number of passes to be made when applying the bubble sort depends upon the original arrangement of the data. Given only the size of the data list, it is not possible to calculate in advance the number of passes required for the bubble sort. However, it is easy to predict the minimum number of passes and the maximum number of passes that will be required.

Example 10.11

Assume that the bubble sort is applied to the following data:

11   15   23   34   35   45

Determine the number of passes and the total number of comparisons needed to

a. Sort the data into ascending order
b. Sort the data into descending order

Solution

a. We quickly determined that the list is in ascending order merely by scanning it. Likewise, the sort procedure must scan the list to determine whether or not it is in order. The bubble sort in Example 10.9 would indicate that no exchanges were made during the first pass and the subroutine would terminate. The sort consists of one pass of five comparisons, which is the minimum number of passes and comparisons.

b. The first pass of the procedure to sort in descending order is illustrated in Figure 10–6. After the first comparison, the first and second items are exchanged, placing the value of 11 in the second position. Likewise, there is an exchange after every comparison. At the completion of the pass, the value of 11 is in the last position of the list. The sequence of the other items is the same as before, but each has shifted up one place on the list.

Figure 10–7 shows the result of each pass. Notice that completion of the fifth pass assures that the entire file is in order. The number of comparisons per pass decreases by 1 after each pass and the total number of comparisons is equal to $5 + 4 + 3 + 2 + 1$, or 15, comparisons. Therefore, in this example, the maximum number of passes is 5 and the maximum number of comparisons is 15. In general, when there are N items in the file, we will consider the minimum number of comparisons to be $N - 1$ and the maximum number of comparisons to be the summation of the integers from 1 to $N - 1$.

End Solution

Figure 10-6.
First Pass of
Manual Bubble Sort
in Ascending Order

First Pass

a. First   11 15 23 34 35 45
   comparison

b. Second   15 11 23 34 35 45
   comparison

c. Third   15 23 11 34 35 45
   comparison

d. Fourth   15 23 34 11 35 45
   comparison

e. Fifth   15 23 34 35 11 45
   comparison

f. Final order— 15 23 34 35 45 11
   first pass

Figure 10-7.
Results of Each
Pass of Manual
Bubble Sort in
Descending Order

a. Original Order   11 15 23 34 35 45
b. After First Pass   15 23 34 35 45 11
c. After Second Pass 23 34 35 45 15 11
d. After Third Pass   34 35 45 23 15 11
e. After Fourth Pass 35 45 34 23 15 11
f. After Fifth Pass   45 35 34 23 15 11

10.6 The Quadratic Sort

The **quadratic sort** algorithm sequences a list of N items by dividing the list into approximately $\sqrt{N}$ groups, each of size $\sqrt{N}$. These groups are then used in sorting the items into the desired sequence. Since the list must be divided into an integral number of groups, the number of items, N, is used to determine a number N', which is the smallest integer equal to or greater than $\sqrt{N}$.

The original list of items is then divided into the N' groups. Each group will have N' items except possibly the last group, which can have fewer than N' items. The name of the sort derives from the use of $\sqrt{N}$ as the basic factor of the size of the group.

The algorithm uses three arrays: X, Y, and AUX. The auxiliary array AUX is defined with N' items and is filled in the following manner for an ascending sort: Find the smallest item in each of the N' groups of the original list in array X and place it in the corresponding position N' of the array AUX. Cross out the original position of X.

After AUX is filled, the algorithm selects the smallest item of AUX and stores it in the first position of array Y, which is to be the sorted array. Assume that the smallest value is in the ith position of AUX. From the method we used to fill AUX, we know that the ith group of X originally contained this smallest value. Go to this ith group and find the smallest remaining item of this group. Place it in the ith position of AUX and "cross out" the original location of that value in the list X.

Then find the smallest item remaining in AUX and place it in the second position of Y. Replace the position of this value in AUX with the remaining smallest item of the group in X corresponding to that position in AUX. This process is continued until all of the items have been transferred to Y. When the procedure terminates, the list in array Y is in ascending order.

Notice that the selection of the smallest item at any time from those in AUX is similar to one pass of the selection sort. Likewise, finding the smallest remaining item of a particular group in X and placing it in the proper location in AUX is again the same as one pass of the selection sort.

The quadratic sort, then, really involves the application of one pass of the selection sort, many times, to lists of size N'. The advantage of the sort lies in the fact that the pass is applied to a list of size N' rather than to a list of size N.

Example 10.12

Apply the quadratic sort to the following list of two-character abbreviations of state names:

NC   MO   CO   MI   CA   OH   NJ   NY

Solution

There are eight items in this list. Since the $\sqrt{8}$ is equal to 2.828, the smallest integer larger than this value is 3. Therefore, the value of N' is 3. The original list, X, is then divided into three groups of three items each and the array AUX will also contain three items.

The arrays are shown in Figure 10–8a; the groups are also indicated in the array X. The array AUX is then filled by finding the smallest item in each of the groups and storing it in AUX. In the first group, one pass of the selection sort will indicate that CO is the smallest item. This will be placed in the first position in AUX and the original position of that value will be crossed out by setting it equal to the string "**."

In a similar manner, the second group in X is searched for the smallest value, which is CA. The value CA is then stored in the second position in AUX and again ** is used to replace CA in the array X. The third value of AUX is determined by the same method. The contents of the three arrays are then as shown in Figure 10–8b.

One pass of the selection sort is then applied to the array AUX. This pass finds that CA, in the second position in AUX, is the smallest item and this value is stored in the first position in Y. The procedure then looks for the smallest item remaining in the second group in X—MI, in the fourth position. The second position in AUX is then filled by this value and the fourth position in X is set equal to **, as shown in Figure 10–8c.

Figure 10-8.
Sample of Manual
Quadratic Sort

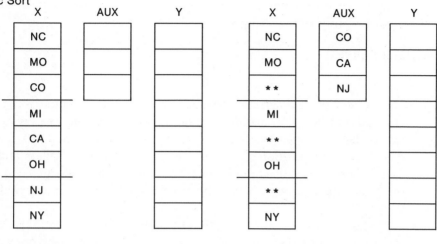

a. Original
   sequence

b. After AUX
   is created

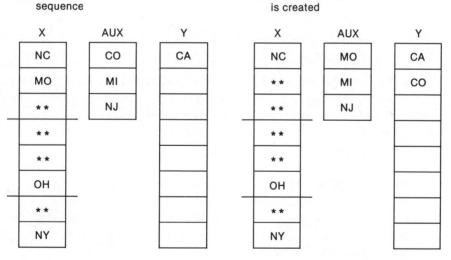

c. After first
   pass on AUX

d. After second
   pass on AUX

After a second pass on AUX, the contents of the arrays are as illustrated in Figure 10–8d. This procedure is continued until the eight items are stored in array Y in ascending order. When array Y is complete, both array X and AUX consist entirely of the string **.

End Solution

The success of the quadratic sort algorithm depends upon the filling of the array AUX. When the smallest item of that array is stored in array Y, the next smaller item is either (1) Already in AUX, or (2) In the group of X corresponding to the position of AUX in which the previous smallest value was found. The method used to fill this ith position of AUX ensures that the smallest value is in AUX before the next smallest value is transferred to array Y.

The subroutine for the quadratic sort algorithm is considerably longer than for the other sorts. However, some aspects of the program are quite similar and the concepts of the program are not difficult. There are several major tasks of the program:

1. Determine the value of N'.
2. Fill the array AUX.
3. Perform the sort by successive applications of one pass of the selection sort to AUX to find the next smallest value, and then applying one pass of the selection sort to the appropriate group of X to find the new value to put in AUX.

Example 10.13

Write a subroutine that uses the quadratic sort to arrange a list in ascending order. The parameters are the one-dimension array to be sorted, the one-dimension array to contain the sorted results, and the variable indicating the number of items in the arrays.

Solution

```
SUBROUTINE QUADSORT (X,Y,N);

    (* X = INPUT ARRAY TO BE SORTED,
       Y = OUTPUT SORTED ARRAY,
       N = NUMBER OF ELEMENTS IN ARRAYS *)

BEGIN
   DUMMY := 10**20;

   N2 := SQRT (N); (* N2 IS LARGEST INTEGER GREATER THAN SQRT(N) *)
```

```
IF (N > N2**2)
THEN
    N2 := N2 + 1;

(* NULLIFY UNUSED ITEMS OF X TO ELIMINATE SELECTION AS SMALLEST *)
FOR I := N + 1 STEP 1 UNTIL (N2**2) DO
    X(I) := DUMMY;

(* INITIALIZE AUX ARRAY WITH SMALLEST ITEM FROM EACH SUBGROUP *)
FOR I := 1 STEP 1 UNTIL N2 DO
BEGIN
    N3 := (I - 1) * N2 + 1;
    N4 := I * N2;
    SMALL := DUMMY;
    FOR J := N3 STEP 1 UNTIL N4 DO
        IF (X(J) < SMALL)
        THEN
            BEGIN
                SMALL := X(J);
                INDX1 := J; (* INDX1 IS SUBSCRIPT OF SMALLEST ITEM IN
                X *)
            END;

    AUX(I) := SMALL; (* STORE SMALLEST ITEM IN AUX *)

    (* NULLIFY POSITION IN X WHERE SMALLEST CAME FROM *)
    X(INDX1) := DUMMY;
END;


(* PICK ITEM FROM AUX AND THEN REFILL UNTIL N ITEMS ARE IN Y *)
(* USE SELECTION SORT ALGORITHM TO PICK SMALLEST FROM X AND AUX *)
(* K POINTS TO NEXT AVAILABLE POSITION IN ARRAY Y *)
K := 0;
FOR I := 1 STEP 1 UNTIL N DO
BEGIN
    SMALL := DUMMY;
    FOR J := 1 STEP 1 UNTIL N2 DO (* FIND SMALLEST ITEM IN AUX *)
        IF (AUX(J) < SMALL)
        THEN
            BEGIN
                SMALL := AUX(J);
                INDX2 := J;
            END;

    K := K + 1; (* PUT SMALLEST INTO NEXT LOCATION IN Y *)
    Y(K) := SMALL;

    (* REPLACE ITEM IN AUX FROM GROUP INDX2 OF ARRAY X *)
    N3 := (INDX2 - 1) * N2 + 1;
    N4 := INDX2 * N2;


    (* N3, N4 ARE THE RANGES OF INDX2 GROUP OF ARRAY X *)
    SMALL := DUMMY
    FOR J := N3 STEP 1 UNTIL N4 DO
```

```
                    IF (X(J) < SMALL)
                    THEN
                        BEGIN
                            SMALL := X(J);
                            INDX1 := J;
                        END;

            AUX(INDX1) := SMALL; (* PUT SMALLEST INTO INDX2 LOCATION OF AUX *)

            X(INDX1) := DUMMY; (* NULLIFY POSITION IN X WHERE SMALLEST CAME
            FROM *)
        END;

END; (* END QUADSORT *)
```

The subroutine is called QUADSORT (X, Y, N). Since this is an ascending order sort, it is necessary to use a high value to cross out the value of an item of an array. We assume that 10^{20} is a sufficiently high value. Since this value will be used in several places in the program, we denote it as the variable DUMMY.

The integer variable N2 is used to denote the N' value of our discussion. It must be remembered that N might not be a perfect square. The integer variable N2 would then be either less than or greater than the square root of N, depending upon the exact value of the square root and whether the computer language rounded or truncated the result. Thus the conditional statement determines whether or not N is greater than $N2^2$. If the conditional is True, the value of N2 is incremented by 1 in order to ensure that N2 is the smallest integer greater than the square root of N.

If the value of N is not a perfect square, the last group of X will have fewer than N' items. In order to make the iterations more general, these items of the array are filled with the dummy value, DUMMY. The first iteration in QUADSORT (X, Y, N) accomplishes this task.

The next iteration is a double nested loop involving the variables I and J. It is used to fill the array AUX with the N2 values. Note that N3 and N4 are calculated for each iteration of I and denote the beginning and the ending items of the Ith group of X.

For example, when I equals 1, the value of N3 is 1 and the value of N4 is N2. When I equals 2, the value of N3 is N2 + 1 and the value of N4 is 2∗N2. The J iteration finds the smallest item of that group and stores it in AUX. You can see in QUADSORT (X, Y, N) that this is practically the same as the selection sort. At the completion of the iteration on I, the entire array AUX is filled with the smallest values from each of the groups of X.

The remainder of the program is an iteration from I= 1 to I= N, representing the size of the original list. The first J iteration finds the smallest value in AUX and places it in array Y. The second iteration of J searches the corresponding group of X to find the smallest of the remaining values in that group to fill the location in AUX. These iterations are similar to the iteration used in filling array AUX. Thus the procedure involves few new concepts.

End Solution

In computing the number of comparisons needed to perform the quadratic sort, it is necessary to count those needed to fill AUX, as well as those needed to create the sorted array, Y. In initiating AUX, there are N' iterations in the I loop, each involving N' comparisons for the nested J loop. Then $(N')^2$ comparisons are needed to fill array AUX.

In sequencing array Y, there are two J iterations within the loop on I. The first requires N' comparisons to find the smallest item of AUX. The second J iteration is needed to search the group in X for the next smallest value to place in AUX and also requires N' comparisons.

Therefore, sequencing array Y requires N iterations for the I loop times 2N' comparisons for the J loops, or $2N * N'$ comparisons. The entire quadratic sort procedure, then, requires $(N')^2 + (2N * N')$, or $N'(N' + 2N)$. Thus for Example 10.12, which has 8 items, the quadratic sort would make $3(3 + 2 * 8)$, or 57, comparisons.

For a small array, the number of comparisons for the quadratic sort is similar to the number of comparisons for the selection sort. Compared to the bubble sort, both of these methods are quite inefficient for a small data set. The inefficiency of the selection sort continues to grow as the number of items to be sorted increases. On the other hand, the quadratic sort becomes considerably more efficient as the size of the data set grows. Solved Problem 10.17 determines the number of comparisons for various examples and shows the advantages of the quadratic sort for larger data sets.

10.7 The Radix Sort

The four sort algorithms developed in the previous sections assumed that each record of the file contains only one field. The common method of storage used for such a file is a one-dimension array. When a file contains records with several fields, it is generally necessary to use either a two-dimension array or parallel arrays to store the records. In the case of two-dimension arrays, a single row can be used to represent one record. Each field of that record can then be stored in one or more columns of that array row.

When there are several fields in a record, the file can be sorted on any of the fields. The field on which the sort is to be performed is called the **sort key.** It is important to remember that records (and not fields) are exchanged in sort algorithms such as the exchange and bubble sorts. Thus the entire array row must be exchanged, rather than merely exchanging two fields of the array. While this is not difficult to program, it does involve a slight change in the logic of the sort. Solved Problem 10.5 provides the logic needed to perform the bubble sort on a two-dimension array. Similar changes would also be appropriate to other sort methods.

In some cases it is necessary to sort a file by several fields. For example, a file might consist of records, each of which contains a name, street address, and city. It might be desirable to perform an initial sort of this file by city. All the records for a particular city could then be sorted by the alphabetical order of the last name of each person. We describe such a file as sorted by name within city. In this example, the city field is called the **primary sort key,** and the name field is referred to as the **secondary sort key.** In general, when we refer to sorting Field Y within Field X, we denote Field X as the primary sort key and Field Y as the secondary sort key.

One method of accomplishing a sort by two fields is called the **radix sort.** The radix sort is not really a different sort algorithm. Rather, it is merely a method of combining the sort algorithms previously described, for the purpose of sorting on two or more fields of a file. In sorting a file with two or more keys, or fields, the order of sorting the fields is important. The following example illustrates the importance of correctly specifying this order.

Example 10.14

A simple file consists of nine records of two fields, one denoting the make of an automobile, and the other the color of that automobile. The original order of the file is

Make Field	Color Field
Ford	Blue
Pontiac	Red
Chevrolet	Red
Ford	Yellow
Dodge	Red
Plymouth	Orange
Ford	Black
Dodge	Black
Chevrolet	Blue

The desired result is to have the records sorted by make of automobile. For all records having the same make, the file is to be ordered by color. In other words, the primary sort key is the MAKE field and the secondary sort key is the COLOR field. Let's sort the file in two different orders to see which order provides the desired result.

a. Order the original file by sorting it first by MAKE of automobile. Then sort this resultant file by the COLOR.

b. Order the original file by sorting it first by COLOR. Then sort this resultant file by MAKE.

Solution

Look at Table 10-1.

a. The original order of the file is shown on the left. The result after the MAKE of the automobile is used as the first sort key, shown in the middle. Using the COLOR to sort this result provides the order shown on the right, which is not the intended result.

b. Table 10-2 provides the results of using the color field as the initial sort key and the make field as the final sort key. Note that the result of this second sort is the desired result.

End Solution

Table 10-1 Result of Radix Sort Using Primary Key First

		Field Used to Perform the Sort			Field Used to Perform the Sort
FORD	BLUE	CHEVROLET	RED	DODGE	BLACK
PONTIAC	RED	CHEVROLET	BLUE	FORD	BLACK
CHEVROLET	RED	DODGE	RED	CHEVROLET	BLUE
FORD	YELLOW	DODGE	BLACK	FORD	BLUE
DODGE	RED	FORD	BLUE	PLYMOUTH	ORANGE
PLYMOUTH	ORANGE	FORD	YELLOW	CHEVROLET	RED
FORD	BLACK	FORD	BLACK	DODGE	RED
DODGE	BLACK	PLYMOUTH	ORANGE	PONTIAC	RED
CHEVROLET	BLUE	PONTIAC	RED	FORD	YELLOW
Original Order		After First Sort		After Second Sort	

Table 10-2 Result of Radix Sort Using Primary Key Last

			Field Used to Perform the Sort		Field Used to Perform the Sort
FORD	BLUE	FORD	BLACK	CHEVROLET	BLUE
PONTIAC	RED	DODGE	BLACK	CHEVROLET	RED
CHEVROLET	RED	FORD	BLUE	DODGE	BLACK
FORD	YELLOW	CHEVROLET	BLUE	DODGE	RED
DODGE	RED	PLYMOUTH	ORANGE	FORD	BLACK
PLYMOUTH	ORANGE	PONTIAC	RED	FORD	BLUE
FORD	BLACK	CHEVROLET	RED	FORD	YELLOW
DODGE	BLACK	DODGE	RED	PLYMOUTH	ORANGE
CHEVROLET	BLUE	FORD	YELLOW	PONTIAC	RED
Original Order		After First Sort		After Second Sort	

The results of these two methods demonstrate an important principle in applying the radix sort: when sorting a file by two fields, the file must first be ordered by the secondary sort key, and then be ordered by the primary sort key. The same principle can be extended to cases where three or more fields are included in the sort. This principle is again illustrated by the following example.

Example 10.15

A file consists of 200 or fewer records of 10 fields each, denoted Field 1 through Field 10. The file is to be sorted by Field 4 within Field 3 within Field 5. Develop an algorithm to read this file, sort it in the desired order, and print out the sorted file.

Solution

The primary sort key is Field 5, the secondary sort key is Field 3, and the tertiary sort key is Field 4. The problem requires the use of a two-dimension sort algorithm. We develop such an algorithm in Solved Problem 10.5 and call it SUBROUTINE BUBSORT2 (A, NR, NC, NS). The formal parameters required are: A, the array to be sorted; NR, the number of rows in A; NC, the number of columns in A; and NS, the column on which the sort is to be conducted.

Program Example 10.15

```
(***** SUBROUTINE BUBSORT2 DECLARED HERE *****)

BEGIN (***** MAIN PROGRAM *****)
   READ (NBR); (* INPUT SIZE OF ARRAY *)

   FOR I := 1 STEP 1 UNTIL NBR DO (* INPUT ARRAY TO BE SORTED *)
      READ (DATA(I,J),J := 1,10);

   CALL BUBSORT2 (DATA, NBR, 10, 4); (* SORT DATA ON FIELD 4 *)

   CALL BUBSORT2 (DATA, NBR, 10, 3); (* SORT DATA ON FIELD 3 *)

   CALL BUBSORT2 (DATA, NBR, 10, 5); (* SORT DATA ON FIELD 5 *)

   FOR I := 1 STEP 1 UNTIL NBR DO (* OUTPUT SORTED ARRAY *)
      WRITE (DATA(I,J),J := 1,10);

END. (* END EXAMPLE 10.15 *)
```

Here is the basic logic of the program. The input and output of the array is designed so that a record corresponds to one data line of input, and one data line of output, respectively. The remainder of the program is merely three calls of the SUBROUTINE BUBSORT2, with the tertiary sort key (Field 4) being used first. This sort is followed by calls on BUBSORT2 using the secondary key (Field 3) and then the primary key (Field 5).

End Solution

10.8 Selection of the Proper Sort Algorithm

The selection of a sort algorithm to apply in a specific situation can be critical if the data set to be processed is large or if the sort algorithm is to be used frequently. The selection of a method in an actual situation depends upon a number of factors. These include the efficiency of the sort algorithm, the particular programming language, the computer that is being used, and the specific program itself. However, we will concentrate our selection criteria on analyzing the general efficiency of the sorting algorithms.

The number of passes and comparisons involved in the sort are two measures of performance. The number of comparisons is useful since it is fairly indicative of the workload: it can be computed for all algorithms under consideration, it is independent of any particular computer, and most of the algorithms involve the same amount of work for a comparison.

Table 10-3 Formulas for Number of Passes

Selection sort	N^2		
Exchange sort	$\dfrac{N(N-1)}{2}$		
Bubble sort	MIN:	$N - 1$	
	MAX:	$\dfrac{N(N-1)}{2}$	
	MEAN:	$\dfrac{N(N-1)}{2} - \dfrac{(N/2)*((N/2)-1)}{2}$	
		$= \dfrac{3N^2 - 2N}{8}$	
Quadratic sort	$N'(N'+2N)$		

Table 10-3 provides a summary of the number of comparisons needed for each of the four sort algorithms that have been discussed in this chapter. The table assumes that each record of the file consists of a single field; that is, a one-dimension array will be considered for evaluating and comparing each algorithm. In the table, N refers to the number of items in the file, and N' is the smallest integer that is greater than or equal to the square root of N.

The mean formula for the bubble sort deserves a comment. The number of comparisons per pass decreases with each pass of the bubble sort. If half of the maximum number of passes are needed for this sort, the number of comparisons will be considerably less than half of the maximum number of comparisons that could be made. The mean formula provides the number of comparisons needed if half of the number of passes (the mean number of passes) is needed to accomplish the sort. This might not be the exact average number of comparisons, but it is a reasonable figure to use in the analysis.

Several of the solved problems in this chapter are designed to introduce additional considerations that must be made when selecting a sort algorithm. Most of these problems will involve the analysis of the number of comparisons. However, we caution the reader that comparisons are not the only way to analyze the various algorithms. When a particular computer or program is being used, there could be other, more valid methods to use.

Solved Problems

10.1
SUBROUTINE SELSORT developed in Example 10.3 sorted a one-dimension array in ascending order. Develop a subroutine similar to SELSORT to sort a one-dimension array in descending order using the selection sort algorithm.

Solution

```
SUBROUTINE SELSORT1 (Al, A2, N);

    (* Al = INPUT ARRAY TO BE SORTED,
       A2 = OUTPUT SORTED ARRAY,
       N = NUMBER OF ELEMENTS IN ARRAYS *)

BEGIN
    DUMMY := -1 * 10**20;

    INDEX := 1;
    K := 0;
    FOR I := 1 STEP 1 UNTIL N DO
    BEGIN
        LARGE := DUMMY;
        FOR J := 1 STEP 1 UNTIL N DO
            IF (Al(J) > LARGE)
            THEN
                BEGIN
                    LARGE := Al(J);
                    INDEX := J;
                END;
        K := K + 1;
        A2(K) := LARGE;
        Al(INDEX) := DUMMY;
    END;

END; (* END SELSORT1 *)
```

The subroutine is named SELSORT1 (A1, A2, N), where A1 is the input array (to be sorted), A2 is the sorted output array, and N is the number of items in the array. The object of each pass in SELSORT1 is to find the largest remaining item, and the variable LARGE is used to hold the largest value found thus far. It is initialized to a very small quantity that is less than any value in the array. The comparison (and exchange, if necessary) is very similar to that of SUBROUTINE SELSORT. The big difference is that the comparison checks to see if A1(K) is larger than LARGE, rather than determining if A1(K) is smaller than a given value. The saving of the largest value in A2 and the crossing out of the corresponding value in A1 follows the same logic as SELSORT.

The relatively minor change reflected in the subroutine as compared to SELSORT is typical of the difference between a subroutine sorting in ascending order and one sorting in descending order. If a particular sort algorithm exists for an ascending sort, it can easily be changed to a descending sort. Therefore, we will generally only show one of these types and let the programmer make the appropriate modifications when the alternate type of sort is needed.

10.2

If an array does not contain negative or 0 values, the selection sort can be modified so that the original array is not destroyed by the sort algorithm. This method can be used when all values in an array are positive numbers, and in some instances it can be used when alphabetical data is to be sorted.

Develop a subroutine that uses this modified selection sort to sequence an array containing only positive values.

Solution

```
SUBROUTINE SELSORT2 (A1, A2, N);

    (* A1 = INPUT ARRAY TO BE SORTED,
       A2 = OUTPUT SORTED ARRAY,
        N = NUMBER OF ELEMENTS IN ARRAYS *)

BEGIN
    INDEX := 1;
    K := 0;
    FOR I := 1 STEP 1 UNTIL N DO
    BEGIN
        SMALL := 10**20;
        FOR J := 1 STEP 1 UNTIL N DO
            IF (A1(J) < SMALL AND A1(J) > 0)
            THEN
                BEGIN
                    SMALL := A1(J);
                    INDEX := J;
                END;
        K := K + 1;
        A2(K) := SMALL;
        A1(INDEX) := -A1(INDEX);
    END;

    FOR I := 1 STEP 1 UNTIL N DO
        A1(I) := -A1(I);

END; (* END SELSORT2 *)
```

SUBROUTINE SELSORT2 (A1, A2, N) is similar to the selection sort pseudo-code for SUBROUTINE SELSORT shown in Example 10.3. There are only three differences:

1. Rather than assigning A1(INDEX) the value 10^{20} when that element of A1 is selected as the next smallest and stored in array A2, A1(INDEX) is assigned the negative of its present value. Since the original value was positive, the revised element is now negative.

2. In making each comparison of the selection sort, there are now two conditions in the subprogram. The additional condition is used to check if

A1(J) is negative. If this is true, the Jth element is no longer eligible for selection and the next element can be examined.

3. The last iteration of the subroutine reverses all of the signs of the A1 array, changing all the negative values to positive values. A1 is then the same as at the beginning of the procedure except that the elements are ordered.

10.3

It is sometimes advantageous to be able to sort either a single column or a single row of a two-dimension array. Develop SUBROUTINE EXCSORT1 (A, N, NR) that uses the exchange sort to order the N items in the NR row of the two-dimension array A.

Solution

```
SUBROUTINE EXCSORT1 (A, N, NR);

   (* A = INPUT ARRAY TO BE SORTED,
      N = NUMBER OF COLUMNS IN ARRAY,
     NR = ROW OF ARRAY A TO BE SORTED *)

BEGIN
   FOR I := 1 STEP 1 UNTIL (N − 1) DO
      FOR J := I + 1 STEP 1 UNTIL N DO
         IF (A(NR,J) < A(NR,I))
         THEN
            BEGIN
               TEMP := A(NR,I);
               A(NR,I) := A(NR,J);
               A(NR,J) := TEMP;
            END;

END; (* END EXCSORT1 *)
```

This algorithm has the same operations as SUBROUTINE EXCSORT (A,N) in Example 10.6. The only changes are the references to array A. Rather than indicating an element of the array as A(I), the elements of the array are denoted as A(NR,I), where NR is the subscript of the row to be sorted.

10.4

There are algorithms in which it is useful to be able to sort only a subset of an array. Develop SUBROUTINE BUBSORT1 (A, K1, K2) that uses the bubble sort to sequence that part of one-dimension array A from A(K1) through A(K2).

Solution

```
SUBROUTINE BUBSORT1 (A, K1, K2);

    (*  A = INPUT ARRAY TO BE SORTED,
       K1 = ROW ON WHICH TO START SORT,
       K2 = ROW ON WHICH TO STOP SORT *)

BEGIN
   FLAG := TRUE;
   FOR I := K1 STEP 1 WHILE (I <= (K2 - 1) AND FLAG) DO
   BEGIN
       FLAG := FALSE;

       FOR J := K1 STEP 1 UNTIL (K2 - I) DO
           IF (A(J) > A(J+1))
           THEN
               BEGIN
                   TEMP := A(J);
                   A(J) := A(J+1);
                   A(J+1) := TEMP;
                   FLAG := TRUE;
               END;
   END;

END; (* END BUBSORT1 *)
```

This algorithm involves few changes from the standard bubble sort. Two operations are different from SUBROUTINE BUBSORT (A,N) in Example 10.9. The outer loop is initialized to K1 and terminates at K2 − 1, where K1, K2 are the lower and upper bounds of the subset of the array to be sorted. The inner loop is initialized to K1 and terminates at K2 − I.

10.5

Although the sorts presented in this chapter were designed for one-dimension arrays, they can be modified in order to be applicable to two-dimension arrays. Develop SUBROUTINE BUBSORT2 (A, NR, NC, NS) that will sort the NR rows of the two-dimension array A. The parameter NS denotes which of the NC columns is to be used as the sort field.

Solution

```
SUBROUTINE BUBSORT2 (A, NR, NC, NS);

    (*  A = INPUT ARRAY TO BE SORTED,
       NR = NUMBER OF ROWS IN ARRAY A,
       NC = NUMBER OF COLUMNS IN ARRAY A,
       NS = COLUMN ON WHICH THE SORT IS TO BE KEYED *)

BEGIN
   FLAG := TRUE;
```

```
FOR I := 1 STEP 1 WHILE (I <= (NR -1) AND FLAG) DO
BEGIN
    FLAG := FALSE;

    FOR J := 1 STEP 1 UNTIL (NR - I) DO
        IF (A(J,NS) > A(J+1,NS)
        THEN
            BEGIN
                FOR K := 1 STEP 1 UNTIL NC DO
                BEGIN
                    TEMP := A(J,K);
                    A(J,K) := A(J+1,K);
                    A(J+1,K) := TEMP;
                END;

                FLAG := TRUE; (* INDICATES THAT A SWAP WAS MADE *)
            END;
END;

END; (* END BUBSORT2 *)
```

The first part of this algorithm is identical to that of the BUBSORT (A, N) in Example 10.9 The conditional, though, must compare A(J,NS) with A(J + 1,NS). If an exchange is to take place, each element of the two rows must be exchanged. This necessitates the use of the K iteration to exchange each A(J,K) with the corresponding element, A(J + 1,K).

10.6

The discussion of the quadratic sort in Section 10.6 pointed out that in most cases the number of items in a list will not be a perfect square. Example 10.13 indicated that dummy values can be used to make the total number of items in the list a perfect square. However, in some cases there are other, more efficient methods of handling this situation. These can be illustrated by applying the quadratic sort to the following list:

STEELERS
CARDINALS
REDSKINS
COWBOYS
BRONCOS
JETS
GIANTS
RAMS
CHARGERS
BEARS
PACKERS

Consider the initialization of the AUX array in applying the quadratic sort procedure to this set of data and suggest two additional methods of handling the situation when the number of items in the list is less than a perfect square.

Solution

There are 11 items to be sorted. The square root of 11 is 3.32 and the smallest integer equal to, or greater than, this number is 4. Therefore, there are 4 groups to be used in array X, each group has 4 items, and there are 4 items in the auxiliary array, AUX. These are portrayed in Figure 10-9a.

Following the method suggested in Example 10.13, the last 5 items can be filled with a dummy value to provide 4 groups of 4 items each. This will result in the last position in AUX also having the dummy value, as shown in Figure 10-9b. Since the J major iteration in Example 10.13 has an upper bound equal to the number of original items in X, none of the dummy values will be transferred to the sorted array Y. Thus although the proper result will be achieved, the disadvantage is that each scan of AUX will perform an unnecessary examination of the last element of array AUX.

An alternative to this method is to make the size of the groups in X smaller, as shown in Figure 10–9c. There are still 4 groups, but each contains only 3 items. This will put items in the fourth group and will reduce the number of comparisons within a group when another value must be added to AUX. Since each group will be reduced by one item and there is a total of N scans of the groups, this method will save N comparisons.

A second alternative is to keep the same number of items in a group but eliminate one of the groups, as shown in Figure 10–9d. There is then one less comparison to be made in each selection of an item from AUX. Since AUX must be scanned N times in a sort, this method would also save N comparisons.

These methods are equivalent when there is only one empty group. But there can be no more than one completely empty group. To be convinced of this, consider N' the computed size and number of groups. The number of items in the list, N, must be less than $(N')^2$ if there are to be any empty spaces; however, N must be greater than $(N' - 1)^2$. If it were not, the integer N' would not be the smallest integer greater than the square root of N (which is the definition). Therefore, the number of empty spaces must be less than $(N')^2 - (N' - 1)^2$ or $2N' - 1$. So, there can only be one completely empty group. Note, however, there need not be a completely empty group, e.g., the case when there are 14 items in the list. But if there is an empty group, then N is less than $(N')^2 - N'$.

Figure 10-9.
Quadratic Sort in
Solved Problem 10.6

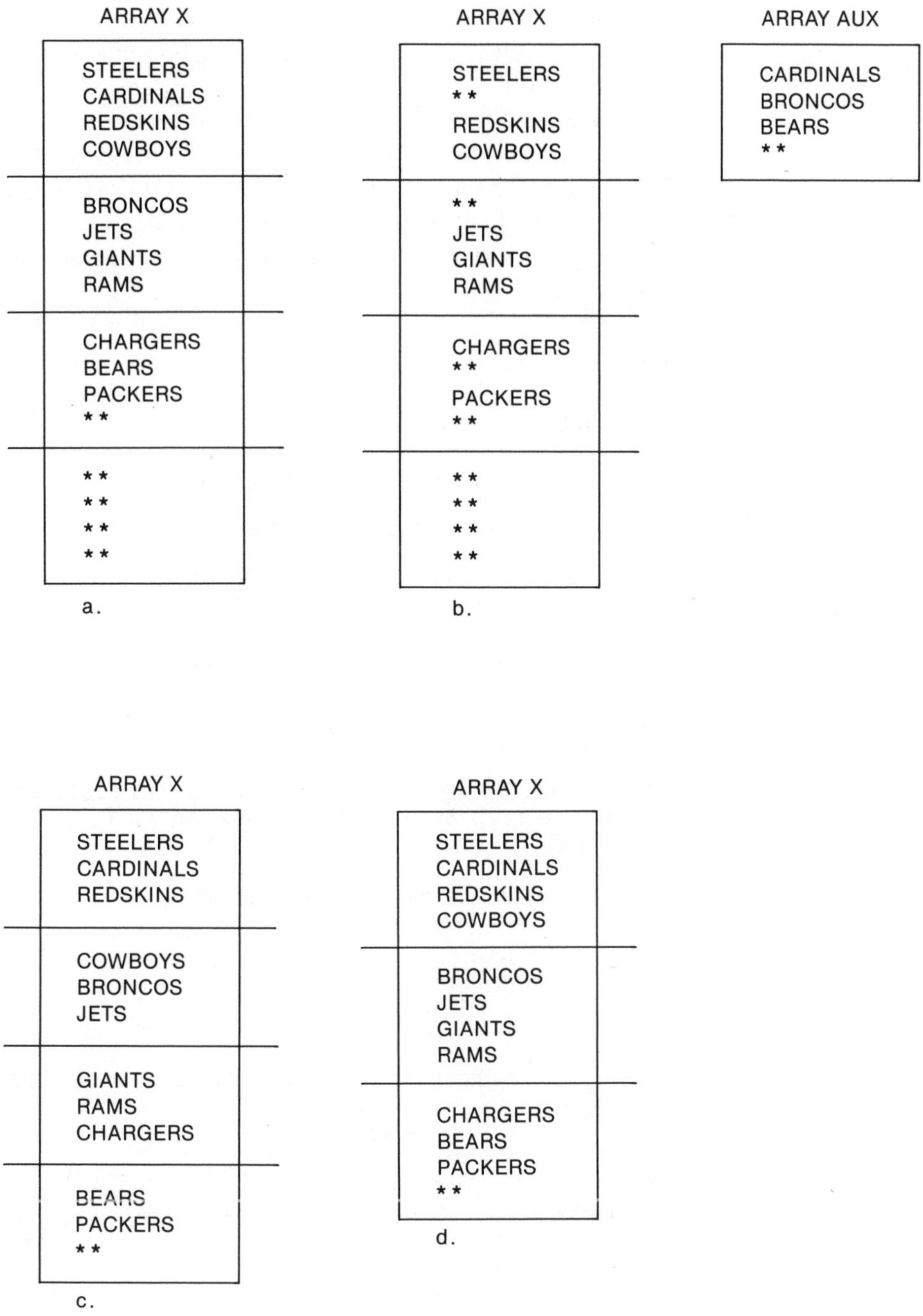

ARRAY X

| STEELERS |
| CARDINALS |
| REDSKINS |
| COWBOYS |
| |
| BRONCOS |
| JETS |
| GIANTS |
| RAMS |
| |
| CHARGERS |
| BEARS |
| PACKERS |
| ** |
| |
| ** |
| ** |
| ** |
| ** |

a.

ARRAY X

| STEELERS |
| ** |
| REDSKINS |
| COWBOYS |
| |
| ** |
| JETS |
| GIANTS |
| RAMS |
| |
| CHARGERS |
| ** |
| PACKERS |
| ** |
| |
| ** |
| ** |
| ** |
| ** |

b.

ARRAY AUX

| CARDINALS |
| BRONCOS |
| BEARS |
| ** |

ARRAY X

| STEELERS |
| CARDINALS |
| REDSKINS |
| |
| COWBOYS |
| BRONCOS |
| JETS |
| |
| GIANTS |
| RAMS |
| CHARGERS |
| |
| BEARS |
| PACKERS |
| ** |

c.

ARRAY X

| STEELERS |
| CARDINALS |
| REDSKINS |
| COWBOYS |
| |
| BRONCOS |
| JETS |
| GIANTS |
| RAMS |
| |
| CHARGERS |
| BEARS |
| PACKERS |
| ** |

d.

10.7

It is not difficult to incorporate one of the two modifications of the previous problem into the algorithm for the quadratic sort. After calculation of the variable N2 in QUADSORT (X, Y, N) in Example 10.13, a conditional can test if N is less than $(N2)^2 - N2$. If this is TRUE, one of the alternative methods can be used. Develop a modification to SUBROUTINE QUADSORT (X, Y, N) of Example 10.13 to reduce the number of groups in AUX when the above conditional is TRUE. (The other modification is considered in Supplementary Problem 10.28).

Solution

```
SUBROUTINE MODQUADSORT (X, Y, N);

    (* X = INPUT ARRAY TO BE SORTED,
       Y = OUTPUT SORTED ARRAY,
       N = NUMBER OF ELEMENTS IN ARRAYS *)

BEGIN
    DUMMY := 10**20;

    N2 := SQRT (N); (* N2 IS LARGEST INTEGER GREATER THAN SQRT(N) *)
    IF (N > (N2**2))
    THEN
        N2 := N2 + 1;

    (* NULLIFY UNUSED ITEMS OF X TO ELIMINATE SELECTION AS SMALLEST *)
    FOR I := N + 1 STEP 1 UNTIL (N2**2) DO
        X(I) := DUMMY;

    (* FOLLOWING ARE CHANGES TO QUADSORT *)
*   IF (N < N2**2 - N2)
*   THEN
*       N5 := N2 - 1
*   ELSE
*       N5 := N2;

*   FOR I := 1 STEP 1 UNTIL N5 DO (* INITIALIZE AUX ARRAY WITH N5 ITEMS *)
    BEGIN
        N3 := (I - 1) * N2 + 1;
        N4 := I * N2;
        SMALL := DUMMY;
        FOR J := N3 STEP 1 UNTIL N4 DO
            IF (X(J) < SMALL)
            THEN
                BEGIN
                    SMALL := X(J);
                    INDX1 := J; (* INDX1 IS SUBSCRIPT OF SMALLEST ITEM IN
                    X *)
                END;

        AUX(I) := SMALL; (* STORE SMALLEST ITEM IN AUX *)
```

```
                 (* NULLIFY POSITION IN X WHERE SMALLEST CAME FROM *)
                 X(INDX1) := DUMMY;
        END;

                 (* PICK ITEM FROM AUX AND THEN REFILL UNTIL N ITEMS ARE IN Y *)
                 (* USE SELECTION SORT ALGORITHM TO PICK SMALLEST FROM X AND AUX *)
                 (* K POINTS TO NEXT AVAILABLE POSITION IN ARRAY Y *)
                 K := 0;
                 FOR I := 1 STEP 1 UNTIL N DO
                 BEGIN
                      SMALL := DUMMY;

                      FOR J := 1 STEP 1 UNTIL N5 DO (* FIND SMALLEST ITEM IN AUX *)
                          IF (AUX(J) < SMALL)
                          THEN
                              BEGIN
                                  SMALL := AUX(J);
                                  INDX2 := J;
                              END;


                      K := K + 1; (* PUT SMALLEST INTO NEXT LOCATION IN Y *)
                      Y(K) := SMALL;

                      (* REPLACE ITEM IN AUX FROM GROUP INDX2 OF ARRAY X *)
                      N3 := (INDX2 - 1) * N2 + 1;
                      N4 := INDX2 * N2;

                      (* N3, N4 ARE THE RANGES OF INDX2 GROUP OF ARRAY X *)
                      SMALL := DUMMY
                      FOR J := N3 STEP 1 UNTIL N4 DO
                          IF (X(J) < SMALL)
                          THEN
                              BEGIN
                                  SMALL := X(J);
                                  INDX1 := J;
                              END;

                      AUX(INDX1) := SMALL; (* PUT SMALLEST INTO INDX1 LOCATION OF AUX *)

                      (* NULLIFY POSITION IN X WHERE SMALLEST CAME FROM *)
                      X(INDX1) := DUMMY;
                 END;

        END; (* END MODQUADSORT *)
```

Although the changes to the algorithm introduce a new integer variable, N5, they are rather simple. The changes to QUADSORT are indicated in MODQUADSORT (X, Y, N) by a * in the leftmost column. The change makes the conditional test, sets N5 to either N2 or to N2 − 1 as appropriate, and establishes the upper bound of the iteration at N5 instead of N2. Thus only N5 items will be included in the array AUX. The only other change is to ensure that only N5 items of AUX are used to select values for the sorted array. This is accomplished by changing the upper bound of the second I iteration in QUADSORT (X, Y, N) from N2 to N5.

10.8

Determine the number of comparisons for applying MODQUADSORT to the data of Solved Problem 10.6. From this example, derive a general formula for the number of comparisons in MODQUADSORT.

Solution

The filling of array AUX involves one pass of the selection sort for each of the 3 groups of 4 items each. Thus there are 12 comparisons in this stage of the algorithm. The selection of the items from AUX takes 11 passes of 3 comparisons each, or 33 comparisons. The replacement of the item in AUX involves a pass of the selection sort using 4 comparisons during each of the 11 times it is performed. The total number of comparisons is then $12 + 33 + 44$, or 89, comparisons.

In general, the modified version involves $N' - 1$ groups of size N'. Therefore, the filling of the AUX array involves $(N' - 1)N'$ comparisons. The searching of AUX for the next smallest value takes $(N' - 1)$ comparisons. The replacement of the value in AUX from the appropriate group results in N' comparisons. Since there are N iterations, that phase of the algorithm will necessitate $N((N' - 1) + N')$ comparisons. The total number of comparisons is then $(N' - 1)N' + N((N' - 1) + N')$, or $(N')^2 + 2NN' - N - N'$, or $N'(N' + 2N) - (N + N')$. The final equation differs from the formula given in Section 10.6 by the subtraction of the factor $N + N'$. Thus the modified method saves $N + N'$ comparisons. Applying this formula to the present problem gives $4(4 + 22) - (11 + 4) = 104 - 15 = 89$, which checks with the above answer.

10.9

The quadratic sort requires a complete scan of the items in a group in order to find the next smallest item to put in array AUX. As pointed out in Section 10.6, this is essentially one pass of the selection sort, a highly inefficient algorithm. In order to improve the overall efficiency of the quadratic sort, a more efficient method can be used to sequence the groups before the main part of the quadratic sort is applied. The next entry for AUX is simply the next order in sequence in the selected group. Apply this concept to the list of football teams in Solved Problem 10.6.

Solution

We will start with MODQUADSORT developed in Solved Problem 10.7 as applied to the data of Solved Problem 10.6. Thus there are 3 groups in array X with 4 items in each group, as shown in Figure 10–10a. Using the bubble

Figure 10-10.

Presorted Quadratic
Sort in Solved-Problem
10.9

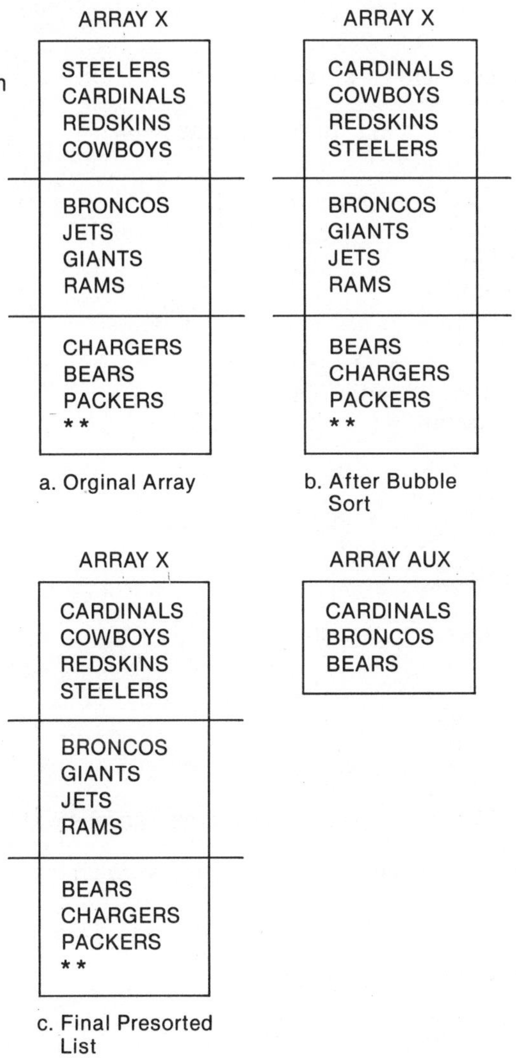

ARRAY X

| STEELERS |
| CARDINALS |
| REDSKINS |
| COWBOYS |
| |
| BRONCOS |
| JETS |
| GIANTS |
| RAMS |
| |
| CHARGERS |
| BEARS |
| PACKERS |
| ＊ ＊ |

a. Orginal Array

ARRAY X

| CARDINALS |
| COWBOYS |
| REDSKINS |
| STEELERS |
| |
| BRONCOS |
| GIANTS |
| JETS |
| RAMS |
| |
| BEARS |
| CHARGERS |
| PACKERS |
| ＊ ＊ |

b. After Bubble
Sort

ARRAY X

| CARDINALS |
| COWBOYS |
| REDSKINS |
| STEELERS |
| |
| BRONCOS |
| GIANTS |
| JETS |
| RAMS |
| |
| BEARS |
| CHARGERS |
| PACKERS |
| ＊ ＊ |

c. Final Presorted
List

ARRAY AUX

| CARDINALS |
| BRONCOS |
| BEARS |

sort to sequence each of the groups provides presorted groups as shown in
Figure 10–10b. Figure 10–10c shows the status after AUX has been filled for
the first time. Note that the original array still contains the sorted groups. A
separate array must be used corresponding to a set of subscripts pointing to
the latest entry in AUX from each group.

10.10

Develop SUBROUTINE MODQUADSORT1 (X, Y, N) to implement the presorted group quadratic sort discussed in Solved Problem 10.9. Use both the
modification of Solved Problem 10.7 and BUBSORT1 in the development of
the algorithm. Recall that BUBSORT1 of Solved Problem 10.4 sorts a designated subset of an array.

Solution

```
SUBROUTINE MODQUADSORT1 (X, Y, N);

(***** SUBROUTINE BUBSORT1 INSERTED HERE *****)

BEGIN
    DUMMY := 10**20;

    N2 := SQRT (N);
    IF (N > N2**2)
    THEN
        N2 := N2 + 1;

    FOR I := 1 STEP 1 UNTIL (N2**2) DO
        X(I) := DUMMY;

    IF (N < N**2 - N2)
    THEN
        N5 := N2 - 1
    ELSE
        N5 := N2;

    FOR I := 1 STEP 1 UNTIL N5 DO
    BEGIN
        N3 := (I - 1) * N2 + 1;
        N4 := I * N2;

        CALL BUBSORT1 (X, N3, N4); (* SORT GROUP FROM N3 TO N4 *)

        AUX(I) := X(N3); (* FILL AUX FROM GROUP STARTING AT N3 *)

        M(I) := 1; (* ARRAY M TRACKS LAST ELEMENT ENTERED INTO AUX *)
    END;

    K := 0;
    FOR I := 1 STEP 1 UNTIL N DO
    BEGIN
        SMALL := DUMMY;

        (* FIND NEXT VALUE FROM AUX TO PLACE INTO Y *)
        FOR J := 1 STEP 1 UNTIL N5 DO
            IF (AUX(J) < SMALL)
            THEN
                BEGIN
                    SMALL := AUX(J);
                    INDX2 := J;
                END;

        K := K + 1;
        Y(K) := SMALL;

        (* FIND NEXT VALUE FROM GROUP INDX2 TO PLACE IN AUX *)
        IF (M(INDX2) <> N2)
```

```
       THEN
           BEGIN
               M(INDX2) := M(INDX2) + 1;
               AUX(INDX2) := X(M(INDX2));
           END
       ELSE
           AUX(INDX2) := DUMMY; (* GROUP INDX2 IS EXHAUSTED *)
END;

END; (* END MODQUADSORT1 *)
```

This algorithm is the same as MODQUADSORT (X, Y, N) in Solved Problem 10.7. The values of N3 and N4 refer to the start and end limits of a group. These are used in the call of BUBSORT1 of Solved Problem 10.4, which uses the bubble sort to order a portion of a one-dimension array. After the sort, the top element of the group is placed in AUX and the index to that sublist, M(I), is initialized to 1.

The searching of AUX is the same as in Solved Problem 10.7. However, the replacement of the item in AUX by the next smallest value from the corresponding group in X is considerably simplified. In most cases this merely involves incrementing the appropriate index M(I) and transferring the appropriate item to the proper position of AUX. The only check needed at this point is to test whether the group has been exhausted and consequently whether the dummy value is needed in AUX. This check consists of comparing the contents of M(INDX2) with N2.

10.11
Determine the number of comparisons needed for applying MODQUADSORT1 to the list of Solved Problem 10.6.

Solution
The bubble sort must be applied to each of the 3 groups of 4 items. Replicating the hand application of the bubble sort portrayed in Example 10.8, shows that there are 6 comparisons needed for the first group, and 5 for each of the other 2 groups, or a total of 16 comparisons to fill AUX. For each of the 11 passes of the main procedure there are 3 comparisons in AUX, or 33 comparisons needed. In moving a new value to AUX for each pass, a comparison is needed to ensure that the end of the group has not yet been reached. This requires another 11 comparisons.

The total number of comparisons is then $16 + 33 + 11$, or 60 comparisons. MODQUADSORT discussed in Solved Problem 10.8 provided 89 comparisons, which means that the number of comparisons for this example will be reduced by approximately one-third by using the presorted version of the algorithm.

10.12

In order to see the magnitude of the difference between the regular quadratic sort and the presorted version when applied to large files, determine the number of comparisons of each algorithm when 3,000 items are to be sorted.

Solution

The square root of 3,000 is 54.77, making 55 the value of the smallest integer greater than or equal to the square root of the size of the list. Since $(N')^2 - N'$ is equal to 2,970, the last group will contain data and it is not possible to use the modifications of Solved Problem 10.7.

As indicated in Section 10.6, the number of comparisons for the regular quadratic sort is equal to $N'(N' + 2N)$. For a 3,000-item list there is, then, $55(55 + 2(3000))$, or 333,025 comparisons.

For the presorted version, there is a maximum of $(N'(N' - 1))/2$, or $55(54)/2$, or 1,485 comparisons per application of the bubble sort. But this sort must be applied N', or 55, times in filling array AUX and a total of 81,675 comparisons could be needed to fill the array. In the selection of the items to put in the sorted array, there are 3,000 scans of the 55 items in AUX or 165,000. In addition there is a comparison for each scan to determine if the end of the respective sublist in X has not been reached, or 3,000. The total number of comparisons is then $81,675 + 165,000 + 3,000$, or 249,675 comparisons.

In general, a quadratic sort with presort will involve a maximum number of comparisons equal to $(N'(N')(N' - 1))/2 + N(N') + N$. Since $(N')^2$ is only slightly more than N, this can be stated as $(N(N' - 1))/2 + N(N') + N$, which can be simplified to $(N(1 + 3N'))/2$.

Note that the above calculation assumes the worst case for the bubble sort. In general, the sort will be better. For example, if the mean figure from Table 10–3 in Section 10.8 had been used in the calculation, there would be another 20,000 fewer comparisons for the presorted version. Using this mean figure, the number of comparisons for the presorted algorithm with the bubble sort is approximately $N(6 + 11N')/8$.

10.13

The insertion sort takes items from an original list and inserts them where they belong in an ordered partial list. The new list is started by moving the first item of the original list A to the first position of the new list B.

Then the second item on list A is compared to the item on list B, i.e., A(2) is compared with B(1). If A(2) is less than B(1), B(1) is moved to B(2), and A(2) becomes B(1). If A(2) is greater than B(1), A(2) is moved to B(2).

Then A(3) is compared with B(1). If A(3) is less than B(1), B(2) is moved to B(3), B(1) is moved to B(2), and A(3) is moved to B(1). If A(3) is greater than B(1) but less than B(2), B(2) is moved to B(3), and A(3) becomes B(2). If A(3) is greater than both B(1) and B(2), A(3) becomes B(3).

This procedure continues with each item of A being inserted in the ever-growing list B.

Apply the insertion method to the following data:

SPAIN
BELGIUM
ITALY
PORTUGAL
FRANCE
AUSTRIA
SWITZERLAND
NORWAY

Solution

Table 10–4 shows the contents of the sorted list after each of the insertions. The procedure is started by SPAIN becoming the first item of the list, as depicted in Table 10–4a. In the second pass (Table 10–4b) BELGIUM, the second item on the original list, is compared to SPAIN. SPAIN becomes the second item on the sorted list and BELGIUM is placed in the first position of the sorted list. Then ITALY is inserted in its place between BELGIUM and SPAIN during the third pass, as shown in Table 10–4c. The algorithm continues until all items in the original list have been inserted in the sorted list, as shown in Table 10–4h.

Table 10-4

a. SPAIN	f. AUSTRIA	h. AUSTRIA
	BELGIUM	BELGIUM
b. BELGIUM	FRANCE	FRANCE
SPAIN	ITALY	ITALY
	PORTUGAL	NORWAY
c. BELGIUM	SPAIN	PORTUGAL
ITALY		SPAIN
SPAIN	g. AUSTRIA	SWITZERLAND
	BELGIUM	
d. BELGIUM	FRANCE	
ITALY	ITALY	
PORTUGAL	PORTUGAL	
SPAIN	SPAIN	
	SWITZERLAND	
e. BELGIUM		
FRANCE		
ITALY		
PORTUGAL		
SPAIN		

10.14

Develop SUBROUTINE INSERT (A, B, N) that uses the insertion sort to sequence the N items in the one-dimension array A into ascending order. Array B is to contain the sorted list after the completion of the subprogram.

Solution

```
SUBROUTINE INSERT (A, B, N);

    (* A = INPUT ARRAY TO BE SORTED,
       B = OUTPUT SORTED ARRAY,
       N = NUMBER OF ELEMENTS IN ARRAYS A AND B *)

BEGIN
   B(1) := A(1);
   FOR I := 2 STEP 1 UNTIL N DO
   BEGIN
       FOUND := FALSE;

       (* SEARCH FOR CORRECT POSITION IN ARRAY B *)
       FOR J := 1 STEP 1 WHILE (J < (I - 1) AND NOT FOUND) DO
           IF (A(I) < B(J))
           THEN
               BEGIN
                   FOUND := TRUE; (* CORRECT LOCATION FOUND IN ARRAY B *)

                   (* MOVE ITEMS J THRU I OF ARRAY B DOWN ONE LOCATION *)
                   FOR K := I STEP -1 UNTIL (J + 1) DO
                       B(K) := B(K - 1);

                   LOC := J; (* LOC KEEPS TRACK OF J FOR PLACEMENT OF A(I) *)
               END;

       IF (FOUND)
       THEN
           B(LOC) := A(I) (* CORRECT LOCATION FOR A(I) IS B(LOC) *)
       ELSE
           B(I) := A(I); (* CORRECT LOCATION FOR A(I) IS B(I) *)
   END;

END; (* END INSRT *)
```

This algorithm starts by assigning the contents of A(1) to B(1). Then the iteration on I considers the second through the Nth items in array A. Each A(I) is compared with the items already in B. The J iteration is controlled by the BOOLEAN variable FOUND and the number of items in B (i.e., $I - 1$). If A(I) is less than any B, then all Bs from that point on are moved down one to make a hole for the A(I), and the loop is terminated by setting FOUND to TRUE. LOC is used to track the correct location in array B for A(I). If FOUND is TRUE, then A(I) is inserted at B(LOC); otherwise it is inserted at the next position (I) in the B array.

10.15

Determine the number of comparisons for applying the insertion sort to the data of Solved Problem 10.13.

Solution

Since the first item on the sorted list is initialized by assigning the first item on the original list to the sorted list, we will consider the algorithm to have N − 1 passes. Table 10–4 can be used to determine the number of comparisons for each of the seven passes. There is only one item on the list at the beginning of the first pass (see Table 10–4a) and therefore there is only one comparison. In the second pass, there must be two comparisons in order to determine that ITALY belongs before SPAIN. There are three comparisons in the third pass. But the fourth pass (see Table 10–4d) only takes two comparisons to determine that FRANCE belongs ahead of ITALY. Continuing in this way it is easy to see that the total number of comparisons is equal to $1 + 2 + 3 + 2 + 1 + 6 + 5$, or 20 comparisons.

10.16

For pass M of the insertion algorithm, there are already M items in the partially sorted list. For any pass of the algorithm, there could be as few as one comparison or as many as M comparisons. On the average, we would expect something like half of the number of the items already in the partially sorted list to be compared with the item of the original list. In fact, it can be shown that the average number of comparisons for pass M is $(M + 1)/2 − 1/M$. If we drop the last term, this will slightly overstate the number of comparisons per pass, but it will simplify the resultant computation. There are then N − 1 passes of the algorithm with approximately $(M + 1)/2$ comparisons per pass. The estimated number of average comparisons can then be expressed mathematically as

$$\sum_{M=1}^{N-1} (M + 1)/2 = N(N + 1)/4$$

We will use this formula in the following problems as the approximate number of average comparisons for the insertion sort.

State the major advantages and disadvantages of this sort compared with the exchange sort.

Solution

The number of comparisons for the exchange sort is equal to $(N − 1)(N)/2$. Thus the major advantage of the insertion sort is that it will only take about half the comparisons the exchange sort will. The major disadvantage of the insertion sort is that a large number of items must be moved in order to insert another item in the partially ordered list. In fact, the number of items moved is roughly the same as the number of comparisons.

10.17

In order to illustrate the differences in comparisons needed for various sorts, develop a table showing the number of comparisons for applying the selection sort, exchange sort, bubble sort, quadratic sort, presorted quadratic sort, and insertion sort to each of four files containing 8, 20, 50, and 100 records. Assume that each record of the file is a single row or item of a one-dimension array.

Solution

The results are summarized in Table 10–5 and are based upon the formulas of Section 10.8, Solved Problem 10.12 and Solved Problem 10.16. From the results it is seen that the selection sort has a great disadvantage that grows as the size of the list increases. The bubble sort is always preferred over the exchange sort since it never involves any more comparisons than the exchange sort and could require considerably fewer comparisons. The insertion sort is also more advantageous than the exchange sort. For the larger list sizes, the quadratic sorts are more advantageous with the presorted version offering increasing advantage as the number of items increases.

Table 10-5. Sort Techniques Compared

	Number of Items			
Sort Algorithm	8	20	50	100
Selection	64	400	2,500	10,000
Exchange	28	190	1,225	4,950
Bubble				
Min	7	19	49	99
Max	28	190	1,225	4,950
Mean	22	145	925	3,725
Quadratic	57	225	864	2,100
Quadratic with Bubble				
Presort				
Max	40	160	625	1,550
Mean	39	153	588	1,450
Insertion				
Average	18	105	638	2,525

10.18

A 1,000-item array is to be sorted, but there is no data storage available in memory for additional storage of arrays. What sorting algorithm would you recommend?

Solution

The selection sort, the quadratic sort, and the insertion sort require additional array storage. Therefore, they are not feasible. This leaves the exchange sort and the bubble sort as the two possibilities. The number of comparisons needed by the exchange sort is $N(N-1)/2$, or $1000(999)/2$, or 499,500 comparisons. The number of comparisons for the bubble sort depends upon the number of passes. The maximum number of passes is N, which here would require 499,500 comparisons. The mean number of comparisons (as defined in Table 10–3 is $N(N-1)/2 - N/2\,(N/2-1)/2$, or $(3N^2 - 2N)/8$, or 374,750.

Thus the number of comparisons for the bubble sort would not exceed the number of comparisons for the exchange sort and they would be considerably less for many cases. If all other factors are relatively equal, the bubble sort should be selected for use in this case.

10.19

Assume that there is sufficient memory space for additional arrays and the 1,000-item array of the previous problem is to be sorted. What sorting algorithm would you recommend under these conditions?

Solution

Table 10–6 shows the formulas and the number of comparisons for each sort algorithm presented in the text, examples, and problems of this chapter. The variable N' is the smallest integer such that $N' >= \sqrt{N}$ and is equal to 32 in this example. The formula for the bubble sort is based upon the mean number of comparisons as presented in Table 10–3. The presorted quadratic sort has been computed on the assumption that the bubble sort is used to sequence the groups and the maximum number of comparisons are taken for the presort.

The table shows the clear superiority of some type of quadratic sort. Although the presorted version of the quadratic sort provides a large savings over the normal quadratic sort, the results could even be somewhat better since the formula was based upon the maximum number of comparisons needed for using the bubble sort as the presort method. One word of caution is needed. The formulas only show the number of comparisons. There could be other factors that would make another method more advantageous for a particular case.

Table 10-6. Sort Techniques Compared for 1,000 Item Array

Sort Algorithm	Formula	Comparisons N = 1000
Selection	N^2	1,000,000
Exchange	$\dfrac{N(N-1)}{2}$	499,500
Bubble (Medium)	$\dfrac{3N^2 - 2N}{8}$	374,750
Quadratic	$N'(N' + 2N)$	65,024
Pre-Sorted Quadratic	$\frac{1}{2}N(1 + 3N')$	48,500
Insertion	$\dfrac{N(N+1)}{4}$	250,250

10.20

A date file contains names and addresses with a 22-character field for the name, three blank characters, a 25-character field for the street address, three blank characters, and a 27-character field for the city. The records in the file are in random order. The file is used to produce a listing in alphabetical order. Develop an algorithm to accomplish this task. Assume that the computer system you are using can hold six characters in one word. Each word occupies one column of an array row. Several words (columns) can be used collectively to constitute a field.

Solution

The 22 characters in the name field will take up 3.67 words. However, the next 3 characters are blank and it is more convenient to consider 24 characters in the name field. This will include 2 blanks in the name field at the end of each name but this cannot possibly affect the sort. In fact, no matter what characters were in this position, they can only affect the sort if the previous 22 characters are the same. In this case, the 2 names are exactly the same and it will not matter which of the names is printed first.

This is an application in which the radix sort is needed. Each record can be read into a row of a two-dimension array. Then the fourth word of the array, which includes the two blanks, can be used as the sort key, followed by sort keys corresponding to the third, second, and first columns, in that order.

Only the name field, which consists of the first 4 words of each array row, is important to this algorithm. The remainder of the columns can then be stored in the computer in any convenient fashion. In this case the easiest method is to store 6 characters in each word of the array except the last column of the array row.

```
(***** SUBROUTINE BUBSORT INSERTED HERE *****)

BEGIN
   READ (N); (* INPUT SIZE OF ARRAY *)

   FOR I := 1 STEP 1 UNTIL N DO (* INPUT ARRAY *)
      READ (X(I,J),J := 1,14);

   CALL BUBSORT2 (X, N, 14, 4); (* SORT ON FIELD 4 *)

   CALL BUBSORT2 (X, N, 14, 3); (* SORT ON FIELD 3 *)

   CALL BUBSORT2 (X, N, 14, 2); (* SORT ON FIELD 2 *)

   CALL BUBSORT2 (X, N, 14, 1); (* SORT ON FIELD 1 *)

   FOR I := 1 STEP 1 UNTIL N DO (* OUTPUT SORTED ARRAY *)
      WRITE (X(I,J),J := 1,14);

END.
```

The actual algorithm to accomplish the task is straightforward. As it is presented here, it consists of 4 calls on the two-dimension sort algorithm BUBSORT2. The sort is performed on the 4 columns forming the name field by calling BUBSORT2 in the reverse order of the sort keys.

Supplemental Problems
10.21

The following data is to be sorted by hand in order to test your understanding of the concepts of the various sorts:

STOKE
LEEDS
ARSENAL
COVENTRY
BIRMINGHAM
SOUTHAMPTON
LIVERPOOL
LEICESTER
NEWCASTLE
IPSWICH
DERBY
CHELSEA

Determine the intermediate results after each pass of the following sorts:

a. Selection sort
b. Exchange sort
c. Bubble sort
d. Quadratic sort
e. Quadratic sort with the bubble sort as the presort method
f. Insertion sort

10.22
Determine the number of comparisons for each of the six sorts when used to sequence the data of the previous problem.

10.23
Develop a subroutine to sort a one-dimension array into descending order using the exchange sort algorithm.

10.24
Develop SUBROUTINE EXCH2(B, START, FINISH) that will use the exchange sort to sequence, in descending order, that part of the one-dimension array B from START through FINISH.

10.25
Develop a subroutine that will use the bubble sort to sequence the contents of a one-dimension array in descending order.

10.26
Develop a subroutine that will use the bubble sort to sort a specified column of a two-dimension array.

10.27
Problem 10.6 suggested two modifications to the quadratic sort and one of these was presented in Solved Problem 10.7. Develop a modification to SUBROUTINE QUADSORT of Example 10.13 using the alternative method.

10.28
Determine the number of comparisons when the algorithm of Supplementary Problem 10.27 is used to sequence a list of 3,000 items. Compare this number with the number of comparisons that would be needed if the modified method of Solved Problem 10.7 had been used in the algorithm.

10.29
Develop SUBROUTINE QUAD2 (X,Y,N) that will use the concepts of the presorted quadratic sort to sequence a one-dimension array in descending order.

10.30

Determine the number of comparisons for the algorithm of the previous problem in order to sequence a list of 1,000 elements.

10.31

Develop an algorithm to use the insertion sort to sequence a two-dimension array in descending order.

11   *Merging and Searching*

11.1 Introduction

Merging is the operation of producing a single sequence of records ordered according to some key from two or more sequences previously ordered by the same key. In other words, merging is the process of combining two or more sorted files into one sorted file. Since the two original files are already sequenced, the process is merely a combination of the two ordered files, an operation that is simpler in concept than sorting.

There are several types of merges. Included in this chapter are discussions on the two-way merge, the three-way merge, and the N-way merge.

The usual purpose of the sorting process is to reorganize a file in such a way that it will be in a better format for further processing or reference. The most frequent operation that is applied to files is searching, an operation strongly affected by whether or not the file is sorted. **Searching** is formally defined as the process of isolating a defined portion, or **subset,** from the entire file. In other words, searching consists of examining the file to find particular records that satisfy certain conditions. This subset of the file could consist of one specific record; it could include a number of records, or it could be a **null set,** (a subset with no records).

Searching is often applied to data that is stored in arrays. In this chapter we discuss two methods of searching array structures: the **linear search** and the **binary search.** Arrays, essentially sequential data organizations, are frequently used, but there are other methods of storing data. Chapter 13 introduces the **list structure** and the **tree data structure** and presents algorithms to search these data organizations.

11.2 The Two-Way Merge

The basic operation of **merging** is simple. Assume that there are three arrays denoted A1, A2, and A3. Arrays A1 and A2, already sorted in ascending order, are to be merged to produce a single list, array A3. Let K1, K2, and K3 be the respective pointers, or indices, to arrays A1, A2, and A3.

The process begins with each index pointing to the first item in its respective array. Compare the two items A1(K1) and A2(K2) and store the smaller of the two in A3(K3). Increment both the index of the array that contained this smaller value and the index K3 by 1. Again compare A1(K1) and A2(K2) and store the smaller of these two values in A3(K3). Then, as before, increment the index of the array that contained the smaller value and also increment K3 by 1.

Array A3 now contains the two smallest items from the combined lists. The two values could have come from the same array or they could have come from different arrays. Continue the process until both lists in A1 and A2 are exhausted. A3 then contains K1 plus K2 items in ascending order.

Example 11.1

Illustrate the merge by showing the operations involved when List A and List B are merged into a single List C in alphabetical order.

List A: BERLIN   GENEVA   LONDON   OSLO   WASHINGTON
List B: LISBON   LONDON   MADRID   OTTAWA   ROME

Solution

The steps involved in applying the merge to this example are shown in Figure 11–1. The arrows point to the two items in each list that are being compared during each step. The smaller of the two items is then added to List C, as shown on the right-hand side of the figure. For instance, the first comparison is between the first item of each list. Since BERLIN comes before LISBON, it is placed in List C. The second item of List A (GENEVA) is then compared with the first item of List B (LISBON), and GENEVA is added to List C. The process continues as shown in the figure. The final order in List C can then be read vertically in the figure.

End Solution

The merge illustrated in Example 11.1 involved two original lists. When there are two lists to be merged, we will refer to the merge as a **two-way merge;** the algorithm we will develop for a two-way merge will apply to data files stored as arrays in main memory, on auxiliary memory, or on magnetic tape. This chapter assumes that all lists to be sorted or merged are contained in arrays.

Most merges assume that the items in the lists are not changed in performing the merge, i.e., the size, structure, and total number of items are not affected by the procedure. Thus if there are duplicates in the lists, the combined list will also contain these duplicates. For example, LONDON appears twice in the final list of Example 11.1. In some applications it is desirable to remove these duplicates while performing the merge. Solved Problem

Figure 11–1.
Sample of Manual
Two-Way Merge

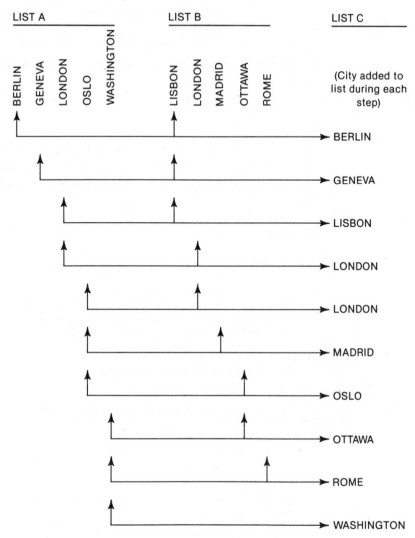

Figure 11-1. Sample of Manual Two-Way Merge

11.1 provides an algorithm that will remove all duplicates while performing the two-way merge.

The subroutine to be presented in the following example, however, is based upon the more common assumption that all items in the two lists are placed in the final merge list.

Example 11.2

Develop a subroutine to implement the two-way merge. The input parameters are the two original arrays and the number of items in each array. The output parameters are the merged array and the number of items in that array.

Solution

```
SUBROUTINE MERGE2 (A1, N1, A2, N2, A3, N3);

   (* A1, A2 = ORIGINAL INPUT ARRAYS,
      N1, N2 = NUMBER OF ELEMENTS IN A1 AND A2,
          A3 = MERGED OUTPUT ARRAY,
          N3 = NUMBER OF ELEMENTS IN A3 *)

BEGIN
   K1 := 1; (* INITIALIZE A1 INDEX *)
   K2 := 1; (* INITIALIZE A2 INDEX *)

   FOR K3 := 1 STEP 1 WHILE ((K1 <= N1) AND (K2 <= N2)) DO
       IF (A1(K1) < A2(K2))
       THEN
           BEGIN
               A3(K3) := A1(K1);
               K1 := K1 + 1;
           END
       ELSE
           BEGIN
               A3(K3) := A2(K2);
               K2 := K2 + 1;
           END;

   IF (K2 > N2) (* A2 IS EXHAUSTED--TRANSFER A1 *)
   THEN
       FOR I := K1 STEP 1 UNTIL N1 DO
       BEGIN
           A3(K3) := A1(K1);
           K3 := K3 + 1;
       END
   ELSE (* A1 IS EXHAUSTED--TRANSFER A2 *)
       FOR I := K2 STEP 1 UNTIL N2 DO
       BEGIN
           A3(K3) := A2(K2);
           K3 := K3 + 1;
       END;
```

```
        N3 := N1 + N2; (* SET NUMBER OF ELEMENTS IN NEW ARRAY A3 *)

    END; (* END MERGE2 *)
```

The three arrays in SUBROUTINE MERGE2 (A1, N1, A2, N2, A3, N3) are denoted A1, A2, and A3, while the number of items in each of these arrays is denoted N1, N2, and N3, respectively. The output parameters in SUBROUTINE MERGE2 (A1, N1, A2, N2, A3, N3) are A3 and N3. The three local variables, K1, K2, and K3, are used as pointers, or indices, to arrays A1, A2, and A3, respectively.

The logic of the algorithm follows the discussion of a merge at the beginning of this section except that this discussion did not indicate the actions to be taken when the index of one array exceeds the number of items in that list. When all items in one list have been assigned to the third list, it is necessary to perform a different operation.

For example, consider the example illustrated in Figure 11–1. When WASHINGTON in List A is compared with ROME in List B, ROME is assigned to List C. The incremented index to List B then no longer points to a data item in the list. Although WASHINGTON in List A *must* be transferred, a test would not be appropriate.

Whenever one of the lists is exhausted, it is necessary to transfer all the remaining items in the other list to the output list. The subroutine implements this logic by using the values of K1 and K2 to control the iteration as compared to their respective terminating values N1 and N2. If the index exceeds the number of items in that list, the items remaining in the other list are transferred to the merged array A3 by one of the two remaining loops. Note that the iterations used in the program will accomplish this transfer properly regardless of the number of items remaining in the list.

End Solution

11.3 The Three-Way Merge

We have explored the concept of the two-way merge; there are also three-way merges, four-way merges, and so on, all of which use essentially the same concept. The major difference is that in these higher order merges, there are more than two input lists, or arrays.

Let's compare the three-way merge to the simpler two-way merge. In order to implement a higher order merge, we want to identify modifications needed in the two-way merge. The major changes occur in the logic of comparing the respective items of the three arrays and in the method of handling the situation when a list is exhausted. The first of these changes is peculiar to the use of three input arrays. The second revision, actually an alternative method of accomplishing the task, could also be used in the two-way merge.

Example 11.3

Develop an algorithm to merge three one-dimension arrays. The input parameters are the three arrays, A1,A2,A3, and their respective sizes, N1,N2,N3. The output parameters are the merged array, A4, and its size, N4.

Solution

```
SUBROUTINE MERGE3 (A1, N1, A2, N2, A3, N3, A4, N4);

    (* A1, A2, A3 = INPUT ARRAYS TO BE MERGED,
       N1, N2, N3 = NUMBER OF ELEMENTS IN A1, A2, A3,
                A4 = MERGED OUTPUT ARRAY,
                N4 = NUMBER OF ELEMENTS ON A4 *)

BEGIN
    BIG := 10**20;

    K1 := 1; (* INITIALIZE A1 INDEX *)
    K2 := 1; (* INITIALIZE A2 INDEX *)
    K3 := 1; (* INITIALIZE A3 INDEX *)

    (* FORCE LAST+1 ELEMENT OF EACH ARRAY TOO BIG TO HANDLE EXHAUSTED LIST *)
    A1(N1+1) := BIG;
    A2(N2+1) := BIG;
    A3(N3+1) := BIG;

    N4 := N1 + N2 + N3; (* SET NUMBER OF ELEMENTS IN NEW ARRAY A4 *)

    FOR K4 := 1 STEP 1 UNTIL N4 DO
        (* TEST TO SEE IF A1(K1) IS SMALLEST OF ALL THREE *)
        IF ((A1(K1) <= A2(K2)) AND (A1(K1) <= A3(K3)))
        THEN
            BEGIN (* A1(K1) WAS SMALLEST *)
                A4(K4) := A1(K1);
                K1 := K1 + 1;
            END
        ELSE
            BEGIN (* A1(K1) WAS NOT SMALLEST *)
                (* TEST TO SEE IF A2(K2) IS SMALLEST *)
                IF (A2(K2) <= A3(K3))
                THEN
                    BEGIN (* A2(K2) WAS SMALLEST *)
                        A4(K4) := A2(K2);
                        K2 := K2 + 1;
                    END
                ELSE
                    BEGIN (* A3(K3) WAS SMALLEST *)
                        A4(K4) := A3(K3);
                        K3 := K3 + 1;
                    END;
            END;

END; (* END MERGE3 *)
```

The naming of the parameters in SUBROUTINE MERGE3 (A1, N1, A2, N2, A3, N3, A4, N4) follows the theme used in SUBROUTINE MERGE2 in Example 11.2, with A4 being the output array and N4 denoting the number of items in that array.

The selection of the smallest value from the three input lists for each iteration is shown by the conditionals in MERGE3. While there are several ways in which this can be achieved, the one shown is as simple as any. The reader might want to verify the fact that this sequence of conditionals will determine the smallest of the three values being considered at the time.

The approach used to determine the end of each list involves the addition of a value to the end of each of the three input arrays. This value is larger than any of the values contained in the arrays and is given the name BIG in the program. The comparison of any other value in the lists with this fictitious value BIG will result in that value being smaller than BIG. Thus the items of the arrays containing BIG will not be transferred to A4 as long as at least one of the input arrays contains one of its original values. The number of iterations used in performing the merge is determined by N4, which is the sum of N1, N2, and N3. This allows all of the original contents of the three arrays to be transferred to A4 and yet prevents any of the added values of BIG being transferred to A4.

Although the algorithm assumes that the lists are in ascending order, the changes required to merge lists in descending order are minor.

End Solution

11.4 The N-Way Merge

The **N-way merge** provides an algorithm that will merge as many lists as desired. It can be used for a two-way merge or a three-way merge as well as for larger numbers of input lists. Although the lists to be merged are considered to be one-dimension arrays, as used in the previous merges, the use of a two-dimension array is needed in order to generalize the procedure. The N rows of the array correspond to the N one-dimension lists to be merged. While the use of a two-dimension array might appear restrictive, this does not cause any real problem. If lists are really one-dimension arrays, these arrays can be stored in the respective rows of the two-dimension array before the procedure is called.

Example 11.4
Develop an algorithm to merge the N rows of a two-dimension array, A, into a one-dimension array, B.

Solution

```
SUBROUTINE MERGEN (A, NA, N, B, NB);

    (*  A = DOUBLY SUBSCRIPTED ARRAY TO BE MERGED,
       NA = PARALLEL ARRAY DESCRIBING LENGTH OF EACH ROW IN ARRAY A,
        N = NUMBER OF ROWS IN ARRAY A,
        B = MERGED SINGLY SUBSCRIPTED OUTPUT ARRAY,
       NB = NUMBER OF ELEMENTS IN ARRAY B *)

BEGIN
    BIG := 10**20;

    NB := 0;
    FOR I := 1 STEP 1 UNTIL N DO (* INITIALIZE ARRAYS AND COUNTERS *)
    BEGIN
        K(I) := 1; (* SET ROW INDICES TO 1 *)

        A(I,NA(I)+1) := BIG; (* SET UP ROW TERMINATOR *)

        NB := NB + NA(I); (* ACCUMULATE TOTAL NUMBER OF ELEMENTS *)
    END;

    FOR KB := 1 STEP 1 UNTIL NR DO (* BEGIN MERGE *)
    BEGIN
        SMALL := BIG;
        FOR J := 1 STEP 1 UNTIL N DO
            IF (A(J,K(J)) < SMALL)
            THEN
                BEGIN
                    SMALL := A(J,K(J));
                    INDEX := J;
                END;

        B(KB) := SMALL; (* TRANSFER ELEMENT *)

        K(INDEX) := K(INDEX) + 1; (* UPDATE ARRAY ROW ELEMENT COUNTER *)
    END;

END; (* END MERGEN *)
```

Since all rows of the input array might not contain the same number of items to be merged, it is necessary to know how many items of each row contain data to be merged. This information is stored in the one-dimension input array NA, with the value of NA(I) denoting the number of items to be merged from the Ith row of array A. The INTEGER variable N is used to store the number of array rows of A to be merged, while the variable NB is used as an output parameter to denote the number of items stored in the merged array B. The subroutine is then denoted as MERGEN (A, NA, N, B, NB).

The first iteration is used to initialize the variables. In order to maintain the generality of the procedure, the indices to the array row must be stored in an array. Array K is used for this purpose and each item of the array is initialized to 1 in the first iteration. The method shown in MERGE3 (Example 11.3) is again used to handle the situation when all items in a particular list (i.e., array row) have been merged. Thus at the beginning of the subroutine, the value of BIG is added at the end of each array row. In order to keep track of the number of items being merged, the number of items to be merged in each array row is added to NR.

The main iteration loop of the program consists of two parts. First, the first item in each of the N rows of A is examined for the smallest value, which is saved in variable SMALL. This value is then stored in the next location of the output array B, with the proper indices being incremented. Note in the pseudocode the use of array K for saving the proper values of the indices to the array rows of A. Thus K(1) is the index to the first row of array A, K(2) is the index to the second row of array A, and so forth. The appropriate reference to array A is then through the use of a subscripted value as its subscript, e.g., A(J,K(J)). In this example J represents the Jth row or list in A, and K(J) represents the next item in that row.

End Solution

11.5 The Linear Search

Searching is the process of isolating a specified portion, or subset, from the entire file. The **search plan** is the method used to search the file.

A **linear search** is a search plan in which the successive items in a file are examined in sequential order. The first item is examined and compared to the item or criteria for which we are searching. Then the second item is examined by the search, and so on; each successive item is examined in turn by the linear search plan.

Linear searches can be divided into two categories: full file searches and sequential searches. A **full file search** is a linear search in which all of the items in a file are examined, regardless of the results of the search. A **sequential search** is a linear search that could be terminated before all records are reviewed if certain conditions are fulfilled. For example, a full file search would be required to find all people in a personnel file who are named John, but a sequential search is adequate to find one person whose name is John.

Solved Problems 11.2 and 11.3 are applications of full file linear searches. This section will be restricted to sequential searches; thus all references to a linear search in the remainder of this chapter imply a sequential search.

In the sequential linear search, each successive item is examined until the desired item is found or until all the items in the file have been examined. If the item is found in the file, the linear search can terminate at that time. If the item is not in the file, the entire file will be examined without success. The data file used for the linear search need not be sorted prior to search. The fact that the file does not have to be ordered is the principal advantage to the linear search. In fact, the primary applications of the linear search are to unordered files.

Example 11.5

Discuss the applications of the linear search to the following data list in order to find Joan's telephone number:

HELEN	321-1678
ANN	223-1369
SUE	321-9512
MARY	303-3625
RUTH	217-4567
JOAN	745-4417
JAN	289-1973
PATTI	745-0647
KATHY	222-6902

Solution

The linear search examines the first name in the list, HELEN, and compares it to the name being sought, JOAN. The first name is not JOAN and, therefore, the second name in the list, ANN, is compared to the name JOAN. Since the two names are not equal, the third name in the list is considered. Again, these two names are not equal and the search continues. When the sixth name is examined, the search is successful and the sequential linear search can be terminated immediately.

End Solution

The linear search algorithm is an extremely simple one. Example 11.6 presents it as a subroutine in which a one-dimension array is searched for a specific value. The result of the subroutine is the index of the item where the value occurs in the array.

Example 11.6

Develop SUBROUTINE LINAR (X, N, DAT, INDEX) that applies the linear search to a one-dimension array. The parameters are the array, X; the number, N, of items in the array; the data, DAT, being searched for in the procedure; and a variable, INDEX, to indicate the subscript of the array where the value exists in the list.

Solution

```
SUBROUTINE LINAR (X, N, DAT, INDEX);

    (*     X = INPUT ARRAY TO BE SEARCHED,
           N = NUMBER OF ELEMENTS IN X,
         DAT = KEY TO BE SEARCHED FOR,
       INDEX = LOCATION OF DAT WITHIN X *)

BEGIN
    FOUND := FALSE; (* FOUND CAUSES LOOP TO TERMINATE *)

    FOR I := 1 STEP 1 WHILE (I <= N AND NOT FOUND) DO
        IF (X(I) = DAT)
        THEN
            FOUND := TRUE;

    IF (FOUND)
    THEN
        (* WHEN LOOP TERMINATED I WAS ALREADY INCREMENTED BY 1 *)
        INDEX := I - 1
    ELSE
        INDEX := 0;

END; (* END LINAR *)
```

The iteration loop compares each successive location in array X to the desired value DAT. The BOOLEAN variable FOUND is used to terminate the search if the item is in the array. Otherwise, the search terminates when the array is exhausted (i.e., $I > N$). INDEX is set to $I - 1$ since I is incremented prior to FOUND being tested for termination. If the value is not found, INDEX has the value of 0. Thus the program calling the subroutine can determine if a value was found in the search by testing the actual parameter corresponding to INDEX. If it is equal to 0, the value DAT was not in the array, while a nonzero value of INDEX indicates the location in the array at which DAT is found.

Note that INDEX will indicate the first item of X containing the value of DAT. Multiple entries with the same value are not considered by the subroutine. Since there is only one variable that is of interest in the output, it is also possible to use a FUNCTION for this example. The FUNCTION would require the appropriate changes in the declaration and subsequent call of the subprogram. Using the linear search, the maximum number of comparisons is N, the minimum is 1, and the average is $N/2$.

End Solution

11.6 The Binary Search

When searching the small list of telephone numbers in Example 11.5, the linear search is practical. But if the list consists of 1,000 students, the method becomes very inefficient. The difficulty is due to the necessity of examining each successive item of the list, since the data are not ordered in the file. When the file is sorted, there are more efficient search algorithms.

Let's use an example out of everyday life: The searching of an ordered list is accomplished when a word is looked up in a dictionary. When you want to find the meaning of "myrmecophagous," you will generally open the dictionary to some page near the center. If the first word on the page is "net," you are past the word "myrmecophagous" and you slip back a few pages. If the first word of that page is "monzonite," you look forward just a few pages. Several pages forward, the definitions start with "mus" and end with "muscarine," so you flip two more pages to where the words on the page are between "Mycenaean" and "mystical." You then look on this page for the word "myrmecophagous."

The use of a dictionary is very simple and fast since it is ordered and you know the sequence of letters in the alphabet. The same factors apply when searching ordered data in a file.

A frequently used search plan for ordered data is the binary search. This search method has some analogies to the dictionary example, although it must be more rigidly specified as an algorithm. The name is derived from the fact that each item examined in the algorithm reduces the number of items remaining to be examined by a factor of two.

The binary search starts by examining the value of the item at the midpoint of the array. If the value of this item is greater than the item for which the list is being searched, then the desired value must be between the first item of the array and the midpoint item of the array. The second half of the list can then be ignored in further searching. Likewise, if the value of the midpoint item is less than the desired item, the desired item must lie between the midpoint item and the last item of the list. In either case, the remaining interval surrounding the desired item has now been reduced to half of the original interval.

The value of the midpoint of the remaining interval is then examined by the procedure. If the value of the item in this location is larger than the desired item, the value must be in the first part of the remaining interval. The second half of that remaining interval need not be considered in further processing. If the value of that item of the array is less than the desired value, the item must be in the second portion and the first part of the remaining interval can be ignored.

Thus by comparing two items of the array with the desired value, the size of the interval containing the desired value has been reduced to one-fourth of its original size. This halving of the remaining interval will occur each time another item of the array is examined. This reduction is due to the judicious selection of the next item.

Figure 11–2.
Sample of
Manual Binary
Sort

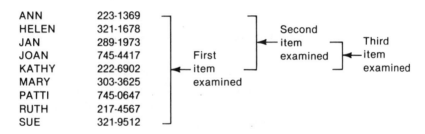

The largest number of items in the list that need to be examined is equal to M, where M is the smallest value such that the number of items in the list is less than 2^n, i.e., M is the smallest integer such that $M >= \log_2 (N)$.

Example 11.7

Apply the binary search to the following ordered list to find Joan's telephone number:

ANN	223-1369
HELEN	321-1678
JAN	289-1973
JOAN	745-4417
KATHY	222-6902
MARY	303-3625
PATTI	745-0647
RUTH	217-4567
SUE	321-9512

Solution

A representation of the operations involved in the search is shown in Figure 11–2. The brackets indicate the remaining interval of interest and the arrows indicate the item that is examined during each iteration.

The original interval includes the whole list and the first item to be examined is the midpoint item of the list, which is the name KATHY. Since KATHY comes after JOAN in alphabetical order, the bottom part of the list can be ignored and the size of the list has been reduced by half. The midpoint item of the remaining list, JAN, is then compared to the desired name, JOAN. Since JAN comes before JOAN, the lower portion of that remaining section is then the interval of interest. The third item looked at by the procedure is JOAN.

Thus it took three comparisons to find the name JOAN in the list. Note that the procedure can also be used to attempt to find the name JUDY. In such a search, the algorithm will determine that the value JUDY is not in the list.

End Solution

In the simple situation of Example 11.7, the binary search does not provide a major advantage over the linear search. But the advantage would become readily apparent when a large list of items is to be searched for a specific value. Solved Problem 11.5 compares the efficiency of these two methods of searching a large data set. In order to perform the search for such large lists, it is desirable to have a simple procedure that applies to lists of INTEGER, REAL, or ALPHANUMERIC data. The following example provides a subroutine that is useful for a one-dimension array.

Example 11.8

Write a subroutine to apply the binary search to a one-dimension array. The input parameters are the array to be searched, X; the number, N, of items in the array; the data being searched for, DAT; and a variable, INDEX, to indicate the location where the value is found in X. Return an INDEX of 0 if DAT is not found in X.

Solution

```
SUBROUTINE BINAR (X, N, DAT, INDEX);

    (*     X = INPUT ARRAY TO BE SEARCHED,
           N = NUMBER OF ELEMENTS IN X,
         DAT = KEY TO BE SEARCHED FOR,
       INDEX = LOCATION OF DAT WITHIN X *)

BEGIN
   LOW := 0;
   HIGH := N + 1;
   MID := HIGH / 2;

   WHILE (X(MID) <> DAT AND (HIGH - LOW) > 1) DO
   BEGIN
       IF (X(MID) > DAT)
       THEN
            HIGH := MID
       ELSE
            LOW := MID;

       MID := (HIGH + LOW) / 2;
   END;

   IF (X(MID) = DAT)
   THEN
        INDEX := MID
   ELSE
        INDEX := 0;

END; (* END BINAR *)
```

The three local variables used in SUBROUTINE BINAR (X, N, DAT, IN-DEX) are important. LOW, which indexes the beginning of the array, and HIGH, which indexes the end of the array, will always be initialized to 0 and N + 1, respectively. This ensures that the endpoints are included in the search. After each iteration, either HIGH or LOW will be moved to MID, depending on the results of the conditional statement, and a new MID will be calculated. The iteration terminates when the data item is found, or HIGH and LOW point to adjacent items. A final test determines whether or not the item was found and INDEX is set to MID or 0, accordingly.

End Solution

While subroutines for the linear search and the binary search have been presented for one-dimension arrays, the search method can be applied to multi-dimension arrays as well. The changes necessary in the search routines are similar to the changes that were necessary to make the sort procedures applicable to two-dimension arrays. Solved Problem 11.4 presents an algorithm that can be used to apply a binary search to a two-dimension array. The extension of the linear search to a two-dimension array is similar.

11.7 Summary

In this chapter we have presented a variety of techniques for merging lists and searching lists. We have by no means exhausted the subject; however, with this foundation you should be able to expand on these algorithms to suit your individual needs. The subject is examined more thoroughly through the following solved problems. The subroutines developed in this chapter are referenced throughout the remainder of the book.

Solved Problems
11.1
Develop an algorithm to perform the two-way merge, eliminating all duplicate data keys from the final list.

Solution

```
SUBROUTINE NEWMERGE2 (A1, N1, A2, N2, A3, N3);

BEGIN
    K1 := 1; (* INITIALIZE A1 INDEX *)
    K2 := 1; (* INITIALIZE A2 COUNTER *)

    FOR K3 := 1 STEP 1 WHILE ((K1 <= N1) AND (K2 <= N2)) DO
    BEGIN
*       IF (A1(K1) = A3(K3)) (* ELIMINATE DUPLICATE A1 AND A3 ITEMS *)
```

```
                THEN
                    K1 := K1 + 1
                ELSE
                    BEGIN
                        (* ELIMINATE DUPLICATE A2 AND A3 ITEMS *)
*                       IF (A2(K2) = A3(K3))
                        THEN
                            K2 := K2 + 1
                        ELSE
                            BEGIN
                                IF (A1(K1) < A2(K2))
                                THEN
                                    BEGIN
                                        A3(K3) := A1(K1);
                                        K1 := K1 + 1;
                                    END
                                ELSE
                                    BEGIN
                                        A3(K3) := A2(K2);
                                        K2 := K2 + 1;
                                    END;
                            END;
                    END;
            END;


        (* ONE OF THE TWO LISTS IS EXHAUSTED *)
        IF (K2 > N2) (* A2 IS EXHAUSTED *)
        THEN
            BEGIN (* TRANSFER A1 *)
                FOR I := K1 STEP 1 UNTIL N1 DO
                BEGIN
*                   IF (A1(K1) <> A3(K3)) (* TEST FOR DUPLICATES *)
                    THEN
                        A3(K3) := A1(K1); (* TRANSFER IF NOT DUPLICATE *)
                    K3 := K3 + 1;
                END;
            END
        ELSE (* TRANSFER A2 *)
            FOR I := K2 STEP 1 UNTIL N2 DO
            BEGIN
*               IF (A2(K2) <> A3(K3)) (* TEST FOR DUPLICATES *)
                THEN
                    A3(K3) := A2(K2); (* TRANSFER IF NOT DUPLICATE *)
                K3 := K3 + 1;
            END;

        N3 := K3; (* SET TOTAL NUMBER OF ELEMENTS IN A3 *)

    END; (* END NEWMERGE2 *)
```

SUBROUTINE NEWMERGE2 (A1, N1, A2, N2, A3, N3) is similar to that of MERGE2 in Example 11.2. The additional conditional checks and operations shown by an asterisk (*) eliminate insertion of the duplicate data into the output list.

11.2

As described in Section 11.5, a full file search is a linear search in which all records in the files or all items in a list are examined regardless of the results of the search. That is, the search does not terminate if one record of the file fulfills the search criteria.

Develop a subprogram that will apply a full file search to determine the number of times that a specified data item occurs in a singly subscripted array.

Solution

```
INTEGER FUNCTION COUNT (X, N, DAT);

    (*   X = INPUT ARRAY TO BE SEARCHED,
         N = NUMBER OF ELEMENTS IN ARRAY,
       DAT = SEARCH KEY *)

BEGIN
    COUNTER := 0; (* NUMBER OF TIMES DAT APPEARS IN X *)

    FOR I := 1 STEP 1 UNTIL N DO
        IF (X(I) = DAT)
        THEN
            COUNTER := COUNTER + 1;

    COUNT := COUNTER; (* RETURN RESULTS *)

END; (* END COUNT *)
```

This subprogram need only determine a single value and consequently a function is appropriate. The INTEGER FUNCTION COUNT (X, N, DAT) is very elementary.

11.3

Develop a subprogram that will apply a full file search to provide the indices of all items in a one-dimension array that equal a specified value.

Solution

```
SUBROUTINE LOCATE (X, N, DAT, IND, M);

    (*   X = INPUT ARRAY TO BE SEARCHED,
         N = NUMBER OF ELEMENTS IN X,
       DAT = SEARCH KEY,
       IND = ARRAY OF INDICES INTO X,
         M = NUMBER OF ELEMENTS IN OUTPUT ARRAY IND *)

BEGIN
    M := 0;

    FOR I := 1 STEP 1 UNTIL N DO
        IF (X(I) = DAT)
```

```
          THEN
             BEGIN
                M := M + 1;
                IND(M) := I;
             END;

END; (* END LOCATE *)
```

Since there is not a single value for the subprogram to provide, a function is not appropriate; a subroutine must be used for this algorithm. The input parameters of LOCATE (X, N, DAT, IND, M) are X, the array to be searched; N, the number of items in X, and DAT, the search value. The output parameters are IND, the array containing the indices of the items of the array that equal DAT, and M, the number of entries made in IND.

11.4

Develop a subroutine to apply the binary search to a doubly subscripted array. Pattern the logic of the subroutine after that of Example 11.8.

Solution

```
SUBROUTINE DBIN2 (X, NR, KCOL, DAT, INDEX);

     (*     X = INPUT ARRAY TO BE SEARCHED,
           NR = NUMBER OF ITEMS IN X,
         KCOL = COLUMN TO BE SEARCHED,
          DAT = SEARCH KEY,
        INDEX = LOCATION OF DAT IN X *)

BEGIN
   LOW := 0;
   HIGH := NR + 1;
   MID := HIGH / 2;

   WHILE ((X(MID,KCOL) <> DAT) AND (HIGH - LOW) > 1) DO
   BEGIN
      IF (X(MID,KCOL) > DAT)
      THEN
          HIGH := MID
      ELSE
          LOW := MID;

      MID := (HIGH + LOW) / 2;
   END;

   IF (X(MID,KCOL) = DAT)
   THEN
       INDEX := MID
   ELSE
       INDEX := 0;

END; (* END DBIN2 *)
```

The parameters of the procedure DBIN2 (X, NR, KCOL, DAT, INDEX) are the same as in Example 11.8, except for one additional parameter, KCOL, to denote the column of the array that is to be used for the sort key. The logic is very close to that of Example 11.8. The only difference is that all references to array X necessitate the use of two subscripts, the second being KCOL.

11.5

A list of 990 items is to be searched for a specific value. What is the maximum number of items that need to be examined in applying (a) the linear search and (b) the binary search?

Solution

a. In the linear search, each successive item in the list is searched until the value is found or the list is exhausted. With one comparison per item examined in the list, the maximum number of comparisons would be 990. If the value is in the list, the average number of comparisons would be half of the items in the list, or 445 in this example.

b. The number of items examined in the binary search is proportional to the power of 2. The value we are looking for is the smallest INTEGER value of N such that $2^n < 990$. Since $2^9 = 512$ and $2^{10} = 1024$, the correct value of N is 10. Therefore, no more than 10 items would have to be examined in the search.

11.6

Most people are familiar with tables that give the mileage between cities. As can be seen from Table 11–1, a square matrix of this type is symmetrical and therefore a table of distances is often shown in a triangular arrangement. Estimated driving times between cities are often provided by automobile associations and are useful in planning trips.

Table 11-1 Mileage Matrix

City	Hometown	Jackson Hollow	Podunk	Slippery Rock
Hometown	0	167	323	892
Jackson Hollow	167	0	2167	555
Podunk	323	2167	0	1667
Slippery Rock	892	555	1667	0

Table 11-2 Mileage Matrix

City	Hometown	Jackson Hollow	Podunk	Slippery Rock
Hometown	0	4.0	5.2	18.5
Jackson Hollow	167	0	40.3	9.3
Podunk	323	2167	0	27.6
Slippery Rock	892	555	1667	0

Assume that a matrix such as Table 11–2 is stored in a two-dimension array such that the upper triangular half contains the estimated travel time in hours between the largest 100 cities in the country and the lower triangular half contains the mileage between these cities. Develop SUBROUTINE FIND (DAT, CITY1, CITY2, MILES, TIME) that will search array DAT containing the mileage information and provide the distance in MILES and the estimated driving time in TIME between CITY1 and CITY2.

Solution

```
SUBROUTINE FIND (DAT, CITY1, CITY2, MILES, TIME);

    (*    DAT = 100X100 ARRAY OF MILES AND TIMES,
        CITY1 = DEPARTURE POINT,
        CITY2 = DESTINATION POINT,
        MILES = DISTANCE BETWEEN CITIES,
         TIME = DRIVING TIME BETWEEN CITIES *)

    (* TOWNS = GLOBAL ARRAY OF 100 CITY NAMES *)

BEGIN

    CALL BINAR (TOWNS, 100, CITY1, C1); (* LOCATE INDEX C1 OF CITY1 IN
    TOWNS *)

    CALL BINAR (TOWNS, 100, CITY2, C2); (* LOCATE INDEX C2 OF CITY2 IN
    TOWNS *)

    IF (C1 > C2)
    THEN
        BEGIN
            TEMP := C1;
            C1 := C2;
            C2 := TEMP;
        END;

    MILES := DAT (C2,C1);
    TIME := DAT (C1,C2);

END; (* END FIND *)
```

The array DAT is essentially a 100×100 matrix that is indexed by a row number and a column number corresponding to two cities. In order to determine which row and column correspond to the two cities, another array, TOWNS, is needed. For simplicity, it is assumed that an abbreviated name of the city can fit into one word (this assumption can be changed as necessary, but a change introduces a slightly more complex search).

Thus TOWNS is a 100-item one-dimension array with each item containing the name of a city. The array TOWNS is arranged in alphabetical order. The sequence of cities in TOWNS corresponds to the sequence of rows and columns in DAT, i.e., the data for the city in TOWNS(I) is stored in Row I and Column I of DAT.

Since TOWNS is not a parameter of the subroutine, it must be a GLOBAL array. Note that it could not be an array local to the procedure. If it were a LOCAL array, the values stored in TOWNS would be lost after each execution of the subroutine.

This algorithm applies the binary search SUBROUTINE BINAR of Example 11.8 to TOWNS to find the indices of the two cities that correspond to CITY1 and CITY2. These indices are denoted C1 and C2, respectively. The indices are checked and exchanged if necessary in order to ensure that C1 is the lower of the two variables.

The rest of the algorithm is then merely the assignment of the proper data items of DAT to MILES and TIME. Since C1 is less than C2, DAT(C1,C2) is in the upper triangular matrix and DAT(C2,C1) is in the lower triangular matrix.

Supplementary Problems
11.7
Develop an algorithm similar to MERGE2 in Example 11.2 that will perform a two-way merge. However, use the method of Example 11.3 to indicate the end of a list.

11.8
Convert SUBROUTINE DBIN2 (X, NR, KCOL, DAT, INDEX), developed in Solved Problem 11.4, into a BOOLEAN function that will return a value of TRUE if DAT is found in array X; otherwise it will return a FALSE.

11.9
One interesting application of search techniques is in determining if a designated string of ALPHANUMERIC characters exists within a second string of characters. Develop a BOOLEAN FUNCTION SEARCH to determine if the string of characters contained in successive rows of the singly dimensioned

array A exists within a second array B. Assume one character per array item. Use the variable NA to indicate the length of the string A, and NB to indicate the length of the string B. The value of SEARCH should indicate whether or not the search of B was successful.

11.10

Modify SEARCH of Supplementary Problem 11.9 such that the beginning location of the string within B is returned as a parameter.

11.11

Further modify SEARCH from Supplementary Problem 11.10 such that the ending location of the string within B is returned as a parameter.

11.12

Discuss how you would allow a lowercase letter to find a match on its equivalent uppercase letter in addition to itself. That is, how would you ensure that 'a' in array A matches either 'a' or 'A' in array B?

12   *Data Processing*

12.1 Introduction

The term **data processing** encompasses the entire spectrum of activity involved with the input, processing, and output of information by some means, manual or otherwise. In this book, we consider data processing to be the use of a computer to manipulate data. Generally, data processing has relatively minor computational requirements as compared to other fields such as numerical analysis; however, it is characterized by large data files that must be maintained and processed with a heavy demand on input/output.

Inherent to any study of data processing is a basic understanding of the organization and structure of that data. In this chapter we will spend considerable time discussing both the logical and the physical aspects of data organization, along with the associated input/output requirements. In our discussion of data manipulation operations as applied to large amounts of data, we include applications requiring the sorting, merging, and searching operations of previous chapters.

One of the major operations involved with data processing is the alteration, changing, or rearranging of data. This operation is categorized as **file maintenance** and will be discussed in detail along with the fundamental differences between **sequential access data files** and **direct access data files.**

This chapter makes extensive use of examples to simplify the presentation of these new concepts. You are encouraged to be sure you have a thorough understanding of the concepts of each example before going on.

12.2 Logical Organization of Data

In referring to the organization of data in certain computer applications, it is common to speak of fields, records, and files. These subdivisions constitute a hierarchy of data organization as follows:

A **field** is defined as a sequence of characters that have a specific relationship or meaning, or that describe some single attribute. For example, a sequence of characters used to describe the name of a person would be called a field.

A **record** is a collection of fields; there is some type of unifying relationship among the various fields in a record. All information relating to a person (e.g., name, address, city, age, height) could constitute a record.

A **file** is a collection of similar records. For example, if we had personnel information for everyone who worked for a particular company, we would have a file.

This hierarchy of data organization is indicated in Figure 12–1.

It is often necessary to discuss the contents of an individual record. There are a number of ways in which this can be done. In this chapter we will present all records in a tabular form. In this form of presentation, each field will be described in a table by the name of the field, the number of characters in the field (the size of the field), the inclusive sequence of character positions within the record that constitute that field, and the type (ALPHA, INTEGER, REAL) of that field. The characters in the record will be numbered from 1 to N, where N is the total number of characters in the record. Character 1 is the leftmost character and character N is the rightmost character of the record. We will refer to this as the layout of the record, or the **record layout.**

Prior to reviewing several examples of accessing records through their tabular description, it is important to review the concept of a word and how it relates to a field. Recall from Chapter 1 that a word consists of a fixed number of bits and that it is an addressable entity in memory. A word can hold ALPHA characters, an INTEGER number, or a REAL number. The number of ALPHA characters or the size of the INTEGER or REAL number the word can hold is determined by the size (number of bits) in the word itself. When information is read into memory, the characters constituting the record are converted into the binary equivalent for their ALPHA, INTEGER, or REAL type and stored into words of memory.

In the case of ALPHA, the READ statement determines the number of characters that are to be stored into one word, within the limits of the size of that word. Recall that 8 bits (a byte) are used to represent a single character. Therefore a 48-bit word could hold 1 to 6 characters at the discretion of the programmer and depending on the way in which the READ statement is coded.

In the case of INTEGER and REAL, the READ statement defines the number of characters (field) used for the number in the record. After converting these characters into binary, the number is rounded (or truncated) to fit into the word size used by the computer. Thus a 5-character numeric field in a record could be converted and stored in a single word in memory.

Since a record on auxiliary storage or on an input device is stored as a sequence of characters, it can be composed of a mix of ALPHA, INTEGER, and REAL information. It would be nice if this same record could be input into a single array row in memory. Unfortunately the array will be defined as containing ALPHA, INTEGER, or REAL information. A mix of any of the three in a single array is not possible. Consequently, records composed of fields of

Figure 12–1.
Sample File
Hierarchy

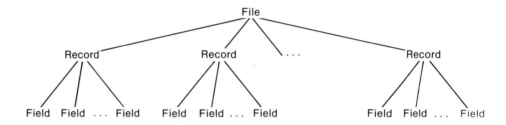

different types will have to be input to separate variables or parallel arrays of the appropriate type.

Example 12.1

Assume that a file contains personal data on all of the employees in a company. In 80 or fewer characters of information, establish a record for an individual employee. Each record is to be broken down into six fields: name, social security number (SSN), street address, city, state, and zip code.

Solution

The tabular form of the record is shown in Table 12–1. Seventy-nine characters have been used for the record. If desired, the remaining (80th) character can be added to the record for various uses. For instance, it could be set to 0 to indicate a present employee or be set to 1 to indicate a previous employee.

End Solution

In Example 12.1, the record length will always be 79 characters. We refer to this as a **fixed length record.** Likewise, the size of a particular field (such as the name field) will be the same for all records. This is called a **fixed length field.**

Table 12-1 Sample Record Layout

Name of Field	Field Size	Character Index In Record	Type
Name	30	1–30	ALPHA
Social security number	9	31–39	INTEGER
Street address	20	40–59	ALPHA
City	13	60–72	ALPHA
State	2	73–74	ALPHA
Zip code	5	75–79	INTEGER

Note that the number of nonblank characters in some fields will always be the same. For example, the social security number will always have nine characters, the state will be represented by two characters, and the zip code will always be represented by five characters.

In contrast, the character string that is needed to represent the name of a person varies in size. The 30-character field used in the example will be too short to represent the full first name, middle name, and last name of some people. On the other hand, it is longer than necessary to represent the alphanumeric string, "John Doe."

It is often desirable to have a field in which the length is determined by the data to be stored there. We refer to these as **variable length fields.** In the previous example, name, address, and city could all be variable length fields.

In using variable length fields, there must be some way to distinguish between two adjacent fields. One method is to use a unique character as a delimiter to separate the fields. Another method of separating variable length fields is to have the first character of a field indicate the number of characters in that field. Both of these methods would result in the use of an additional character for each field and could increase the difficulty of processing. However, the use of variable length fields could be desirable in order to save storage space that would be wasted in most records if fixed length fields were used.

In addition to distinguishing between fixed length and variable length fields, there are also fixed length and variable length records. The size of the **variable length record** varies according to the amount of data that is stored in it. A record made up of a number of variable length fields will constitute a variable length record.

Example 12.2

Consider a specific record whose layout is as described in Example 12.1. The record is to contain the data for John Joseph Jones, who lives at 1111 Main St., Anywhere, California 99999, and who has the social security number 123-12-3123.

1. Illustrate the record when it is a fixed length record following the format of Example 12.1.
2. Illustrate the record when it is a variable length record containing variable length fields separated by the delimiter #.

Solution

The two formats are depicted in Figure 12–2. They are shown on a coding sheet in order to illustrate the number of blank characters that exist in each format.

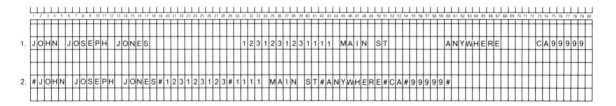

Figure 12–2.
Fixed Versus
Variable Length
Records

1. The fixed length record is shown on line 1. The fields are placed in the character positions previously indicated in Table 12–1.

2. The variable length record is shown on line 2. The delimiter # is used to separate the fields. Although sufficient blanks are inserted to separate the words, no extra blanks are retained at the end of each field. The entire record can fit in 60 characters, providing a savings in record length of approximately 25 percent over the fixed length record.

End Solution

There are instances in which there could be a number of fields of the same type. These are referred to as repeating fields. For instance, golf scores for the members of a club can be kept on a computer. In addition to an average score, a golf handicap, and certain identifying information, it could be desirable to record each of the scores for an individual golfer. There would then be a number of identical fields for recording the scores; these score fields would be repeating fields. The number of repeating fields can vary in each record or there can be a set number of such fields. Thus with repeating fields of constant size, the record could be either a variable length record or a fixed length record.

Example 12.3
Consider a file of golfers' scores in which each record contains the identification of the golfer, the average score, the handicap of the golfer, the number of scores, and a series of repeating fields containing the various scores.

1. Develop the record layout for a variable length record in which there is a field for each score and there can be any number of scores up to 99.

2. Develop the record layout for a fixed length record in which the repeating fields allow for 15 scores to be kept. Assume a word consists of 48 bits and thus can hold a maximum of 48 / 8, or 6 characters.

Solution

1. The record layout for a suitable variable length record is shown in Table 12–2. As many fields for the scores can be added to the record as are needed for an individual. The number of scores is recorded in the first two characters of the record. There are four (24 / 6) words necessary for the input of the name. One word of storage is required for each of the other quantities. Thus the number of words needed to store the record in memory would be eight plus the number of scores. The number of characters in the record is 37 plus three times the number of scores. The first two characters of the word can be used during processing to determine the size of the variable length record. New scores can be added by writing the new scores at the end of the record and changing the value of the first field of the record.

2. Table 12–3 illustrates the record layout for a fixed length record of 82 characters. The significant difference from the variable length record is that the number of fields for scores will always be equal to 15. If the number of valid scores is less than 15, zeros will be stored in some of the fields. If a golfer has over 15 scores, only 15 scores will be saved, e.g., the latest 15 scores.

   The order of the fields is different from that of Table 12–2 but either of the two sequences of fields would be adequate for the fixed sized record. The record layout of Table 12–3 can be used for the variable length record; however, the record layout of Table 12–2 facilitates processing by having the score count in the first field and the repeating fields expanded at the end of the record.

End Solution

While the previous example involved only one type of repeating field, a record could contain several types of repeating fields. For example, the above record could contain repeating fields for bowling scores as well as for golf scores. In addition, a grouping of fields could be repeated within the record. That is, a field that is a repeating field could have several subfields. An illustration of this is presented in the following example.

Example 12.4

Develop the record layout for recording the utility usage and account balance in the customer file of a utility company. The record contains an account number, the customer's name and address, and a repeating field to record the information for each of two utilities. Each of these repeating fields is to consist of five subfields: the rate charged for the utility, the previous meter

Table 12-2 Golfer Variable Length Record Layout

Name of Field	Field Size	Character Index In Record	Type
Number of scores	2	1–2	INTEGER
Identification	4	3–6	INTEGER
Name	24	7–30	ALPHA
Average	5	31–35	REAL
Handicap	2	36–37	INTEGER
Repeating fields	3	38–40	INTEGER
of scores	.	.	.
as necessary,	.	.	.
up to 99	.	.	.

Table 12-3 Golfer Fixed Length Record Layout

Name of Field	Field Size	Character Index In Record	Type
Identification	4	1–4	INTEGER
Name	24	5–28	ALPHA
Number of scores	2	29–30	INTEGER
Repeating field of	3	31–33	INTEGER
scores,	.	.	.
up to 15	.	.	.
	.	.	.
	3	73–75	INTEGER
Average	5	76–80	REAL
Handicap	2	81–82	INTEGER

reading, the present meter reading, the previous account balance, and the present account balance.

Solution

The suggested layout of the record is shown in Table 12–4. Note that the repeating fields consist of five subfields and each of these is repeated in the same order. The first of these could refer to the gas account and the second could be the electric account. The record is a single fixed length record of 116 characters.

End Solution

The previous examples illustrated the major considerations for fixed length and variable length fields, as well as fixed length and variable length records. Most of these records are used in later examples of this chapter. Before closing this section, we present one further example that will be referred to later in the chapter.

Example 12.5

The motor vehicle departments of all states maintain computerized records of vehicle registrations. Develop a simple vehicle record for use with a vehicle registration file. The record should contain information relating to the personal identification of the owner including the owner's address, a description of the vehicle, and registration data. Describe the fields to be included in the record, the size of each field, and the total record size.

Solution

The personal identification includes the name, address, city, state, and zip code. The social security number provides a unique identity. The vehicle description includes the make, year, model, type (convertible, sedan, station wagon, truck, van, and so forth), color, horsepower, and cubic-inch displacement. The registration data includes the state of registration and the registration number (i.e., license number).

   Although there are a number of possible record layouts, Table 12-5 provides one acceptable format. Note that the first six fields are the same size as those in Example 12.1. There are many possible variations in the size of the fields. In specific applications, it could be necessary to modify the size of some fields from those shown in the table. However, the 128-character record layout shown in Table 12-5 is fairly typical.

End Solution

Table 12-4 Utility File Record Layout

Name of Field	Field Size	Character Index In Record	Type
Account number	6	1–6	INTEGER
Customer name	20	7–26	ALPHA
Customer address	20	27–46	ALPHA
Utility rate	7	47–53	INTEGER
Utility previous reading	7	54–60	INTEGER
Utility present reading	7	61–67	INTEGER
Utility previous balance	7	68–74	REAL
Utility present balance	7	75–81	REAL
Utility rate	7	82–88	INTEGER
Utility previous reading	7	89–95	INTEGER
Utility present reading	7	96–102	INTEGER
Utility previous balance	7	103–109	REAL
Utility present balance	7	110–116	REAL

Table 12-5 Vehicle Registration File Record Layout

Name of Field	Field Size	Character Index In Record	Type
Name of owner	30	1–30	ALPHA
Social security number	9	31–39	INTEGER
Address	20	40–59	ALPHA
City	13	60–72	ALPHA
State	2	73–74	ALPHA
Zip code	5	75–79	INTEGER
Year of manufacture	2	80–81	INTEGER
Make of vehicle	10	82–91	ALPHA
Model of vehicle	8	92–99	ALPHA
Type of vehicle	8	100–107	ALPHA
Color of vehicle	6	108–113	ALPHA
Horsepower	3	114–116	INTEGER
Cubic-inch displacement	3	117–119	INTEGER
State registered	2	120–121	ALPHA
Registration number	7	122–128	ALPHA

12.3 Physical Data Organization

All our pseudocodes have assumed that we are using a video terminal keyboard as the input device and a video display or line printer as the output device. There are a number of other input and output devices, as described in Chapter 3. The general concepts of reading and writing data with these other devices are similar to those which we have previously discussed. The particulars vary, but many of the variations are due to the specific computer more than anything else.

Some of the basic concepts of other I/O devices and some of the factors influencing tape and disk I/O are presented in this section. Considerations for other devices will be similar. This section also illustrates some of the differences in using sequential access files stored on magnetic tape and random access files stored on disk.

A. Input/Output Buffers

In studying input and output devices, it is necessary to understand the general concept of input/output buffers. The speed of reading a data record from a keyboard is extremely slow compared to the internal speed of the central processing unit (CPU). Although the speed of magnetic tape for input and output is faster, it is still considerably slower than the speed of the CPU. Even the fastest I/O devices such as disks are considerably slower than the CPU.

In the early computers, such differences in speed were not a matter of concern. However, as computers became faster, the variations in input and output speed compared with the speed of the CPU created inefficiencies. The use of buffering helps to overcome some of these disadvantages.

An **input/output buffer** is a portion of memory in which the contents of a record are stored temporarily before the data is moved to the proper storage locations or moved to an I/O device. For example, a buffer for a card reader will be large enough to hold the 80 characters contained on each card. In effect, it is an array that is used to store the contents of a data card until the information is moved to the storage locations corresponding to the variables in the variable list. Thus it gets its name from the fact that it acts as a buffer between the I/O device and the memory of the computer.

Another example is the output buffer, which will contain the number of characters that are included in one line of output. In performing output the buffer is filled before the data is released to the proper output device.

Buffers can be used effectively to speed up the input/output operation of the computer. The buffer can be filled while the computer is doing other processing. For example, the card image can be transmitted from the card reader to the input buffer while the computer is performing other computations. When the program encounters a READ operation, the information can be obtained from the buffer. If the buffer is not full by the time the READ operation is to be performed, the program can wait until the data is in the buffer.

Buffers can be particularly useful when there is **multiple buffering.** As one buffer is being used, other buffers can be filled. There is then rotation of the buffers and each new READ operation accesses the next buffer in turn. This can speed up the I/O operations by reducing the delays of waiting for input and output. There is of course a trade-off in terms of storage space as additional buffers are introduced. Generally those computer systems, compilers, or programs using multiple buffering will use two or three buffers.

The storage space to be used for the buffers must be set aside in main storage. Some languages such as COBOL have special instructions to allocate this storage space. Other languages will allocate storage space for the buffers the first time the file is used. In some instances, the information about the number of buffers and their size must be provided in declarations or control statements; other systems will assume a default value for buffer parameters if more specific information is not provided. In any case, you must find out the details of establishing buffers for the language and computer you are using.

B. Physical Records

The records described so far in this chapter were logical records. A **logical record** contains specific information or data about an entity, i.e., it is a record in the sense of the definition at the beginning of Section 12.2. But all transfers between an I/O device and a buffer area occur in a fixed length group of characters called a physical record. Thus the **physical record** is the size of the data that is actually transferred to and from the buffer; the logical record is the size of the record as seen by the program.

The size of the physical record is sometimes influenced or limited by the specific I/O device or by the need to transfer relatively large blocks of data to increase the efficiency of the data transfer. On the other hand, the logical record size is determined by the application or program.

A physical record can consist of more than one logical record. A physical record that consists of two or more logical records is referred to as a **block** or a **blocked record**. An **unblocked record** is a physical record that contains only one logical record, i.e., the size of the physical and logical record is identical.

Example 12.6

The data of the vehicle registration file of Example 12.5 is to be stored in physical records that have a maximum size of 1000 characters each. If as much of the physical record is used as possible, describe the relationship between the logical and physical records.

Solution

As described in Example 12.5, each logical record of the vehicle registration file consists of 128 characters. Since 1000 divided by 128 equals 7.8, a maximum of 7 complete logical records can fit in 1000 characters of storage. Therefore, we make the physical record equal to 7 times 128, or 896 characters, and a blocked physical record contains 7 logical records.

End Solution

C. Tape Files

Magnetic tape storage is analogous to a home tape recording system except that, instead of a continuous audio signal being recorded, discrete digital signals are recorded across and along the tape. The number of signals, i.e., bits, across the tape ranges from 7 to 9, depending on the manufacturer's coding scheme. In general, one row of bits across the tape represents a single character of information. Information is read or written as the tape moves across a set of read/write heads.

Due to the physical design of magnetic tape, the records on a tape file must be stored sequentially. To access any particular record it is necessary to move the tape until the desired record is under the read/write head. Magnetic tapes are known as **sequential access devices.** Because advancing the tape its full length can take several minutes, tape processing is relatively time consuming.

Although tapes are organized into sequential files, there are ways to make tape processing more efficient and productive. One way is to sort the records on the file before storing them on the tape. For example, they could be organized in alphabetical order by name of employee, by social security number, by transaction order number, by date and time information, or by numerous alternative key fields. This ordering of information is the basis of the concepts of merging files and of the data processing techniques for tape files.

A simple example is a computerized inventory control system in which the basic file is kept on a magnetic tape. In this case it is desirable to order the stock records by some field such as stock number. The transactions to be processed in updating the information in the file can be sorted by stock number prior to processing. These sorted transactions can then be matched against the sequenced stock control records on the tape. This method of processing is efficient enough to justify the existence of many tape-oriented systems.

Tape fields can contain variable length or fixed length records. Likewise, the records can be blocked or unblocked records. Blocked records can be particularly useful for tape files. Since tape is read while it is moving at full speed, the tape must be started before the record can be read and it must be stopped after the read operation. Since this takes time, there must be a portion of the tape left blank between records to allow time for the tape drive to start and stop. This portion of the tape, referred to as the **interrecord gap,** varies considerably in length up to a maximum of three-quarters of an inch.

Since these gaps only occur between blocks that are in fact physical records, the larger the blocked records, the greater the savings in storage space. Consider the space used by the vehicle registration file, in which records are blocked (see Example 12.6), versus the space that would be required if the file contained unblocked records.

If the processing of a magnetic tape merely involves the reading of the file, only one tape is necessary. The tape can be read in a sequential manner and at the conclusion of the program, the tape is rewound and the program is terminated. But if the information on the file is to be changed, a different method must be used.

After the information in a record has been read from a tape file, the beginning of the next record is under the read head. When changes have been made, it is necessary to store the record back on tape. One possible way to store the record at its proper space is to move the tape back to the beginning of the last record. This is referred to as **backspacing.** After a tape is backspaced to the beginning of the record just read, the record could be stored in its former position on the original tape.

There are several disadvantages to this method. First, it takes extra processing time to backspace the tape, which could significantly slow down the overall program. Another disadvantage occurs when a revised variable length record is a different size than the original one. If this situation occurs, part of the following record could be lost due to the increase in the size of the revised record. This impractical approach is not used.

Instead, a second tape is generally used for the revised output. Upon completion, the revised tape becomes the latest updated data file, and the old tape file can be used for a backup historical file.

The following example illustrates the operation of a magnetic tape file when a separate output tape is used in the processing.

Example 12.7

Assume that the utility records of Example 12.4 are stored as a sequential file on magnetic tape. Develop an algorithm that will prepare the bills for all customers in the file by computing charges for one of the two utilities. Preparation of the bill involves calculating the cost, which is based on the rate for the utility and the amount consumed. Then the balances contained in the record must be updated. The bill is printed and the updated record is saved on a separate tape.

Solution

```
PROGRAM EXAMPLE 12.7;

    (* PREPARE GAS AND ELECTRIC UTILITY BILL FOR ALL ACCOUNTS *)

    FILE TAPEOLD, TAPENEW;

    (* TAPEOLD = PREVIOUS UTILITY FILE,
       TAPENEW = UPDATED UTILITY FILE *)

BEGIN
    READ (CODE, MONTH, DAY, YEAR); (* INPUT FIRST TRANSACTION *)

    (* INPUT FIRST RECORD *)
    READ (TAPEOLD, ACCOUNT, (CUSTOMER[I],I := 1,7),
        GASRATE, PREVGASREAD, PRESGASREAD, PREVGASBAL, PRESGASBAL,
        ELECTRATE, PREVELECTREAD, PRESELECTREAD, PREVELECTBAL,
        PRESELECTBAL);

    WHILE (ACCOUNT <> 999999) DO
    BEGIN
        IF (CODE = 0) (* GAS UTILITY *)
        THEN
            BEGIN
                USAGE := PRESGASREAD - PREVGASREAD;
                COST := GASRATE * USAGE;
                PREVGASBAL := PRESGASBAL;
                PRESGASBAL := PRESGASBAL + COST;

                (* OUTPUT GAS BILL *)
                WRITE (ACCOUNT, (CUSTOMER[I],I := 1,7), "GAS USED =", USAGE,
                    "AMOUNT OWED =", PRESGASBAL, MONTH, DAY, YEAR);
            END
        ELSE (* PROCESS ELECTRIC UTILITY *)
            BEGIN
                USAGE := PRESELECTREAD - PREVELECTREAD;
                COST := ELECTRATE * USAGE;
                PREVELECTBAL := PRESELECTBAL;
                PRESELECTBAL := PRESELECTBAL + COST;

                (* OUTPUT ELECTRIC BILL *)
                WRITE (ACCOUNT, (CUSTOMER[I],I := 1,7), "ELECTRIC USED =",
                USAGE,
                    "AMOUNT OWED =", PRESELECTBAL, MONTH, DAY, YEAR);
            END;

        (* WRITE CUSTOMER RECORD TO UPDATE FILE *)
        WRITE (TAPENEW, ACCOUNT, (CUSTOMER[I],I := 1,7), GASRATE,
            PREVGASREAD, PRESGASREAD, PREVGASBAL, PRESGASBAL, ELECTRATE,
            PREVELECTREAD, PRESELECTREAD, PREVELECTBAL, PRESELECTBAL);

        (* INPUT NEXT RECORD *)
        READ (TAPEOLD, ACCOUNT, (CUSTOMER[I],I := 1,7), GASRATE,
```

```
                   PREVGASREAD, PRESGASREAD, PREVGASBAL, PRESGASBAL, ELECTRATE,
                   PREVELECTREAD, PRESELECTREAD, PREVELECTBAL, PRESELECTBAL);
         END;

    END. (* EXAMPLE 12.7 *)
```

Two tape files are used in this algorithm; one is the input utility file and the other is the updated output utility file. The variable, CODE, indicates whether the gas (CODE = 0) or the electric (CODE = 1) will be processed. The usage of the appropriate utility is calculated as the present reading minus the previous reading. The cost is the amount used times the rate for that utility. The previous balance becomes the present balance. The new present balance is the cost plus the present balance.

The bill is printed and the updated record is written to the new output tape. The next sequential record is read and processing continues until the trailer value is encountered.

After each record is updated, it is written to the new tape. Upon completion of processing, the new tape is the latest and most accurate record. In the next processing cycle, this new tape would be the input to the program. Although the old tape is no longer needed, it would be retained for some time in most computer installations as a backup tape; should the new tape not be usable later (e.g., some gross error in the program or inadvertent destruction of the tape), the old one would still be available. Eventually the old tape would be "destroyed" by writing over it for some other purpose.

End Solution

Example 12.7 illustrated the use of a sequential access tape file. To distinguish one tape file from another, it is necessary to include certain information at the beginning of the tape. Thus most systems provide a **header** or **label,** at the start of a tape to provide such information as the name of the file, the tape number, the date written, and the size and number of the physical records on the tape. Most systems have some form of OPEN and CLOSE command that checks and records this information in the header.

In manipulating tape storage devices, there are generally a number of input/output commands needed besides READ and WRITE. Although these commands differ among languages, the languages themselves do not account for all the differences. A particular computer can have a major impact upon these instructions; therefore, the vendor's language manual must be consulted when using tapes. Although the specifics vary, the general concepts of many of these commands are similar. The following list indicates the nature of some of these operations.

1. Backspace

The **BACKSPACE command** allows the computer to go back a number of records, i.e., it reverses the tape. A particular command might imply that only one block is to be backspaced at a time, but most languages will allow you to specify any INTEGER number of blocked records to be backspaced. In any case the tape must be backspaced by blocks, since the interrecord gap is used to count the number of blocks passed over.

2. Skip

The **SKIP command** moves the tape forward without reading the contents of the blocks. Thus it is similar to the backspace, but it is used to go in a forward direction. Again the number of records skipped refers to blocks or physical records.

3. Rewind

The **REWIND command** causes the tape to be rewound to the beginning of the tape.

4. Write End-of-File

On a magnetic tape, it is necessary to have some type of marker to denote the end of the file; this is usually referred to as an **end-of-file marker.** Sometimes a specialized command, such as a **WRITE END-OF-FILE command,** is used. In some languages, there is a single command that does several things. For example, a command to close a file might also write the end-of-file mark, rewind the tape, and release the buffer space back to the system.

5. Sense End-of-File Mark

It is often desirable to know when the end of the file is reached. For example, if we are processing all the records of a file, we might need to know when we reach the end of the tape so that we can terminate the program. Or we might want to get to the end of a file so that we could add more records. Thus there is generally some provision for a **SENSE END-OF-FILE MARK** command.

Due to the differences in the implementation of these concepts, we do not believe it is advantageous to provide examples using them. If you understand the general concepts of these commands, you can use the language manual for your computer to understand them in detail.

D. Direct Access Files

Magnetic disk storage is analogous to your home phonograph system. Instead of a single, reducing spiral track of continuous, audio recording, the magnetic disk can be considered to be composed of a number of concentric circles, or tracks, composed of discrete bits of information. Each of these tracks can be written on and read from by a read/write head that "flies" above the surface of the disk.

Although the individual bits are organized sequentially around a track, the disk is not considered a sequential storage device, because the position of the read/write head can be moved from track to track. Each track can be thought of as being divided into pie-shaped slices called **sectors.**

All tracks are numbered for ease of addressing. Sectors are also numbered, with each sector having a unique address. The address of the sector is written into the sector as a header so that the disk controller can read the address and determine the position of the read/write head.

Due to a disk's physical design, the time necessary to retrieve data from a disk is considerably less than the time to read data from a magnetic tape and in general any record can be accessed as readily as any other. Thus a disk is referred to as a **direct access device.**

Because of the differences in physical characteristics, files on disks are stored somewhat differently than files on tapes. Disks constantly rotate at their full operating speed, up to 3600 RPM, and do not need to speed up or slow down to read and write; thus there is no need for interrecord gaps.

There is another difference in storage techniques on disks. Most disks are organized into **fixed length sectors** to facilitate the transfer of information. Each track of the disk contains a number of sectors, as illustrated in Figure 12–3. All transfers to and from the disk start at the beginning of a sector. A physical record on the device is aligned with the beginning of a sector, but it may require more than one sector.

Figure 12–3.
Schematic View of a
Disk Surface

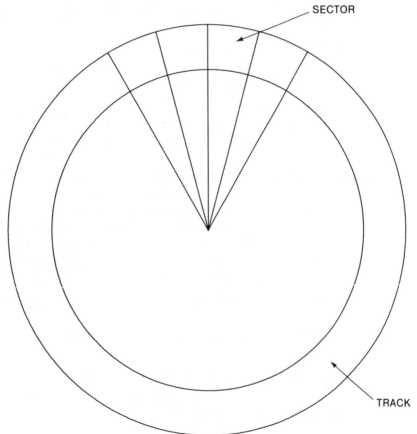

An efficient physical record size would be one that is close to a multiple of the sector size. The use of the blocking factor describing the relationship between the logical and physical record must then consider the size of the sector. This is illustrated in the following example.

Example 12.8

A particular computer system has disk sectors of 240 characters each. One application to be run on the system has a logical record of 70 characters. Discuss the contents of the disk file when

a. The physical record and logical record are the same size
b. The physical record contains three logical records
c. The physical record contains 24 logical records.

Solution

a. This physical record contains 70 characters. Since all disk transfers occur in terms of physical records and each physical record involves at least one sector, there will only be one physical record in each sector. Thus only 70 of the 240 characters in a sector will be used; over 70 percent of the disk file will be wasted space.

b. This physical record contains 210 characters. There will only be 30 unused characters of the available 240; thus only 12.5 percent of the disk space will be wasted in each sector.

c. The 24 logical records will take 24 times 70, or 1680, characters. Since there are 240 characters in a sector, the entire physical record will take 7 sectors, but there will be no wasted space. Although you might want to use this size physical record to avoid wasting space, other factors must be considered. For example, if two buffers are to be used for this file, each buffer must be 1680 characters and there would be 3360 characters of main memory used for these buffers. If these buffers were considered too large for the system, a reasonable compromise might be a blocking factor of 10. Ten logical records would require 700 characters, or three disk sectors. This would require a smaller buffer and less than 3 percent (20 divided by 720) of the disk space would be wasted. Thus, selecting the blocking factor is a matter of judgment, based upon various considerations.

End Solution

Direct access files can be organized in several ways. Although various languages and systems provide different types, the following three methods of organization are common.

1. Sequential

In a **sequential disk file organization** records are stored in the order in which they are encountered in the program. Although it is very much like a sequential tape file, a disk is generally much faster than tape. If the records are sorted in some manner before processing, the sequential disk file can be used advantageously, just as tape files can be. There are numerous other cases in which the sequential disk file is useful.

2. Direct Random

A **random file** is one in which any given record can be accessed without first accessing all the intervening records. With a direct access device, or disk, the time needed to access an arbitrary record is a constant, independent of the position of the record in the file.

A **direct random disk file** is one type of random organization. The location of a record can be found directly, using one of several methods. One way to access a record is to know the physical location of the record on the device. A more beneficial way is to perform some transformation upon one of the fields that is used as a key. This transformation will consist of a calculation or some operation upon the key, resulting in a physical address, or location. This method of address calculation is sometimes called **scrambling,** or **hash coding.**

3. Indexed Sequential

An **indexed sequential disk file** is another type of random file organization. In the indexed sequential disk file, the records are stored in a sequential manner, but each record has a key. This key could be a name, social security number, account number, and so on. The key and the corresponding record number, or record address, are then stored in an **index,** or **dictionary.** When a particular record is to be retrieved, this index can be used to look up the physical location of the record.

The general concept of this dictionary, or index, is illustrated in Figure 12–4. If the keys stored in the dictionary are in sequential order, a binary search routine can be used to locate a particular key and the corresponding location of the record to which it refers. The process of locating the record in the main file is then quite rapid.

If the dictionary is not too large and if it is used frequently, it can be kept in main memory as an array. If the dictionary is not held in main memory, several other alternatives are available. If the dictionary is used infrequently it can be stored on disk and be read into memory as needed.

In this chapter we will assume that the dictionary is stored permanently on disk. At the beginning of a program that accesses an indexed sequential file, the dictionary relating to that file will be read into an array in main memory where it will remain while the program is being executed. After the comple-

Figure 12-4.
Dictionary of
Indexed Sequential
Disk File

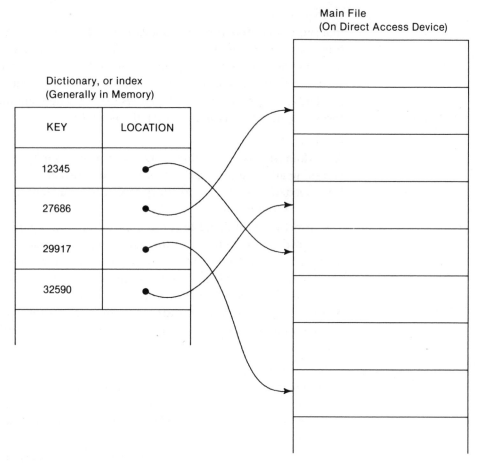

tion of processing, the dictionary is no longer saved in main memory. If changes have been made in the dictionary, the revised version is written over the original version still on disk. If no changes have occurred, the original dictionary on disk is still accurate, and the duplicate dictionary in main memory is destroyed.

Dictionaries are developed and maintained by the applications program. In all computer systems there must also be a **directory** that shows the location of various files on the systems storage devices. These systems directories are controlled by the operating system software and pertain to the locations of files. The dictionaries we have been discussing provide information on the locations of records within these files.

When referencing a disk in our pseudocode, it is necessary to distinguish in our I/O statements between a sequential file and a random file. A reference to a sequential file will be denoted by a single name, e.g., FILEZ, but a random file will be denoted by the name of the file and a variable used to distinguish a particular record on that file, e.g., FILEZ[INDEX].

The name of the file must be explicitly declared at the beginning of the program in a file statement that has the form of the reserved word FILE followed by the name of the file. For example, the statement

FILE ABC;

declares that ABC is the name of a file. The name of the file must always appear as the first name within the parentheses of a READ or WRITE statement. Thus, given the previous declaration, the statement

READ (ABC, X, Y, Z);

causes the next record on file ABC to be read and the appropriate fields of the record to be stored in variables X, Y, and Z. The statement READ (ABC[INDEX], X, Y, Z) causes the INDEX record of file ABC to be read and the appropriate fields of that record to be stored in variables X, Y, and Z.

The use of a direct access file differs somewhat from the use of a magnetic tape file. When a record of a disk file is changed, the record is almost always stored back in its original file. In the case of a fixed length record, the record is usually placed in its original position. Since any record of the file can be accessed as readily as any other record, there is no extra processing time involved in storing the record at its original location. In fact, it can be faster since the previous location has already been determined and the dictionary does not need to be used to find a new location.

If the record is a variable length record and its size is increased as a result of changes to the record, it might not fit in its original position. In this case, a new location might need to be found.

The following example utilizes a disk and its corresponding dictionary. It is based on the use of the utility file described in Table 12–4. This provides a comparison of the processing of a disk with the processing of a magnetic tape file that was used in Example 12.7.

Example 12.9

Assume that the utility records of Example 12.4 are stored as an indexed sequential file (FILE2) on a disk. Develop a program that will record a new reading for either or both of the two utilities in the record. After updating the record, the account number along with the old and new readings of one or both utilities are to be output on the line printer. The updated record is then to be stored in its original location.

Solution

```
PROGRAM EXAMPLE 12.9;

(* RECORD GAS AND ELECTRIC UTILITY METER READINGS *)

FILE FILE1, FILE2;

   (* FILE1 = DICTIONARY OF POINTERS INTO FILE2,
      FILE2 = UTILITY RECORDS BY ACCOUNT *)

BEGIN
   (* INPUT DICTIONARY *)
   READ (FILE1, NBR);
   READ (FILE1, (KEY(I),LOC(I),I := 1,NBR));

   READ(ACCOUNT, ELECT, GAS); (* INPUT FIRST CUSTOMER TRANSACTION *)

   WHILE (ACCOUNT <> 999999) DO (* PROCESS CUSTOMERS UNTIL TRAILER VALUE *)
   BEGIN
       CALL BINAR (KEY, NBR, ACCOUNT, PTR); (* SEARCH KEY FOR ACCOUNT *)

       IF (PTR <> 0) (* ACCOUNT IS IN KEY AT POSITION PTR *)
       THEN
           BEGIN
               READ (FILE2[LOC(PTR)], ACCOUNT, (CUSTOMER[I],I := 1,7),
                   GASRATE, PREVGASREAD, PRESGASREAD, PREVGASBAL,
                   PRESGASBAL, ELECTRATE, PREVELECTREAD, PRESELECTREAD,
                   PREVELECTBAL, PRESELECTBAL);

               IF (ELECT <> 0) (* PROCESS ELECTRIC READING *)
               THEN
                   BEGIN
                       PREVELECTREAD := PRESELECTREAD;
                       PRESELECTREAD := ELECT;
                   END;

               IF (GAS <> 0) (* PROCESS GAS READING *)
```

```
                        THEN
                            BEGIN
                                PREVGASREAD := PRESGASREAD;
                                PRESGASREAD := GAS;
                            END;

                        (* PRINT OUT UTILITY READINGS *)
                        WRITE (ACCOUNT,(CUSTOMER[I],I := 1,7),
                            "PREVIOUS GAS READING =", PREVGASREAD,
                            "PRESENT GAS READING =", PRESGASREAD,
                            "PREVIOUS ELECTRIC READING =", PREVELECTREAD,
                            "PRESENT ELECTRIC READING =", PRESELECTREAD);

                        (* OUTPUT TO UPDATE FILE *)
                        WRITE (FILE2[LOC(PTR)], ACCOUNT, (CUSTOMER[I],I := 1,7),
                            GASRATE, PREVGASREAD, PRESGASREAD, PREVGASBAL,
                            PRESGASBAL, ELECTRATE, PREVELECTREAD, PRESELECTREAD,
                            PREVELECTBAL, PRESELECTBAL);
                END
            ELSE
                WRITE("ERROR--ACCOUNT NOT FOUND", ACCOUNT, ELECT, GAS);

            READ (ACCOUNT, ELECT, GAS); (* GET NEXT TRANSACTION *)
        END;

    END. (* END EXAMPLE 12.9 *)
```

Let's assume that the dictionary for FILE2 is stored on the same disk as a sequential file (FILE1). The first item in the index provides the size of the index. At the start of the program, this value is read into the variable NBR. Using this value, the remainder of FILE1 is read into the parallel arrays KEY, containing account numbers, and LOC, containing pointers to the associated records in FILE2.

The input record for each transaction contains three items of information: the account number (ACCOUNT), the gas reading (GAS), and the electric reading (ELECT). Using the trailer card termination technique, the last transaction is signalled by an account number of 999999.

For valid account numbers, KEY is searched using SUBROUTINE BINAR, which is the binary search previously developed in Example 11.8. If the resulting pointer (PTR) does not equal zero, the record was found by BINAR and is read from FILE2, location LOC(PTR). This is the initial item in the READ statement and uses the annotation FILE2[LOC(PTR)]. The utility accounts are then updated for nonzero electric and gas readings, output to the printer, and rewritten into the appropriate location, [LOC(PTR)], in FILE2. Since no changes were made to KEY or LOC, there is no need to rewrite FILE1 when processing terminates.

End Solution

As with tape files, it is necessary to consult the vendor's programming manual when performing disk input/output operations. Due to these variations, we will not illustrate the operations with an example. The following comments merely point out some of the concepts of disk input/output.

The READ and WRITE commands referring to disk are generally similar to those used in this text so far. A number of the other I/O commands previously discussed for tapes are available for use with disks although the actual implementation might be different. Some of these differences are because disks rotate. Remember that a tape file will actually stop at the position where the next record to be read is located. But because the disk is rotating, it obviously does not stop at the position of the next record; the location of the next record to be accessed is merely recorded in the disk controller.

Thus a BACKSPACE command, if supported in the language, does not involve a physical movement of the disk. It merely decrements (decreases) the value of the pointer so that it is pointing to the previous record. Likewise, the SKIP command will merely move the pointer by incrementing it.

The REWIND command might or might not be defined for a disk. In any case this instruction will not cause the disk to go in the opposite direction. In some computers, the command is used to reset the variable pointing to the disk file to the first record in the file.

The WRITE END-OF-FILE and SENSE END-OF-FILE commands can also be useful in determining the end of a disk file but this does not necessarily imply that a physical end of file is written on a disk as it is with a tape. The end of a disk file can be determined by keeping track of the number of records in the file and comparing the current value of the pointer to the maximum value. Thus the end of the file can be sensed by the operating system and be indicated to the user program by using the information in memory without any actual reference to the disk itself.

12.4 File Maintenance Operations

The routine operations associated with data processing can be grouped in the following categories:

• Sorting
• Merging
• Searching and data retrieval
• File maintenance
• Full file processing

The concepts included in sorting were discussed at some length in Chapter 10; merging and searching were covered in Chapter 11. Although most of the major aspects of searching a file were covered, the various examples and problems in this chapter will introduce other considerations in searching and data retrieval.

One of the major concepts discussed in this chapter is file maintenance; several examples will be provided. The term **full file processing** is used to denote those actions that are applied to every record in a file and that are not necessarily pure file maintenance. For example, every record in an inventory file might be examined in order to compute the total value of stock that is on hand at a given time.

File maintenance is the alteration of a file. There are several types of file maintenance transactions, including

- Addition of records to a file
- Deletion of records from a file
- Changing the value of a field of a record
- Changing the structure of a record or of a file

The last type of file maintenance occurs infrequently. For example, changing a file structure from a sequential to a random organization would be a major change in the file structure. In another instance, every record in a file might be expanded from 20 words to 30 words, again a major change. Although infrequent, these are important operations that require special, individually designed programs.

File maintenance can be applied to several types of files, namely, sequential arrays held in main memory, sequential tape files, and disk files. The methods of maintaining files on different media vary; the next two sections will discuss examples of file maintenance operations on tape and disk files. The following example covers changes to an array. In this situation, the addition and deletion of a record involves the movement of data within the array either to make room for a new record being added or to fill the gap left by a deleted record.

Example 12.10

A two-dimension array contains five columns of data for each array row. Three types of changes are to be made to the array: addition of an array row, deletion of an array row, and change of data in an array row.

Each change is specified by a separate transaction data entry in which the first field denotes the required action or transaction. A value of 1 will denote an addition to the array, a value of 2 will denote a deletion from the array, and a value of 3 will indicate a change in one element of the array. In all three cases, the second data element provides the row involved in the change. For an addition, the third through seventh data elements provide the values of the five elements of the array row. For a change, the third and fourth data elements indicate the column to be changed and the new value.

Figure 12–5.

$$
\begin{bmatrix}
11 & 93 & 13 & 14 & 15 \\
21 & 22 & 91 & 24 & 25 \\
31 & 32 & 33 & 34 & 35 \\
41 & 42 & 43 & 44 & 45 \\
51 & 52 & 53 & 92 & 55
\end{bmatrix}
$$

a. Array After First Three
   Transactions

$$
\begin{bmatrix}
11 & 93 & 13 & 14 & 15 \\
21 & 22 & 91 & 24 & 25 \\
31 & 32 & 33 & 34 & 35 \\
51 & 52 & 53 & 92 & 55
\end{bmatrix}
$$

b. Array After Fourth Transaction

$$
\begin{bmatrix}
11 & 93 & 13 & 14 & 15 \\
21 & 22 & 91 & 24 & 25 \\
31 & 32 & 33 & 34 & 35 \\
51 & 52 & 53 & 92 & 94
\end{bmatrix}
$$

c. Array After Fifth Transaction

$$
\begin{bmatrix}
11 & 93 & 13 & 14 & 15 \\
81 & 82 & 83 & 84 & 85 \\
21 & 22 & 91 & 24 & 25 \\
31 & 32 & 33 & 34 & 35 \\
51 & 52 & 53 & 92 & 94
\end{bmatrix}
$$

d. Array After Sixth Transaction

$$
\begin{bmatrix}
11 & 93 & 13 & 14 & 15 \\
81 & 82 & 83 & 84 & 85 \\
21 & 22 & 91 & 24 & 25 \\
95 & 32 & 33 & 34 & 35 \\
51 & 52 & 53 & 92 & 94
\end{bmatrix}
$$

e. Array After Last Transaction

$$
\begin{bmatrix}
11 & 93 & 13 & 14 & 15 \\
81 & 82 & 91 & 84 & 85 \\
21 & 22 & 23 & 24 & 25 \\
95 & 42 & 43 & 44 & 45 \\
51 & 52 & 53 & 92 & 55
\end{bmatrix}
$$

f. Array If Transaction Order Had
   Been Reversed

Show the final contents of this array after processing the changes shown in Table 12–7.

Solution

The first three file maintenance actions involve a change in the contents of the record. After these three changes have been processed, the array is as shown in Figure 12–5a. The fourth file maintenance action deletes the fourth row of the array. Thus the fifth row is moved up and there are only four rows in the array, as shown in Figure 12–5b. The next set of data revises the present fourth row (originally the fifth row), providing the results in Figure 12–5c. The next action is the addition of a new second row. This necessitates the movement of three rows to make room, as shown in Figure 12–5d. The last data set calls for a change action, resulting in the final array shown in Figure 12–5e.

These file maintenance operations are sequence sensitive, i.e., the final array contents are dependent upon the sequence in which the changes are processed. For example, if the changes are processed in the reverse order of that shown in Table 12–7, the final array would appear as shown in Figure 12–5f. This result is obviously different from Figure 12–5e.

End Solution

Table 12-6 Original Two-Dimension Array

	Column				
Row	1	2	3	4	5
1	11	12	13	14	15
2	21	22	23	24	25
3	31	32	33	34	35
4	41	42	43	44	45
5	51	52	53	54	55

The original array contents are shown in Table 12–6.

Table 12-7 Sample Input Transactions

Code	Row	Column	Values
3,	2	3	91
3,	5	4	92
3,	1	2	93
2,	4		
3,	4	5	94
1	2		81 82 83 84 85
3	4	1	95

The operations necessary for addition or deletion of array rows are developed in the following example.

Example 12.11

Develop an algorithm in the form of a subroutine that will accomplish the file maintenance actions outlined in the preceding example.

Solution

```
SUBROUTINE MAINT (DATA, NR, NC, ROW, COL, CODE, TRANS);

    (*  DATA = ARRAY TO BE UPDATED,
          NR = NUMBER OF ROWS IN DATA,
          NC = NUMBER OF COLUMNS IN DATA,
         ROW = ROW TO BE UPDATED,
         COL = COLUMN TO BE UPDATED,
        CODE = INDICATES UPDATE TO BE MADE,
       TRANS = UPDATE INFORMATION *)

BEGIN
   IF (CODE = 1)
   THEN
        CALL ADD (DATA, NR, NC, ROW, TRANS)
   ELSE
       BEGIN
           IF (CODE = 2)
           THEN
               CALL DELETE (DATA, NR, NC, ROW)
           ELSE
              BEGIN
                  IF (CODE = 3)
                  THEN
                      CALL UPDATE (DATA, ROW, COL, TRANS)
                  ELSE
                      WRITE ("ERROR--INVALID CODE", CODE);
              END;
       END;

END; (* END MAINT *)
```

The pseudocode for SUBROUTINE MAINT implements the solution through calls to four subroutines: MAINT, ADD, DELETE, and UPDATE. These maintain the array DATA and correspond to the three file maintenance transactions previously discussed. Assume that the call to MAINT (DATA, NR, NC, ROW, COL, CODE, TRANS) provides the array (DATA) to be processed, the number (NR) of rows, the number (NC) of columns, the row (ROW) to be processed, the column (COL) to be processed, the transaction code (CODE), and the transaction data (TRANS). Not all of these variables are necessary to each transaction.

```
SUBROUTINE ADD (DATA, NR, NC, ROW, TRANS);

    (*  DATA = TO BE UPDATED,
          NR = NUMBER OF ROWS IN DATA,
          NC = NUMBER OF COLUMNS IN DATA,
         ROW = POSITION AT WHICH TO INSERT TRANS,
       TRANS = DATA TO BE INSERTED AT ROW *)

BEGIN
    FOR I := NR STEP (-1) WHILE (I >= ROW) DO (* MOVE ROWS DOWN BY ONE *)
      FOR J := 1 STEP 1 UNTIL NC DO
        DATA(I+1,J) := DATA(I,J);

    FOR J := 1 STEP 1 UNTIL NC DO (* INSERT TRANS AT ROW *)
      DATA(ROW,J) := TRANS(J);

    NR := NR + 1; (* UPDATE ROW COUNT *)

END; (* END ADD *)
```

In SUBROUTINE ADD (DATA, NR, NC, ROW, TRANS), a row is added to to the array. The ROW through NR rows of DATA must be moved down one position starting with row NR. The value of NR must be incremented by 1 to reflect the addition. Note that the value of COL is not applicable and is not passed from MAINT to ADD as a formal parameter.

```
SUBROUTINE DELETE (DATA, NR, NC, ROW);

    (* DATA = ARRAY TO BE UPDATED,
         NR = NUMBER OF ROWS IN DATA,
         NC = NUMBER OF COLUMNS IN DATA,
        ROW = ROW TO BE DELETED *)

BEGIN
    FOR I := ROW STEP 1 WHILE (I < NR) DO (* MOVE ROWS UP BY ONE *)
      FOR J := 1 STEP 1 UNTIL NC DO
        DATA(I,J) := DATA(I + 1,J);

    NR := NR - 1; (* UPDATE ROW COUNT *)

END; (* END DELETE *)
```

In SUBROUTINE DELETE (DATA, NR, NC, ROW), an array row is deleted. All rows are moved up one, starting at ROW+1 through NR. The value of NR is decremented by 1 to reflect the deletion. Note that the variables COL and TRANS are not applicable and are not passed from MAINT to DELETE as formal parameters.

```
SUBROUTINE UPDATE (DATA, ROW, COL, TRANS);

    (*  DATA = ARRAY TO BE UPDATED,
         ROW = ROW TO BE UPDATED,
         COL = COLUMN TO BE UPDATED,
       TRANS = UPDATE ELEMENT *)

BEGIN

    DATA(ROW,COL) := TRANS(1);

END; (* END UPDATE *)
```

SUBROUTINE UPDATE (DATA, ROW, COL, TRANS) assumes that the update consists of a single element in TRANS(1) for DATA (ROW, COL).

End Solution

12.5 A Tape-Oriented File System

Example 12.3 provides a record layout format for a file of golf averages and handicaps. The next two examples outline a simple data processing system that treats this file as a sequential tape file. Although you might not normally associate the game of golf with computers, the principles involved in manipulating this golf file are the same as those used in many other data processing problems.

Example 12.12

Develop a file maintenance algorithm for golf scores using the record format discussed in Example 12.3 and presented in Table 12–3. The sample transaction record format is shown in Table 12–8.

Table 12-8 Golfer Transaction Record Layout

Name of Field	Field Size	Character Index In Record	Type
Transaction code	1	1	INTEGER
Identification	4	2–5	INTEGER
Name	24	6–29	ALPHA
Number of scores	2	30–31	INTEGER
Score 1	3	32–34	INTEGER
.	.	.	.
.	.	.	.
.	.	.	.
Score 15	3	74–76	INTEGER

The allowable transactions are as follows:

Code	Action
1	A new record is to be created from the input. This includes the golfer's name, identification code, and the scores to date (maximum of 15).
2	A golfer's record is to be deleted from the file.
3	Additional scores are to be added to an existing record. If the total number of scores is more than 15, only the latest 15 scores will be kept in the record.

Solution

```
PROGRAM EXAMPLE 12.12;

FILE TAPE1, TAPE2;

   (* TAPE1 = INPUT MASTER,
      TAPE2 = OUTPUT MASTER *)

(* COMMON VARIABLES--CODE, IDENTGOLFER, IDENTTRANS, NAMEGOLFER, NAMETRANS,
   SCORESGOLFER, SCORESTRANS, NUMSCORESGOLFER, NUMSCORESTRANS,
   AVERAGE, HANDICAP *)

SUBROUTINE GETGOLFER;

(* COMMON VARIABLES AND FILES FROM MAIN PROGRAM REPEATED HERE *)

BEGIN
   READ (TAPE1, IDENTGOLFER, (NAMEGOLFER(I),I := 1,4), NUMSCORESGOLFER,
      (SCORESGOLFER(I),I := 1,15), AVERAGE, HANDICAP);
END; (* END GETGOLFER *)

SUBROUTINE GETTRANS;

(* COMMON VARIABLES FROM MAIN PROGRAM REPEATED HERE *)

BEGIN
   READ (CODE, IDENTTRANS, (NAMETRANS(I),I := 1,4), NUMSCORESTRANS,
      (SCORESTRANS(I),I := 1,15));
END; (* END GETTRANS *)


SUBROUTINE PUTGOLFER;

(* COMMON VARIABLES AND FILES FROM MAIN PROGRAM REPEATED HERE *)

BEGIN
   WRITE (TAPE2, IDENTGOLFER, (NAMEGOLFER(I),I := 1,4), NUMSCORESGOLFER,
      (SCORESGOLFER(I),I := 1,15), AVERAGE, HANDICAP);
END; (* END PUTGOLFER *)
```

```
SUBROUTINE NEWSCORES;

(* COMMON VARIABLES FROM MAIN PROGRAM REPEATED HERE *)

BEGIN
    SCORECOUNT := NUMSCORESGOLFER + NUMSCORESTRANS;
    IF (SCORECOUNT <= 15)
    THEN
        BEGIN
            (* SAVE OLD AND NEW SCORES *)
            FOR I := 1 STEP 1 UNTIL NUMSCORESTRANS DO
                SCORESGOLFER(NUMSCORESGOLFER + I) := SCORESTRANS(I);

            NUMSCORESGOLFER := SCORECOUNT;
        END
    ELSE
        (* MORE THAN 15 SCORES, SAVE ALL NEW AND SOME OLD *)
        BEGIN
            OLDSCORES := 15 - NUMSCORESTRANS;
            J := 1;
            (* MOVE OLD SCORES, SAVING LATEST OF OLD SCORES *)
            FOR I := NUMSCORESGOLFER - OLDSCORES + 1 STEP 1 UNTIL
            NUMSCORESGOLFER DO
            BEGIN
                SCORESGOLFER(J) := SCORESGOLFER(I);
                J := J + 1;
            END;

            (* COPY NEW SCORES *)
            J := 1;
            FOR I := OLDSCORES + 1 STEP 1 UNTIL SCORECOUNT DO
            BEGIN
                SCORESGOLFER(I) := SCORESTRANS(J);
                J := J + 1;
            END;
        END;

END; (* END NEWSCORES *)


(***** MAIN PROGRAM BEGINS HERE *****)
BEGIN
    CALL GETGOLFER; (* INPUT NEXT GOLFER RECORD *)

    CALL GETTRANS; (* INPUT NEXT TRANSACTION RECORD *)

    (* PROCESS TRANSACTIONS UNTIL TRAILER RECORD *)
    WHILE ((IDENTGOLFER <> 9999) AND (IDENTTRANS <> 9999)) DO
    BEGIN
        (* GET FIRST RECORD THAT IS >= IDENTTRANS *)
        WHILE (IDENTGOLFER < IDENTTRANS) DO
        BEGIN
            CALL PUTGOLFER;
            CALL GETGOLFER;
        END;
```

```
            IF (IDENTGOLFER = IDENTTRANS)
        THEN
            BEGIN
                IF (CODE = 2) (* DELETE RECORD FROM TAPE1 *)
                THEN
                    BEGIN
                        CALL GETGOLFER;
                        WRITE ("DELETED IDENT=", IDENTTRANS);
                    END
                ELSE
                    BEGIN
                        IF (CODE = 3) (* CHANGE SCORES *)
                        THEN
                            BEGIN
                                CALL NEWSCORES;
                                CALL PUTGOLFER;
                                CALL GETGOLFER;
                            END
                        ELSE
                            WRITE ("ERROR--ADD RECORD EXISTS",
                                IDENTTRANS);
                    END;
            END
        ELSE (* IDENTGOLFER > IDENTTRANS *)
            BEGIN
                IF (CODE = 1) (* ADD NEW GOLFER *)
                THEN
                    BEGIN
                        TEMPAVERAGE := 0;
                        TEMPHANDICAP := 0;
                        WRITE (TAPE2, IDENTTRANS, (NAMETRANS(I),I := 1,4),
                                NUMSCORESTRANS, (SCORESTRANS(I),I := 1,15),
                                TEMPAVERAGE, TEMPHANDICAP);
                        WRITE ("RECORD ADDED =", IDENTTRANS);
                    END
                ELSE
                    WRITE ("ERROR--RECORD OUT OF SEQUENCE", IDENTGOLFER);
            END;

        CALL GETTRANS; (* INPUT NEXT TRANSACTION *)
    END;

    WHILE (IDENTGOLFER <> 9999) DO (* SAVE REMAINDER OF FILE *)
    BEGIN
        CALL PUTGOLFER;
        CALL GETGOLFER;
    END;

    CALL PUTGOLFER; (* SAVE TRAILER RECORD *)

END. (* END EXAMPLE 12.12 *)
```

In this program it is assumed that the input transaction file and input golfer file are sorted in ascending order. Files are input and output via calls to the respective subroutines: GETGOLFER, GETTRANS, and PUTGOLFER. After initializing the first iteration by inputting the first transaction record (GETTRANS) and the first golfer record (GETGOLFER), iteration continues until a trailer value (9999) is input as the identifier from either file. Regardless of the transaction code, no action is appropriate until a golfer record (IDENTGOLFER) is input that is greater than or equal to the transaction record (IDENTTRANS). When this condition is satisfied, this iteration terminates and a check is made for matching identifiers. If a match is found, only code 2 or 3 is acceptable; otherwise an error condition exists.

In the case of CODE = 1, the addition code, an error condition exists if the record to be added already exists. If the transaction identifier is less than the golfer identifier, an error exists; either the golfer file or the transaction file is out of sequence.

In the case of CODE = 2, the deletion code, a new golfer record is read and the previous record is deleted by not writing it to the update file.

In the case of CODE = 3, the update code, a check is made to see if the total number of scores exceeds 15. If so, all the new scores and the latest of the old scores, equal to 15 minus the number of new scores, are retained. If the total number of scores is less than 15, the new scores are appended to the old scores. These calculations occur in SUBROUTINE NEWSCORES.

After each iteration the next transaction record is input (GETTRANS). Upon termination of the iteration, care is taken that the remaining records in the golfer file are transferred to the update file. This must include the final trailer record.

End Solution

The next example illustrates a full file process in which the entire master tape is read and a computation is performed for each record. Although values in the records are changed, there is no input file of updated data. All modifications to the records are based on the information already contained in the record. They are not the result of addition, deletion, or modification of the basic data of the file.

Example 12.13

Develop an algorithm to process the entire golf score file and compute an average for each golfer. If there are five or more scores, a handicap is calculated using the formula:

Handicap = .80 * (Average − Rating),

where the rating is a par score assigned to that particular golf course.

Solution

```
PROGRAM EXAMPLE 12.13;

FILE TAPE1, TAPE2;

   (* TAPE1 = INPUT MASTER,
      TAPE2 = OUTPUT MASTER *)

(* COMMON VARIABLES—CODE, IDENTGOLFER, NAMEGOLFER, SCORESGOLFER,
         NUMSCORESGOLFER, AVERAGE, HANDICAP *)


SUBROUTINE GETGOLFER;

(* COMMON VARIABLES AND FILES FROM MAIN PROGRAM REPEATED HERE *)

BEGIN
   READ (TAPE1, IDENTGOLFER, (NAMEGOLFER(I),I := 1,4), NUMSCORESGOLFER,
       (SCORESGOLFER(I),I := 1,15), AVERAGE, HANDICAP));
END; (* END GETGOLFER *)


SUBROUTINE PUTGOLFER;

(* COMMON VARIABLES AND FILES FROM MAIN PROGRAM REPEATED HERE *)

BEGIN
   WRITE (TAPE2, IDENTGOLFER, (NAMEGOLFER(I),I := 1,4), NUMSCORESGOLFER,
       (SCORESGOLFER(I),I := 1,15), AVERAGE, HANDICAP);
END; (* END PUTGOLFER *)


BEGIN (***** MAIN PROGRAM BEGINS HERE *****)
   READ (RATE); (* INPUT COURSE RATING *)

   CALL GETGOLFER; (* INPUT FIRST GOLFER *)

   (* PROCESS GOLF RECORDS UNTIL TRAILER VALUE *)
   WHILE (IDENTGOLFER <> 9999) DO
   BEGIN
      (* TOTAL SCORES AND CALCULATE AVERAGE *)
      SUM := 0;
      FOR I := 1 STEP 1 UNTIL NUMSCORESGOLFER DO
          SUM := SUM + SCORESGOLFER(I);

      IF (NUMSCORESGOLFER <> 0)
      THEN
          AVERAGE := SUM / NUMSCORESGOLFER
      ELSE
          AVERAGE := 0;
```

```
        IF (NUMSCORESGOLFER >= 5) (* CALCULATE HANDICAP *)
        THEN
            HANDICAP := .8 * (AVERAGE - RATE);

        CALL PUTGOLFER; (* OUTPUT RESULTS *)

        WRITE ("GOLFER RECORD", IDENTGOLFER, (NAMEGOLFER(I),I := 1,4),
            NUMSCORESGOLFER, (SCORESGOLFER(I),I := 1,15), AVERAGE,
            HANDICAP);

        CALL GETGOLFER; (* INPUT NEXT GOLFER *)
    END;
        CALL PUTGOLFER; (* SAVE TRAILER RECORD *)

    END. (* END EXAMPLE 12.13 *)
```

The individual records in the golf score file have fields reserved for an average and a handicap. The computation of these quantities will modify the information in some of the records. Since this is a sequential tape file, the modified records will be refiled on a new master tape. In this algorithm, the old and new master tapes are referred to as TAPE1 and TAPE2, respectively.

The program is initialized by reading the rating of the golf course into the variable RATE. In turn, each record is input by a call to SUBROUTINE GETGOLFER. The total of the golfer's scores is accumulated in the variable SUM by the iteration going from 1 to NUMSCORESGOLFER, which contains the number of valid scores in the record. The average score is then computed and stored in AVERAGE if the number of scores is greater than 0; otherwise AVERAGE is set to 0.

If the number of scores is equal to or greater than 5, the handicap formula is applied and the result is stored in HANDICAP. The updated record is then output to TAPE2 via a call to SUBROUTINE PUTGOLFER. An updated record is also output to the line printer. When the dummy identification number of 9999 is encountered for IDENTGOLFER, the processing is terminated. Note that the dummy record must be written to the new tape via a final call to PUTGOLFER so that it is available to terminate the next processing cycle.

End Solution

12.6 A Disk-Oriented File System

The vehicle record layout of Example 12.5 can be used in a computerized vehicle registration file. Such a file could be used for data retrieval; requests would access a single record of the file. Since this would be the normal mode of operation, efficient processing would demand that the file be maintained as a random file on a disk. A sequential file organization would be possible but extremely inefficient.

The next three examples develop a simple system implementing the vehicle registration file on a disk.

Example 12.14

Develop the record layouts for the input transactions to a vehicle registration file of a system with the record layout of Table 12–5. In designing the layouts, assume that the system must handle the addition, deletion and modification of records. In adding a new record to the file, the input must read an entire data record of 128 characters from the vehicle registration file. Assume the length of the input data record is restricted to a maximum of 80 characters and that the driver's Social Security Number (SSN) is the key to the record. Because of the record length restriction it is necessary to divide the input transaction record into two separate lines of input of up to 80 characters each, if needed.

Solution

A full transaction record will require two READ statements to input the entire record. In the case of a deletion transaction, however, only the value of the SSN is required from the transaction record. Thus only the first line of a deletion record is input and a single READ statement is sufficient. The same is true for modification transactions that apply to only the name or address fields. For efficiency the program reads two data lines for addition and for vehicle and registration modification transactions. One data line is read for deletion and for name and address modification transactions.

The layout of the first line of the transaction record is shown in Table 12–9. To determine the type of file maintenance action requested, a one-digit number is used as the transaction code; it appears as the first character in the record. The Social Security Number is used to match the first line of the record to the second whenever a second input line is required. It is also used as the key for matching the input transaction record to the records input from the vehicle registration file. The name and the address information take up the remainder of the 80 characters of the first line of the transaction record. This input can be used for deletion of the record, for modification of the name or address, or for the first line of input for a new record. Table 12–10 provides the layout of the second line of the transaction record; it is actually a continuation of the first line. In addition to the transaction code and the social security number, it contains the fields relating to vehicle description and registration. The Social Security Number is not needed in this second line; however, it provides a means of ensuring that the second line of the transaction input record matches the first.

End Solution

Table 12-9 Record Layout of First Line of Transaction

Name of Field	Field Size	Character Index In Record	Type
Code	1	1	INTEGER
Social security number	9	2–10	INTEGER
Name of owner	30	11–40	ALPHA
Address	20	41–60	ALPHA
City	13	61–73	ALPHA
State	2	74–75	ALPHA
Zip code	5	76–80	INTEGER

Table 12-10 Record Layout of Second Line of Transaction

Name of Field	Field Size	Character Index In Record	Type
Code	1	1	INTEGER
Social security number	9	2–10	INTEGER
Year	2	11–12	INTEGER
Make of vehicle	10	13–22	ALPHA
Model of vehicle	8	23–30	ALPHA
Type of vehicle	8	31–38	ALPHA
Color of vehicle	6	39–44	ALPHA
Horsepower	3	45–47	INTEGER
Cubic-inch displacement	3	48–50	INTEGER
State registered	2	51–52	ALPHA
Registration number	7	53–59	INTEGER

The following example for the vehicle registration file uses nine transaction codes. Basically these provide for file maintenance by changing various fields of the record without affecting other fields. Since the file is on disk, the sequence of records to be processed is not important.

Example 12.15

Develop an algorithm that will perform file maintenance actions on the master vehicle registration file, which is an indexed sequential disk file with 128-character records described in Table 12–5. The input transaction records are the two-line records described by Table 12–9 and Table 12–10. The following transactions are to be included:

Code	Action
1	Add a record to the file
2	Delete a record from the file
3	Modify the name field
4	Modify the address field
5	Modify the name and address field
6	Modify the car description
7	Modify the registration data
8	Terminate processing
9	Read the second line of transaction input

Solution

```
PROGRAM EXAMPLE 12.15;

FILE VEHICLE, DRTY;

    (* VEHICLE = AUTOMOBILE REGISTRATION FILE,
         DRTY = DIRECTORY OF POINTERS INTO VEHICLE *)

(* COMMON VARIABLES--FNAME, FSSN, FADDRESS, FCITY, FSTATE, FZIPCODE,
         FYEAR, FMAKE, FMODEL, FTYPE, FCOLOR, FHP, FCID, FREGSTATE,
         FREGNUMBER, CODE1, TNAME, TSSN, TADDRESS, TCITY, TSTATE,
         TZIPCODE, TYEAR, TMAKE, TMODEL, TTYPE, TCOLOR, THP, TCID,
         TREGSTATE, TREGNUMBER, CODE2, SSN1, SSN2 *)

(***** SUBROUTINE DUALSORT INSERTED HERE *****)


SUBROUTINE GETVEHICLE (INDEX);
    (* COMMON VARIABLES AND FILES FROM MAIN PROGRAM REPEATED HERE *)
BEGIN
    READ (VEHICLE[LOC(INDEX)], (FNAME(I),I := 1,5), FSSN,
        (FADDRESS(I),I := 1,4), (FCITY(I),I := 1,3), (FSTATE(I),I := 1,2),
```

```
                    FZIPCODE,  FYEAR,  (FMAKE(I),I  :=  1,2),  (FMODEL(I),I  :=  1,2),
                (FTYPE(I),I := 1,2), FCOLOR, FHP, FCID, FREGSTATE, FREGNUMBER);
      END; (* END GETVEHICLE *)


      SUBROUTINE PUTVEHICLE (INDEX);
         (* COMMON VARIABLES AND FILES FROM MAIN PROGRAM REPEATED HERE *)
      BEGIN
         WRITE (VEHICLE[LOC(INDEX)], (FNAME(I),I := 1,5), FSSN,
             (FADDRESS(I),I := 1,4), (FCITY(I),I := 1,4), (FSTATE(I),I := 1,2),
             FZIPCODE,  FYEAR,  (FMAKE(I),I  :=  1,2),  (FMODEL(I),I  :=  1,2),
             (FTYPE(I),I := 1,2), FCOLOR, FHP, FCID, FREGSTATE, FREGNUMBER);
      END; (* END GETVEHICLE *)


      SUBROUTINE PUTNEWVEHICLE (INDEX);
         (* COMMON VARIABLES AND FILES FROM MAIN PROGRAM REPEATED HERE *)
      BEGIN
         WRITE (VEHICLE[LOC(INDEX)], (TNAME(I),I := 1,5), TSSN,
             (TADDRESS(I),I := 1,4), (TCITY(I),I := 1,3), (TSTATE(I),I := 1,2),
             TZIPCODE,  TYEAR,  (TMAKE(I),I  :=  1,2),  (TMODEL(I),I  :=  1,2),
             (TTYPE(I),I := 1,2), TCOLOR, THP, TCID, TREGSTATE, TREGNUMBER);
      END; (* END PUTNEWVEHICLE *)


      SUBROUTINE GETFIRSTTRANSACTIONRECORD;
         (* COMMON VARIABLES FROM MAIN PROGRAM REPEATED HERE *)
      BEGIN
         READ (CODE1, SSN1, (TNAME(I),I := 1,5), (TADDRESS(I),I := 1,4),
             (TCITY(I),I := 1,3), (TSTATE(I),I := 1,2), TZIPCODE);
      END; (* END GETFIRSTTRANSACTIONRECORD *)


      SUBROUTINE GETSECONDTRANSACTIONRECORD;
         (* COMMON VARIABLES FROM MAIN PROGRAM REPEATED HERE *)
      BEGIN
         READ (CODE2, SSN2, TYEAR, (TMAKE(I),I := 1,2), (TMODEL(I),I := 1,2),
             (TTYPE(I),I := 1,2), TCOLOR, THP, TCID, TREGSTATE, TREGNUMBER);
      END; (* END GETSECONDTRANSACTIONRECORD *)

      BEGIN (***** MAIN PROGRAM BEGINS HERE *****)
         BIG := 10**20;

         READ (DRTY, NDIR, NRFREE); (* INDEX SIZE AND NUMBER OF FREE RECORDS *)

         READ (DRTY, (KEY(I),LOC(I),I := 1,NDIR)); (* INPUT DICTIONARY *)

         READ (DRTY, (FREE(I),I := 1,NRFREE)); (* INPUT LIST OF FREE SPACE *)

         NDIR1 := NDIR;

         CALL GETFIRSTTRANSACTIONRECORD; (* INPUT FIRST TRANSACTION *)
```

```
(* CONTINUE UNTIL TRANSACTION CODE = 8 *)
WHILE (CODE1 <> 8) DO
BEGIN
    IF (CODE1 = 1 OR CODE1 >= 6) (* SECOND DATA CARD REQUIRED *)
    THEN
        CALL GETSECONDTRANSACTIONRECORD;

    (* TEST FOR MATCHING SSN AND CODE = 9 *)
    IF (SSN1 = SSN2 AND CODE2 = 9) (* SECOND CARD MATCHES FIRST *)
    THEN
        BEGIN
            CALL BINAR (KEY, NDIR1, SSN1, INDEX); (* SEARCH FOR SSN *)

            IF (INDEX = 0) (* SSN NOT FOUND UP TO NDIR1 *)
            THEN
                (* SEARCH ADDED RECORDS *)
                CALL LINZ (KEY, NDIR1, NDIR, SSN1, INDEX);

            IF (CODE1 = 1) (* ADD A RECORD *)
            THEN
                BEGIN
                    IF (INDEX <> 0 AND LOC(INDEX) <> BIG)
                    THEN
                        WRITE ("ERROR--RECORD ALREADY EXISTS", SSN1)
                    ELSE
                        BEGIN
                            IF (INDEX = 0)
                            THEN
                                BEGIN
                                    NDIR := NDIR + 1;
                                    INDEX := NDIR;
                                END;

                            KEY(INDEX) := SSN1;

                            IF (NRFREE > 1) (* ASSIGN A FREE RECORD *)
                            THEN
                                BEGIN
                                    LOC(INDEX) := FREE(NRFREE);
                                    NRFREE := NRFREE - 1;
                                END
                            ELSE (* NO FREE RECORDS AVAILABLE *)
                                BEGIN
                                    LOC(INDEX) := FREE(1);
                                    FREE(1) := FREE(1) + 1;
                                END;

                            (* CREATE NEW RECORD *)

                            CALL PUTNEWVEHICLE (INDEX);

                        END; (* INDEX <> 0 AND LOC(INDEX) <> BIG *)

                END
            ELSE (* CODE1 <> 1 *)
```

```
BEGIN
    IF (CODE1 = 2) (* DELETE A RECORD *)
    THEN
        BEGIN
            NRFREE := NRFREE + 1;
            FREE(NRFREE) := LOC(INDEX);
            LOC(INDEX) := BIG;
        END
    ELSE (* CODE1 <> 1 OR 2 *)
        BEGIN
            CALL GETVEHICLE (INDEX);

            IF (CODE1 = 3) (* CHANGE NAME *)
            THEN
                FOR I := 1 STEP 1 UNTIL 5 DO
                    FNAME(I) := TNAME(I);

            IF (CODE1 = 4) (* CHANGE ADDRESS *)
            THEN
                FOR I := 1 STEP 1 UNTIL 4 DO
                    FADDRESS(I) := TADDRESS(I);

            IF (CODE1 = 5) (* CHANGE NAME AND ADDRESS *)
            THEN
                BEGIN
                    FOR I := 1 STEP 1 UNTIL 5 DO
                        FNAME(I) := TNAME(I);
                    FOR I := 1 STEP 1 UNTIL 4 DO
                        FADDRESS(I) := TADDRESS(I);
                END;

            IF (CODE1 = 6) (* CHANGE CAR DESCRIPTION *)
            THEN
                BEGIN
                    FYEAR := TYEAR;
                    FOR I := 1 STEP 1 UNTIL 2 DO
                    BEGIN
                        FMAKE(I) := TMAKE(I);
                        FMODEL(I) := TMODEL(I);
                        FTYPE(I) := TTYPE(I);
                    END;
                    FCOLOR := TCOLOR;
                    FHP := THP;
                    FCID := TCID;
                END;

            IF (CODE1 = 7) (* CHANGE REGISTRATION *)
            THEN
                BEGIN
                    FREGSTATE := TREGSTATE;
                    FREGNUMBER := TREGNUMBER;
                END;

            IF (CODE1 = 9)
            THEN
                WRITE ("ERROR--ILLEGAL TRANSACTION",
                SSN1);
```

```
                              (* OUTPUT MODIFIED RECORD *)
                              CALL PUTVEHICLE (INDEX);
                        END;
                  END;
            END
      ELSE
            WRITE ("ERROR--FIRST/SECOND TRANSACTION MISMATCH", SSN1);

      CALL GETFIRSTTRANSACTIONRECORD; (* INPUT NEXT TRANSACTION *)
END;

(* CODE = 8 *)
FOR I := 1 STEP 1 UNTIL NDIR DO (* DESTROY KEY FOR DELETED RECORDS *)
      IF (LOC(I) = BIG)
      THEN
            KEY(I) := BIG;

CALL DUALSORT (KEY,LOC,NDIR); (* SORT KEY AND LOC ON ELEMENTS IN KEY *)

(* ELIMINATE ALL DELETED RECORDS *)
FOR I := NDIR STEP(-1) WHILE (I >= 1 AND KEY(I) = BIG) DO
      NDIR := NDIR - 1;

REWIND (DRTY);

(* RESTORE DICTIONARY AND AMOUNT OF FREE SPACE *)
WRITE (DRTY, NDIR,NRFREE);

(* RESTORE UPDATED DICTIONARY *)
WRITE (DRTY, (KEY(I),LOC(I),I := 1,NDIR));

(* RESTORE UPDATED FREE SPACE *)
WRITE (DRTY, (FREE(I),I := 1,NRFREE));

END. (* END EXAMPLE 12.15 *)
```

A dictionary is required when using an indexed sequential disk file. In this example, the addition or deletion of records in the vehicle registration file will cause changes in the dictionary. To conserve disk space, the storage locations on the disk that are released by the deletion of a record should be reused for the storage of new records. Therefore, an array of available disk space is maintained along with the dictionary of pointers.

The first process in this pseudocode is to read the dictionary into the parallel arrays KEY and LOC and the list of available storage locations into array FREE. These are input from the sequential disk file DRTY.

By the call to SUBROUTINE GETFIRSTTRANSACTIONRECORD the first line of a transaction record is read, with CODE1 as the transaction code number and SSN1 as the owner identification key. The remainder of the fields in the transaction record are read into the appropriate COMMON array and simple variables.

A code of 8 signals the termination of processing and the first iteration tests CODE1 for this value. Since transaction codes 1, 6, and 7 require the second line of the transaction record, CODE1 is tested for these values and a second input is performed as appropriate by a call to SUBROUTINE GETSECONDTRANSACTIONRECORD. If a second input is performed, the SSN of the two inputs must match (SSN1 = SSN2) and the code on the second line of the transaction record must be 9, (CODE2 = 9). If either of these conditions is not TRUE, an error exists and an appropriate message is printed.

After the input is completed, the binary search SUBROUTINE BINAR, of Example 11.8 is used to find the social security number in the dictionary. If not in the dictionary, the value of INDEX is 0. If it is in the dictionary, INDEX is equal to the row in which SSN1 appears in the array KEY. Note that BINAR only searches the dictionary to NDIR1, which is the size of the dictionary at the start of processing. During processing the algorithm adds new records to the end of the dictionary in the order that they are created. This is done to avoid resorting the dictionary for each record added; therefore, if no match was found for SSN1 by BINAR to row NDIR1, the entries between NDIR1 and NDIR are searched via a linear search. The SUBROUTINE LINZ is assumed to be an algorithm similar to LINAR of Example 11.6, which will perform a linear research of a designated portion of a single-dimension array from KEY(NDIR1) to KEY(NDIR).

The rest of the program details the proper action to take for each of the eight transaction codes. The conditionals for these checks are in the ascending order of 1 to 7. If sufficient data is available to indicate the relative percentage of use of each code, the conditionals could be arranged in the sequence of highest to lowest usage, which would increase the efficiency of the program. However, this efficiency would result only if the conditionals were nested through use of IF . . . THEN . . . ELSE constructs.

Although the transaction code of 1 for addition is checked first, we will initially discuss the action for a transaction code of 2 for deletion. This is one of the simpler actions and the result of the deletion process affects the algorithm that handles additions. When a record is to be deleted, the pointer to the disk for that item, i.e., LOC(INDEX), is set to 10**20. It is assumed that this constant is larger than any possible address on disk. In effect, this value indicates that the record corresponding to KEY(INDEX) does not exist on the disk. The value of KEY(INDEX) is not changed in order to maintain the KEY in ascending sequence so the binary search can be applied.

Prior to changing LOC(INDEX), the disk location of the record being deleted is stored in the next element of FREE. Thus the location is available for storing a new record. Note that no action is taken to change the contents on the disk. Since there is no longer any mechanism to access that location through the dictionary, the contents of that location are immaterial. That is, we delete a record by removing it from the dictionary.

The algorithm for the addition of a record (CODE = 1) is the most complicated of the actions. First we must ensure that we are not trying to add a record for a key that already exists. If the key is in the dictionary, we cannot add the record to this file unless the pointer to the disk location is equal to 10**20. In this latter case, a record for that key existed at one time, but the record has been deleted. Although this situation would not be expected to occur very often, it is a possibility that the algorithm must allow for.

If a record with this SSN already exists, an error message is output. If not, the dictionary is expanded to include the new key as its last entry. The corresponding available disk location is determined from the contents of FREE. FREE is designed so that all available locations corresponding to deleted records are listed in elements of FREE(2) and higher; the value of FREE(1) contains the starting address of the additional space that has been reserved at the end of the file for new records.

If the number of locations in FREE is greater than 1 at the time a new record is to be added, one of the deleted locations can be used for the new record and the address of that location is stored in LOC(INDEX). When there are no locations open, the space at the end of the file is used to store the new record. When this occurs, the value of FREE(1) is incremented each time to record the location of the next available disk record. The remainder of the task for addition consists of writing the updated record back to AUTO at location INDEX via a call to SUBROUTINE PUTNEWVEHICLE.

The processing for transaction codes 3 through 8 (updates of an existing record on AUTO) involves similar actions. The LOC(INDEX) record is read from AUTO into the appropriate COMMON arrays and simple variables by the call to SUBROUTINE GETVEHICLE. Depending on the transaction code, the transaction input variables are transferred to the associated vehicle registration file variables. After the update, the record is stored back in its original location on AUTO by the call to SUBROUTINE PUTVEHICLE.

After all transactions have been processed, the dictionary is assumed to be out of order for two reasons. First of all, the deletion of a record results in a key in the dictionary not pointing to a usable location, i.e., the pointer has a value of 10**20. This row of the dictionary is really wasted, but it had to be retained during processing to ensure that KEY was in sequence for the binary search. Second, the new records listed at the end of the dictionary should be placed in their proper sequence.

Therefore the dictionary array KEY must be sorted before storing it back on the disk. The first step is to set the keys of the deleted records to 10**20 in order that they will be in the last positions of the array after the sort. Then the sort is done using SUBROUTINE DUALSORT, which sorts parallel arrays on the first array listed. In the next iteration, rows with a value of 10**20 are dropped from KEY and LOC. This is accomplished by iterating from I = NDIR to I = 1 and decrementing I.

Although the iteration theoretically goes to I = 1, it terminates early when the value of KEY(I) is not equal to 10**20. The arrays KEY, LOC, and FREE are then saved on the sequential disk file DRTY.

End Solution

The following example involves a full file search of the vehicle registration file, which is treated as a disk file.

Example 12.16

Develop an algorithm that will examine the entire vehicle registration file in order to provide a count of the number of vehicles of each color.

Solution

```
PROGRAM EXAMPLE 12.16;

FILE DRTY, VEHICLE;

    (*    DRTY = DIRECTORY OF POINTERS INTO VEHICLE,
       VEHICLE = REGISTRATION FILE *)

(***** SUBROUTINE BINAR INSERTED HERE *****)

BEGIN
    READ (NR);
    READ (SHADE(I),I := 1,NR); (* INPUT NR POSSIBLE COLORS *)

    LAST := NR + 1;
    (* INPUT DICTIONARY *)
    READ (DRTY, NDIR, NRFREE);
    READ (DRTY, (KEY(I),LOC(I),I := 1,NDIR));

    SHADE(LAST) := "OTHER"; (* ALLOW FOR NO MATCHING COLOR *)

    FOR I := 1 STEP 1 UNTIL LAST DO (* ZERO OUT COUNTERS *)
       COLORCOUNT(I) := 0;

    FOR I := 1 STEP 1 UNTIL NDIR DO
    BEGIN
        READ (VEHICLE[LOC(I)], COLOR);

        (* SEARCH FOR COLOR IN ARRAY SHADE *)
        CALL BINAR (SHADE, NR, COLOR, PTR);

        IF (PTR <> 0) (* COLOR MATCHES *)
        THEN
            COLORCOUNT(PTR) := COLORCOUNT(PTR) + 1
        ELSE (* NO MATCHING COLOR *)
```

```
                    COLORCOUNT(LAST) := COLORCOUNT(LAST) + 1;
         END;

         FOR I := 1 STEP 1 UNTIL LAST DO (* OUTPUT RESULTS *)
            WRITE ("COLOR =", SHADE(I), "COUNT =", COLORCOUNT(I));

   END. (* END EXAMPLE 12.16 *)
```

Before processing the file, the possible colors are input to the array SHADE so they can be compared with the vehicle colors in the file. As shown in the pseudocode, there are NR colors of six characters each. The dictionary is input from the sequential disk file DRTY to the parallel arrays KEY and LOC. This is the same dictionary that was used in the preceding example.

Although the variable NRFREE is not needed in this particular program, it is stored on the disk immediately after the variable NDIR and it is read so that the values for the arrays KEY and LOC are read into the correct locations. The array FREE, at the end of DRTY, is not read since it is not needed in the algorithm and does not affect the input of the dictionary.

The array COLORCOUNT is used to accumulate the count for each color. Therefore one of the first tasks of the program is to zero the array. Each record of the file is then examined in turn. LOC contains the pointers to all of the records in the file. Thus by iterating LOC(I) from I = 1 to I = NDIR, all records in the file will be accessed. The vehicle color from each of these NDIR records is read into the variable COLOR. Although the complete record from disk will be transferred into the buffer, only one field in each record needs to be referenced. In most programming languages this will be handled through the format declaration associated with the READ statement.

The variable COLOR is then matched against the elements of SHADE by means of the binary search. Note that this assumes the elements of SHADE are in ascending order. If the color is in the array, the corresponding element of the COLORCOUNT is incremented by 1. If COLOR does not match a value in SHADE, the value for COLORCOUNT(NR + 1) is incremented. This element corresponds to all other colors that do not appear in SHADE. Note that the six characters in a row of COLOR are compared against six characters in a row of SHADE. Therefore the location of blanks in the array row is particularly important. Assuming that "ˆ" represents a blank in a string, the computer will consider the six-character strings REDˆˆˆ to be different from the six-character string ˆˆREDˆ. Thus failure to match COLOR with an element of SHADE can be due to the method of storing a short string, as well as the absence of the color in the array. In order to avoid this problem, some convention must be followed in storing the color in the original record. For instance, one simple rule that is often used is to left-justify the short string in the field. Thus the color red will always be stored as REDˆˆˆ.

After the entire file has been examined, the colors and their corresponding counts are printed. This includes the OTHERˆ category, which includes all items not matched against those in SHADE. Since the dictionary was not changed by the processing of the file, there is no need to save it; thus the program can be terminated after printing the results.

End Solution

12.7 A Sample Data Processing Application: An Inventory Control System

One of the important applications of data processing is the area of inventory, or stock, control. In this section we will develop a simple inventory control system to provide a unified example in which to summarize and further illustrate some of the data processing concepts. Although the sample system is directed to inventory control, many of its aspects are equally useful in other applications.

In the inventory file, a stock control record is kept on each item. When stock is received or issued, the stock records are updated. The system also provides data regarding the time to reorder stock and the size of such an order. A number of inputs and outputs are included in the system.

The four examples in this section present the format of the basic stock record, the formats of the inputs, the formats of the outputs, and the general algorithm of the main program. There are four subroutines corresponding to four processes used in the system; these are discussed in Solved Problems 12.4 through 12.7. The examples also provide the framework for other features of an inventory control system; some of these additional enhancements are presented in Solved Problems 12.8 through 12.11.

Each stock control record reflects information and inventory status related to that specific stock item. The file STOCK is assumed to be stored as an indexed sequential disk file.

Example 12.17

Design the format of the basic record for the stock control system. The stock record should contain the following items:

1. The identification of the stock item. This consists of the stock number and the name.
2. Information relating to the quantity of stock. This includes the quantity of goods on hand, the quantity on order, the quantity on backorder (if any), and the quantity issued.
3. Reorder information. This is the stock level at which another order is placed (the reorder point), the size of the order (reorder quantity), and the date of the last reorder.
4. Unit cost of the item.

Table 12-11 Stock Control Record Layout

Name of Field	Field Size	Character Index In Record	Type
Stock number	8	1–8	INTEGER
Stock item	18	9–26	ALPHA
Quantity on hand	6	27–32	INTEGER
Quantity on order	6	33–38	INTEGER
Quantity on backorder	6	39–44	INTEGER
Quantity issued	6	45–50	INTEGER
Reorder point	6	51–56	INTEGER
Reorder quantity	6	57–62	INTEGER
Reorder date	6	63–68	INTEGER
Unit cost	8	69–76	REAL

Solution

The stock control record format is depicted in Table 12–11. The first two fields relate to the identification of the stock item. It is assumed that the stock number has 8 or fewer characters and that 18 characters are sufficient for the name. The system allows for quantities up to 999,999. The reorder date will be stored as a 6-character code with 2 characters each for month, day, and year (in that order). The unit cost is assumed to consist of 5 places to the left of the decimal point, the decimal point, and 2 decimal places.

End Solution

There are three major inputs to the system. The information in these inputs and their formats are covered in the following example. All input records are limited to 80 characters.

Example 12.18

Design the formats of the inputs in the inventory control system. These are

1. Receipt document—This indicates the identification of the stock item, quantity of goods received from the vendor, the total cost of the goods received, the identification of the vendor, and the date.

2. Request—This is the basic document that causes an issue to be made from the system. It contains the identification of the stock item, the quantity requested, the identification of the customer, and the date.

3. Backorder request—When goods are not in stock, they must be back-ordered. The backorder request, which contains the same information as the basic request, is the document that initiates subsequent filling of the order. After goods are received, these backorders must be processed and filled. The backorder requests are generated by the system when an order cannot be completely filled.

In designing these three formats it is necessary that the three inputs be distinguished from each other. However, it is also desirable to make the inputs as compatible as possible.

Solution

The three input formats are depicted in Table 12–12 through Table 12–14. Note the similiarity among them. The major distinction is made by a two-digit code in the first field. The identification of the vendor is organized like the identification of the customer; both consist of a five-character identification number and an eighteen-character name. The stock item identification and the quantity follow the same format as the basic stock record. The cost field, however, is increased to ten characters, since the cost refers to total cost rather than the unit cost.

End Solution

There are four outputs of the inventory control system. Three are line printer outputs and the fourth is output to the backorder file, BACKORDER, which will be used as input when backordered stock items are received. These are all designed to fit in an 80-character record format.

Example 12.19
Design the formats of the outputs of the inventory control system. The four outputs are

1. Receipt acknowledgment—This document is printed when a stock record is updated from the receipt document. It can be used for several purposes including the acknowledgment to the vendor that the order has been received or the notification to the accounts payable department to pay the vendor. It contains the identification of the stock item, the quantity received, the total cost of the item, the date, and the identification of the vendor.

Table 12-12 Stock Received Record Layout

Name of Field	Field Size	Character Index In Record	Type
Code	2	1–2	INTEGER
Stock number	8	3–10	INTEGER
Stock item	18	11–28	ALPHA
Quantity received	6	29–34	INTEGER
Total cost	10	35–44	REAL
Vendor number	5	45–49	INTEGER
Vendor name	18	50–67	ALPHA
Date	6	68–73	INTEGER

Table 12-13 Stock Request Record Layout

Name of Field	Field Size	Character Index In Record	Type
Code	2	1–2	INTEGER
Stock number	8	3–10	INTEGER
Stock item	18	11–28	ALPHA
Quantity issued	6	29–34	INTEGER
Unused	10	35–44	REAL
Customer number	5	45–49	INTEGER
Customer name	18	50–67	ALPHA
Date	6	68–73	INTEGER

Table 12-14 Backorder Record Layout

Name of Field	Field Size	Character Index In Record	Type
Code	2	1–2	INTEGER
Stock number	8	3–10	INTEGER
Stock item	18	11–28	ALPHA
Quantity backordered	6	29–34	INTEGER
Unused	10	35–44	REAL
Customer number	5	45–49	INTEGER
Customer name	18	50–67	ALPHA
Date	6	68–73	INTEGER

2. Issue document—This is the document that provides the information relating to the filling of a request. It can be used as the shipping document, or it can be the basis for preparing the customer's bill. It includes the identification of the stock item, the quantity issued, the total cost, the date of the issue, and the identification of the customer.

3. Order document—This document provides the information necessary to reorder stock. It is produced as a result of the stock level falling below the reorder point. This output contains the identification of the stock item, the order quantity, and the date.

4. Backorder request—This record is output to the backorder file and becomes the basic document that will be used as the input to fill a backorder when the item is again in stock. It is in the same format as the input.

Solution

The first three outputs are shown in Table 12–15 through Table 12–17. As with the inputs to the system, the three line printer outputs have a compatible format. Since the output is generated as the associated transaction is processed, the three types will be interspersed.

The format of the backorder request is the same as that depicted in Table 12–14. In other words, this file output is the same as the input and, in fact, this output product is later used as an input to the system.

End Solution

Figure 12–6 is a representation of the system showing the stock records, the inputs, and the outputs. The dashed line indicates that the backorder request output becomes the input at some later point. The main program of the system is covered in the following example.

Example 12.20

Develop the general algorithm that will process the various transactions of the inventory control system. The transactions will be identified as follows:

Code	Action
1	Receipt of stock items for inventory
2	Request for issue of parts from inventory
3	Backorder request
9	Marker to indicate the end of the transactions, i.e., a signal to stop processing

Table 12-15 Receipt Acknowledgment Record Layout

Name of Field	Field Size	Character Index In Record	Type
Stock number	8	1–8	INTEGER
Stock item	18	9–26	ALPHA
Quantity received	6	27–32	INTEGER
Total cost	10	33–42	REAL
Date	6	43–48	INTEGER
Vendor number	5	49–53	INTEGER
Vendor name	18	54–71	ALPHA
"RECEIPT"	7	72–78	ALPHA

Table 12-16 Stock Issue Record Layout

Name of Field	Field Size	Character Index In Record	Type
Stock number	8	1–8	INTEGER
Stock item	18	9–26	ALPHA
Quantity issued	6	27–32	INTEGER
Total cost	10	33–42	REAL
Date	6	43–48	INTEGER
Customer number	5	49–53	INTEGER
Customer name	18	54–71	ALPHA
"ISSUE"	7	72–78	ALPHA

Table 12-17 Stock Backorder Record Layout

Name of Field	Field Size	Character Index In Record	Type
Stock number	8	1–8	INTEGER
Stock item	18	9–26	ALPHA
Quantity ordered	6	27–32	INTEGER
Unused	10	33–42	REAL
Date	6	43–48	INTEGER
Vendor number	5	49–53	INTEGER
Vendor name	18	54–71	ALPHA
"ORDER"	7	72–78	ALPHA

Figure 12-6.
Inventory Control
System

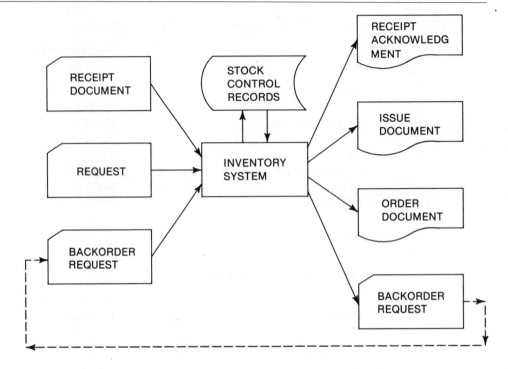

Solution

```
PROGRAM EXAMPLE 12.20;

FILE DICT, STOCK, BACKORDERS;

   (*  DICT = POINTERS INTO ARRAY STOCK,
      STOCK = ARRAY OF INVENTORY DATA,
 BACKORDERS = FILE OF BACKORDER REQUESTS *)

(* COMMON VARIABLES--CODE, STOCKNUMBER, STOCKITEM, CUSTOMER,
   CUSTOMERNUMBER, QUANTITY, QTOH, BKORD, QTISS, REORDPT, REORDQT,
   REORDDATE, COST, DATE *)

(***** SUBROUTINE BINAR INSERTED HERE *****)

SUBROUTINE GETTRANSACTION;
   (* COMMON VARIABLES FROM MAIN PROGRAM REPEATED HERE *)
BEGIN
   READ (CODE, STOCKNUMBER, (STOCKITEM(I),I := 1,3), QUANTITY, COST,
       CUSTOMERNUMBER, (CUSTOMER(I),I := 1,3), DATE);
END; (* END GETTRANSACTION *)


SUBROUTINE GETSTOCKRECORD (INDEX);
   (* COMMON VARIABLES AND FILES FROM MAIN PROGRAM REPEATED HERE *)
BEGIN
   READ (STOCK[LOC(INDEX)], STOCKNUMBER, (STOCKITEM(I),I := 1,3), QTOH,
       QTORD, BKORD, QTISS, REORDPT, REORDQT, REORDDATE, COST);
END; (* END GETSTOCKRECORD *)


SUBROUTINE PUTSTOCKRECORD (INDEX);
(* COMMON VARIABLES FROM MAIN PROGRAM REPEATED HERE *)
BEGIN
   WRITE (STOCK[LOC(INDEX)], STOCKNUMBER, (STOCKITEM(I),I := 1,3), QTOH,
       QTORD, BKORD, QTISS, REORDPT, REORDQT, REORDDATE, COST);
END; (* END PUTSTOCKRECORD *)


BEGIN (***** MAIN PROGRAM BEGINS HERE *****)
   READ (DATE); (* MONTH, DAY, YEAR *)

   (* INPUT DICTIONARY *)
   READ (DICT, NBR); (* SIZE OF DICTIONARY FILE *)
   READ (DICT, (PARTNR(I),LOC(I),I := 1,NBR));

   CALL GETTRANSACTION; (* INPUT FIRST TRANSACTION *)

   (* PROCESS TRANSACTIONS UNTIL TRAILER VALUE *)
   WHILE (CODE <> 9) DO
   BEGIN
       (* SEARCH FOR STOCKNUMBER IN PARTNR *)
       CALL BINAR (PARTNR, NBR, STOCKNUMBER, INDEX);

       IF (INDEX = 0)
```

```
        THEN
            WRITE("ERROR--RECORD NOT FOUND", STOCKNUMBER)
        ELSE
            BEGIN
                CALL GETSTOCKRECORD (INDEX);

                IF (CODE = 1)
                THEN
                    CALL RECEIPT (QUANTITY, COST);

                IF (CODE = 2)
                THEN
                    CALL ISSUE (QUANTITY);

                IF (CODE = 3)
                THEN
                    CALL BACKORDER (QUANTITY);

                IF (CODE >= 4 AND CODE <> 9)
                THEN
                    WRITE ("ERROR--ILLEGAL CODE", STOCKNUMBER)
                ELSE
                    CALL PUTSTOCKRECORD (INDEX);

            END; (* INDEX <> 0 *)

        CALL GETTRANSACTION;
    END;

END. (* END EXAMPLE 12.20 *)
```

There are two major actions in initializing the program. First, the date is read as a six-character INTEGER with two INTEGERS each for month, day, and year, in that order. Next, NBR records of the dictionary are input to the parrallel arrays PARTNR and LOC from the disk file DICT.

Each transaction is read into the appropriate COMMON arrays and simple variables by the call to SUBROUTINE GETTRANSACTION. The stock number is checked against the dictionary to determine the location of the record in the stock control file. Since the dictionary is assumed to be in sequential order by stock number, the binary search SUBROUTINE BINAR can be used to return the value of INDEX, which in turn is a pointer to LOC, which contains the actual disk address to be accessed. If INDEX = 0, the record was not found in the dictionary and an error message is generated for the stock number, STOCKNUMBER. If STOCKNUMBER is found in the array PARTNR, the stock record is read from location LOC(INDEX) in file STOCK into the appropriate COMMON arrays and variables.

The action taken for each of the three types of transactions is accomplished by subroutine calls. These subroutines are developed in the solved problems. If the input code does not relate to one of these transactions or if it does not indicate the end of processing, an error message is printed with the stock-number of the transaction. When the transaction code is a 9, processing is terminated. Note that the contents of the dictionary will not be saved at the end of processing since there has been no change to the arrays PARTNR or LOC during processing; thus the existing copies of these arrays on disk are still accurate.

End Solution

Solved Problems
12.1

Example 12.12 provided an algorithm for doing file maintenance operations on a file of golf scores on a tape. Develop an algorithm to perform the same file maintenance operations on this file maintained on a disk.

Solution

```
PROGRAM PROBLEM 12.1;

FILE REC; (* REC = FILE OF GOLFER RECORDS *)

(* COMMON VARIABLES--CODE, IDENTGOLFER, IDENTTRANS, NAMEGOLFER,
          NAMETRANS, SCORESGOLFER, SCORESTRANS, NUMSCORESGOLFER,
          NUMSCORESTRANS, AVERAGE, HANDICAP *)


SUBROUTINE GETGOLFER (INDEX);
    (* COMMON VARIABLES AND FILES FROM MAIN PROGRAM REPEATED HERE *)
BEGIN
    READ (REC[INDEX], IDENTGOLFER, (NAMEGOLFER(I),I := 1,4),
    NUMSCORESGOLFER, (SCORESGOLFER(I), I := 1, 15), AVERAGE, HANDICAP));
END; (* END GETGOLFER *)



SUBROUTINE GETTRANS;
    (* COMMON VARIABLES FROM MAIN PROGRAM REPEATED HERE *)
BEGIN
    READ (CODE, IDENTTRANS, (NAMETRANS(I),I := 1,4), NUMSCORESTRANS,
        (SCORESTRAN(I),I := 1,15));
END; (* END GETTRANS *)


SUBROUTINE PUTGOLFER (INDEX);
    (* COMMON VARIABLES AND FILES FROM MAIN PROGRAM REPEATED HERE *)
BEGIN
    WRITE (REC[INDEX], IDENTGOLFER, (NAMEGOLFER(I),I := 1,4),
        NUMSCORESGOLFER, (SCORESGOLFER(I),I := 1,15), AVERAGE, HANDICAP);
END; (* END PUTGOLFER *)
```

```
SUBROUTINE PUTNEWGOLFER (INDEX);
    (* COMMON VARIABLES AND FILES FROM MAIN PROGRAM REPEATED HERE *)
BEGIN
    TEMPAVERAGE := 0;
    TEMPHANDICAP := 0;
    WRITE (REC[INDEX], IDENTTRANS, (NAMETRANS(I),I := 1,4), NUMSCORESTRANS,
        (SCORESTRANS(I),I := 1,15), TEMPAVERAGE, TEMPHANDICAP);
END; (* END PUTNEWGOLFER *)


SUBROUTINE PRINTRECORD;
(* COMMON VARIABLES FROM MAIN PROGRAM REPEATED HERE *)
BEGIN
    WRITE ("GOLFER RECORD =", IDENTGOLFER, (NAMEGOLFER(I),I := 1,4),
        NUMSCORESGOLFER, (SCORESGOLFER(I),I := 1,15), AVERAGE, HANDICAP);
END; (* END PRINTRECORD *)


SUBROUTINE NEWSCORES;
(* COMMON VARIABLES FROM MAIN PROGRAM REPEATED HERE *)
BEGIN
    SCORECOUNT := NUMSCORESGOLFER + NUMSCORESTRANS;
    IF (SCORECOUNT <= 15)
    THEN
        BEGIN
            (* SAVE OLD AND NEW SCORES *)
            FOR I := 1 STEP 1 UNTIL NUMSCORESTRANS DO
                SCORESGOLFER(NUMSCORESGOLFER+I) := SCORESTRANS(I);
            NUMSCORESGOLFER := SCORECOUNT;
        END
    ELSE
        (* MORE THAN 15 SCORES, SAVE ALL NEW AND SOME OLD *)
        BEGIN
            OLDSCORES := 15 - NUMSCORESTRANS;
            J := 1;

            (* MOVE OLD SCORES, SAVING LATEST OF OLD SCORES *)
            FOR I := NUMSCORESGOLFER - OLDSCORES + 1 STEP 1 UNTIL
            NUMSCORESGOLFER DO
            BEGIN
                SCORESGOLFER(J) := SCORESGOLFER(I);
                J := J + 1;
            END;

            (* COPY NEW SCORES *)
            J := 1;
            FOR I := OLDSCORES + 1 STEP 1 UNTIL SCORECOUNT DO
            BEGIN
                SCORESGOLFER(I) := SCORESTRAN(J);
                J := J + 1;
            END;
        END;

END; (* END NEWSCORES *)
```

```
BEGIN (***** MAIN PROGRAM BEGINS HERE *****)
    DUMMY := 10**20;

    CALL GETTRANS; (* INPUT TRANSACTION CODE AND UPDATE DATA *)

    (* PROCESS ALL TRANSACTIONS UNTIL TRAILER VALUE *)
    WHILE (IDENTTRANS <> 9999) DO
    BEGIN
        IF (CODE = 1) (* ADD A NEW GOLFER *)
        THEN
            CALL PUTNEWGOLFER (IDENTRANS)
        ELSE
            BEGIN
                IF (CODE = 2) (* DELETE A GOLFER *)
                THEN
                    BEGIN
                        OLDIDENT := IDENTTRANS;
                        IDENTTRANS := 0;

                        CALL PUTNEWGOLFER (OLDIDENT);
                        WRITE ("DELETED GOLFER =", OLDIDENT);
                    END (* CODE = 2 *)
                ELSE
                    BEGIN
                        IF (CODE = 3) (* ADD LATEST SCORES UP TO 15 *)
                        THEN
                            BEGIN
                                CALL GETGOLFER (IDENTGOLFER);
                                CALL NEWSCORES;
                                CALL PUTGOLFER (IDENTGOLFER);
                                CALL PRINTRECORD;
                            END; (* CODE = 3 *)
                    END; (* CODE <> 2 *)
            END; (* CODE <> 1 *)
    END; (* IDENTGOLFER <> 9999*)

END. (* END PROBLEM 12.1 *)
```

With the exception of input and output, the basic operations of this pseudocode closely resemble the general flow of Example 12.12. One significant difference is the omission of the comparison of the keys of the old master file and the inputs. In a tape file, the inputs must be arranged in the same sequence as the master file and the transactions must be matched against the records of the master file. Since there is direct access capability in this case, the update transactions can be in any sequence. This eliminates the need for several conditionals in the program.

The disk file could be handled as in Example 12.15 with the use of a dictionnary to relate the key and the location of the record on disk. However, another method is used for this problem to illustrate a simple direct random type of file organization. Records in a disk file have their locations indexed from 1 to the number of locations, in the same manner that arrays are indexed. If the keys are numbered in the same manner, the key can be used as the index to the location and a dictionary relating the key and the location index is not necessary. In this problem, we assume that the golfer identification number is assigned in this way. Therefore, the pseudocode does not show any use of the dictionary, but the value of IDENTGOLFER is used to determine the location of the record.

Because the key is the index to the disk file, the deletion process differs somewhat from that in Example 12.15. In this problem, a zero is stored as the golfer identification in the disk record when the golfer's record is deleted. The record index is temporarily saved in OLDIDENT until the record with the zero identification code is output to the file. Since the records can be obtained from the file directly without reference to a dictionary, the zero identification code indicates that this is an invalid record if it is again accessed during processing.

The remainder of the pseudocode is generally self-explanatory and follows the flow of Example 12.12.

12.2

Example 12.13 computed an average and a handicap for all of the golfers whose records were maintained in a sequential file. Develop an algorithm to perform a similar task for the direct random disk file, REC, described in Solved Problem 12.1.

Solution

```
PROGRAM PROBLEM 12.2;

FILE REC; (* REC = FILE OF GOLFER RECORDS *)

(* COMMON VARIABLES--CODE, IDENTGOLFER, NAMEGOLFER, SCORESGOLFER,
   NUMSCORESGOLFER, AVERAGE, HANDICAP *)


SUBROUTINE GETGOLFER (INDEX);
   (* COMMON VARIABLES AND FILES FROM MAIN PROGRAM REPEATED HERE *)
BEGIN
   READ (REC[INDEX], IDENTGOLFER, (NAMEGOLFER(I),I := 1,4),
   NUMSCORESGOLFER, (SCORESGOLFER(I), I := 1,15), AVERAGE, HANDICAP);
END; (* END GETGOLFER *)


SUBROUTINE PUTGOLFER (INDEX);
   (* COMMON VARIABLES AND FILES FROM MAIN PROGRAM REPEATED HERE *)
BEGIN
   WRITE (REC[INDEX], IDENTGOLFER, (NAMEGOLFER(I),I := 1,4),
      NUMSCORESGOLFER, (SCORESGOLFER(I),I := 1,15), AVERAGE, HANDICAP);
END; (* END PUTGOLFER *)


SUBROUTINE PRINTRECORD;
   (* COMMON VARIABLES FROM MAIN PROGRAM REPEATED HERE *)
```

```
BEGIN
    WRITE ("GOLFER RECORD =", IDENTGOLFER, (NAMEGOLFER(I),I := 1,4),
        NUMSCORESGOLFER, (SCORESGOLFER(I),I := 1,15), AVERAGE, HANDICAP);
END; (* END PRINTRECORD *)


BEGIN (***** MAIN PROGRAM BEGINS HERE *****)
    READ (RATE); (* INPUT GOLFCOURSE RATING *)

    READ (NBR); (* INPUT NUMBER OF RECORDS IN FILE *)

    FOR NEXTRECORD := 1 STEP 1 UNTIL NBR DO
    BEGIN
        CALL GETGOLFER (NEXTRECORD); (* GET FIRST GOLFER RECORD *)

        IF (IDENTGOLFER <> 0 ) (* VALID RECORD *)
        THEN
            BEGIN
                SUM := 0;
                (* ACCUMULATE SCORES AND CALCULATE AVERAGES *)
                FOR I := 1 STEP 1 UNTIL NUMSCORESGOLFER DO
                    SUM := SUM + SCORESGOLFER(I);

                IF (NUMSCORESGOLFER <> 0)
                THEN
                    AVERAGE := SUM / NUMSCORESGOLFER
                ELSE
                    AVERAGE := 0;

                IF (NUMSCORESGOLFER > 5) (* CALCULATE HANDICAP *)
                THEN
                    HANDICAP := .8 * (AVERAGE - RATE);

                CALL PUTGOLFER (NEXTRECORD); (* RESTORE RECORD *)
                CALL PRINTRECORD; (* PRINT RESULT *)
            END;
        END;

END. (* END PROBLEM 12.2 *)
```

Each record of the file is read from the disk in the iteration on INDEX. The variable INDEX ranges from 1 to NBR, which is the index to the last record in REC with valid data. Since GOLFERIDENT, the key to the record, designates the relative location of the record, a dictionary is not needed.

Each record is input by a call to SUBROUTINE GETGOLFER (INDEX). If the value of the golfer's identification, GOLFERIDENT, is not 0, the record contains useful data and the average and handicap are computed in the same manner as in Example 12.13. If GOLFERIDENT is equal to 0, a valid record does not exist at this location in the disk and the next record is read. This continues until all valid golfer records have been examined and their average and handicap computed.

12.3

Example 12.4 provides the formats of records that constitute a utility file; Examples 12.7 and 12.9 illustrated two operations on this file. Develop another program for the utility file that will record the payment of an account. The utility file is a sequential tape file. Data relating to the payment of the accounts is read into a two-dimension array PAY. PAY is then sorted and the result is processed against the master utility file. A new master utility file is generated that contains the updated records.

Solution

```
PROGRAM PROBLEM 12.3;

FILE TAPE1, TAPE2;

    (* TAPE1 = INPUT UTILITY FILE,
       TAPE2 = UPDATED OUTPUT UTILITY FILE *)

    (* PAYMENTS COL. 1 = ELECTRIC,
                 COL. 2 = GAS *)

(***** SUBROUTINE SORTARRAYS INSERTED HERE *****)

BEGIN
    (* INPUT ALL TRANSACTIONS TO PAYMENTS (ELECTRIC,GAS) *)
    READ (ID(1), PAYMENTS(1,1), PAYMENTS(1,2));

    NBR := 0; (* NUMBER OF PAYMENTS MADE *)

    (* FILL PAYMENTS UNTIL TRAILER RECORD *)
    FOR I := 2 STEP 1 WHILE (ID(I-1) <> 999999) DO
    BEGIN
        READ (ID(I), PAYMENTS(I,1), PAYMENTS(I,2));
        NBR := NBR + 1;
    END;

    (* SORT PAYMENTS BY ACCOUNT NUMBERS IN ID *)
    CALL SORTARRAYS (ID, NBR, PAYMENTS, 2);

    (* INPUT SIZE OF UTILITY FILE AND INITIALIZE NEW FILE *)
    READ (TAPE1,NR);
    WRITE (TAPE2,NR);

    K := 1; (* INDEX TO PAY *)

    (* J IS INDEX TO TAPE1 *)
    FOR J := 1 STEP 1 UNTIL NR DO
    BEGIN
        READ (TAPE1, ACCOUNT, (CUSTOMER(I),I := 1,7), GASRATE,
            PREVGASREAD, PRESGASREAD, PREVGASBAL, PRESGASBAL, ELECTRATE,
            PREVELECTREAD, PRESELECTREAD, PREVELECTBAL, PRESELECTBAL);
```

```
(* CHECK FOR FILE OUT OF SEQUENCE *)
WHILE (ID(K) < ACCOUNT) DO
BEGIN
    WRITE ("ERROR--TRANSACTION OUT OF SEQUENCE", ID(K));
    K := K + 1;
END;

        IF (ID(K) = ACCOUNT) (* MATCHING ACCOUNTS *)
        THEN
            BEGIN
                (* UPDATE ELECTRIC BILL BALANCE *)
                PRESELECTBAL := PRESELECTBAL - PAYMENT(K,1);

                (* UPDATE GAS BILL BALANCE *)
                PRESGASBAL := PRESGASBAL - PAYMENT(K,2);

                K := K + 1;
            END;

        (* UPDATE NEW UTILITY FILE *)
        WRITE (TAPE2, ACCOUNT, (CUSTOMER(I),I := 1,7), GASRATE,
            PREVGASREAD, PRESGASREAD, PREVGASBAL, PRESGASBAL, ELECTRATE,
            PREVELECTREAD, PRESELECTREAD, PREVELECTBAL, PRESELECTBAL);
    END;

END. (* END PROBLEM 12.3 *)
```

The first task in the algorithm is to read all of the data that corresponds to the payment of the accounts. The account number is read into the array ID and the payments are read into the parallel array PAYMENTS. The first column of PAYMENTS contains the amount of the electric payment, and the second column contains the amount of the gas payment. A dummy record of 999999 terminates the processing with the variable NBR indicating the number of payments to be processed. PAYMENTS is then sorted with the parallel array ID as the key by a call to SUBROUTINE SORTARRAYS, which sorts parallel arrays using the first array as the sort key.

The number of records in the master tape (TAPE1) is read and stored in NR; the new tape (TAPE2) is initialized by storing NR in the first record. The remainder of the program involves two iteration variables. J refers to the record on the tape; K refers to the next transaction in PAYMENTS. The Jth record of the master tape is read and checked against the Kth row of PAY. There are three possible actions:

1. If the account number, ACCOUNT, equals the transaction account number ID(K), the file is updated. The amount of the electric payment, PAYMENTS(K,1), is subtracted from the present electric balance. Then the same operation is performed for the gas charge. There are two variations from the normal that the algorithm must process properly. First, if there is a payment for only one of the utilities, the present balance for the other

utility must not be changed. When no payment is made for a utility, the value of 0 is subtracted from the present balance and the balance remains unchanged. The other possibility is that the customer might pay more than the present balance. In this case, the payment will result in a negative balance. The negative balance will be retained, indicating the customer has a credit toward the next payment. Subsequent reference to the file will provide the correct information.

2. If the account number, ACCOUNT, is greater than the transaction account number, ID(K), the account number in ID(K) does not match an existing account in the utility file and an error message is printed that the transaction file is out of sequence.

3. If the account number, ACCOUNT, from the utility file is less than the transaction account number, ID(K), no payment was received and no action is taken. In both this case and the case in which a payment is used to update the record, the record is written to the new utility file, TAPE2.

After the entire utility file has been processed, the program terminates. Note that all records on TAPE1 will be read even if all rows in the array PAYMENTS have been processed before the end of the tape. If this were not done, the last few records on the old tape would not be transferred to the new tape.

12.4

The inventory control system presented in Section 12.7 calls SUBROUTINE RECEIPT to record a receipt of stock. Develop RECEIPT to update the stock record and print out the receipt acknowledgment whenever stock is received.

Solution

```
SUBROUTINE RECEIPT (QTRECEIVED, RECCOST);

(* COMMON VARIABLES FROM MAIN PROGRAM REPEATED HERE *)

BEGIN
    TOTALCOST := QTOH * COST + RECCOST;
    QTOH := QTOH + QTRECEIVED;
    COST := TOTALCOST / QTOH;
    QTORD := QTORD - QTRECEIVED;

    (* REDUCE QTORD TO 0 IF MORE STOCK RECEIVED THAN WAS ORDERED *)
    IF (QTORD < 0)
    THEN
        QTORD := 0;

    WRITE (STOCKNUMBER, (STOCKITEM(I),I := 1,3), QTRECEIVED, RECCOST,
            DATE, CUSTOMERNUMBER, (CUSTOMER(I),I := 1,3)), "RECEIPT");

END; (* END RECEIPT *)
```

The two parameters of RECEIPT (QTRECEIVED, RECCOST) correspond to the quantity of stock (QUANTITY) that has been received and the cost of this stock (COST). These two parameters must be used to update the quantity of stock on hand (QTOH) and the unit cost (UNITCOST) contained in the stock record. The new quantity on hand is simply the sum of the quantity on hand and the quantity received. The new unit cost necessitates computation of the total cost of the stock previously on hand. To determine the new unit cost, the sum of the two costs (TOTALCOST) is then divided by the new quantity on hand.

TOTALCOST must be computed before QTOH is updated, since the original value of QTOH enters into the calculation for TOTALCOST. The quantity on order (QTORD) is then decremented by the size of the order received. QTORD is set to 0 if the quantity received (QTRECEIVED) is greater than the quantity ordered (QTORD). The receipt acknowledgment is then printed according to the format shown in Table 12–15.

In examining the pseudocode of Example 12.20, note that the formal parameters of SUBROUTINE RECEIPT correspond to the actual parameters read from the input transaction, i.e., QUANTITY and COST. The data in the stock record are treated as common variables. The transaction variables QUANTITY and COST could also be treated as COMMON variables; this is a matter of choice. One advantage to this method is that specifying the formal parameters makes SUBROUTINE RECEIPT more readable. Note that the files and formats are assumed to be global variables.

The question arises whether the unit cost is the cost of the stock item for our company or the price at which we sell the item. Many service and manufacturing firms find it necessary to maintain their inventory cost in the stock records; however, for a retail firm, the selling price might be more useful. For the sake of convention our inventory control system assumes that this is the cost of goods to the firm. But either assumption can be made for this simple system. In more sophisticated systems, both purchase cost and selling price might be included in the computer records.

12.5

Develop SUBROUTINE ISSUE, which is called by the inventory control system in Example 12.20. ISSUE handles the issue of stock by determining the amount to be issued (QTISS), updating the stock record, reordering the stock item if necessary, determining if a backorder must be made, and printing out the issue document.

Solution

```
SUBROUTINE ISSUE (QTISSUE);

(* COMMON VARIABLES AND FILES FROM MAIN PROGRAM REPEATED HERE *)
```

```
BEGIN
    IF QTISSUE > QTOH)
    THEN
        BEGIN
            (* INSUFFICIENT STOCK ON HAND *)
            BACKORDERAMOUNT := QTISSUE - QTOH;
            BKORD := BKORD + BACKORDERAMOUNT);
            QTISSUE := QTOH;

            (* SET CODE = 3 FOR BACKORDER AND OUTPUT TO BACKORDER FILE *)
            WRITE (BACKORDER, 3, STOCKNUMBER, (STOCKITEM(I),I := 1,3),
            BACKORDERAMOUNT, 0, CUSTOMERNUMBER, (CUSTOMER(I),I := 1,3),
            DATE);
        END;

    QTOH := QTOH - QTISSUE; (* UPDATE QUANTITY ON HAND *)

    ISSUECOST := QTISSUE * COST; (* TOTAL COST OF ISSUE *)

    QTISS := QTISS + QTISSUE; (* UPDATE TOTAL ISSUED IN STOCK RECORD *)

    WRITE (STOCKNUMBER, (STOCKITEM(I),I := 1,3), QTISSUE, ISSUECOST,
        DATE, CUSTOMERNUMBER, (CUSTOMER(I),I := 1.3), "ISSUE");

    (* CHECK TO SEE IF STOCKLEVEL REQUIRES A NEW ORDER TO BE WRITTEN *)
    CURRENTLEVEL := QTOH + QTORD - BKORD;
    IF (CURRENTLEVEL < REORDPT)
    THEN
        CALL ORDER (CURRENTLEVEL);

END; (* END ISSUE *)
```

This pseudocode provides the logic of SUBROUTINE ISSUE (QTISSUE). The parameter (QTISSUE) provides the quantity of stock requested, and it corresponds to the actual parameter QUANTITY in the main program.

The subroutine must first determine if there is sufficient quantity on hand to fill the requisition. If QTISSUE is greater than QTOH, some of the stock must be backordered. If stock is backordered, a backorder request must be output to file BACKORDER and the amount on backorder (BKORD) must be updated in the stock record. Note that if stock is backordered, the quantity issued is only equal to the quantity on hand. In all cases, the stock on hand is decremented by the amount of stock that will be issued and the issue document is printed for billing purposes.

The inventory system is designed to reorder stock whenever the stock falls below a certain point, called the reorder point. There are a number of ways to establish this inventory level. A simple method is to determine the reorder point arbitrarily, based upon an evaluation of past history. A more formal but common method is to use the economic order quantity. Other more sophisticated methods are available. In any case, the stock record contains the reorder point as well as the reorder quantity. When the stock position falls below the reorder point, an order is placed through the call to SUBROUTINE ORDER. In determining the stock position, it is necessary to include the amount of stock on order and the quantity on backorder, i.e., that quantity already reserved to fill other orders.

12.6

Develop SUBROUTINE ORDER to be called by SUBROUTINE ISSUE of the inventory control system; SUBROUTINE ORDER will determine the size of the order, update the stock record, and print the order document.

Solution

```
SUBROUTINE ORDER (AMOUNT);

(* COMMON VARIABLES FROM MAIN PROGRAM REPEATED HERE *)

BEGIN
   NEWORDER := REORDPT - AMOUNT + REORDQT;
   QTORD := QTORD + NEWORDER;

   WRITE (STOCKNUMBER, (STOCKITEM(I),I := 1,3), NEWORDER, 0,
      DATE, CUSTOMERNUMBER, (CUSTOMER(I),I := 1,3), "ORDER");
END; (* END ORDER *)
```

SUBROUTINE ORDER (AMOUNT) is very simple. The parameter AMOUNT corresponds to the present stock position as determined by SUBROUTINE ISSUE, i.e., the sum of the quantity of stock on hand and the quantity on order minus the quantity backordered. The amount to be ordered (NEWORDER) consists of the reorder quantity plus the amount by which the stock position is below the reorder point. Thus the stock position after the order will fill all the backorders plus the amount equal to the reorder quantity and the reorder point.

12.7

Develop a SUBROUTINE BACKORDER that will process any backorder request received by the inventory control system.

Solution

```
SUBROUTINE BACKORDER (BACKORDERAMOUNT);

(* COMMON VARIABLES AND FILES FROM MAIN PROGRAM REPEATED HERE *)

BEGIN
   IF (QTOH > 0)
   THEN
       BEGIN
           BKORD := BKORD - BACKORDERAMOUNT;
```

```
                   IF (BKORD < 0)
                   THEN
                        BKORD := 0;

                   CALL ISSUE (BACKORDERAMOUNT);
               END
           ELSE
               (* SET CODE = 3 FOR BACKORDER AND OUTPUT TO BACKORDER FILE *)
               WRITE (BACKORDER, 3, STOCKNUMBER, (STOCKITEM(I),I := 1,3),
                   BACKORDERAMOUNT, 0, CUSTOMERNUMBER, (CUSTOMER(I),I := 1,3),
                   DATE);

       END; (* END BACKORDER *)
```

In SUBROUTINE BACKORDER (BACKORDERAMOUNT) the parameter
BACKORDERAMOUNT provides the order quantity and corresponds to the
actual parameter QUANTITY. A check must be made to see if there is any
stock on hand. If there is no stock on hand, a backorder is made.

In this simple system, it is assumed that the input documents are only
used for one input. Therefore, when there is zero inventory, a second backorder request identical to the first one is produced by BACKORDER. If stock
exists, the quantity on backorder is reduced by the size of this backorder request and ISSUE is called to handle this transaction as a normal issue. This
will correctly handle the various conditions that could occur. If enough stock
is not available to satisfy the order, ISSUE will issue the stock on hand and
then produce a new backorder request for a smaller amount.

12.8

In many inventory control systems it is necessary to determine the monetary
value of the inventory for tax purposes and for profit and loss statements.
Develop a program to use with our inventory control system that will determine the cost of the inventory, estimate the value of the stock on order, and
estimate the value of the backorders.

Solution

```
PROGRAM PROBLEM 12.8;

FILE DICT, STOCK;

    (*  DICT = POINTERS INTO ARRAY STOCK,
        STOCK = ARRAY OF INVENTORY DATA *)

BEGIN
    (* INPUT DICTIONARY *)
    READ (DICT, NBR);
    READ (DICT, (PARTNR(I), LOC(I),I:=1, NBR));
    ICOST := 0;
    ORDVALUE := 0;
    BKORDVALUE := 0;
```

```
FOR I := 1 STEP 1 UNTIL NBR DO
BEGIN
    READ (STOCK[LOC(I)], QTOH, QTORD, BKORD, COST);

    ICOST := ICOST + QTOH * COST; (* COST OF INVENTORY *)

    ORDVALUE := ORDVALUE + QTORD * COST; (* VALUE OF GOODS ON ORDER *)

    BKORDVALUE := BKORDVALUE + BKORD * COST; (* VALUE OF BACKORDERS *)
END;

WRITE ("COST OF INVENTORY =", ICOST,
       "VALUE OF STOCK ON ORDER =", ORDVALUE,
       "VALUE OF BACKORDERS =", BKORDVALUE);

END. (* END PROBLEM 12.8 *)
```

All records in the inventory file must be examined to determine the contribution of each stock item to the total figures. The dictionary of record locations on disk must be read into memory. Then a straightforward iteration through the dictionary is used to ensure that all records are examined.

The cost of the inventory (ICOST), the estimated value of the stock on order (ORDVALUE), and the estimated value of the backorders (BKORD-VALUE) are calculated and accumulated for each stock item in the file STOCK.

The algorithm provides an exact or true cost of the inventory due to the method in which the unit cost is determined within the system (see the discussion for Solved Problem 12.4). The value of the quantity of stock on order, however, is only an estimate. When the stock is received, the cost could be higher or lower than the unit cost carried in the stock records. Likewise, the value of the backorders can only be considered an estimate.

12.9

In many inventory systems there are several categories of inventory, and different management techniques are applied to the stock items in each of these categories. This enables the stock items that account for the majority of the inventory investment to be given special treatment. There are different techniques to isolate these high-value items, including high unit cost, large inventory values (unit cost times inventory on hand), and high volume of activity (unit cost times the annual number issued).

Develop an algorithm that will identify stock items as likely candidates for special controls. The criteria to be used are

1. Unit cost greater than a fixed value DCOST
2. Inventory value of the stock item greater than the value DINV
3. Volume of activity greater than the value DISS

Solution

```
PROGRAM PROBLEM 12.9;

FILE DICT, STOCK;

    (*  DICT = POINTERS INTO ARRAY STOCK,
       STOCK = ARRAY OF INVENTORY DATA;

BEGIN
    (* INPUT DICTIONARY *)
    READ (DICT, NBR);
    READ (DICT, (PARTNR(I), LOC(I),I := 1,NBR));

    READ (DCOST, DINV, DISS); (* INPUT HI-VALUE TEST CRITERIA *)

    FOR I := 1 STEP 1 UNTIL NBR DO
    BEGIN
        READ (STOCK[LOC(I)], STOCKNUMBER, QTOH, QTISS, COST);
        IF (COST >= DCOST)
        THEN
            WRITE (STOCKNUMBER, QTOH, QTISS, COST,
                "HIGH UNIT COST ITEM")
        ELSE
            BEGIN
                IF (QTOH * COST >= DINV)
                THEN
                    WRITE (STOCKNUMBER, QTOH, QTISS, COST,
                        "HIGH INVENTORY VALUE")
                ELSE
                    IF (QTISS * COST >= DISS)
                    THEN
                        WRITE (STOCKNUMBER, QTOH, QTISS, COST,
                            "HIGH VOLUME OF ACTIVITY");
            END;
    END;

END. (* END PROBLEM 12.9 *)
```

This pseudocode contains a number of similarities with the preceding problem. Three tests are applied to the information contained in each stock record. If the stock item meets any of the three criteria, the stock record is printed with the first condition that the item fulfills. It is possible that an item might exceed more than one of the criteria; however, this is not indicated in the output. To indicate each condition the item meets, only minor modifications would be needed in the algorithm.

12.10

In the inventory control system of Section 12.7, there were four codes used for the input transactions (see Example 12.20). The two-digit field used in the inputs provides for the expansion of the system to handle up to 99 different transactions as part of a more sophisticated system. One such possibility is the clearing of a backorder without shipping the stock. We've stated that an item is backordered when a request is received and the item is not in stock. Before we obtain additional stock, our customer might decide to cancel his order and make other arrangements to get his supplies.

Provide this cancellation process for our stock inventory system by accomplishing the following:

a. Describe the record layouts of the input for the cancellation transaction and for the printed cancellation message.

b. Develop SUBROUTINE CANCEL that will delete a backorder from the system without shipment of the stock.

c. Discuss the changes in the main program (see Example 12.20) if the input code for the transaction is a 4.

Solution

a. The record layout for the transaction can follow the same layout as the backorder transaction, as shown in Table 12–14. The only difference is the transaction code used in the first two characters. The record layout for the printed cancellation message is identical to the issue document in Table 12–16 except that the last field contains the word "CANCEL."

```
SUBROUTINE CANCEL (CANCELAMOUNT);

(* COMMON VARIABLES FROM MAIN PROGRAM REPEATED HERE *)

BEGIN
    IF (CANCELAMOUNT < BKORD)
    THEN
        BKORD := BKORD - CANCELAMOUNT
    ELSE
        BKORD := 0;

    WRITE (STOCKNUMBER, (STOCKITEM(I),I := 1,3), CANCELAMOUNT, 0, DATE,
        CUSTOMERNUMBER, (CUSTOMER(I),I := 1,3), "CANCEL");

END; (* END CANCEL *)
```

b. SUBROUTINE CANCEL (CANCELAMOUNT) is shown here. The backorder figure (BKORD) of the stock record is reduced by CANCELAMOUNT, which corresponds to the value of the actual parameter quantity. A check is made that an inadvertent error does not result in the number of backorders dropping below 0.

c. The changes necessary in the pseudocode in Example 12.20 are a test on CODE = 4, a call to SUBROUTINE CANCEL, and modification of the test for illegal codes. If CODE = 4, then CANCEL should be called.

12.11

The sample inventory control system does not include provisions for inserting new items in the stock control records or for deleting stock items. Modify the algorithm presented in Example 12.20 to allow the insertion and deletion of stock items. Use transaction codes 5 and 6 for insertion and deletion, respectively.

Solution

```
PROGRAM PROBLEM 12.11;

FILE DICT, STOCK, BACKORDERS;

   (*  DICT = POINTERS INTO ARRAY STOCK,
       STOCK = ARRAY OF INVENTORY DATA,
  BACKORDERS = FILE OF BACKORDER REQUESTS *)


(* COMMON VARIABLES--CODE, STOCKNUMBER, STOCKITEM, CUSTOMER,
   CUSTOMERNUMBER, QUANTITY, QTOH, BKORD, QTISS, REORDPT, REORDQT,
   REORDDATE, COST, DATE *)


(***** SUBROUTINES BINAR, DUALSORT, AND LINZ INSERTED HERE *****)


SUBROUTINE GETTRANSACTION;
   (* COMMON VARIABLES FROM MAIN PROGRAM REPEATED HERE *)
BEGIN
   READ (CODE, STOCKNUMBER, (STOCKITEM(I),I := 1,3), QUANTITY, COST,
       CUSTOMERNUMBER, (CUSTOMER(I),I := 1,3), DATE);
END; (* END GETTRANSACTION *)


SUBROUTINE GETSTOCKRECORD (INDEX);
   (* COMMON VARIABLES AND FILES FROM MAIN PROGRAM REPEATED HERE *)
BEGIN
   READ (STOCK[LOC(INDEX)], STOCKNUMBER, (STOCKITEM(I),I := 1,3), QTOH,
       QTORD, BKORD, QTISS, REORDPT, REORDQT, REORDDATE, COST);
END; (* END GETSTOCKRECORD *)


SUBROUTINE PUTSTOCKRECORD (INDEX);
   (* COMMON VARIABLES AND FILES FROM MAIN PROGRAM REPEATED HERE *)
BEGIN
   WRITE (STOCK[LOC(INDEX)], STOCKNUMBER, (STOCKITEM(I),I := 1,3), QTOH,
       QTORD, BKORD, QTISS, REORDPT, REORDQT, REORDDATE, COST);
END; (* END PUTSTOCKRECORD *)


BEGIN (***** MAIN PROGRAM BEGINS HERE *****)
   BIG := 10**20;
   READ (DATE);

   (* INPUT DICTIONARY *)
   READ (DICT, NBR);
```

```
          READ (DICT, (PARTNR(I),LOC(I),I := 1,NBR));

          CALL GETTRANSACTION; (* INPUT FIRST TRANSACTION *)

          NBR1 := NBR; (* NBR1 IS LENGTH OF ORIGINAL ARRAY PARTNR *)

          (* PROCESS TRANSACTIONS UNTIL TRAILER VALUE *)
          WHILE (CODE <> 9) DO
          BEGIN
              (* SEARCH FOR STOCKNUMBER IN ORIGINAL LIST *)
              CALL BINAR (PARTNR, NBR, STOCKNUMBER, INDEX);

*         IF (INDEX = 0) (* SEARCH FOR STOCKNUMBER IN ADDED LIST *)
*         THEN
*             CALL LINZ (PARTNR, NBR1, NBR, STOCKNUMBER, INDEX);
*         IF (CODE = 5) (* INSERT NEW PART INTO SYSTEM *)
*         THEN
*             BEGIN
*                 READ (STOCKNUMBER, (STOCKITEM(I),I := 1,3), QTOH, QTORD,
                        BKORD, QTISS, REORDPT, REORDQT, REORDDATE, COST);

                    IF (INDEX = 0) (* PART DID NOT PREVIOUSLY EXIST *)
                    THEN
                        BEGIN
                          (* GET NEXT AVAILABLE DISK SPACE USING
                             INTRINSIC FUNCTION NEXT *)
*                         INDEX := NEXT (STOCK);
*                         NBR := NBR + 1;
*                         PARTNR(NBR) := STOCKNUMBER;
*                         LOC(NBR) := INDEX;

                          CALL PUTSTOCKRECORD (INDEX);
                        END
                    ELSE
                        WRITE ("ERROR--STOCKNUMBER EXISTS", STOCKNUMBER);
                END;

*         IF (CODE = 6) (* DELETE PART FROM SYSTEM *)
*         THEN
*             BEGIN
*                 IF (INDEX <> 0)
*                 THEN
*                     LOC(INDEX) := BIG;
*                 ELSE
*                     WRITE ("ERROR--RECORD DOESN'T EXIST", STOCKNUMBER);
*             END;

*         IF ((CODE <> 5) AND (CODE <> 6))
*         THEN
                  BEGIN
                    IF (INDEX = 0)
                    THEN
                        WRITE ("ERROR--RECORD NOT FOUND", STOCKNUMBER)
                    ELSE
                        BEGIN
                          CALL GETSTOCKRECORD (INDEX);
```

```
                              IF (CODE = 1)
                              THEN
                                   CALL RECEIPT (QUANTITY, COST);

                              IF (CODE = 2)
                              THEN
                                   CALL ISSUE (QUANTITY);

                              IF (CODE = 3)
                              THEN
                                   CALL BACKORDER (QUANTITY);

                              IF (CODE = 4)
                              THEN
                                   CALL CANCEL (QUANTITY);

                              IF (CODE = 7 OR CODE = 8)
                              THEN
                                   WRITE ("ERROR--ILLEGAL CODE", STOCKNUMBER)
                              ELSE
                                   CALL PUTSTOCKRECORD (INDEX);
                         END; (* INDEX <> 0 *)
                    END;

               CALL GETTRANSACTION; (* INPUT NEXT TRANSACTION *)

          END;

     (* STOP CODE = 9 SO SAVE THE DICTIONARY *)
*    FOR I := 1 STEP 1 UNTIL NBR DO (* DESTROY KEY FOR DELETED RECORDS *)
*        IF (LOC(I) = BIG)
*        THEN
*               PARTNR(I) := BIG;

     (* SORT PARTNR AND LOC ON PARTNR INCLUDING NEW RECORDS UP TO NBR *)
*    CALL DUALSORT (PARTNR, LOC, NBR);

     (* ELIMINATE DELETED RECORDS FROM LIST *)
*     FOR I := NBR STEP (-1) WHILE (I >= 1 AND PARTNR(I) = BIG) DO
*        NBR := NBR - 1;

     (* RESTORE DICTIONARY *)
*    WRITE (DICT, NBR);
*    WRITE (DICT, (PARTNR(I),LOC(I),I := 1,NBR));

END. (* END PROBLEM 12.11 *)
```

The modifications to the previous system of Example 12.20 are shown in this pseudocode by asterisks (*) in the left-most column. These changes result in a considerable increase in the size of the algorithm. Although the other transactions are based on the fact that the stock item is in the file, insertion is based on the absence of the item from the file. If the item is found in the file, there must be an error in either the input or in the file, i.e., a stock record cannot be added if it already exists in the file.

To determine if the item is in the file, the dictionary PARTNR is searched using a combination of the binary and linear searches, as shown in Example 12.15. The original array is searched via the binary search (BINAR), and the linear search (LINZ) is applied to the additions to the file (i.e., entries between NBR1 and NBR) that may result from previous add transactions.

If a record is to be added to the file, the second line of the input transaction must be read with the data of the new stock record. This record is read before the check to see if the stock item is included in the file. If the item is found in the file, the second line of the transaction must still be read. If it was not input, the program would assume that this was the next transaction and the processing of this input as another transaction would introduce an error into the system.

If the item is valid for insertion, entries are made in the dictionary and the information is output to the stock control file. Assume that NEXT is an intrinsic function that provides the next available disk address for the file STOCK.

If an item is to be deleted, the corresponding entry in the dictionary is set to 10**20, but there is no need to change the contents on the disk. Since there is no way to get to the information by means of the dictionary, the stock record does not exist as far as this inventory control system is concerned.

The additional code added before the end of the program saves the contents of the dictionary. In the previous algorithms of this inventory control system, there were no changes made to the dictionary and therefore it was not necessary to save it at the conclusion of processing. In this algorithm the insertion and deletion of stock items will cause the dictionary to be revised and thus it must be stored for future use. The actions necessary to rearrange the dictionary file are similar to those presented in Example 12.15.

Supplementary Problems
12.12
Develop a program to use with the inventory control system in Section 12.7 that will estimate the values of the issues made to date. (This involves full file processing. The quantity issued field and the unit cost field need to be considered.)

12.13
In most inventory systems there is a need for the inventory manager to check the status of certain information in the computerized stock record. Although this is a simple procedure, our inventory system does not contain a provision for this type of query. Modify the algorithm of Solved Problem 12.11 to handle a transaction code of 7, which causes a printout of the information in the file for a specified stock item.

12.14

Most systems require some means to correct errors in the computer records. In the inventory system, assume that the errors in the stock records are corrected by inputting the entire stock record. This will be very much like the insertion of a new record except that the stock number will appear in the dictionary. Modify the algorithm of Solved Problem 12.11 to handle a transaction code of 8, which will correct a record by reading in the new data for the entire record.

12.15

The inventory control system developed in this chapter assumed a disk file. But the system might also be used with a sequential file, probably magnetic tape. Change the algorithm of Solved Problem 12.11 to handle a sequential inventory control file.

12.16

Develop the linear search SUBROUTINE LINZ (KEY, NDIR1, NDIR, SSN, INDEX) required by Example 12.15.

12.17

Develop the parallel array sort SUBROUTINE DUALSORT (KEY, LOC, NDIR) required by Example 12.15.

12.18

Modify the algorithm developed in Supplementary Problem 12.17 to allow the second parallel array to be a two-dimension array as required by Solved Problem 12.3. The subroutine should be called SORTARRAYS (FIRSTARRAY, ARRAYSIZE, SECONDARRAY, COLUMNS).

12.19

Modify the algorithm of Solved Problem 12.11 to process the file BACK-ORDER whenever stock is received.

13 *Normal Data Structures*

13.1 Introduction   The algorithms in previous chapters assumed data are stored as simple variables or in sequential data organizations. A **sequential data organization** is one in which the logical relationships between records in a file are indicated by the physical location of the records in the file. When the Ith + 1 record follows the Ith record in logical sequence, it also follows the Ith data item in the physical arrangement, i.e., it uses contiguous storage locations.

The simplest example of a sequential data organization is a one-dimension array. If the values in an array X are arranged logically in ascending order, the physical organization of that array is such that $X(I+1) >= X(I)$. This can also be stated as $X(J) >= X(I)$ for all $J > I$. Thus the physical organization of the array is the same as the logical organization.

Although the simple sequential data organization is adequate for a large number of applications, a number of other data structures are frequently found to be more beneficial. One that separates the logical and physical organization is the **linked list,** or **chain.** In a linked list each record contains not only a data value, but it also indicates the next record in the logical arrangement. Thus the physical arrangement need not use contiguous locations; a record can be located anywhere in memory.

In a **singly linked list** there are two parts to the record. The first part, called the **symbol,** contains the value of the data item of the record; the second part, called the **link,** contains a pointer to the location of the next record in the sequence. Although the application is not completely analogous, the concept of a pointer is exhibited in a manual file system in which the records contain notations such as "See also Record XYZ123."

A singly linked list has only one pointer to the next record in a sequence. An extension is the **doubly linked list,** which contains a pointer to the previous record (a **backward link**) as well as a pointer to the next record (a **forward link**). Singly linked lists and doubly linked lists are discussed in Sections 13.2 and 13.3, respectively.

A different data structure is the **tree structure.** A tree structure uses pointers in a manner similar to linked lists, but it is a slightly more sophisticated arrangement. In many cases it provides additional processing advantages over the use of linked lists. Most people are familiar with the general concepts as exhibited in a family tree. Section 13.4 will give a formal definition of trees.

There are many advantages in the use of linked lists and trees instead of sequential structures. Some of these relate to flexibility in allocation of storage due to the removal of the need for contiguous storage. A second group of advantages relates to the flexibility in processing. Linked lists and trees can facilitate operations such as insertion, deletion, appending, and editing.

Some uses of linked lists and tree structures are rather complicated. Programming languages such as LISP and SNOBOL have been designed especially for linked list processing. This chapter concentrates upon basic considerations of these data structures and emphasizes the fundamental searching and update actions. This should enable the reader to use the basic structures as well as provide adequate background for those who wish to study this area in greater detail.

13.2 Singly Linked Lists

Each data item of Table 13–1 consists of a city and a postal zip code. This information can be stored in alphabetical order in a two-dimension array of 2 columns and 13 rows. This is a sequential organization in that the position of the record in the file denotes the order of the file, i.e., the name of the city determines the location of the data item in the file.

The binary search can be used to search this data structure for the name of a particular city. This same file can be used to determine what city corresponds to a particular zip code; however, since the zip codes are not sequential, a linear search must be used. Obviously the file can be sorted by zip code and this would also be a sequential organization.

The same data as shown in Table 13–2 can also be considered a sequential organization. However, in this case the file is not ordered by either of the two columns in the array. It may be in a random order, in the order that the data was derived, or in the order of frequency of use of the city name.

In a linked list the logical organization of a file is divorced from the physical structure. In a singly linked list each record points to the location of the next record in the logical sequence. In the case shown in Table 13–2, each entry is numbered from 1 to 13. A third word can be used to indicate the next item in the list and the order of the logical organization is then determined by these **pointers,** or **links.**

Example 13.1
Organize the data of Table 13–2 into a linked list by alphabetical order of the city name.

Table 13-1 Alaska Cities in Ascending Order

Index	City	Zip Code
1	BARTH	32532
2	CAMDEN	04843
3	CHENEY	99004
4	CLINTON	52732
5	DALLAS	75247
6	DAYTON	45409
7	ELM CITY	27822
8	ERWIN	37650
9	LAMBERT	38643
10	LAWTON	73501
11	MONROE	71201
12	NORFOLK	23511
13	QUINCY	62301

Table 13-2 Alaska Cities in Random Order

Index	City	Zip Code
1	QUINCY	62301
2	DAYTON	45409
3	NORFOLK	23511
4	DALLAS	75247
5	ELM CITY	27822
6	CLINTON	52732
7	ERWIN	37650
8	MONROE	71201
9	LAWTON	73501
10	CHENEY	99004
11	LAMBERT	38643
12	CAMDEN	04843
13	BARTH	32532

Table 13-3 Alaska Cities Ordered by Linked List

Index	City	Zip Code	Pointer
1	QUINCY	62301	0
2	DAYTON	45409	5
3	NORFOLK	23511	1
4	DALLAS	75247	2
5	ELM CITY	27822	7
6	CLINTON	52732	4
7	ERWIN	37650	11
8	MONROE	71201	3
9	LAWTON	73501	8
10	CHENEY	99004	6
11	LAMBERT	38643	9
12	CAMDEN	04843	10
13	BARTH	32532	12

Head ◁13|

Solution

The first city in an alphabetical list would be BARTH, which is at location 13 in the list. Therefore, the head of the linked list is location 13. The second city in alphabetical order would be CAMDEN, which is in position 12. Therefore, location 13 must contain a pointer to location 12. Likewise location 12 must contain a pointer to location 10, which contains the third city in alphabetical order, CHENEY.

These pointers are stored in a third column of the resultant linked list, shown in Table 13–3 with the beginning of the list indicated in the box marked Head. Note that the last city in the list is QUINCY. Therefore, the pointer for QUINCY does not point to another location. It is necessary that the pointer for QUINCY indicate the end of the linked list. In this case the value 0 is used for this purpose.

End Solution

Searching a linked list consists of beginning at the head of the list and following the chain until the required data item is found or until the search procedure determines that the item is not in the list. This latter condition can be met in two ways depending upon whether or not the linked list is ordered on the key used for the search. The two methods are the **ordered linked list** and the **unordered linked list.**

A. Ordered List

Assume the value being searched for is called DATA. If the key of the record being examined is greater than DATA and the item has not been found, then it is not in the list. In the above example, assume the search key is by city and the value of DATA is CHICAGO. After comparing DATA to all earlier items, when DATA is compared with CLINTON, it is evident that CHICAGO is not in the linked list since the cities are linked alphabetically.

B. Unordered List

Assume the value of DATA being searched for in the above example is zip code 80909. Since the list is ordered by city, there is no order to the zip codes. Therefore, to be assured that 80909 is not a zip code in the list, all items of the linked list must be examined.

Example 13.2

Develop an algorithm that will search a singly linked list to find the zip code, given the name of the city. The linked list is stored in a two-dimension array LL in which the first column of any row is the name of a city, the second column is the corresponding zip code, and the third column is the pointer to the next item in the list. The list is assumed to be in ascending order by the name of the city.

Solution

```
INTEGER FUNCTION ZIP (CITY);

(* COMMON VARIABLE--START *)

BEGIN

    FOUND := FALSE;

    K := START; (* K POINTS TO NEXT RECORD IN THE LIST LL *)

    ZIP := 0;
    WHILE (NOT FOUND AND K <> 0) DO
    BEGIN
        IF (CITY = LL(K,1))
        THEN
            BEGIN
                FOUND := TRUE;
                ZIP := LL(K,2);
            END
        ELSE
            BEGIN
                IF (CITY < LL(K,1)) (* CITY IS NOT IN LIST LL *)
                THEN
                    K := 0 (* UPDATE POINTER TO NEXT RECORD *)
```

```
                              ELSE
                                  K := LL(K,3);
                          END;
                END;

          END; (* END ZIP *)
```

In the INTEGER FUNCTION ZIP (CITY), the start, or head, of the linked
list LL is assumed to be stored in the global variable START, and K is initialized to this value. In order to terminate the iteration, the BOOLEAN variable
FOUND is used to determine when the desired value of CITY has been
found. An additional test $(K=0)$ is made on K to determine the end of the
list. Since the list is ordered, the search should be terminated if CITY is less
than the current value of LL(K,1). If no match is found during the current
pass, the value of K is updated to the next pointer value found in LL(K,3).
The function terminates with a valid zip code value LL(K,2) when found, or 0
when not found.

End Solution

Although the above example is oriented to a specific linked list, the general
principles of following the list apply to any linked list, or chain. Supplementary Problem 13.9 develops a somewhat more general subroutine to search a
linked list.

Since the linked list structure is considerably different from a sequential
organization, adding or deleting data items in a linked list must be different
from adding or deleting items in an array. When adding a new data item to a
linked list, the physical location of the data within the linked list is not important. It is only necessary that the links in the chain be changed so that the
data item is placed in its proper logical sequence. The algorithm for performing insertion requires the linked list to be followed until the proper place for
the new item is determined. The pointers are then changed to include the
new data item. There are slight variations of the algorithm when the inserted
item becomes the first or last item in the list.

Example 13.3
Develop an algorithm to insert a new item in its proper place in a singly
linked list that is in ascending order.

Solution

```
SUBROUTINE INSERT (LL, START, KEY, LINK, IND);
```

```
BEGIN

    IF (LL(IND,KEY) < LL(START,KEY))
    THEN
        BEGIN (* INSERTION SHOULD BE AT START *)
            LL(IND,LINK) := START,
            START := IND;
        END
    ELSE
        BEGIN
            KPREV := START; (* SAVE PREVIOUS POINTER IN KPREV *)
            K := LL(START,LINK); (* GET POINTER TO NEXT RECORD IN K *)
            FOUND := FALSE;

            WHILE (NOT FOUND) DO
            BEGIN
                IF (LLK,LINK) = 0) (* MAKE NEW RECORD LAST *)
                THEN
                    BEGIN
                        LL(IND,LINK) := K;
                        LL(KPREV,LINK) := IND;
                        FOUND := TRUE;
                    END
                ELSE (* TEST FOR LAST RECORD *)
                    BEGIN
                        IF (LL,LINK) = 0) (* MAKE NEW RECORD LAST *)
                        THEN
                            BEGIN
                                LL(IND,LINK) := 0;
                                LL(K,LINK) := IND;
                                FOUND := TRUE;
                            END
                        ELSE (* UPDATE FOR NEXT RECORD *)
                            BEGIN
                                KPREV := K;
                                K := LL(K,LINK);
                            END;
                    END;
            END;
        END;

END; (* END INSERT *)
```

We assume that the linked list is stored in a two-dimension array LL with each row corresponding to a data item in the list. The column of the array used for the search key is denoted KEY; the column containing the link, or pointer, to the next item of the list is called LINK. The start, or head, of the list is stored in a simple variable START. Except for the value of the pointer, the data to be entered in the list is stored at some available row IND of LL.

The algorithm, which has no global variables, is shown as SUBROUTINE INSERT (LL, START, KEY, LINK, IND). The first condition in INSERT checks to see if the item belongs at the head of the list. Since the list is in ascending order, if the value of the key of the new item is less than the key of the first item in the list, i.e., LL(IND,KEY) < LL(START,KEY), the new item becomes the start of the list. If the new item does not become the start of the linked list, the values of K and KPREV are used to indicate the index of the next data item to be examined and the previous data item examined, respectively. These two values must be kept since two links must always be changed for any inserted item.

The items in the chain are then checked until either the key of the new item is less than the key of the next item in the list or the list is exhausted. In the former case, the link of the item pointing to position K and the link of the new item are changed. If the list is exhausted, the new item is placed at the end of the list. Its link is set to 0 and the link of the previous final item is changed to point to IND.

An insertion anywhere involves changing the pointer of the previous values, if any, and the pointer of the new item. It is critical that these changes be made correctly.

End Solution

Deletion of a data item from a linked list necessitates changing the values of the pointers so that the chain bypasses the record to be eliminated. Once this modification has been made, the item cannot be accessed as a member of the list even though the data is still stored in the array. The data need not be eliminated from the array and, in fact, it may be necessary to keep the item in the array.

Example 13.4

Develop an algorithm to delete an item from a singly linked list in which the keys are in ascending order.

Solution

```
SUBROUTINE DELETE (LL, START, KEY, LINK, DAT);

BEGIN
   IF (DAT <> LL(START,KEY)) (* CHECK FIRST POSITION *)
   THEN
        BEGIN
           KPREV := START;
           K := LL(START,LINK);
           FOUND := FALSE;

           WHILE (NOT FOUND) DO
           BEGIN
```

```
                       IF (DAT = LL(K,KEY))
                       THEN
                           BEGIN (* ITEM FOUND--MODIFY POINTERS *)
                               LL(KPREV,LINK) := LL(K,LINK);
                               FOUND := TRUE;
                           END
                       ELSE
                           BEGIN

                               IF (DAT > LL(K,KEY))
                               THEN (* ITEM NOT FOUND IN LIST *)
                                   FOUND := TRUE
                               ELSE
                                   BEGIN
                                       IF (LL(K,LINK) = 0)
                                       THEN (* END OF LIST--ITEM NOT FOUND *)
                                           FOUND := TRUE
                                       ELSE (* SET POINTER FOR NEXT ITEM *)
                                           BEGIN
                                               KPREV := K;
                                               K := LL(K,LINK);
                                           END;
                                   END;
                           END;
                   END
               ELSE (* MATCH ON START OF LIST *)
                   START := LL(START,LINK);

  END; (* END DELETE *)
```

In SUBROUTINE DELETE (LL, START, KEY, LINK, DAT), DAT is the key of the data item to be deleted. The other parameters and the structure of the array are the same as in Example 13.3. K and KPREV are pointers to the current and previous records, respectively.

The search algorithm requires a comparison between the key field of each record and DAT. If equal, pointers are adjusted to bypass the record. If the end of the list is encountered or DAT becomes greater than LL(K,KEY), the item is not in the list and the procedure can terminate. The algorithm could be modified to indicate that the search terminated without the item being deleted because it was not found in the list.

End Solution

13.3 Doubly Linked Lists

A **doubly linked list** has two pointers associated with each data item: one points to the next item in the list (the **successor link,** or forward link) and one points to the preceding item in the list (the **predecessor link,** or the backward link). Thus there is both a forward and a backward pointer. This type of chain can provide advantages in a number of instances. The following example provides an illustration of a doubly linked list.

Example 13.5

Table 13–4 contains a list of the cities in Alaska with a population greater than 1,500. While keeping the list in alphabetical order, develop a doubly linked list in descending order by population.

Solution

Two additional columns are added to the list: one for the forward pointer and the other for the backward pointer. The final result is shown in Table 13–5. ANCHORAGE, the largest city, has a forward pointer to location 4 (FAIR-BANKS), which is the second largest city. The backward pointer for FAIR-BANKS then points to location 1 (ANCHORAGE). The forward link for FAIRBANKS is location 5 (JUNEAU), which in turn has a backward link pointing to FAIRBANKS. All towns are then linked in this manner.

Since SEWARD (Index 12) is the smallest city and thus last on the list, its forward pointer is a 0, which indicates the tail of the list. And there is no backward pointer 12 because no city points back to it.

Likewise, since ANCHORAGE (Index 1) is the largest city and thus first on the list, its backward pointer is a 0, which indicates the head of the list. And there is no forward pointer 1 on the list because no city points ahead to it.

Searching a doubly linked list is similar to searching a singly linked list. However, a doubly linked list can be searched in a forward or backward direction. For use in a search in either direction, the algorithm of the procedure for searching a singly linked list needs only slight modification for it to be used for a doubly linked list.

The insertion and deletion algorithms for a doubly linked list are slightly more complicated than for a singly linked list, due to the necessity to update more than one type of pointer. The following example provides an algorithm for insertion; Solved Problem 13.1 provides an algorithm for deletion.

End Solution

Example 13.6

Develop an algorithm to insert a new item into its proper place in a doubly linked list that is arranged in ascending order.

Solution

```
SUBROUTINE DINSRT (LL, START, KEY, LINKF, LINKB, IND);

(* KEY IS DATA FIELD--IND POINTS TO NEW ITEM *)

BEGIN
   IF (LL(IND,KEY) > LL(START,KEY))  (* CHECK HEAD OF LIST *)
   THEN
      BEGIN
```

Table 13-4 Alaska Cities with Population over 1,500

Index	City	Population
1	ANCHORAGE	48,029
2	BARROW	2,104
3	BETHEL	2,416
4	FAIRBANKS	14,771
5	JUNEAU	13,556
6	KENAI	3,553
7	KETCHIKAN	6,994
8	KODIAK	3,798
9	KOTZEBUE	1,696
10	NOME	2,488
11	PETERSBURG	2,042
12	SEWARD	1,587
13	SITKA	3,370
14	WRANGELL	2,029

Table 13-5 Double Linked List by Population

Index	City	Population	Forward Pointer	Backward Pointer
1	ANCHORAGE	48,029	4	0
2	BARROW	2,104	11	3
3	BETHEL	2,416	2	10
4	FAIRBANKS	14,771	5	1
5	JUNEAU	13,556	7	4
6	KENAI	3,553	13	8
7	KETCHIKAN	6,994	8	5
8	KODIAK	3,798	6	7
9	KOTZEBUE	1,696	12	14
10	NOME	2,488	3	13
11	PETERSBURG	2,042	14	2
12	SEWARD	1,587	0	9
13	SITKA	3,370	10	6
14	WRANGELL	2,029	9	11

HEAD   ◁1

TAIL   ◁12

```
(* NOT HEAD--FOLLOW CHAIN--K ALWAYS POINTS TO SUCCESSOR *)
K := LL(START,LINKF);
FOUND := FALSE;

WHILE (NOT FOUND) DO
BEGIN (* TEST FOR CORRECT POSITION *)
    IF (LL(IND,KEY) < LL(K,KEY))
    THEN
        BEGIN (* POSITION FOUND *)
            (* SET FORWARD LINK OF NEW *)
            LL(IND,LINKF) := K;

            (* SET BACKWARD LINK OF NEW *)
            LL(IND,LINKB) := LL(K,LINKB);

            (* SET FORWARD LINK OF PREVIOUS *)
            LL(LL(K,LINKB),LINKF) := IND;

            (* SET BACKWARD LINK OF SUCCESSOR *)
            LL(K,LINKB) := IND;

            FOUND := TRUE;
        END
    ELSE
        BEGIN
            IF (LL(K,LINKF) = 0) (* TEST FOR LAST IN LIST *)
            THEN
                BEGIN (* INSERT AT TAIL *)
                    (* SET FORWARD LINK OF NEW *)
                    LL(IND,LINKF) := 0;

                    (* SET BACKWARD LINK OF NEW *)
                    LL(IND,LINKB) := K;

                    (* SET FORWARD LINK OF PREVIOUS *)
                    LL(K,LINKF) := IND;

                    FOUND := TRUE;
                END
            ELSE
                K := LL(K,LINKF);
        END;
    END;
END
ELSE (* HEAD IS CORRECT POSITION *)
    BEGIN
        (* SET FORWARD LINK OF NEW *)
        LL(IND,LINKF) := START;

        (* SET BACKWARD LINK OF NEW *)
        LL(IND,LINKB) := 0;

        (* SET BACKWARD LINK OF OLD HEAD *)
        LL(START,LINKB) := IND;
```

```
                          (* SET NEW HEAD INDICATOR *)
                          START := IND;
                    END;

          END; (* END DINSRT *)
```

SUBROUTINE DINSRT (LL, START, KEY, LINKF, LINKB, IND) is patterned after the subroutine for insertion into a singly linked list (Example 13.3). The procedure involves both a forward link to the successor item in the list (LINKF) and a backward link to the predecessor in the list (LINKB). In general, this means that four links must be changed as a result of an insertion: two pointers in the new item, one pointer in the predecessor, and one pointer in the successor. As with the singly linked list, there is a variation in the procedure when an item is inserted at either the head or the tail of the list.

End Solution

The changing of the links must be studied closely in order to understand the changes that are being made. Figure 13–1 contains a simple illustration of the changes when the data item with the key COW is to be inserted between those items corresponding to the keys CAT and DOG.

The original contents of the pointers are as shown in Figure 13–1a, in which the three data items are at locations 17, 35, and 53. The algorithm in Example 13.6 can then be examined in light of this illustration.

The algorithm would determine that the word COW at location 53 should be inserted before DOG. The first of the four assignment operations changes the 92 of COW to 35 (the present value of K), the second operation changes the 91 to 17 (the present contents of the backward pointer of the data item K). The third operation involves a subscripted value as a subscript. In the example, LL(K,LINKB) is equal to 17 and therefore LL(LL(K,LINKB)LINKF) is LL(17,LINKF) and thus the value of 35 in the word with the key of CAT is changed to 53 (value of IND). The last operation changes the backward pointer of the data item at location 35 to the value of 53. The result is then as shown in Figure 13–1b.

There are a couple of instances in which caution must be exercised in making the insertion. First, the algorithm must be sure that the value of a pointer is not changed before it is to be used in another assignment statement. For example, if the operation in the pseudocode with START := IND were interchanged with the one immediately before it, the wrong action would occur. Second, note that if the new item is to be stored at the end of the list, there is no successor and, therefore, the backward link of the successor cannot be changed. Thus there are only three assignment operations in that case.

Figure 13–1.
Doubly Lined List

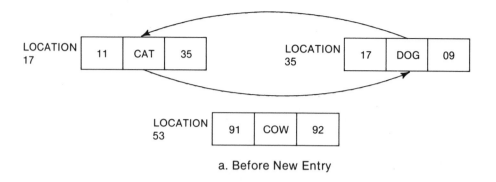

a. Before New Entry

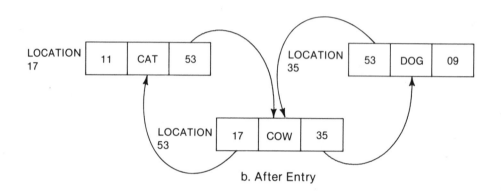

b. After Entry

13.4 Trees

A **tree** can be defined as a set of **nodes** that are organized in a relationship so that (1) there is a specially designated node called the **root** of the tree and (2) the remaining nodes of the tree are divided into independent (or disjoint) sets so that each of these sets is a tree (called a **subtree**).

One form of tree structure familiar to most people is a family tree. Another example of a tree is shown in Figure 13–2a. This representation of a tree, as well as the other trees in this chapter, has the root at the top of the diagram, following the convention used in most computer texts. In this tree, the root is Washington and there are three subtrees: (TRUMAN, JEFFERSON, HOOVER), (ROOSEVELT), and (LINCOLN, MADISON, JOHNSON, EISENHOWER). A node that has no subtrees is defined as a **null node, or leaf.** To follow a tree from its root node to any other node is defined as traversing the tree. In traversing the tree in Figure 13–2b from WASHINGTON to ROOSEVELT, the sequence WASHINGTON, TRUMAN, JEFFERSON, ROOSEVELT would be recorded.

Figure 13–2.
Tree Structures

a. Sample Tree
Structure

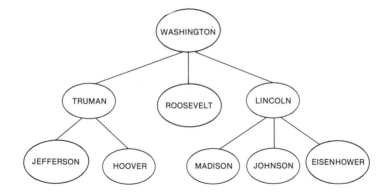

b. Binary Tree
Structure

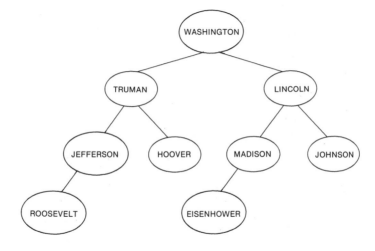

c. Ordered Binary
Tree Structure

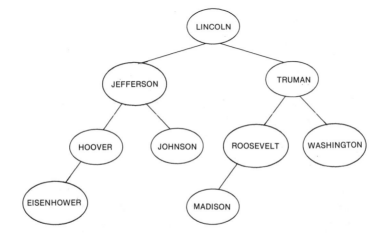

Example 13.7

Figure 13–2b depicts the data from Figure 13–2a in the form of a **binary tree.** That is, there are no more than two branches leading from any given node. The binary tree in Figure 13–2b does not appear to have a particular sequence. Reorder the tree so that it is in alphabetical order.

Solution

The binary tree in Figure 13–2c is arranged in alphabetical order when traversed in a particular sequence. The basic rules for this traversal are as follows:

1. Start at the root and follow the left-most branches until a leaf, or null node, is encountered, i.e., a node with no branches. Record the leaf.

2. Back up to the root of the subtree of the leaf. Record the root.

3. Traverse the right branch of this node (if it exists), treating it as a new tree. In traversing the tree in Figure 13–2b from WASHINGTON to ROOSEVELT, the sequence WASHINGTON, TRUMAN, JEFFERSON, ROOSEVELT would be recorded.

In traversing Figure 13–2c in alphabetical sequence, follow the left-most subtrees until a null node, or leaf, is encountered (EISENHOWER). The node EISENHOWER is then the first in the sequence. Since the right subtrees of (EISENHOWER) are also null, the root of the tree (EISENHOWER, HOOVER), i.e., HOOVER, is added to the sequence. The node HOOVER does not have a right subtree, so the node JEFFERSON is added to the sequence.

The right subtree of JEFFERSON, i.e., JOHNSON, is now traversed. Continuing the process shows the tree to be in alphabetical order. Trees can, of course, be reordered by various attributes. For example, the above tree could be reordered in the chronological sequence by which the individuals held the office of President.

End Solution

The above method of traversing a tree is technically called a **postorder traversal.** Two other methods of traversal are introduced in Solved Problem 13–5. Traversing trees is related to searching; a problem of this type is provided in Problem 13–6. The following example illustrates how a tree can be stored in a computer.

Example 13.8

Organize the data of Table 13–2 into a binary tree structure by alphabetical order of the city name. Develop a method of storing this data in a computer.

Figure 13–3.
Ordered Tree
Structure

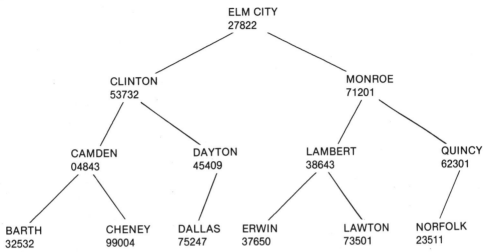

Solution

A graphic view of a suitable binary tree is shown in Figure 13–3. Although there are obviously a number of variations of a particular tree structure, this figure shows one of the balanced arrangements of this tree, i.e., each subtree has basically the same number of nodes.

In developing a method to store the tree, we will assume that the tree is stored in an array arrangement with each row corresponding to an entry for a city. The first column of the array is the pointer to the root of the left subtree, the second column is the pointer to the right subtree, the third column contains the city name, and the fourth column contains the corresponding zip code. Assuming the order of the cities in the array to be the same as that in Table 13–2, the tree array structure is stored as shown in Table 13–6.

The root of the tree is ELM CITY at location 5 and therefore the value of root is 5. The left link for ELM CITY is 6, which indicates the root of that subtree is CLINTON. Likewise, the right pointer for ELM CITY is 8, which indicates that MONROE is the root of the right subtree. The remainder of the tree can then be determined by following these two subtrees.

A useful exercise is to draw the tree based upon the array. The final result should agree with Figure 13–3. The value of 0 is used as a marker to show the end of a branch, i.e., the absence of any other subtrees. Note the number of times these markers occur.

End Solution

Table 13-6 Array Implementation of Tree Structure

Index	Column 1 Left Link	Column 2 Right Link	Column 3 City	Column 4 Zip Code
1	3	0	QUINCY	62301
2	4	0	DAYTON	45409
3	0	0	NORFOLK	23511
4	0	0	DALLAS	75247
5	6	8	ELM CITY	27822
6	12	2	CLINTON	52732
7	0	0	ERWIN	37650
8	11	1	MONROE	71201
9	0	0	LAWTON	73501
10	0	0	CHENEY	99004
11	7	9	LAMBERT	38643
12	13	10	CAMDEN	04843
13	0	0	BARTH	32532

ROOT   5

The advantages of tree structures are in the ease of searching and the relatively rapid insertion and deletion of individual items. Searching a tree is an excellent application of a recursive subroutine and it is presented as such in the following example.

Example 13.9

Develop a subprogram to search a tree structure stored in an array arrangement. If the data being sought is in the tree, the result of the procedure is the index of the array row. If the data is not in the tree, a value of 0 is returned from the subprogram. Make the algorithm general enough to handle any tree in which the first column is the left pointer and the second column is the right pointer.

Solution

```
INTEGER FUNCTION TREE1 (M1, M2, DAT);

BEGIN
   IF (DAT <> X(M1,M2)) (* CHECK FIRST NODE *)
   THEN
       BEGIN
           IF (DAT < X(M1,M2)) (* FOLLOW LEFT BRANCH *)
```

```
              THEN
                  BEGIN
                      IF (X(M1,1) = 0)
                      THEN
                          TREE1 := 0
                      ELSE
                          TREE1 := TREE1(X(M1,1),M2,DAT);
                  END
              ELSE (* FOLLOW RIGHT BRANCH *)
                  BEGIN
                      IF (X(M1,2) = 0)
                      THEN
                          TREE1 := 0
                      ELSE
                          TREE1 := TREE1(X(M1,2),M2,DAT);
                  END;
          END
      ELSE (* MATCH ON FIRST NODE *)
          TREE1 := M1;

  END; (* END TREE1 *)
```

In FUNCTION TREE1 (M1, M2, DAT), M1 is the index of the node (array row) under consideration, M2 is the column of the array containing the search key, and DAT is the data that the procedure is attempting to find. The array X, which contains the tree structure in array form, is a GLOBAL array.

If DAT is equal to X(M1,M2), then the value of the function is M1; otherwise the search continues. If DAT is less than X(M1,M2), the left subtree is used for the further search. The right subtree is used if DAT is greater than X(M1,M2). If the pointer to the appropriate subtree is 0, there is no subtree, DAT is not in the tree, and a value of 0 is returned by the function. If the appropriate subtree does exist, TREE1 is called recursively. The calls eventually stop with TREE1 having a value equal to M1 or to 0.

End Solution

TREE1 is a general algorithm for searching a tree that could easily be applied to the zip code problem.

Example 13.10
Assume an array X contains the zip code information in tree form as shown in Table 13–4. If the root of the tree is stored at ROOT and the name of the city being searched for is stored in CITY, devise an algorithm to find the zip code.

Solution

```
INTEGER FUNCTION ZIP (CITY);

BEGIN
   ZIP := X(TREE1(ROOT,3,CITY),4);

END; (* END ZIP *)
```

The name of the city is in column 3 of the array. Therefore, the location of the row for that city is the value of the function corresponding to TREE1(ROOT,3,CITY). Accessing the array with this index and the fourth column yields the corresponding zip code. This trivial algorithm consists of one statement, which is called from within an assignment statement in FUNCTION ZIP(CITY).

End Solution

The insertion of a new data item in a tree can best be accomplished by a recursive procedure. An algorithm using a recursive procedure is portrayed in the following example.

Example 13.11

Develop an algorithm to insert a new record into its proper place in a tree structure that is arranged in ascending order by the sort key.

Solution

```
SUBROUTINE TREE2 (M1, M2, MNEW);

BEGIN
   IF (X(MNEW,M2) < X(M1,M2)) (* TEST LEFT PATH *)
   THEN
       BEGIN
           IF (X(M1,1) = 0)
           THEN
               BEGIN (* NULL NODE FOUND *)
                   X(M1,1) := MNEW;
                   X(MNEW,1) := 0;
                   X(MNEW,2) := 0;
               END
           ELSE
               CALL TREE2 (X(M1,1), M2, MNEW);
       END
   ELSE (* RIGHT PATH *)
       BEGIN
           IF (X(M1,2) = 0)
           THEN
```

```
                        BEGIN (* NULL NODE FOUND *)
                            X(M1,2) := MNEW;
                            X(MNEW,1) := 0;
                            X(MNEW,2) := 0;
                        END
                    ELSE
                            CALL TREE2 (X(M1,2), M2, MNEW);
                END;

END; (* END TREE2 *)
```

Assume that the tree is stored in a manner similar to that used in Example 13.8. The array X is GLOBAL to the subprogram containing this algorithm, the first column of the array is the left pointer, the second column is the right pointer, M1 refers to the row index of the node under consideration, and M2 is the column number of the sort key. The information to be entered into the tree is already stored in row MNEW of X; the procedure merely needs to fix the pointers in this word and the node that points to it.

SUBROUTINE TREE2 (M1, M2, MNEW) is a recursive subroutine. It follows the tree, comparing the value of the key of the new item, i.e., X(MNEW,M2), with that of the node being considered, i.e., X(M1,M2), as if searching for the key in the tree. This eventually leads to a null subtree. Since the algorithm branches to the left when X(MNEW,M2) < X(M1,M2) and branches to the right when X(MNEW,M2) > X(M1,M2), this null subtree must then be the proper position for the new entry. The pointer for the node with the null subtree is changed to point to MNEW and the two pointers in the new node are set to 0, i.e., null subtrees.

End Solution

13.5 Treesort: An Example of Using the Concepts of a Tree

The concepts underlying trees are often useful, even though the actual data storage might not be a tree structure. One example is a sort routine called TREESORT3, which is based upon an algorithm developed by Robert W. Floyd and published in the algorithms section of the *Communications of the ACM* (Association of Computing Machinery) (December 1968). Although the actual data structure is a one-dimension array, this sort algorithm considers the data in the array to be in the form of a binary tree.

The N items in a one-dimension array M are to be sorted. Consider each item of the array to be the node of a binary tree. For each item that is an even integer, $I > 2$, the node M(I/2) is assumed to be the parent or father node of M(I). If I is an odd integer and $I > 1$, the father node of M(I) is M((I − 1)/2). Thus if N = 3, the array M can be visualized as the tree shown in Figure 13–4. If N = 5, the items M(4) and M(5) have M(2) as a parent node. Thus a binary tree can be described by a one-dimension array.

Figure 13–4.
Sample Tree
Structure

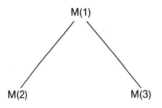

M(1)

M(2)   M(3)

Example 13.12

The following list of names is to be sorted in alphabetical order: TERRY, LEN, MARGE, KATE, STEVE, EDDIE, TOM, LIBBY, BILL, BARB. The data is stored in a one-dimension array M in the order listed. Depict the data as a tree, utilizing the above concepts.

Solution

The root of the binary tree is the first item of the array, TERRY. The two nodes at the next level of the tree are M(2) and M(3), which correspond to LEN and MARGE, respectively. The construction of this concept results in the tree shown in Figure 13–5a.

End Solution

The heart of the TREESORT3 algorithm is based upon the concept that for any particular subtree, the largest or smallest value is to be placed at the root of the tree. For example, in the subtree in Figure 13–5b, the largest value is not stored in the root of the subtree. Therefore, the algorithm would change the subtree so that LIBBY becomes the root of the tree. This can be done in this case by merely exchanging the contents of M(4) and M(8). The revised subtree is then as shown in Figure 13–5c. One algorithm for making this change compares the two nodes M(8) and M(9) to find the larger of the two; it then compares the larger node at the lower level with the root. Finally, it moves the larger node from the lower level to the root, if necessary.

Example 13.13

Consider that three items (M(I),M(2I),M(2I+1)) of a one-dimension array constitute a binary tree with M(I) as the root. Develop SUBROUTINE SIFT (I, N) that will ensure that the largest of the three values is at the root of the tree. The algorithm should handle any value of I so that $1 <= I <= N$.

Figure 13–5.
Tree Structures

a. Unordered Tree
Structure

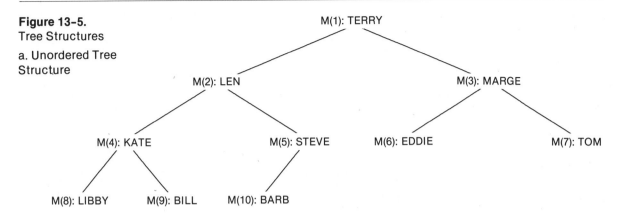

b. Unordered
Subtree Structure

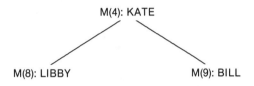

c. Largest Item on
Top Subtree
Structure

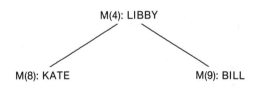

Solution

```
SUBROUTINE SIFT (I, N);

BEGIN
    COPY := M(I); (* SAVE CURRENT NODE *)
    J := 2 * I;

    IF (J <= N)
    THEN
        BEGIN
            (* SET J TO LARGEST OF M(J+1) AND M(J) *)
            IF (J < N AND M(J+1) > M(J))
            THEN
                J := J + 1;

            (* IF M(J) > M(I) MAKE SWAP *)
            IF (M(J) > COPY)
            THEN
                BEGIN
                    M(I) := M(J);
                    I := J;
                END;

            M(I) := COPY;
        END;

END; (* END SIFT *)
```

The binary tree can have one or both subtree(s) null. For example, if I = N, there are obviously two null subtrees. In fact, if I > N/2, the binary tree will always consist of the root and two null subtrees. The tree has one null subtree and one nonnull subtree when I = N/2. The algorithm must take this into account.

This algorithm begins by saving the value of M(I) in COPY and computes J as 2*I. The value of J is then compared with the value of N. If J > N, each succeeding binary tree consists solely of the node M(I) and the algorithm can terminate. If J = N, there is only one nonnull subtree and that node, M(J), is compared with COPY. If J < N, there are two nodes at the lower level and the larger of these two nodes must be found before comparisons with COPY. If M(J) > COPY, then M(J) > M(I) and the exchange is made.

The observant reader might notice that the exchange of M(I) and M(J) is somewhat less efficient than the previous method we used to make exchanges. Normally the exchange involves the following three assignment operations:

```
COPY := M(I);
M(I) := M(J);
M(J) := COPY;
```

In this algorithm it is handled as follows:

```
COPY := M(I);
M(I) := M(J);
  I  := J;
M(I) := COPY;
```

In fact, the first and last assignment statements are performed every time regardless of whether or not an exchange has been made. Although this introduces some inefficiency, it is included here to make the algorithm more suitable for later modification.

End Solution

Since the SIFT algorithm handles a tree consisting of at most three nodes, it is desirable to extend the algorithm to larger binary trees. This is rather easy if it is assumed that each of the two subtrees is already set up so that the largest node of the subtree is at the root of that subtree.

SIFT only needs to consider the root of the tree and the root of the two subtrees. If the original root is the largest of the three values, then the tree is ordered with the largest value at the root. If an exchange is made, the largest value would be at the root of the tree, but the subtree that originally contained the largest value might not be in the proper order. The SIFT algorithm can then put the largest value of that subtree at the root of the subtree. This process can continue through as many levels as necessary.

For example, consider the left subtree of Figure 13–5a, with M(2):LEN as its root. If the two subtrees of that tree are in order with their largest value at the roots, the tree would appear as in Figure 13–6a. The task is then to apply the SIFT algorithm to get the largest value in M(2).

The SIFT algorithm is applied to the tree consisting of M(2), M(4), and M(5). This results in STEVE being stored in M(2) and LEN being stored in M(5), as shown in Figure 13.6b. Since the node M(5) was changed, it is then necessary to examine the tree consisting of M(5) and M(10) using the SIFT routine. In this case the tree is in order, but this will not necessarily always be so. For example, consider the case where M(2) might have originally contained the name ANDY instead of LEN.

Example 13.14

The application of the SIFT algorithm to order a large binary tree need not involve successive subroutine calls. Develop algorithm SIFTDN (I, N) that sifts down the value of M(I) to its correct level in the tree. Start with SUBROUTINE SIFT (I, N).

Figure 13–6.
Tree Structures

a. Tree Structure
with Largest Item at
Root of Subtrees

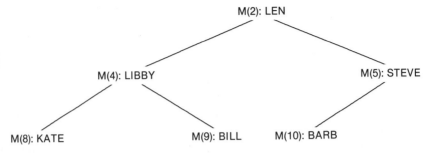

b. Tree Structure
with Largest Item at
Root

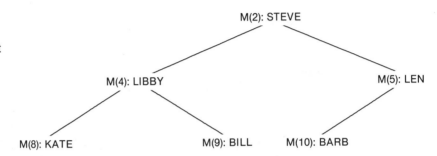

Solution

```
SUBROUTINE SIFTDN (I, N);

BEGIN
*  DONE := FALSE;

   COPY := M(I); (* SAVE CURRENT NODE *)

*  WHILE (NOT DONE) DO (* CONTINUE UNTIL NO SWAP IS MADE *)
*  BEGIN
        J := 2 * I;

        IF (J <= N)
        THEN
            BEGIN
                (* SET J TO LARGEST OF M(J+1) AND M(J) *)
                IF (J < N AND M(J+1) > M(J))
                THEN
                    J := J + 1;

                IF (M(J) > COPY)
                THEN
```

```
                        BEGIN (* SWAP ELEMENTS *)
                            M(I) := M(J);
                            I := J;
                        END
 *             ELSE (* NO SWAP MADE SO QUIT *)
 *                 DONE := TRUE;
 *                 M(I) := COPY;
            END
        ELSE
            DONE := TRUE;
 *  END;

END; (* END SIFTDN *)
```

The changes in the SIFT algorithm from Example 13.13 are labelled with an asterisk (*) in the margin of the SIFTDN algorithm. The current value of I is doubled and the algorithm is applied to the subtree from which the largest values came. The algorithm terminates when all nodes have been searched or when no exchange takes place. The method of exchanging M(I) and M(J), as pointed out in the last example, is an advantage in this subroutine.

End Solution

Example 13.15
Develop an algorithm to implement the TREESORT3 procedure outlined above.

Solution

```
SUBROUTINE TREESORT3 (M, N);

BEGIN
   (* PUT LEFT AND RIGHT SUBTREES IN ORDER *)
   FOR I := N / 2 STEP (-1) WHILE (I >= 2) DO
      CALL SIFTDN (I, N);

   (* PERFORM STEP 3 AND 4 OF PROCEDURE DESCRIBED *)
   FOR I := N STEP (-1) WHILE (I >= 2) DO
   BEGIN
      CALL SIFTDN (1, I);

      TEMP := M(1);
      M(1) := M(I);
      M(I) := TEMP;
   END;

END; (* END TREESORT3 *)
```

SUBROUTINE SIFTDN is the heart of the TREESORT3 algorithm. The sort algorithm can be broadly outlined as follows:

1. Consider that the one-dimension array M to be sorted is a binary tree in which M(I/2) is the father of M(I). This is merely a conceptual step, a way of looking at the problem; there are no operations in the algorithm for this step.

2. Rearrange the left subtree and the right subtree of the M binary tree so that each subtree is an ordered tree. For the purposes of this algorithm, we will consider an ordered tree to be one in which the root of that tree has a higher value than any node in its two subtrees and each subtree is, in turn, an ordered tree. Note that this definition is recursive and that therefore the subtrees at all levels must be ordered. SUBROUTINE SIFTDN can be used to order the trees at the lowest levels with nonnull subtrees and then to order each successive tree through all levels of the M binary tree.

3. Apply SIFTDN (1, N) to array M. At the conclusion of the preceding step, the left subtree is ordered and the right subtree is ordered, but an arbitrary value is at the root of the entire binary tree, i.e., at M(1). The call of SIFTDN (1, N) will then check to see if M(1) is the largest value. If not, the algorithm will move the largest value (which must be at either the root of the left subtree or at the root of the right subtree) to the root of the tree. As explained in Example 13.14, it will also ensure the respective subtree continues to be ordered.

4. Exchange M(1) with M(N). This takes the largest value from M(1) and places it in M(N). The location M(1) then contains an arbitrary (i.e., unknown) value.

5. Decrement N by 1. Terminate the algorithm if N = 1; otherwise, go to step 3. When N = 1, array M is sorted and the algorithm stops. If N > 1, the repetition of the procedure works with an array that has one data item fewer. Thus that part of the array to be considered as a tree gets smaller by one item with each application of the subroutine.

Although the TREESORT3 algorithm appears rather short, it contains successive calls on the SIFTDN subroutine. The first iteration accomplishes step 2 above. All nodes M(I), for which I > N / 2, have two null subtrees. Therefore, the loop starts at I = N/2 and goes to 2 by decrementing the control variable I. This starts with the subtrees at the lowest level and works successively up the main tree. For the node M(I) being considered at any time, each of the two subtrees for that node is already ordered. Therefore, the SIFTDN (I, N) procedure will order the tree that has M(I) as its root. Since the iteration terminates at I= 2, the only tree not ordered is the one with M(1) as its root, i.e., the entire M binary tree.

The second iteration performs steps 3 and 4 of the TREESORT3 procedure outlined above. The call on SIFTDN orders the subtree consisting of data items of the array M(1) through M(I), placing the largest value in M(1). The values of M(1) and M(I) are then exchanged. The iteration reduces the value of I by 1 (step 5 of the TREESORT3 procedure) and the subroutine is applied to the smaller tree.

End Solution

Example 13.16

Apply the TREESORT3 algorithm to the data of Example 13.12.

Solution

The starting position is in Figure 13–5a. Since N= 10, the first iteration in the TREESORT3 algorithm in Example 13.15 goes from I= 5 to I= 2. Therefore, the first call of SIFTDN considers the subtree M(5), M(10) and no change is made in the subtree. The second call of the subroutine considers the subtree consisting of nodes M(4), M(8), and M(9). As a result, the names LIBBY and KATE are exchanged.

The next application of the subroutine considers nodes M(3), M(6), and M(7). In this case TOM is moved to M(3), and MARGE replaces TOM at M(7). The fourth and last call of SIFTDN in this iteration starts with the subtree of Figure 13–6a and stops with the subtree of Figure 13–6b. The end result for the first iteration is shown in Figure 13–7a.

The second iteration does the actual sorting. The first application of SIFTDN will result in the names TERRY and TOM being exchanged. The subtree with TERRY as its root in location M(3) is then found to be ordered. Upon return from the subroutine, the contents of M(1) and M(10) are exchanged and the tree appears as in Figure 13–7b.

The second application of SIFTDN only considers the tree from M(1) through M(9). In this case TERRY moves up to M(1) and BARB replaces TERRY in M(3). Then in the subtree with node M(3), BARB moves to M(7); M(3) is filled by MARGE. The exchange of M(1) and M(9) is made and the tree appears as in Figure 13–7c. The algorithm continues in this manner until the final position of Figure 13–7d is obtained.

End Solution

Figure 13-7.
Tree Structures

a. Tree Structure
After First Iteration

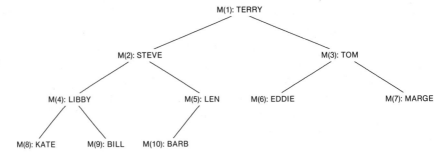

b. Tree Structure
After Second
Iteration

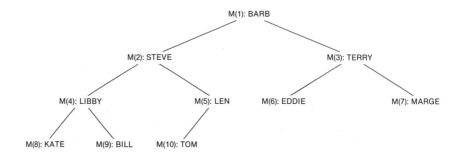

c. Tree Structure
After Third Iteration

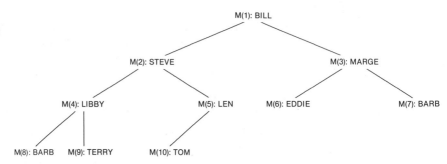

d. Tree Structure
After Final Iteration

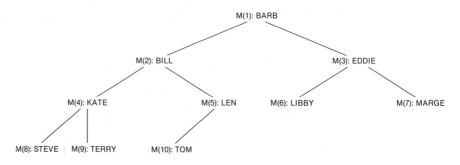

Solved Problems

13.1

Develop an algorithm to delete an item from a doubly linked list in which the keys are in ascending order.

Solution

```
SUBROUTINE DDELET (LL, START, KEY, LINKF, LINKB, DAT);

BEGIN
    IF (DAT <> LL(START,KEY)) (* TEST FOR MATCH AT HEAD *)
    THEN
        BEGIN
            K := LL(START,LINKF); (* K ALWAYS POINTS TO NEXT NODE *)
            DONE := FALSE;

            WHILE (NOT DONE) DO
            BEGIN
                IF (DAT = LL(K,KEY))
                THEN
                    BEGIN
                        DONE := TRUE;

                        (* SET FORWARD LINK OF PREDECESSOR *)
                        LL(LL(K,LINKB),LINKF) := LL(K,LINKF);

                        IF (LL(K,LINKF) <> 0) (* CHECK FOR LAST *)
                        THEN
                            (* SET BACKWARD LINK OF SUCCESSOR *)
                            LL(LL(K,LINKF),LINKB) := LL(K,LINKB);
                    END
                ELSE
                    BEGIN
                        IF (DAT < LL(K,KEY))
                        THEN
                            BEGIN
                                (* CHECK FOR END OF LIST *)
                                IF (LL(K,LINKF) <> 0)
                                THEN
                                    (* UPDATE K TO SUCCESSOR *)
                                    K := LL(K,LINKF)
                                ELSE
                                    DONE := TRUE;
                            END
                        ELSE
                            DONE := TRUE;
                    END;
            END;
        END
    ELSE (* MATCH AT HEAD OF LIST *)
```

```
        BEGIN
            START := LL(START,LINKF);
            LL(START,LINKB) := 0;
        END;

END; (* END DDELET *)
```

SUBROUTINE DDELET (LL, START, KEY, LINKF, LINKB, DAT) is a combination of the concepts of DELETE (Example 13.4) and of DINSRT (Example 13.6). As shown in DELETE, it is simpler to delete an item from a list than to add one. However, it is still necessary to be careful in the individual operations of the procedures.

You can follow the general techniques of deletion by considering the elimination of the data item with COW in Figure 13–1b. It is also necessary to be sure that the data item being deleted is not the last one in the list. Thus there is a conditional check to see if LL (K,LINKF)= 0 and, if so, the algorithm bypasses the changing of the backward pointer of the successor (since there is none). There is a second check to see if LL(K,LINKF)= 0, which is used to determine if the list has been exhausted without finding the desired data item.

13.2

Section 13.2 discusses the use of a singly linked list. Some data applications involve more than one linked list. Design a file of the 50 states containing the following information for each state:

• Total area in square miles
• Population as of the last census
• State capital
• Date of admission of the state to the Union

The file is to be ordered in some manner for each of the following:

• Alphabetically by state
• Descending order of square miles
• Descending order of population
• Ascending order of date of admission to the Union

Solution

The file can be arranged with 50 row entries, one for each state. This list can be in alphabetical order, taking care of the first ordering requirement. The other data items can be ordered by means of three linked lists, one each for area, population, and date of admission. There is no need to link the names of the capitals in this example. A possible arrangement of the file with the

Table 13-7 1970 Population Figures

State	Capital	Area	Area Linked List	1970 Population	Population Linked List	Date Admitted to the Union	Admission Date Linked List
ALABAMA	MONTGOMERY	51,609	32	3,444,165	47	Dec 14, 1819	19
ALASKA	JUNEAU	586,412	43	302,173	0	Jan 3, 1959	11
ARIZONA	PHOENIX	113,909	28	1,772,482	48	Feb 14, 1912	2
ARKANSAS	LITTLE ROCK	53,104	33	1,923,295	3	Jun 15, 1836	22
CALIFORNIA	SACRAMENTO	158,693	26	19,953,134	32	Sep 9, 1850	23
COLORADO	DENVER	104,247	50	2,207,259	37	Aug 1, 1876	34

first few items is in Table 13–7. The numbers in the linked lists are pointers to the appropriate rows of the file corresponding to the next state in the chain.

13.3

There are a variety of ways to use the data file of the preceding problem in order to answer queries. Outline the necessary search strategy to answer each of the following questions:

a. What is the capital of MONTANA?
b. What is the population of UTAH?
c. What state consists of 104,247 square miles?
d. What was the 33rd state admitted to the Union?
e. How many states have a population greater than 5 million?
f. How many states have a population density per square mile greater than 100?
g. Assume that there are two additional linked lists: one for population in ascending order and another for area in ascending order. You are allowed to examine only ten items in the file and on the basis of this sample, you must predict the state with the largest population density. Without any knowledge of the data base, what is a reasonable search strategy?

Solution

a. Since the list is arranged in a sequential manner by state name, perform a binary search on the state name to find MONTANA. Then output HEL-

ENA from the column corresponding to the capital.

b. Use the binary search to find UTAH. The result (1,059,273) is output from the corresponding population column.

c. This can be found by a linear search of the file checking the area column for each state. When the value is found, print out the name of the state. An alternative method is to follow the area linked list until the value of 104,247 is found and COLORADO is output from the state field.

d. The date of admission linked list is needed for an efficient search. Follow the list, keeping track of the number of items being searched. When the 33rd item on the list is encountered, print out the name of the state (ORE-GON).

e. The population is linked in descending order. Follow this list and increment a counter for each item until the population figure for a state drops below 5,000,000 (11 states).

f. Population density is the population of the state divided by the area. Thus a computation must be made for each data item that is examined. In order to answer this question from the file, there must be a full file search, i.e., each item in the file must be examined. Note that this is the first search so far in which this was necessary. (The answer is 16 states.)

g. Intuitively, one would expect the state with the highest population density to be one of the smallest states in area or one of the largest in population. One might then select the first five states from the descending population list and the first five states from the ascending area list. The population density would then be computed for this sample of 10 items with the highest value serving to predict the state with the highest population density. Using this method, NEW JERSEY (the fifth smallest state), with a population density of 9148, would be selected. This is, in fact, the state with the highest population density.

13.4

In many computer applications there is frequent use of search methods to retrieve data. In these applications it is necessary that the data be organized in a reasonably efficient manner to facilitate the search. This problem considers an example of such a situation. Population information is to be kept for all towns and cities in the U.S. with more than 1,500 people (close to 7500 towns and cities). The major types of questions to be answered by this data falls into the following categories:

a. Population of specific cities (e.g., What is the population of Pennington Gap, Virginia? Is the population of Farmers Branch, Texas, greater than 20,000? How much larger is Houston than Atlanta?).

b. Population data related to specific states (e.g., What are the ten largest cities in Vermont? How many cities in Illinois have a population between

20,000 and 80,000? Is the combined population of the eight largest cities in Texas greater than the combined population of the eight largest cities in Ohio? What is the smallest city in the state of Arizona?).

c. Population data related to the entire U.S. (e.g., What are the ten largest cities in the U.S.? How many cities in the U.S. have a population of between 1800 and 1900?).

Due to the need for lists in ascending and descending order and the requirement for certain calculations, all linked lists are to be doubly linked lists. In addition, it has been deemed necessary to keep all data about a state in alphabetical order by city name in order to facilitate certain queries and the output of state-related information. Within these two design criteria, outline a suitable method of computer storage of the data.

Solution

There are obviously a number of possible solutions. The type of computer, the programming language, available software, and so forth, can affect the efficiency. What is efficient in one system might not be efficient in another. If you are familiar with a particular computer system, you can orient your solution in that direction. We will present here a rather general solution.

One idea that can be pursued is to have 50 two-dimension arrays of the type used for the Alaska data of Example 13.5 (one array per state). It would be a reasonable approach to have each array on a disk file. But we will assume that all arrays are stored in memory. It would then be clumsy and inefficient to try to manipulate 50 arrays in the program.

An alternative would be to have a three-dimension array with the first dimension being 50 two-dimension arrays to represent each of the 50 states. But we must consider the size requirements. As shown later, there must be at least two doubly linked lists in order to perform the searches efficiently. Using three words for the city name, one word for population, and one word for each of the four pointers, there would be eight words per city. In some systems two pointers could be stored in one word. Even so, it appears that a minimum of five words would be needed in any case.

The array dimensions would then contain (50 states)*(525 cities/state)*(5 words/city), or 131,250 words. (The 525 in the second dimension is necessary since we must allow for the maximum number of cities per state, i.e., 525 in Pennsylvania.) Since there are 7500 cities in the data, only 7500*5 words (37,500) contain data. Thus only 37,500/131,250 words, i.e., 28.6 percent, of the array space is actually filled. In most instances it is not feasible to waste this much memory. Therefore, another method must be found.

A more desirable approach would be to have an array of 7,500 rows so that all array space is effectively used; this is the method we will utilize. Each city will be listed in the array alphabetically within state and the data for each state will be organized alphabetically within the array. Thus the data for Alabama (with cities in alphabetical sequence) would be first in the array, followed by the data for Alaska, followed by the data for Arizona, and so on.

But there must then be a method to get to the data for a particular state rapidly. A separate array will be used for this purpose. The first few data items of the array are shown in Table 13–8. Thus there are 160 cities in Alabama with more than 1500 inhabitants and these cities are in locations 1 to 160 of the main array. Alaska has 14 cities in this category; they are in locations 161 to 174. Likewise, Arizona has 49, starting at location 175. A binary search can then be applied to this state array to find the proper starting point for any state.

If the goal was to find a particular city in a state, a second binary search could be applied to the starting and ending points of the data for that state. For example, in order to find the population of Cotton Plant, Arkansas, a binary search of the 50-item state array will provide the bounds of 224 and 334 for the main array. Then the binary search could be applied to the city array between locations 224 and 334. Note that the number of cities and the ending row of the city array need not both be included in the state array since one can be computed from the other.

In fact, only the name of the state and the starting location are needed. The other values can be obtained by calculation from the starting location of the next state in sequence. But for some arrays, it might be advantageous to keep this information rather than compute it each time. We will assume the information is kept in the array.

Questions about state population, type b above, can be handled easily if there is a doubly linked list. Within each state, chain the cities by ascending and descending population. This doubly linked list would then be the same as that presented in Example 13.5 for Alaska. To indicate the starting forward pointer and backward pointer for each state, the state array must contain two additional columns, as shown in Table 13–9.

The data structure in the preceding problem would be sufficient to answer queries of types a and b. But efficient handling of the questions of type c requires another series of linked lists.

Although all cities in the U.S. could be included in one linked list ordered by population, it would take a linked list of 7500 items. This would be entirely too unwieldy to search and would not be efficient. A list of 100 or so items is generally not too large a list. So we might create 75 lists of 100 each by size of population.

For example, there are 63 cities with 200,000 or more inhabitants. This could constitute one linked list. There are then 90 cities with a population between 100,000 and 200,000, which would constitute a second linked list. Thus, efficient linked lists are available for questions of type c.

Table 13-8 Pointer Array to Population Array

State	Number of Cities With Population Over 1,500	Starting Location	Ending Location
ALABAMA	160	1	160
ALASKA	14	161	174
ARIZONA	49	175	223
ARKANSAS	111	224	334

Table 13-9 Pointer Array to Population Array

State	Number of Cities	Starting Location	Ending Location	Forward Pointer	Backward Pointer
ALABAMA	160	1	160	19	29
ALASKA	14	161	174	161	172
ARIZONA	49	175	223	204	189
ARKANSAS	111	224	334	283	285

Table 13-10 Pointer Array to Other Linked Lists

Lower Bound of Size	Number of Cities	Starting Location	Ending Location
200,000	63	4563	2147
100,000	90	3038	2744
70,000	95	2968	3191

There must then be a size array to reflect the data for each of these chains. The format can be similar to the array shown in Table 13–10. In contrast to Table 13–8, note that all columns are needed in this size array. A binary search can be applied to this size array to find the starting and ending locations for a particular size of city.

13.5

The text has described the **postorder traversal** of a binary tree that considers the sequence generated from traversing the tree in the following order: (left subtree)—root—(right subtree). The **preorder traversal** follows the tree in the order: root—(left subtree)—(right subtree). A tree traversed in the order:

Figure 13–8.
Binary Tree
Structure

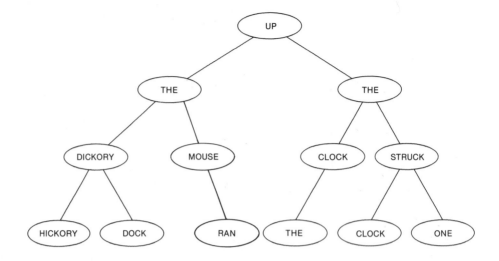

(left subtree)—(right subtree)—root is called an **endorder traversal.** Determine the sequence that the tree in Figure 13–8 represents under (a) postorder traversal, (b) preorder traversal, and (c) endorder traversal.

Solution

Following the respective traversal rules provides the following results:

a. Postorder traversal: (Left Subtree)—Root—(Right Subtree)
    HICKORY DICKORY DOCK
    THE MOUSE RAN UP THE CLOCK
    THE CLOCK STRUCK ONE

b. Preorder traversal: Root—(Left Subtree)—(Right Subtree)
    UP THE DICKORY HICKORY DOCK
    MOUSE RAN THE CLOCK
    THE STRUCK CLOCK ONE

c. Endorder traversal: (Left Subtree)—(Right Subtree)—Root
    HICKORY DOCK DICKORY
    RAN MOUSE THE THE CLOCK
    CLOCK ONE STRUCK THE UP

13.6

Example 13.7 and solved Problem 13.5 illustrate the postorder traversal of a tree. Traversal is related to searching and it is useful to have a means of printing out the sequence of a tree. Develop an algorithm in the form of a recursive subroutine that will output the tree in sequential order using postorder traversal.

Solution

```
SUBROUTINE TREE3 (M1, M2);

BEGIN
    IF (X(M1,1) <> 0) (* FOLLOW LEFT SUBTREE TO NULL NODE *)
    THEN
        CALL TREE3 (X(M1,1), M2);

    WRITE (X(M1,M2)); (* OUTPUT NODE *)

    IF (X(M1,2) <> 0) (* FOLLOW RIGHT SUBTREE TO NULL NODE *)
    THEN
        CALL TREE3 (X(M1,2), M2);

END; (* END TREE3 *)
```

The subroutine TREE3 (M1, M2) uses a GLOBAL array X in which M2 is the column number of the key to be printed. The parameter M1 indicates the row index of the node under consideration. Column 1 is the pointer to the left subtree and Column 2 is the pointer to the right subtree.

The algorithm is very compact. It involves the left subtree, the node corresponding to the present value of M1, and the right subtree. If there is a left subtree, $(X(M1) <> 0)$, TREE3 is called recursively for that subtree. The value of the present node is printed followed by a recursive call on the right subtree if it exists. The only operation besides the two recursive calls is printing X(M1,M2). This will occur for each call of TREE3, which will be called recursively as many times as there are nodes in the tree. To ensure that you understand the algorithm, follow one of the examples (e.g., Figure 13–2c) through the algorithm.

13.7

The TREESORT3 algorithm presented in Section 13.5 is a very efficient sort algorithm. The maximum number of comparisons is approximately equal to $2N(\log_2(N) - 1)$. Compute the maximum number of comparisons needed for values of N equal to 8, 20, 50, 100, and 1000 items. Compare the results with the solutions of Solved Problems 10.17 and 10.19.

Solution

We will round $\log_2(N)$ to the next highest integer when it is not an integer. The maximum number of comparisons is then as shown in Table 13.11. The table also shows the best sort method and number of comparisons, as found in Solved Problems 10.17 and 10.19. To determine the previous best sort, the mean number of comparisons was used when the bubble sort was considered.

Table 13-11 Comparison of Sorting Algorithms

N	Maximum Number of Comparisons TREESORT	Previous Best Sort Number of Comparisons	Algorithm
8	32	18	Insertion
20	160	105	Insertion
50	500	588	PreSorted Quadratic with Bubble PreSort
100	1,200	1,450	PreSorted Quadratic with Bubble PreSort
1000	18,000	48,500	PreSorted Quadratic with Bubble PreSort

Supplementary Problems
13.8

Example 13.2 presents a method for searching a particular singly linked list. Develop a general algorithm in the form of a subroutine to search a linked list in the same sense in which Example 13.9 is a general search algorithm for a tree.

13.9

Devise a data structure (file organization) for the state information and linked list of Solved Problem 13.2 that will be suitable on a computer. (Note that this could mean using more than one word for storing such information as the name of the capital). Then develop the algorithms necessary to access the data structure to answer each of the search queries posed in Solved Problem 13.3.

13.10

Develop an algorithm to create the data base of Solved Problem 13.2 from a transaction file in which each record contains a state name, the capital, the population, the area in square miles, and the date of admission to the Union. The transaction file is initially in random order, but the final data structure should be in alphabetical order by state name and should include the three linked lists outlined in Solved Problem 13.3.

(Hint: After input of the data, the file can be organized in sequential order by sorting the array row using a procedure similar to BUBSORT2 of Solved Problem 10.5. Each of the linked lists can then be created in turn. The simplest way to create a linked list is to make a list of one with the first state (Alabama) and then use the insertion algorithm (e.g., INSERT of Example 13.3) to insert the values for each succeeding state.)

13.11

Use the algorithm of Supplementary Problem 13.10 to create the state data base using only the first 48 states (i.e., without Alaska and Hawaii). Develop an algorithm to read a record with a new state and change the data structure to add that state.

Test your program with the input data for Alaska and Hawaii, but be sure the algorithm is general and is not specifically oriented to only these two states. When a new state, e.g., Alaska, is inserted in the data base, all of the states below that point must be moved down by one position. This will change the row indices, which in turn will change the references to the locations in the linked list. One solution is to rebuild the linked lists each time a state is added.

Attempt to do this problem without reconstructing the entire linked list from scratch. In order to test the generality of your procedure, assume that Puerto Rico and the Virgin Islands are to be included in the state data base.

13.12

The description of Solved Problem 13.4 poses a number of queries to the city population data base. Outline the search strategy to process each of these requests.

13.13

Using the assumptions on the structure of the data base from Solved Problem 13.4, develop the algorithms to implement two or three of the search strategies from Solved Problem 13.3. Several of these algorithms could necessitate additional assumptions about the data structure.

13.14

Develop an algorithm to delete an existing record from a binary tree structure that is arranged in ascending order by the sort key. Deletion from a tree is more difficult than insertion and the algorithm will probably consist of several recursive procedures. Most methods would involve the movement of a node from the lowest level to replace the node being eliminated.

For example, consider the deletion of the node corresponding to CLINTON in Figure 13–3. The algorithm can, in effect, have CHENEY or DALLAS take the place of CLINTON. Besides a method to find the node, e.g., DALLAS, one pointer must be changed in ELM CITY, one pointer changed in DAYTON, and two pointers changed in DALLAS.

Glossary

Absolute Address
The actual or physical address of a variable or instruction in memory, usually determined at execution time when the program code is loaded into memory.

Access Time
The time interval between initiation and completion of a memory READ/WRITE function.

Address
The location within memory where information is stored. This may be a Relative or an Absolute address.

Algorithm
A finite sequence of operations which defines the process for effectively solving a particular problem within a finite period of time.

Arithmetic Expression
A single variable or a combination of one or more variables and/or constants separated by arithmetic operators, which, when evaluated, yields a numerical value.

Array
A data structure within which a set of elements is arranged in a prescribed fashion such that individual elements may be addressed by a single variable name and a relative position within the data structure, i.e., a subscript.

Assembler
A program which converts English-like, higher level language statements into machine code on a one-for-one basis.

Assembly Language
The syntax for constructing programming statements acceptable to the AS-SEMBLER.

Assignment Statement
A statement which causes the value of the expression on the right hand side of the assignment operator (:=) to be stored in the variable on the left hand

side of the operator. The assignment operator is sometimes referred to as a Replacement Operator.

Auxiliary Memory
See MASS STORAGE.

Backspace
An Input/Output operation which provides the ability to move backwards one logical or physical record in a file.

Binary Operators
An operator which affects two operands. The LOGICAL Operators AND and OR which establish the relationship between the BOOLEAN expression immediately preceding and following their appearance are BINARY OPERATORS. The Arithmetic Operators (*,/,**) are also BINARY OPERATORS. The Arithmetic Operators (+,−) when they represent the addition and subtraction operation respectively are also BINARY OPERATORS.

Binary Search
A search algorithm which isolates the desired element by repeatedly dividing the search list in half.

Bit
A binary digit (0,1) or the smallest unit of data in binary notation.

Block
A physical record consisting of two or more logical records.

Blocked Record
Same as a BLOCK.

BOOLEAN Expression
A simple BOOLEAN variable or two or more variables and/or BOOLEAN (TRUE/FALSE) constants separated by relational operators, which when evaluated yields a BOOLEAN value.

BOOLEAN Value
A TRUE or FALSE.

Bottom Up Design
A design philosophy which starts at the lowest level and builds the solution from that point.

Bracketing
A programming concept which allows a group of statements to be treated as a unit.

Buffer
A section of memory reserved to temporarily store data during an Input/Output transaction matching the high speed of the processor to the low speed of the I/O device.

Byte
A grouping of eight consecutive bits, which may be treated or referenced as a unit.

Chain
The relationship formed when a series of data elements are linked together in a way which allows access to the next logical data item from the current data item.

Closed Subprogram
A subprogram within which only one copy of the code exists and program flow is redirected to execute it as necessary.

Coding
The process of developing a set of program instructions from a logical description of a solution procedure or algorithm.

Comments
Remarks which may be interspersed within program statements for the purpose of documenting the process.

Comparison
The act of comparing two values to determine their logical relationship with regard to equality, greater than, or less than.

Compiler
A computer program which converts English-like, higher level language programming statements into machine language statements on a one-to-many basis.

Computer Science
The study of information processing through the use of a computer.

Conditional Processing
The ability to select between alternative courses of action based on some decision criteria.

Constant
A BOOLEAN or arithmetic entity which has a fixed value.

Contents
The information stored at a given address in memory.

Control Variable
A variable which is used to determine when the terminating criteria for an iterative process has been satisfied.

Data Item
The smallest element of identifiable information in a record.

Declaration
A programming construct which defines the attributes of a variable, array, or file to the remainder of the program.

Decomposition
The process of dividing a large, unmanageable problem into smaller, more understandable subproblems.

Direct Access Devices
A physical storage device on which the time to access any given record is independent of its location on the device.

Doubly Linked List
A linked list in which each data record contains both a forward and reverse pointer.

Field
The location within a record for a particular data item location. All records are composed of data items in specific FIELDs.

File
A collection of related data records.

File Maintenance
The process of altering, updating, rearranging, or deleting records in a data file.

Fixed Length Field
A field within a record which has a fixed size and does not vary from record to record within the file.

Fixed Length Record
A record within a data file which has a fixed size and does not vary from record to record within the file.

Fixed Size Field
Same as FIXED LENGTH FIELD.

Flowchart
A graphical representation of the flow of operations in a program.

Four-Way Merge Sort
A sort algorithm which uses four data sets to simultaneously merge and sort two unsorted, input data files.

Full File Processing
A file maintenance procedure requiring access to every record in the file.

Function
A specific type of subprogram which calculates and returns a single value by assigning that value to the name of the subprogram itself. It is referenced as an expression.

Hash Coding
A process of applying some transformation algorithm to a data item to provide the actual location of a record in a data structure or file.

Header Value
A terminating technique in which the number of times an iteration is to be performed is input from the head of the list of data records to be processed.

High-Level Language
A computer programming language which allows a programmer to write his computer instructions in English-like statements. High-level languages require COMPILERS to convert their single statements into multiple machine language instructions.

Identifier
A name applied to a simple variable or an array to uniquely specify or address it.

Increment
The process of updating the CONTROL VARIABLE in an iteration.

I/O
An acronym for Input/Output.

I/O Bound
A computer system in which the slow processing speed of the I/O devices causes the central processing unit to constantly wait for completion of I/O functions.

I/O Limited
Same as I/O BOUND.

Indexed Sequential File
A RANDOM file structure in which each record is stored in sequential order and has a key assigned to it. The key is then used to form an index which can be accessed to determine the location of the record in the file.

Input Statements
Programming statements which cause the computer to accept the next data record from an input device, convert it into an internal binary format, and store it in main memory for processing.

Instruction
A command to the computer to perform a specific sequence of steps when decoded by the Control Unit.

Inter-Record Gap
The space between records on a sequential access storage device. This space helps delineate one record from the next.

Iterative Processing
A computer process which allows a set of program steps to be repeated a number of times based on some terminating criteria.

Key
A data item which uniquely defines a record within a file.

Language
A specific set of words and the rules governing their usage from which statements may be constructed for communicating instructions and/or information to the computer.

Layout of the Record
A diagrammatic representation of a record organization showing the location of fields and their respective sizes within the record.

Leaf
A node in a TREE structure which has no descendents or subtrees.

Linear Search
A search plan in which elements of the search list are examined in sequential order.

Link
A field within a linked list record which points to the next record in the list.

Linked List
The relationship formed when a series of data elements are linked together in some way. Same as CHAIN.

Logical Operators
Operators which connect BOOLEAN expressions according to a set of rules in order to form new BOOLEAN expressions. The LOGICAL operators are AND, OR, and NOT.

Logical Record

The Record as it appears to the application program without regard to physical storage limitations or blocking factors.

Main Memory

A high-speed, small-capacity storage device connected to the Central Processing Unit. It is used for temporary program and data storage while a program is actually being executed.

Mantissa

The magnitude or decimal portion of a REAL (Fixed Point or Floating Point) number.

Mass Storage

A storage device used in conjunction with main memory. Generally having a much larger capacity, but slower access time than main memory. Same as AUXILIARY MEMORY.

Merging

The process of producing a single sequence of records according to some KEY from two or more sequences of records previously ordered by the same KEY.

Mnemonic Operation Code

An Operation Code which is expressed by a series of characters rather than numbers. Although cryptic, the code generally relates to English words, such as CMP for COMPARE.

Multiple Buffering

An arrangement of buffers allowing one buffer to be accessed while another is being filled (READ) or emptied (WRITE).

Normalize

The process of converting a number to scientific notation by moving the decimal point to a position in the number where a single non-zero digit exists to its left, and then adjusting the exponent to reflect this shift accordingly.

N-Way Merge

A general merge algorithm for as many input lists as desired.

Open Subprogram

A subprogram that is inserted in line within the calling program at each point where it is referenced during compilation or assembly.

Operand

That part of a computer instruction containing the data or the address of the data upon which the instruction is to operate.

Ordered List

A list within which the elements are arranged according to some defined sequence.

Output Statement

A computer instruction that first causes data to be converted from internal, binary form into the form required by the output device. The data is then transferred to the output device from memory.

Pass

One complete iteration of a sorting algorithm through the list of data being sorted.

Physical Record

The record as it actually appears on the Input/Output device. It is the size of the record as it is transferred to and from the data buffers.

Pointer

See LINK.

Postorder Traversal

Traversal through a Tree structure following the order of (Left Subtree)—Root—(Right Subtree).

Preorder Traversal

Traversal through a Tree structure following the order of Root—(Left Subtree)—(Right Subtree).

Primary Sort Key

The highest priority sort field in the data record.

Procedural Language

See HIGH-LEVEL LANGUAGE.

Program

A series of instructions that can solve a problem or accomplish a task when executed on a computer.

Random File

A file stored on a Direct Access Device in which the time to access any given record in the file is independent of that record's position in the file, relative to any other record in the file.

Real Number

A number which has both a whole portion and a decimal portion.

Record

A collection of related data items or fields.

Relative Address
The address of a variable or instruction with respect to the starting address of the program or another point of reference.

Rewind
An Input/Output instruction causing the pointer to the file to be reset to the first record in the file.

Root
Any node in a Tree structure from which other nodes branch.

Scrambling
See HASH CODING.

Searching
The process of examining the data in a list or file to locate a specific data item.

Secondary Sort Key
A data item or field which has second priority to the primary sort key.

Sectors
A track on a disk may be separated into segments called SECTORS which contain a fixed amount of data.

Sense-End-Of-File-Mark
An Input/Output instruction detecting the end of a file and reporting this situation to the program.

Sequential Access File
Records in a file arranged in sequential order. That is, to access the N-th record in the file, the previous N−1 records must first be accessed.

Sequential Data Organization
A file structure in which the logical relationships between the records in the file are indicated by the physical location of the records in the file.

Sign-Bit
The leftmost bit in an N-bit word designating the sign of the word.

Singly Linked Lists
A data structure having only a single pointer associated with each record. This pointer points to the next logical record in the list.

Skip
An Input/Output instruction that causes the record pointer to be incremented by 2 versus 1, effectively bypassing the next logical record.

Sorting
The process of arranging a list of data into ascending or descending order on a designated data field or key.

Sort Key
The specific data item or field on which sorting is to be performed.

Special Condition
A terminating technique for iterative processing in which the iteration is terminated when a specific set of conditions has been met, i.e., when a particular data item is found in a list.

Stepwise Refinement
The structured problem-solving technique of repetitively subdividing the problem.

Structured Approach
A disciplined approach to problem solving that encompasses a set of techniques making the art of problem solving more rigorous.

Structured Programming
A method for developing good quality software using a system engineering approach.

Subprogram
A self-contained set of instructions which, when executed, yields a desired result.

Subscript
An arithmetic expression which yields the relative address of a particular data element in an array.

Subroutine
A specific type of subprogram used to calculate several values, or to provide a specific effect or series of actions. Subroutines are executed through explicit Call statements.

Subtrees
A set of nodes having all the properties of a Tree, but which are subordinate to another node.

Symbol
The part of a record in a linked list containing the actual data.

Terminating Value
The value against which the control variable is compared in an iteration to determine when the iteration is to be terminated.

Testing
The term applied to the process of comparing the control variable in an iteration process to the terminating value for that iteration.

Three-Way Merge
The process of combining three presorted input lists into a single, sorted, output list.

Top Down Design
A design philosophy that starts at the highest level and continuously refines the problem until the solution is determined at the lowest level.

Tracks
Concentric circles about a disk platter containing data and grouped into aggregates of data called sectors.

Trailer Value
A technique used in inputting data. The input process terminates when a designated data item attains a designated value, which differs from all normal values for that data item.

Traversing
The term applied to the process of searching or examining elements of a Tree structure.

Tree Structure
A method of organizing data, consisting of a set of nodes which are organized so that one specific data element is considered the root node, and the successor nodes are divided into independent sets so that each of these sets also forms a tree.

Two-Way Merge
The process of combining two presorted input lists into a single, sorted, output list.

Unary Operator
Any operator which affects only a single operand. The arithmetic operators plus (+) and minus (−) may be considered unary operators such as in −A. The logical operator NOT is a unary operator such as in NOT TRUE.

Unblocked Record
A physical record that contains only one logical record, i.e., the size of the physical and logical record are identical.

Unordered List
A list of data that has no particular sequence with regard to a designated field.

Variable

A name assigned to an identifier in a program that can assume different values during processing.

Variable Length Fields

A field in which the length of the field itself varies depending on the data to be stored in the field.

Variable Length Record

A record in which the length of the record itself varies depending on the data to be stored in the record. A variable length record can be composed of one or more variable length fields.

Word

A unit of data, an instruction, or a grouping of bits that are treated as an entity by the Central Processing Unit. The amount of information that is generally accessed by one reference to memory.

Write-End-Of-File

Generally a special Input/Output instruction associated with tapes that causes an end-of-file mark to be placed on the tape itself.

Index

About the Authors

John M. Hartling is Manager of Engineering Information Systems at Digital Equipment Corporation's Colorado Springs facility. Prior to that John was an Assistant Professor of Computer Science at the United States Air Force Academy. He received his M.S. from the Naval Postgraduate School.

Larry E. Druffel has been an Associate Professor at the United States Air Force Academy and a Program Manager for Defense Advanced Research Projects Agency managing computer science research projects. Larry received his Ph.D. from Vanderbilt University and he has authored or co-authored more than 30 articles in Computer Science.

F. Jack Hilbing is Assistant Director, Electronics and Applied Physics Department, Borg-Warner Corporation. Jack has also been an Assistant Professor of Computer Science at the United States Air Force Academy. He received his Ph.D. from Stanford University.